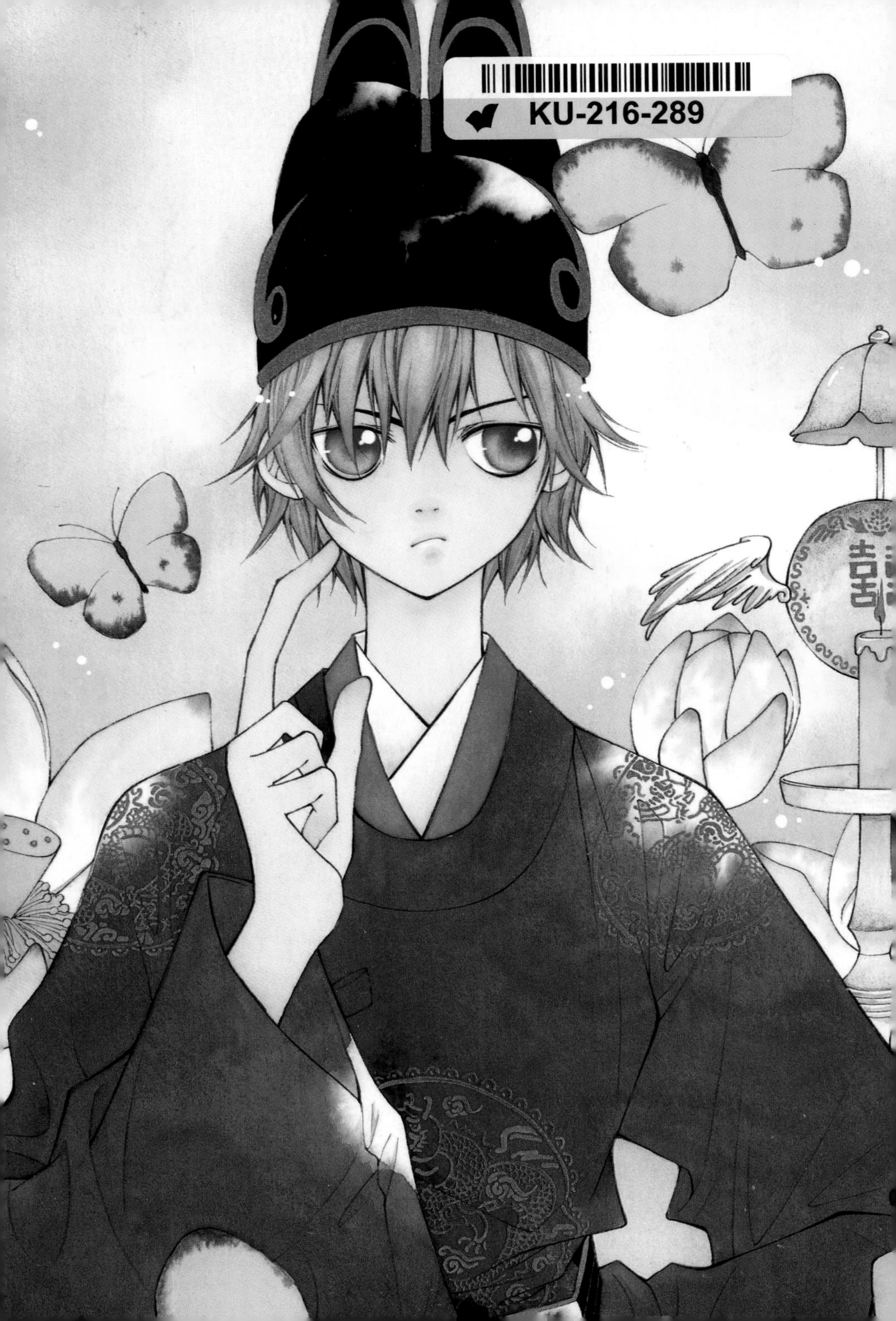

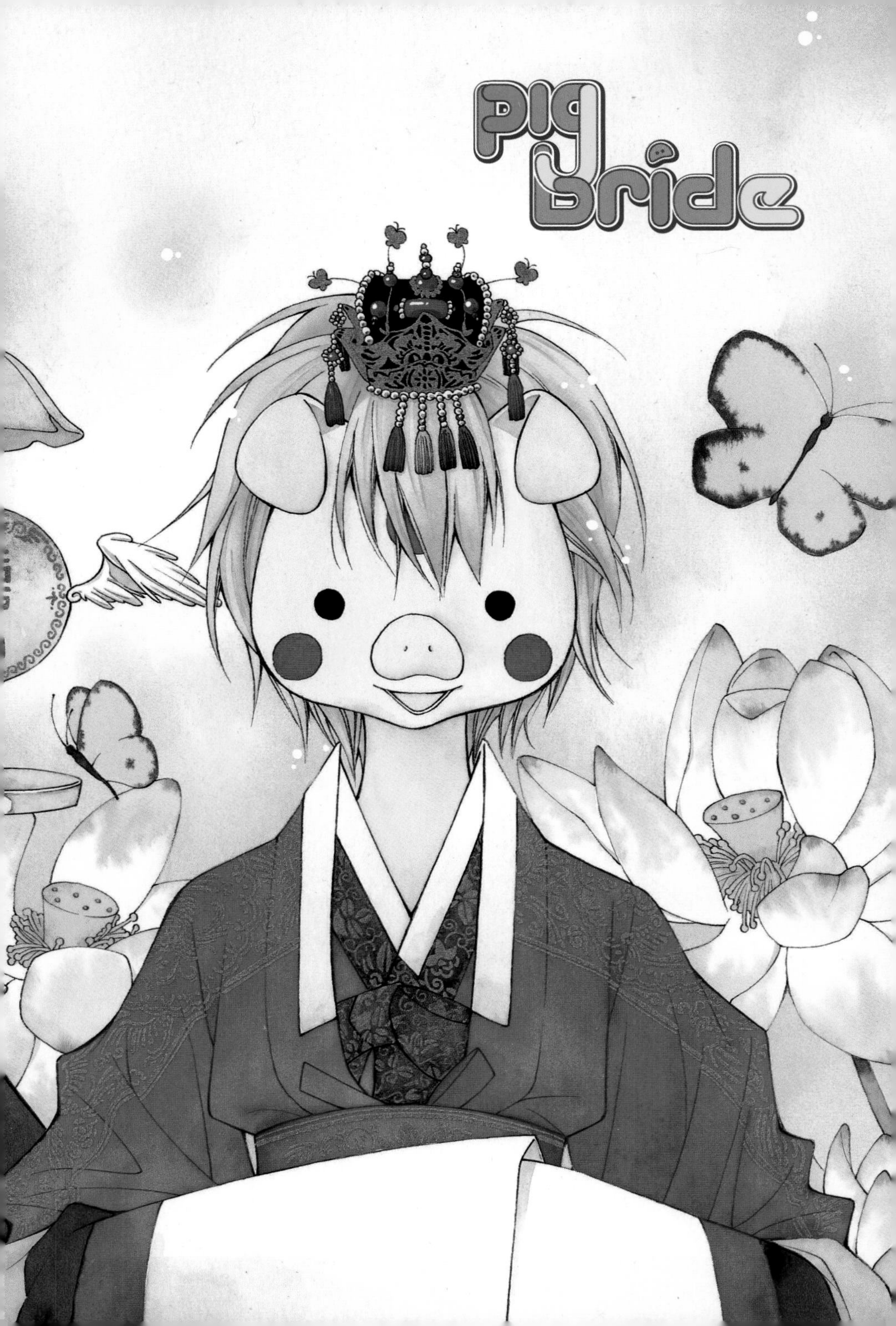
pig
bride

Story by **KookHwa Huh**
Art by **SuJin Kim**

pig bride

PLEASE READ IT WITH LOVE!

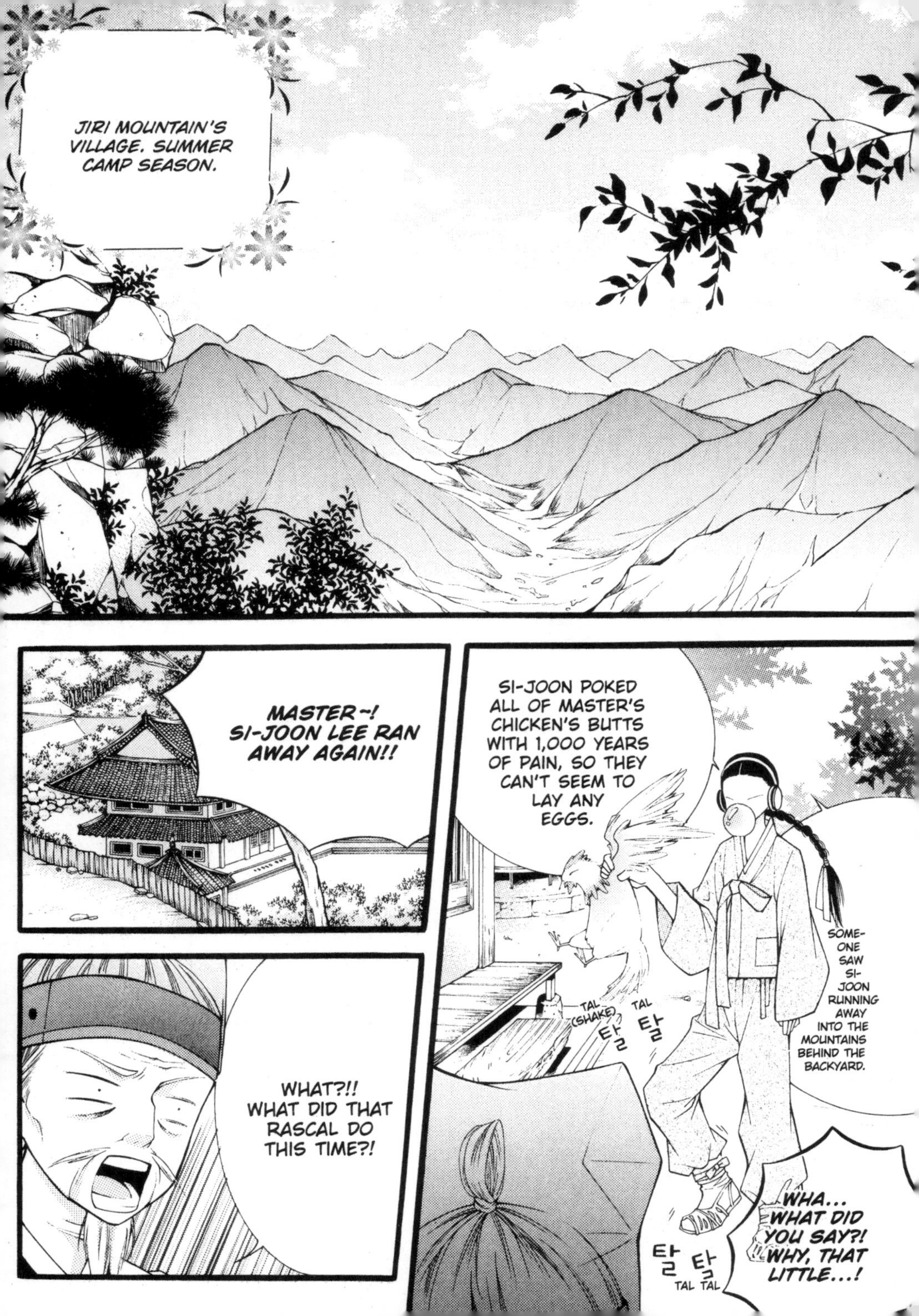
JIRI MOUNTAIN'S VILLAGE. SUMMER CAMP SEASON.
MASTER~! SI-JOON LEE RAN AWAY AGAIN!!
SI-JOON POKED ALL OF MASTER'S CHICKEN'S BUTTS WITH 1,000 YEARS OF PAIN, SO THEY CAN'T SEEM TO LAY ANY EGGS.
SOME-ONE SAW SI-JOON RUNNING AWAY INTO THE MOUNTAINS BEHIND THE BACKYARD.
TAL (SHAKE) TAL
탈 탈
WHAT?!! WHAT DID THAT RASCAL DO THIS TIME?!
WHA... WHAT DID YOU SAY?! WHY, THAT LITTLE...!
탈 탈
TAL TAL

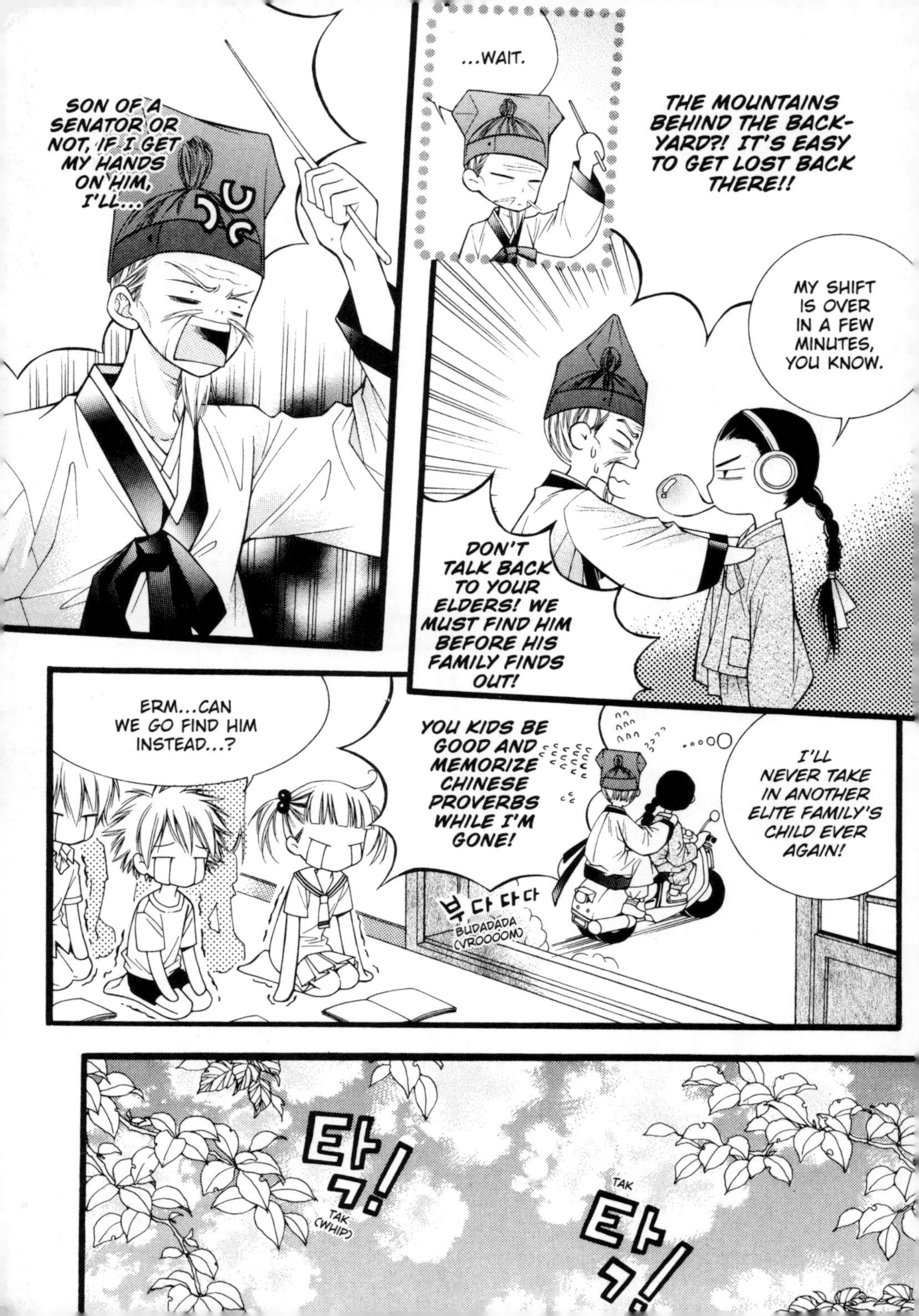
SON OF A SENATOR OR NOT, IF I GET MY HANDS ON HIM, I'LL...
...WAIT.
THE MOUNTAINS BEHIND THE BACK-YARD?! IT'S EASY TO GET LOST BACK THERE!!
MY SHIFT IS OVER IN A FEW MINUTES, YOU KNOW.
DON'T TALK BACK TO YOUR ELDERS! WE MUST FIND HIM BEFORE HIS FAMILY FINDS OUT!
ERM...CAN WE GO FIND HIM INSTEAD...?
YOU KIDS BE GOOD AND MEMORIZE CHINESE PROVERBS WHILE I'M GONE!
I'LL NEVER TAKE IN ANOTHER ELITE FAMILY'S CHILD EVER AGAIN!
부다다다
BUDADADA (VROOOOM)
탁!
TAK (WHIP)
TAK
탁!

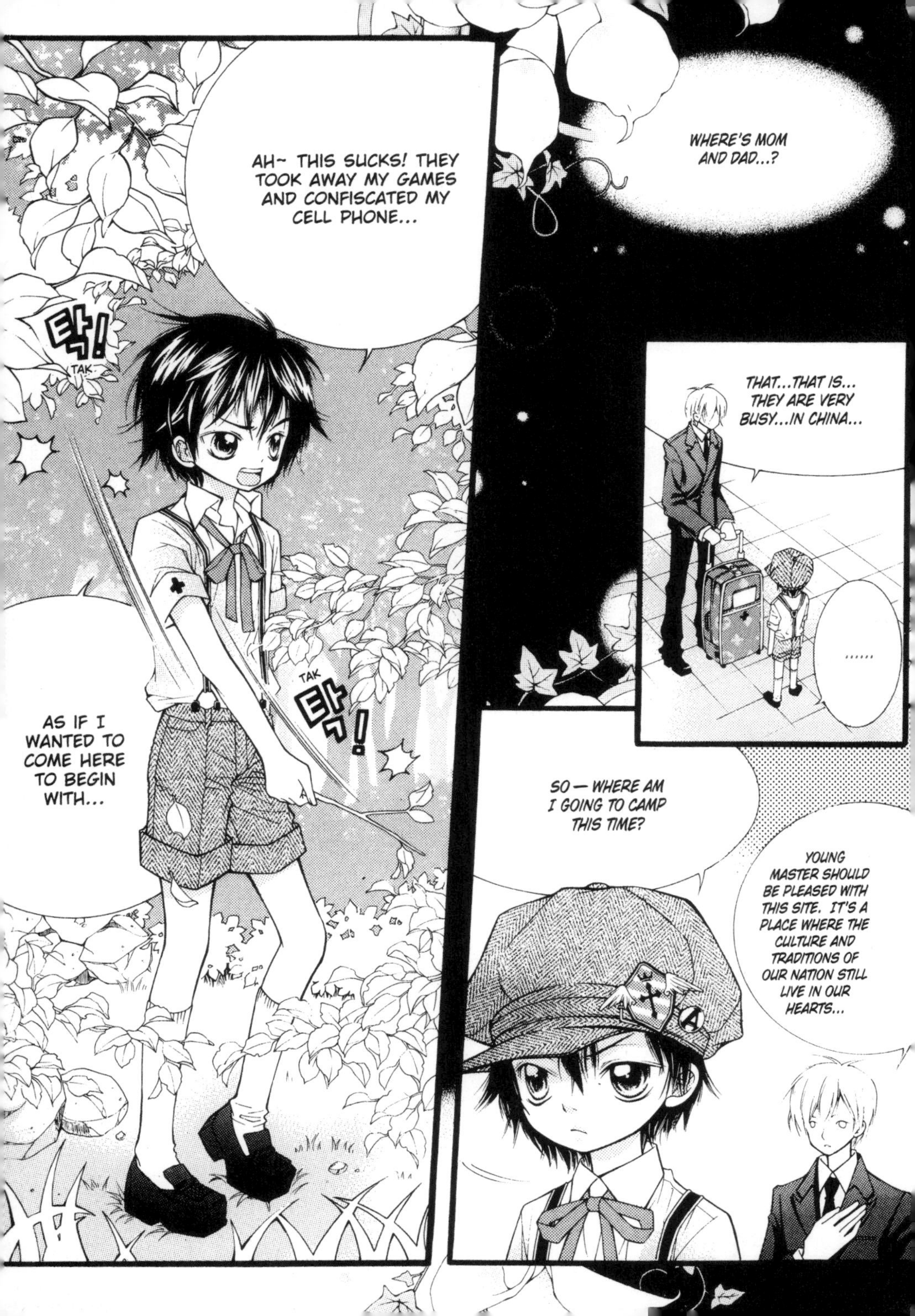
WHERE'S MOM AND DAD...?
AH~ THIS SUCKS! THEY TOOK AWAY MY GAMES AND CONFISCATED MY CELL PHONE...
TAK
TAK
AS IF I WANTED TO COME HERE TO BEGIN WITH...
THAT...THAT IS... THEY ARE VERY BUSY...IN CHINA...
......
SO — WHERE AM I GOING TO CAMP THIS TIME?
YOUNG MASTER SHOULD BE PLEASED WITH THIS SITE. IT'S A PLACE WHERE THE CULTURE AND TRADITIONS OF OUR NATION STILL LIVE IN OUR HEARTS...

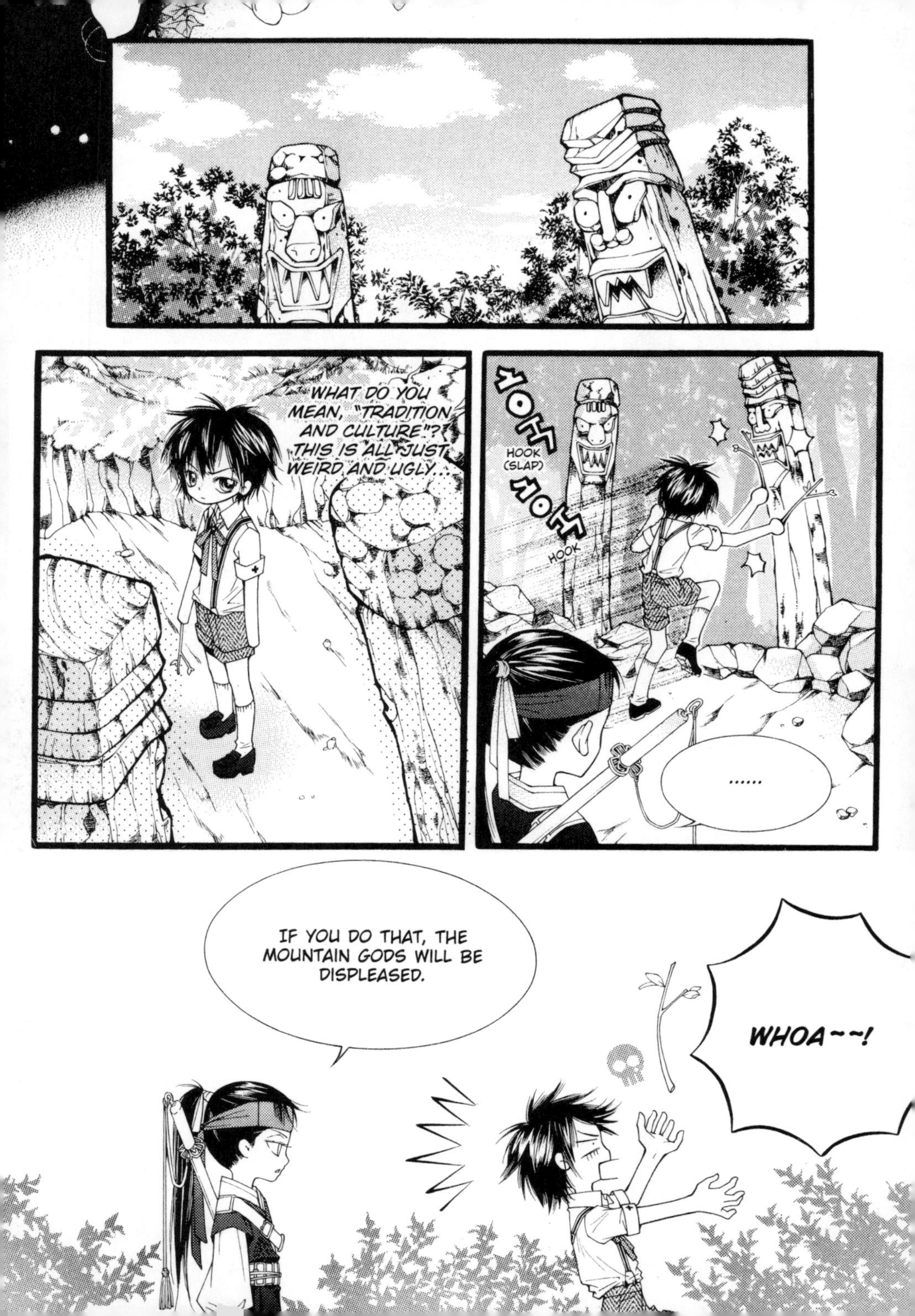
WHAT DO YOU MEAN, "TRADITION AND CULTURE"? THIS IS ALL JUST WEIRD AND UGLY...
HOOK (SLAP)
HOOK
......
WHOA~~!
IF YOU DO THAT, THE MOUNTAIN GODS WILL BE DISPLEASED.

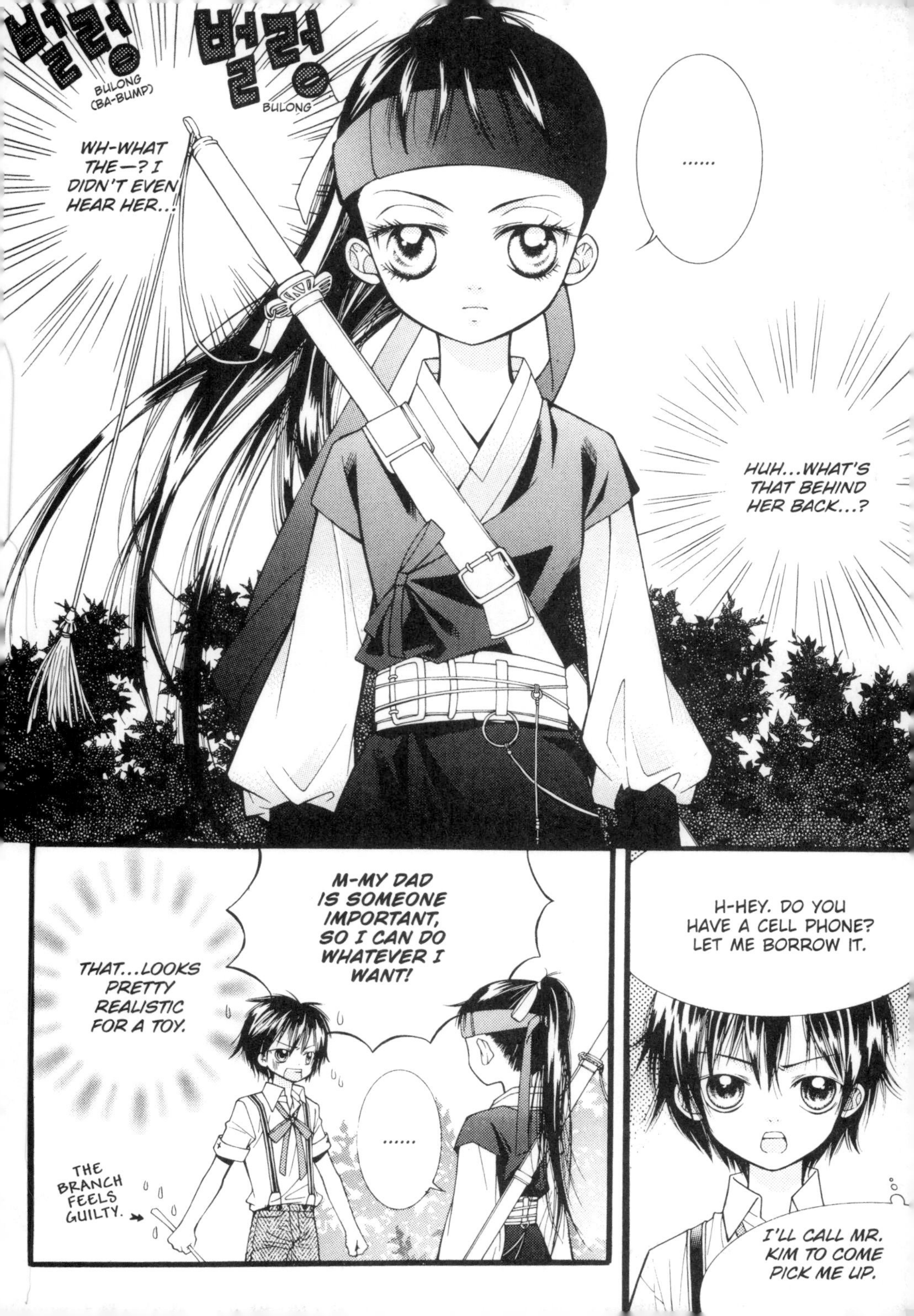

벌렁 벌렁
BULONG (BA-BUMP)
BULONG
WH-WHAT THE—? I DIDN'T EVEN HEAR HER...
......
HUH...WHAT'S THAT BEHIND HER BACK...?
H-HEY. DO YOU HAVE A CELL PHONE? LET ME BORROW IT.
I'LL CALL MR. KIM TO COME PICK ME UP.
M-MY DAD IS SOMEONE IMPORTANT, SO I CAN DO WHATEVER I WANT!
THAT...LOOKS PRETTY REALISTIC FOR A TOY.
......
THE BRANCH FEELS GUILTY.

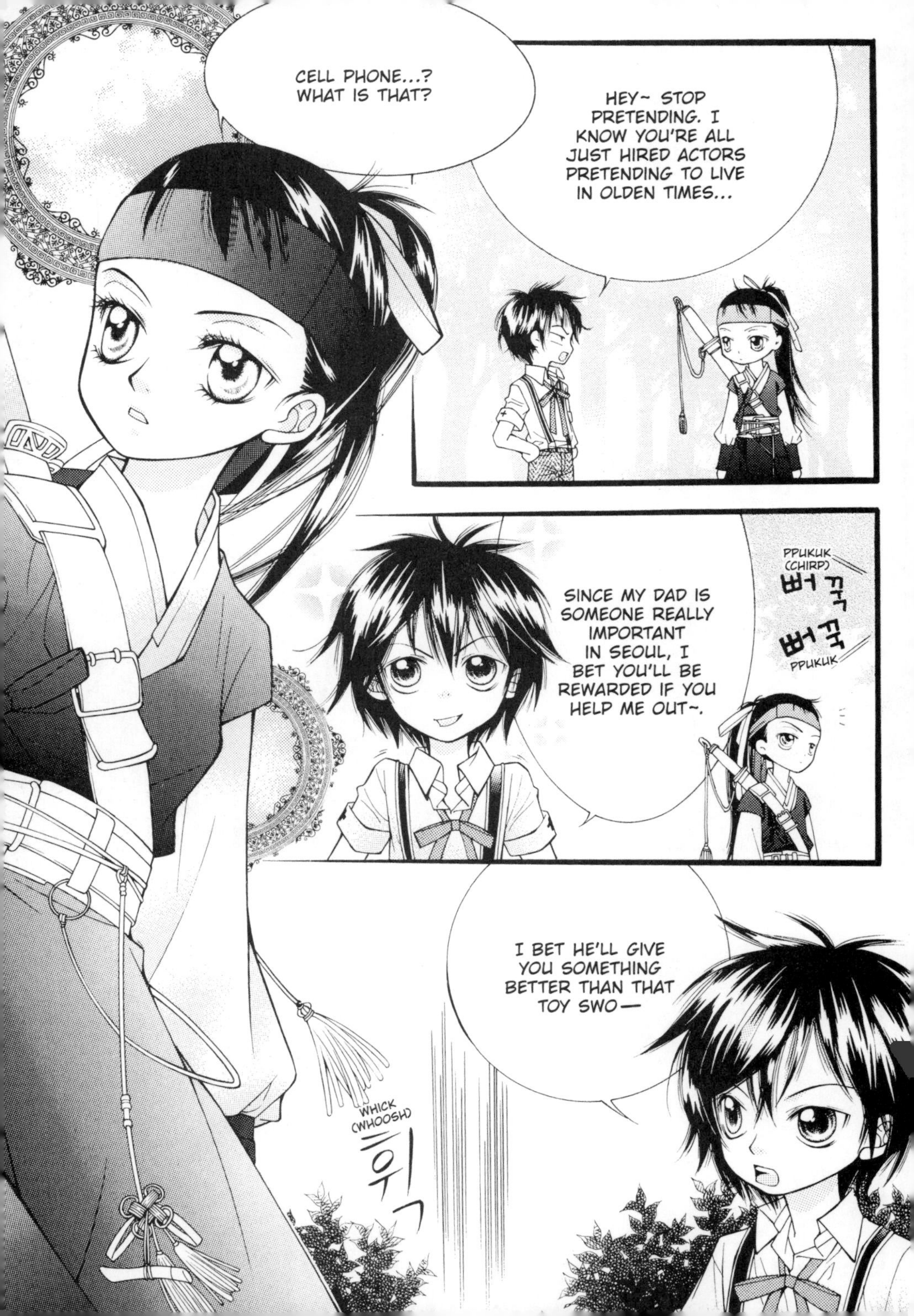
HEY~ STOP PRETENDING. I KNOW YOU'RE ALL JUST HIRED ACTORS PRETENDING TO LIVE IN OLDEN TIMES...
CELL PHONE...? WHAT IS THAT?
PPUKUK (CHIRP)
뻐꾹 뻐꾹
PPUKUK
SINCE MY DAD IS SOMEONE REALLY IMPORTANT IN SEOUL, I BET YOU'LL BE REWARDED IF YOU HELP ME OUT~.
I BET HE'LL GIVE YOU SOMETHING BETTER THAN THAT TOY SWO—
WHICK (WHOOSH)
휘익

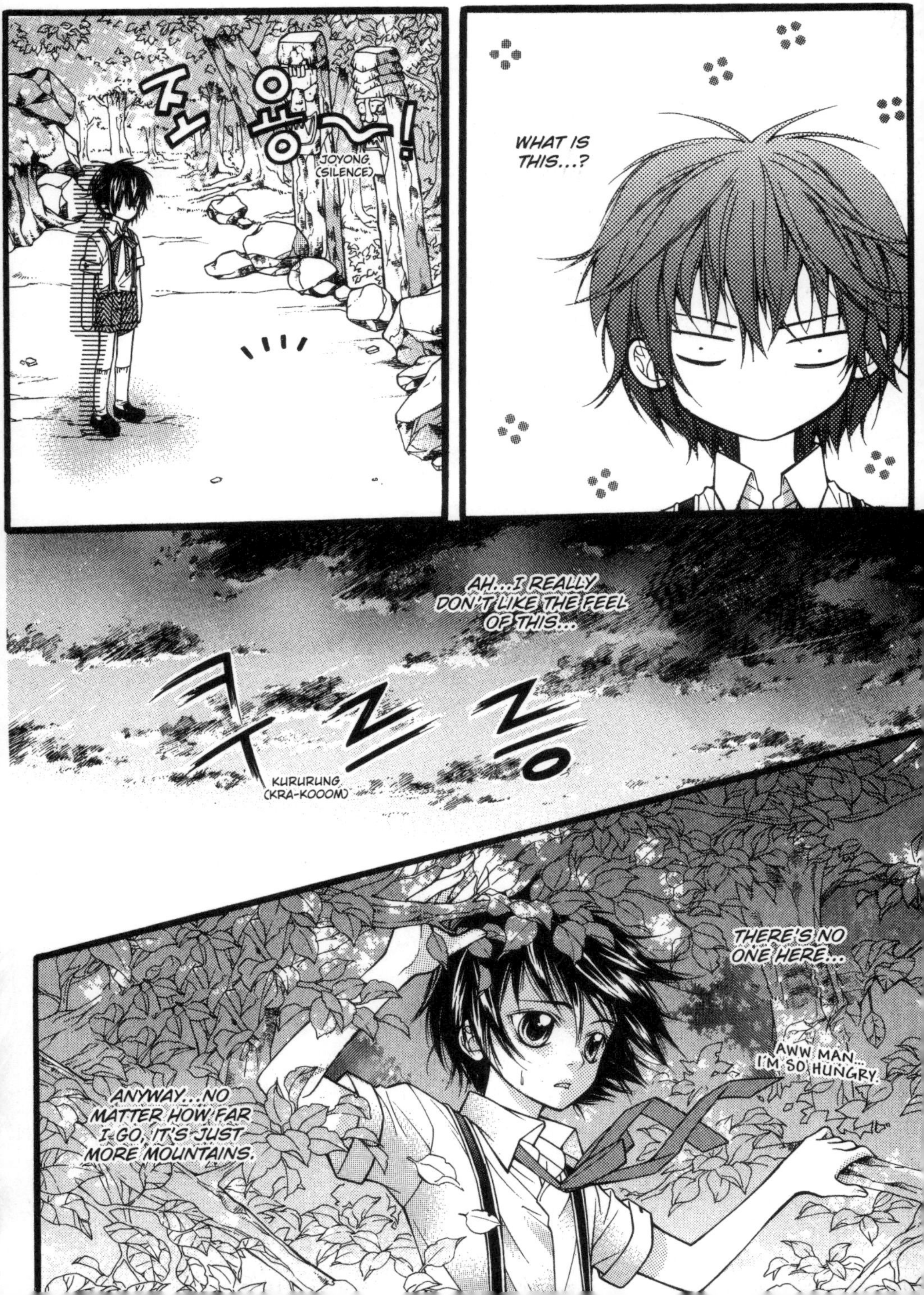

WHAT IS THIS...?
조용~!
JOYONG (SILENCE)
AH...I REALLY DON'T LIKE THE FEEL OF THIS...
쿠르릉
KURURUNG (KRA-KOOOM)
THERE'S NO ONE HERE...
AWW MAN... I'M SO HUNGRY.
ANYWAY...NO MATTER HOW FAR I GO, IT'S JUST MORE MOUNTAINS.

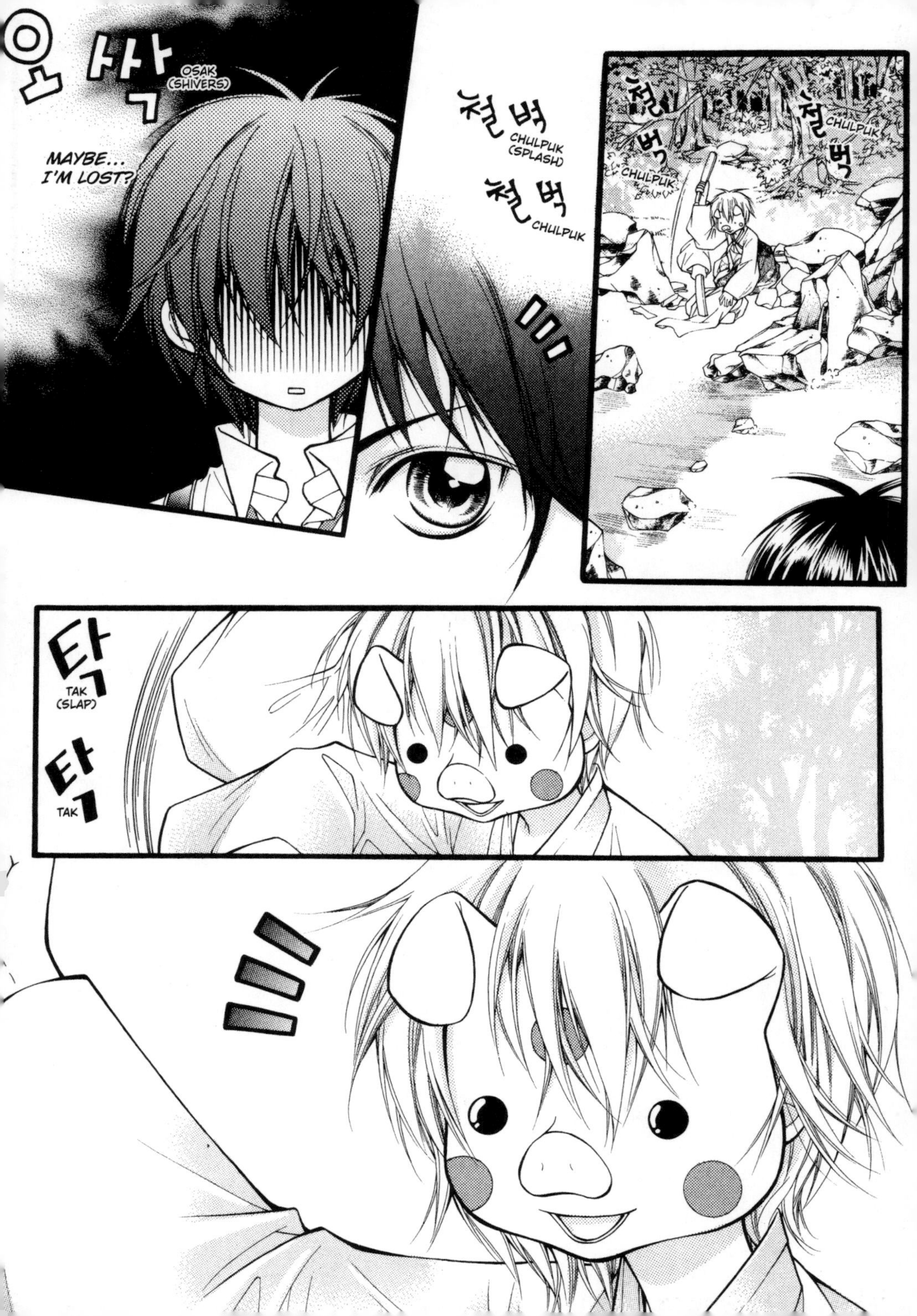
오싹
OSAK (SHIVERS)
MAYBE... I'M LOST?
철벅
CHULPUK (SPLASH)
철벅
CHULPUK
철벅
CHULPUK
철벅
CHULPUK
탁
TAK (SLAP)
탁
TAK

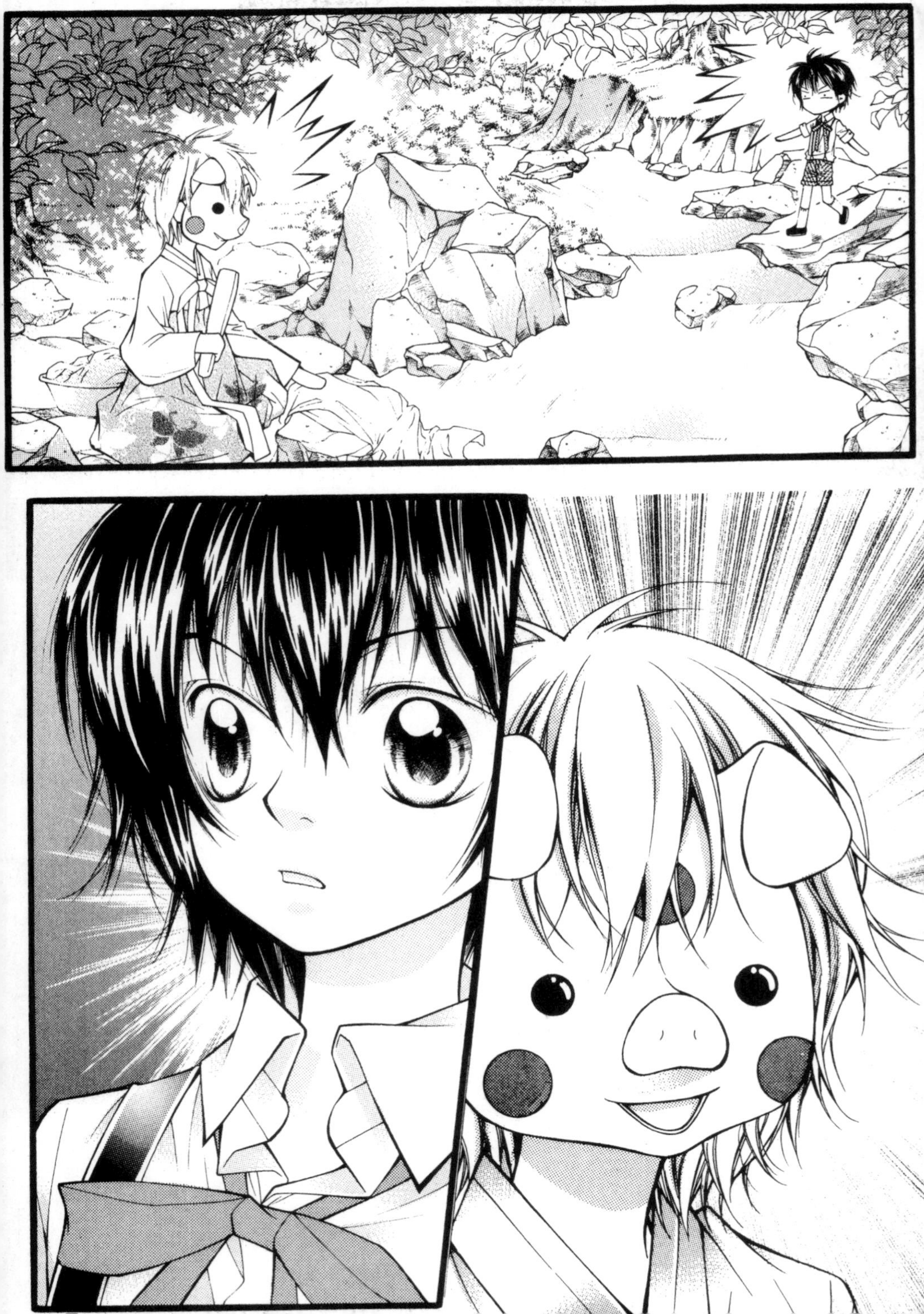

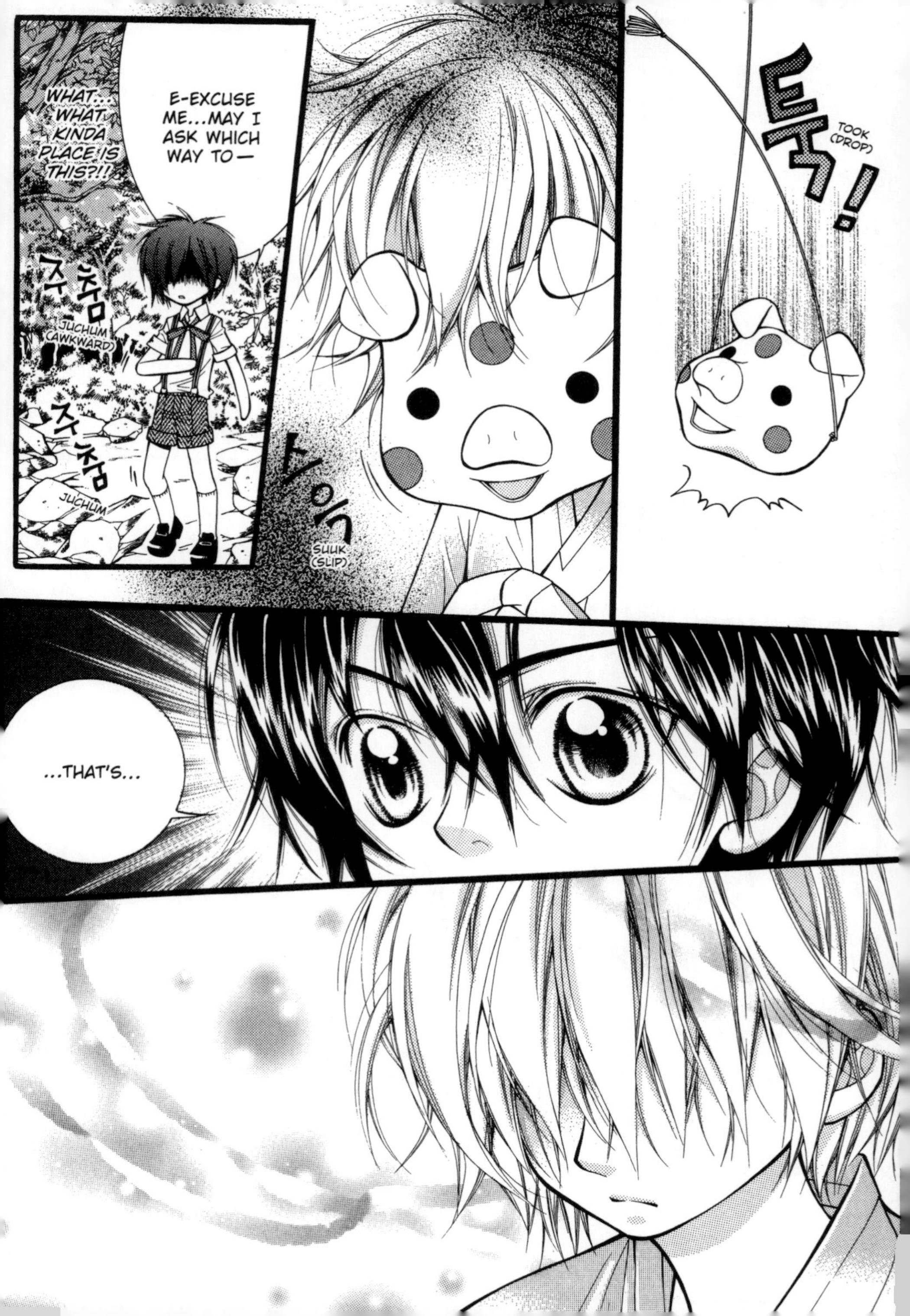

E-EXCUSE ME...MAY I ASK WHICH WAY TO—
WHAT... WHAT KINDA PLACE IS THIS?!!
JUCHUM (AWKWARD)
JUCHUM
SUUK (SLIP)
TOOK (DROP)
...THAT'S...

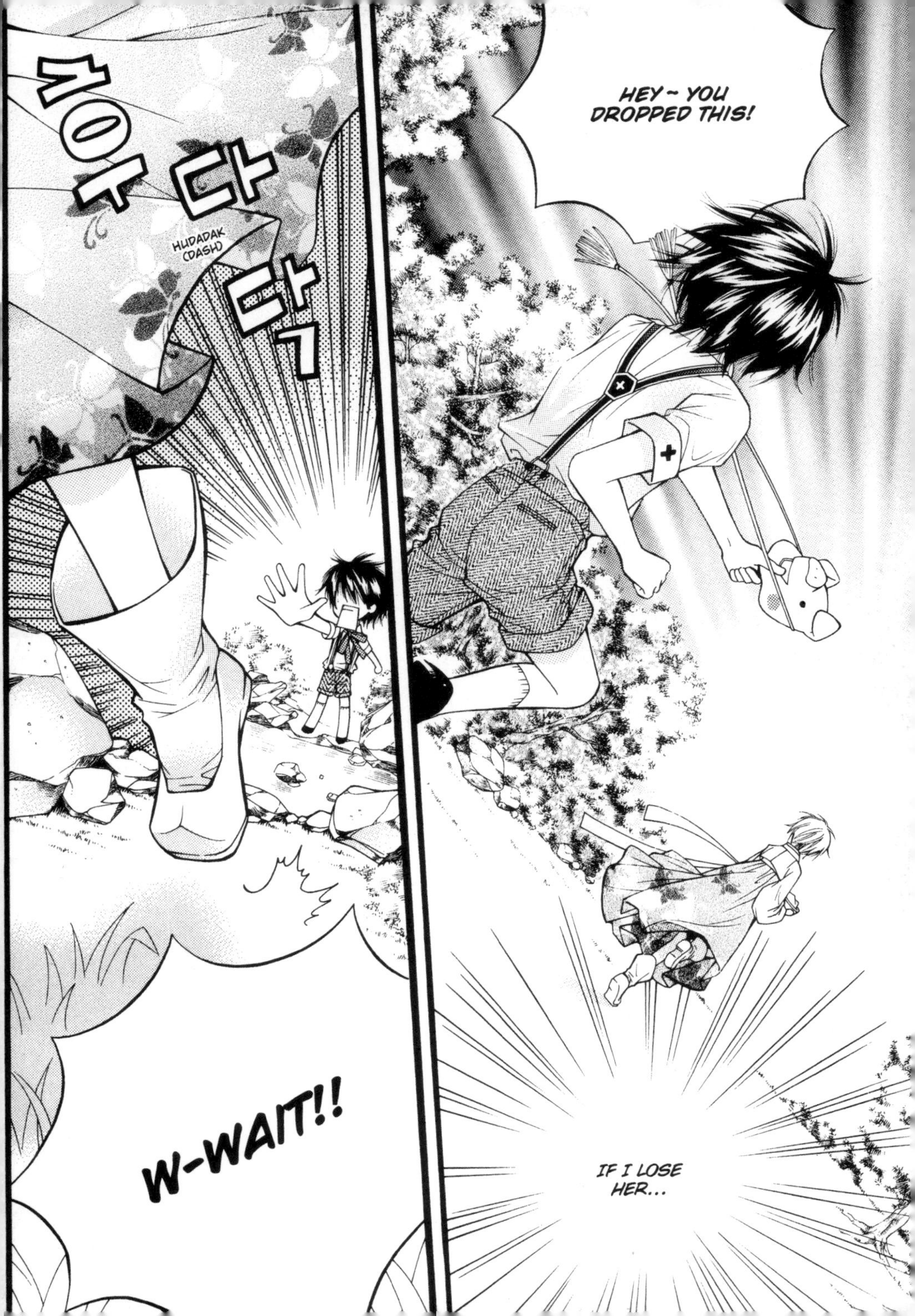
후다닥
HUDADAK (DASH)
W-WAIT!!
HEY~ YOU DROPPED THIS!
IF I LOSE HER...

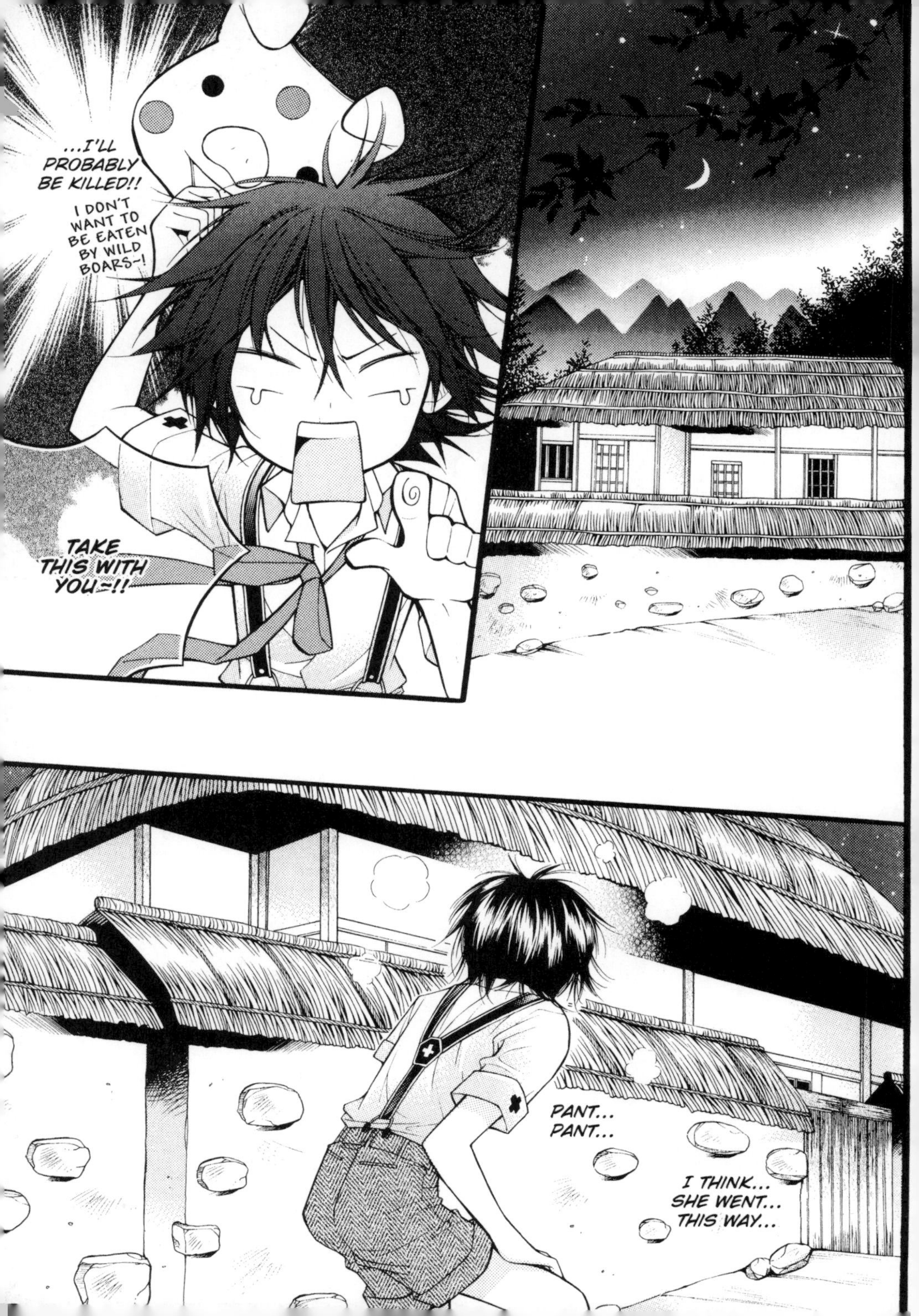
...I'LL PROBABLY BE KILLED!!
I DON'T WANT TO BE EATEN BY WILD BOARS~!
TAKE THIS WITH YOU~!!
PANT... PANT...
I THINK... SHE WENT... THIS WAY...

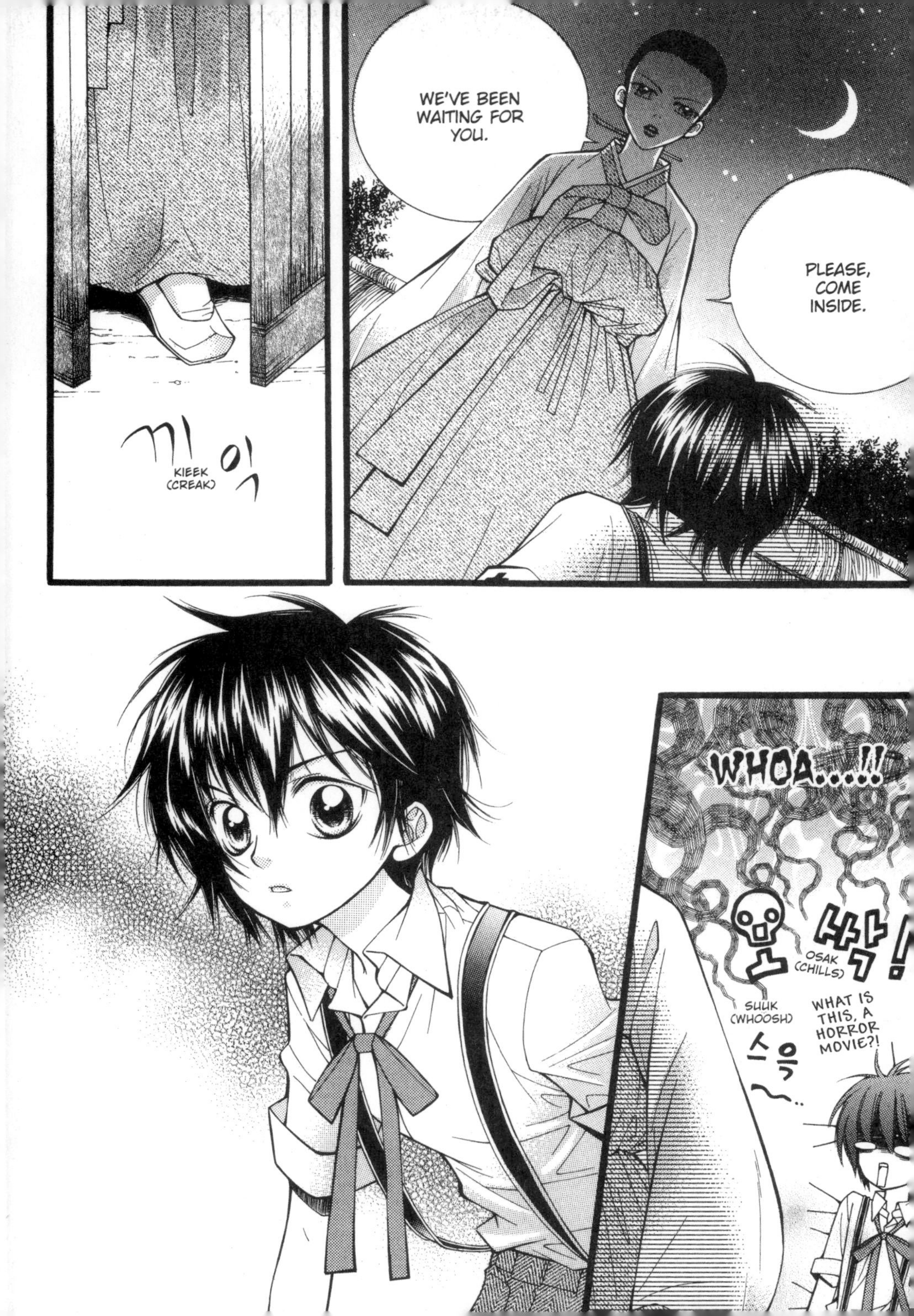

WE'VE BEEN WAITING FOR YOU.
PLEASE, COME INSIDE.
끼익
KIEEK (CREAK)
WHOA...!!
오싹!
OSAK (CHILLS)
WHAT IS THIS, A HORROR MOVIE?!
스읍~..
SUUK (WHOOSH)

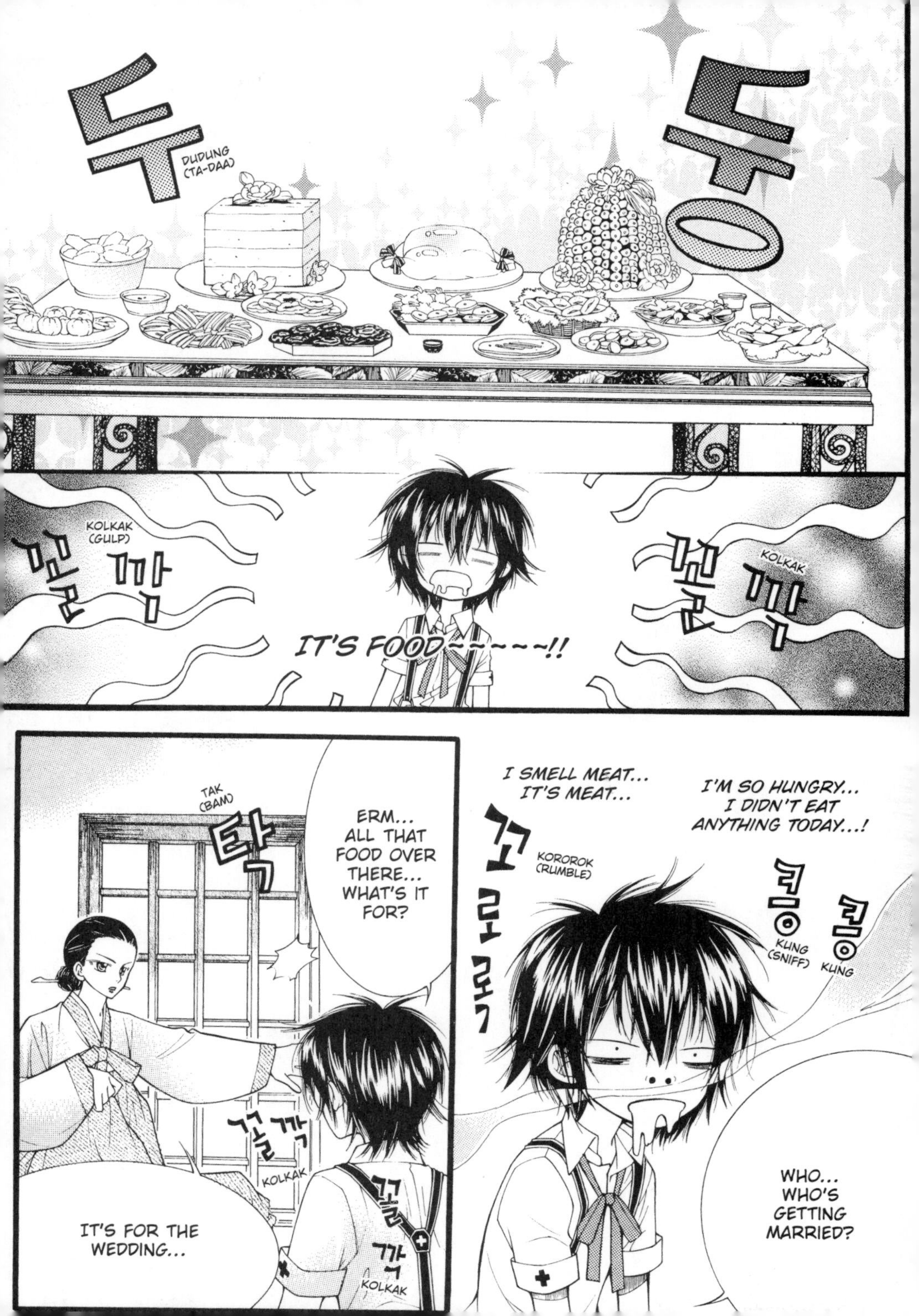

두둥
DUDUNG (TA-DAA)
꼴깍
KOLKAK (GULP)
IT'S FOOD~~~~~~!!
꼴깍
KOLKAK
탁
TAK (BAM)
ERM... ALL THAT FOOD OVER THERE... WHAT'S IT FOR?
IT'S FOR THE WEDDING...
꼴깍
KOLKAK
꼴깍
KOLKAK
I SMELL MEAT... IT'S MEAT...
꼬르륵
KOROROK (RUMBLE)
I'M SO HUNGRY... I DIDN'T EAT ANYTHING TODAY...!
킁킁
KUNG (SNIFF) KUNG
WHO... WHO'S GETTING MARRIED?

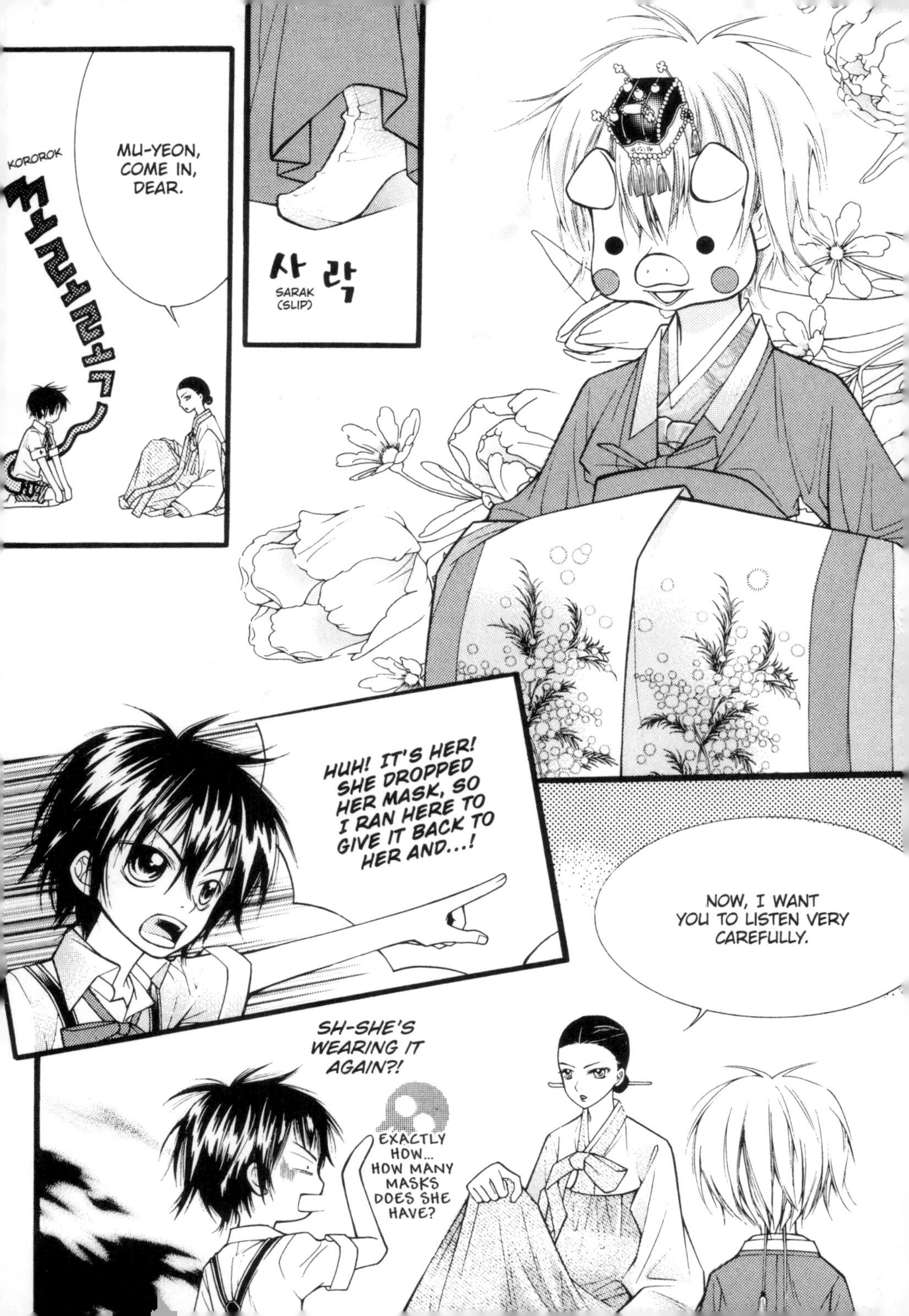

사락
SARAK (SLIP)
MU-YEON, COME IN, DEAR.
KOROROK
HUH! IT'S HER! SHE DROPPED HER MASK, SO I RAN HERE TO GIVE IT BACK TO HER AND...!
NOW, I WANT YOU TO LISTEN VERY CAREFULLY.
SH-SHE'S WEARING IT AGAIN?!
EXACTLY HOW... HOW MANY MASKS DOES SHE HAVE?

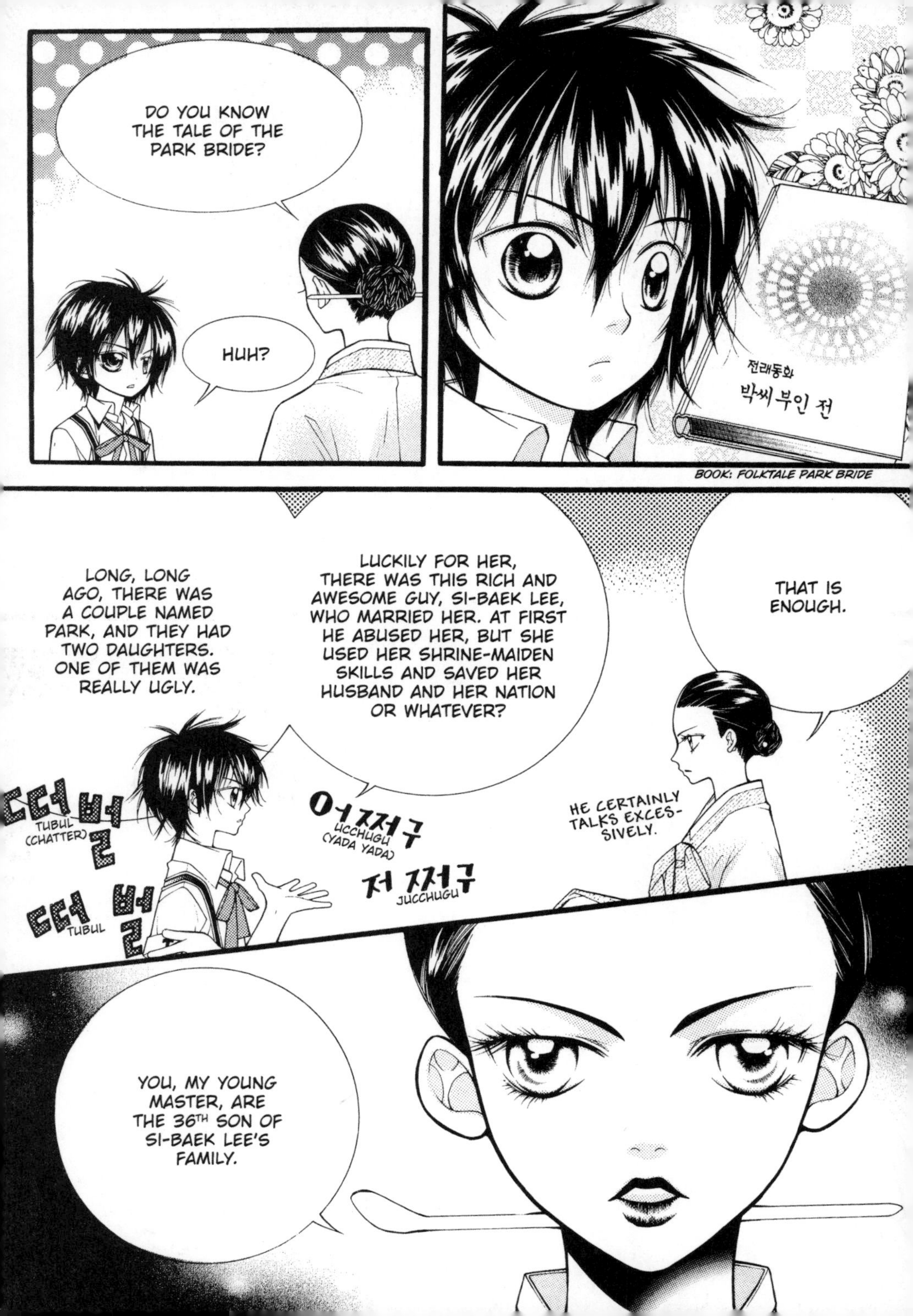

DO YOU KNOW THE TALE OF THE PARK BRIDE?
HUH?
전래동화
박씨부인 전
BOOK: FOLKTALE PARK BRIDE
LONG, LONG AGO, THERE WAS A COUPLE NAMED PARK, AND THEY HAD TWO DAUGHTERS. ONE OF THEM WAS REALLY UGLY.
LUCKILY FOR HER, THERE WAS THIS RICH AND AWESOME GUY, SI-BAEK LEE, WHO MARRIED HER. AT FIRST HE ABUSED HER, BUT SHE USED HER SHRINE-MAIDEN SKILLS AND SAVED HER HUSBAND AND HER NATION OR WHATEVER?
THAT IS ENOUGH.
떠벌
TUBUL (CHATTER)
떠벌
TUBUL
어쩌구
UCCHUGU (YADA YADA)
저쩌구
JUCCHUGU
HE CERTAINLY TALKS EXCES-SIVELY.
YOU, MY YOUNG MASTER, ARE THE 36TH SON OF SI-BAEK LEE'S FAMILY.

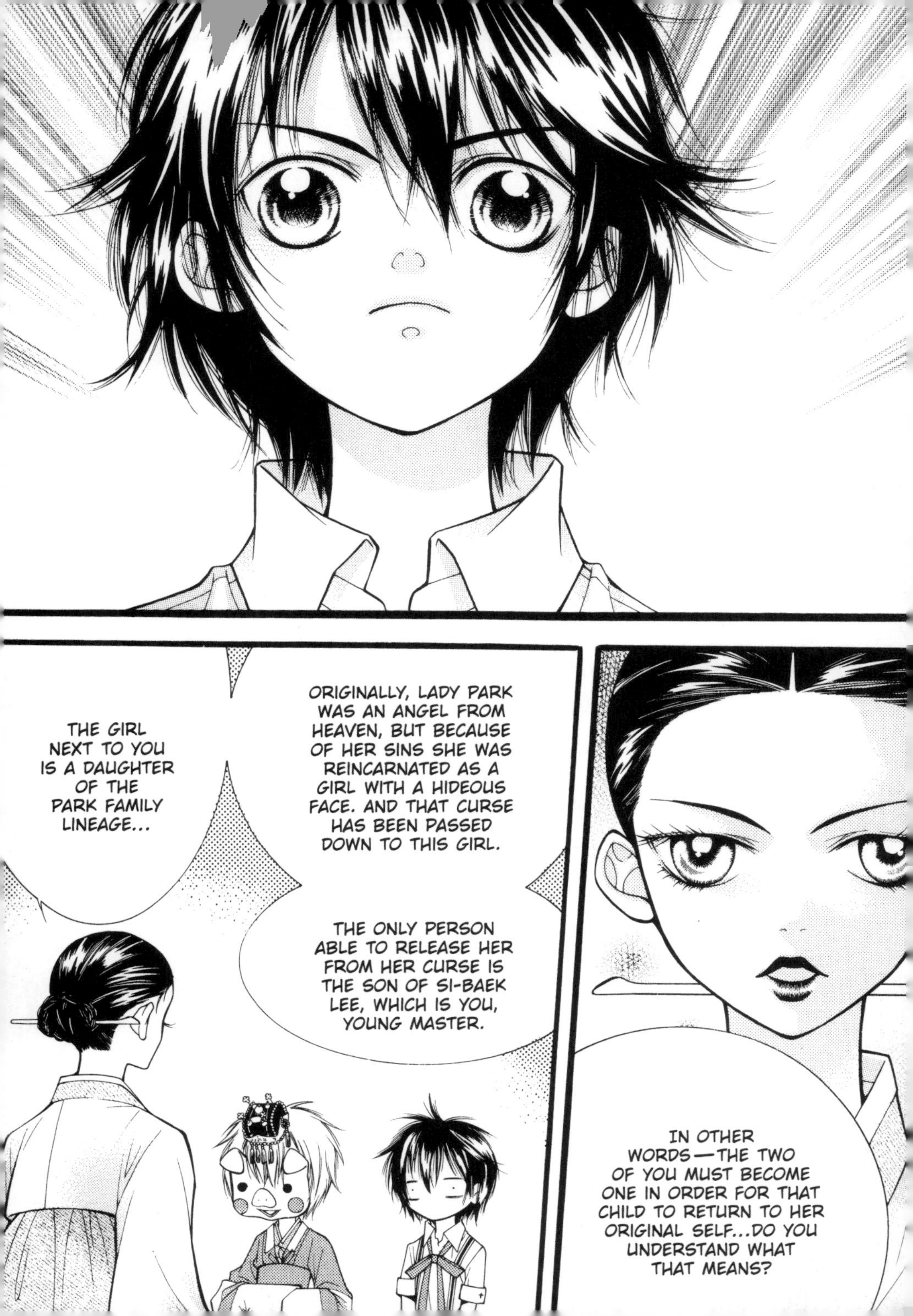
ORIGINALLY, LADY PARK WAS AN ANGEL FROM HEAVEN, BUT BECAUSE OF HER SINS SHE WAS REINCARNATED AS A GIRL WITH A HIDEOUS FACE. AND THAT CURSE HAS BEEN PASSED DOWN TO THIS GIRL.
THE GIRL NEXT TO YOU IS A DAUGHTER OF THE PARK FAMILY LINEAGE...
THE ONLY PERSON ABLE TO RELEASE HER FROM HER CURSE IS THE SON OF SI-BAEK LEE, WHICH IS YOU, YOUNG MASTER.
IN OTHER WORDS—THE TWO OF YOU MUST BECOME ONE IN ORDER FOR THAT CHILD TO RETURN TO HER ORIGINAL SELF...DO YOU UNDERSTAND WHAT THAT MEANS?

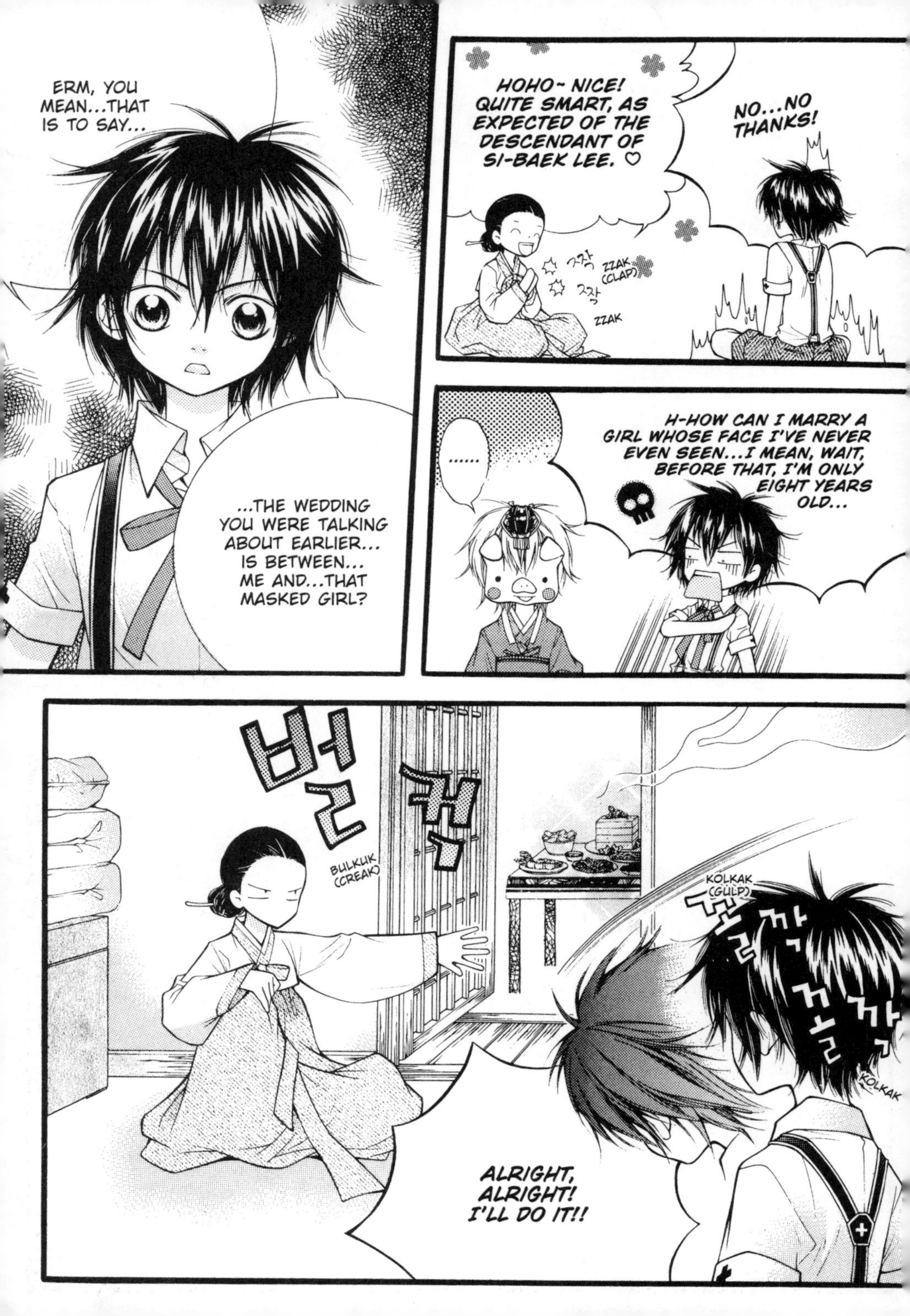
ERM, YOU MEAN...THAT IS TO SAY...
...THE WEDDING YOU WERE TALKING ABOUT EARLIER... IS BETWEEN... ME AND...THAT MASKED GIRL?
HOHO~ NICE! QUITE SMART, AS EXPECTED OF THE DESCENDANT OF SI-BAEK LEE. ♡
짝 ZZAK (CLAP)
짝 ZZAK
NO...NO THANKS!
......
H-HOW CAN I MARRY A GIRL WHOSE FACE I'VE NEVER EVEN SEEN...I MEAN, WAIT, BEFORE THAT, I'M ONLY EIGHT YEARS OLD...
벌컥
BULKUK (CREAK)
KOLKAK (GULP)
꼴깍 꼴깍
KOLKAK
ALRIGHT, ALRIGHT! I'LL DO IT!!

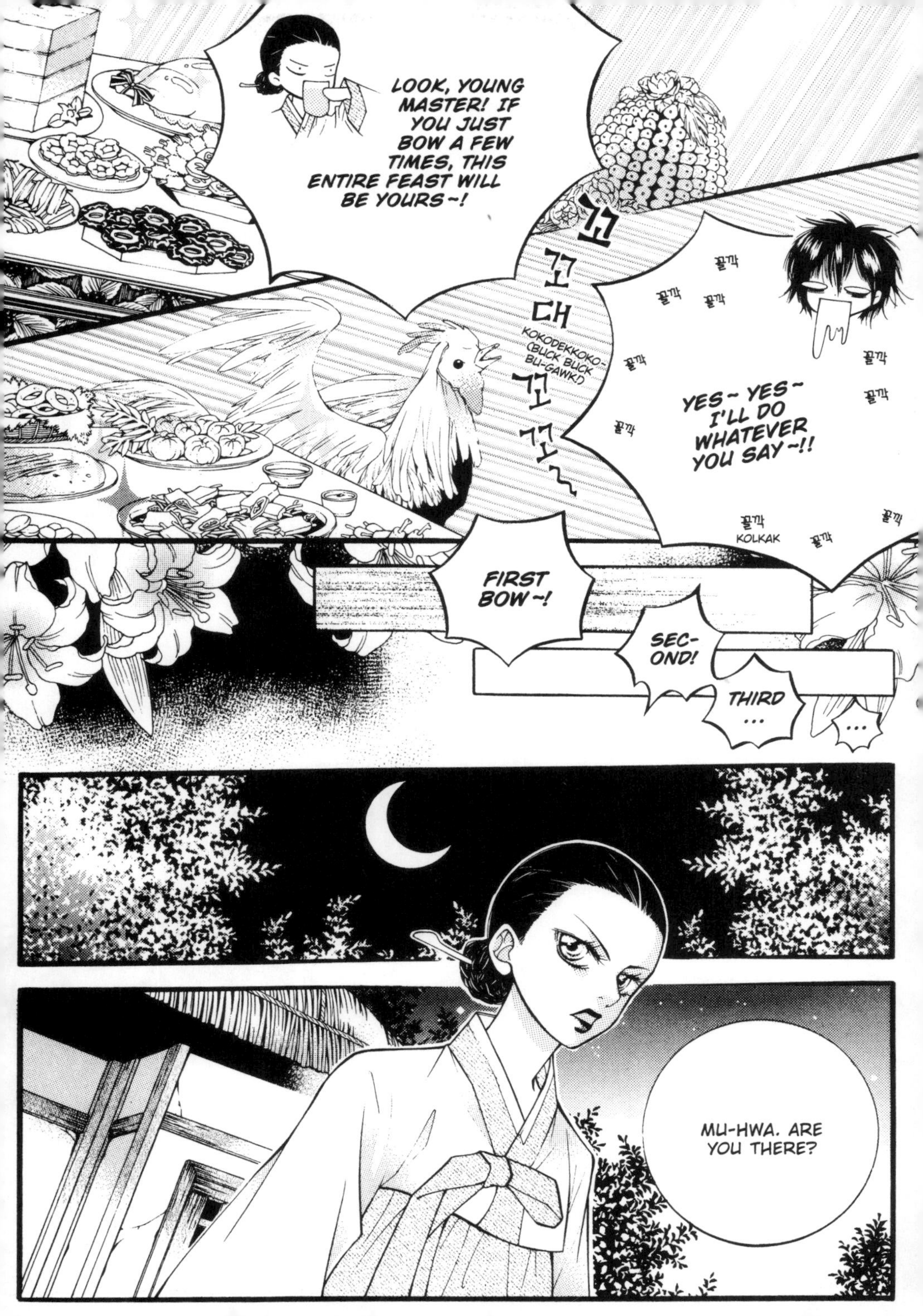
LOOK, YOUNG MASTER! IF YOU JUST BOW A FEW TIMES, THIS ENTIRE FEAST WILL BE YOURS~!
KOKODEKKOKO~ (BUCK BUCK BU-GAWK!)
꼴깍
KOLKAK
YES~ YES~ I'LL DO WHATEVER YOU SAY~!!
FIRST BOW~!
SEC-OND!
THIRD ...
...
MU-HWA. ARE YOU THERE?

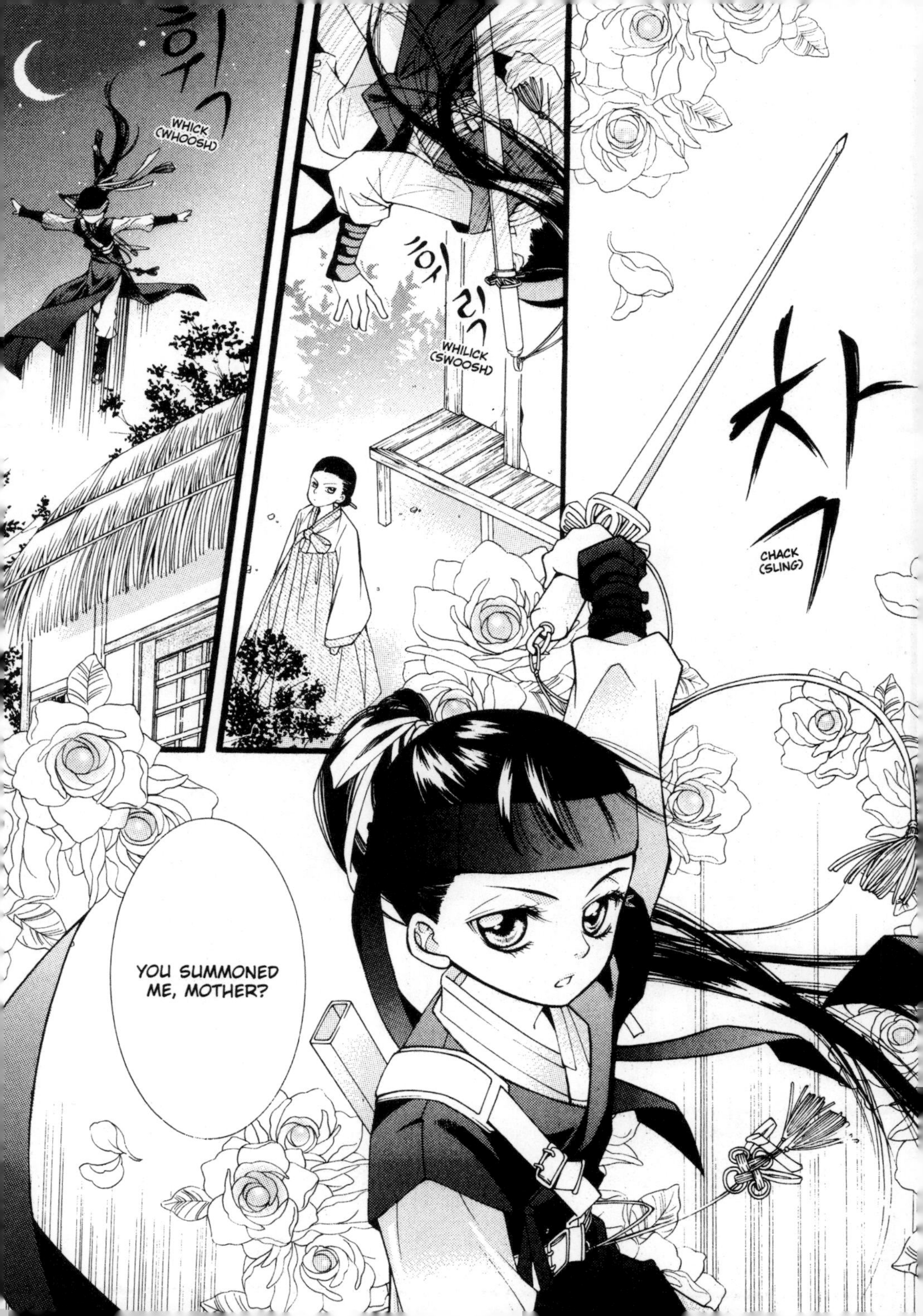

휘익
WHICK (WHOOSH)
휘리릭
WHILICK (SWOOSH)
착
CHACK (SLING)
YOU SUMMONED ME, MOTHER?

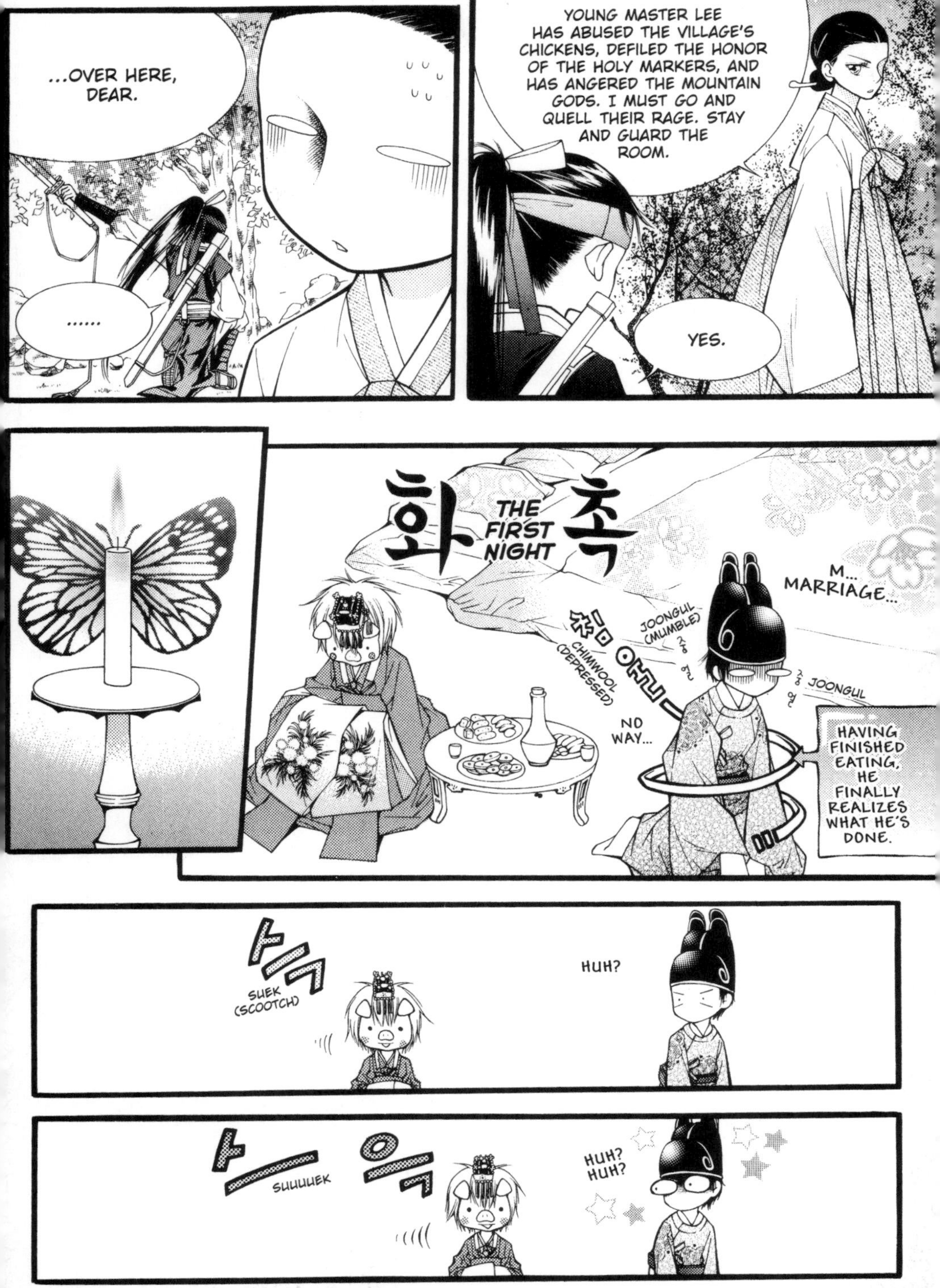
YOUNG MASTER LEE HAS ABUSED THE VILLAGE'S CHICKENS, DEFILED THE HONOR OF THE HOLY MARKERS, AND HAS ANGERED THE MOUNTAIN GODS. I MUST GO AND QUELL THEIR RAGE. STAY AND GUARD THE ROOM.
YES.
...OVER HERE, DEAR.
......
화촉
THE FIRST NIGHT
M... MARRIAGE...
JOONGUL (MUMBLE)
JOONGUL
침울
CHIMWOOL (DEPRESSED)
NO WAY...
HAVING FINISHED EATING, HE FINALLY REALIZES WHAT HE'S DONE.
HUH?
SUEK (SCOOTCH)
HUH? HUH?
SUUUUEK

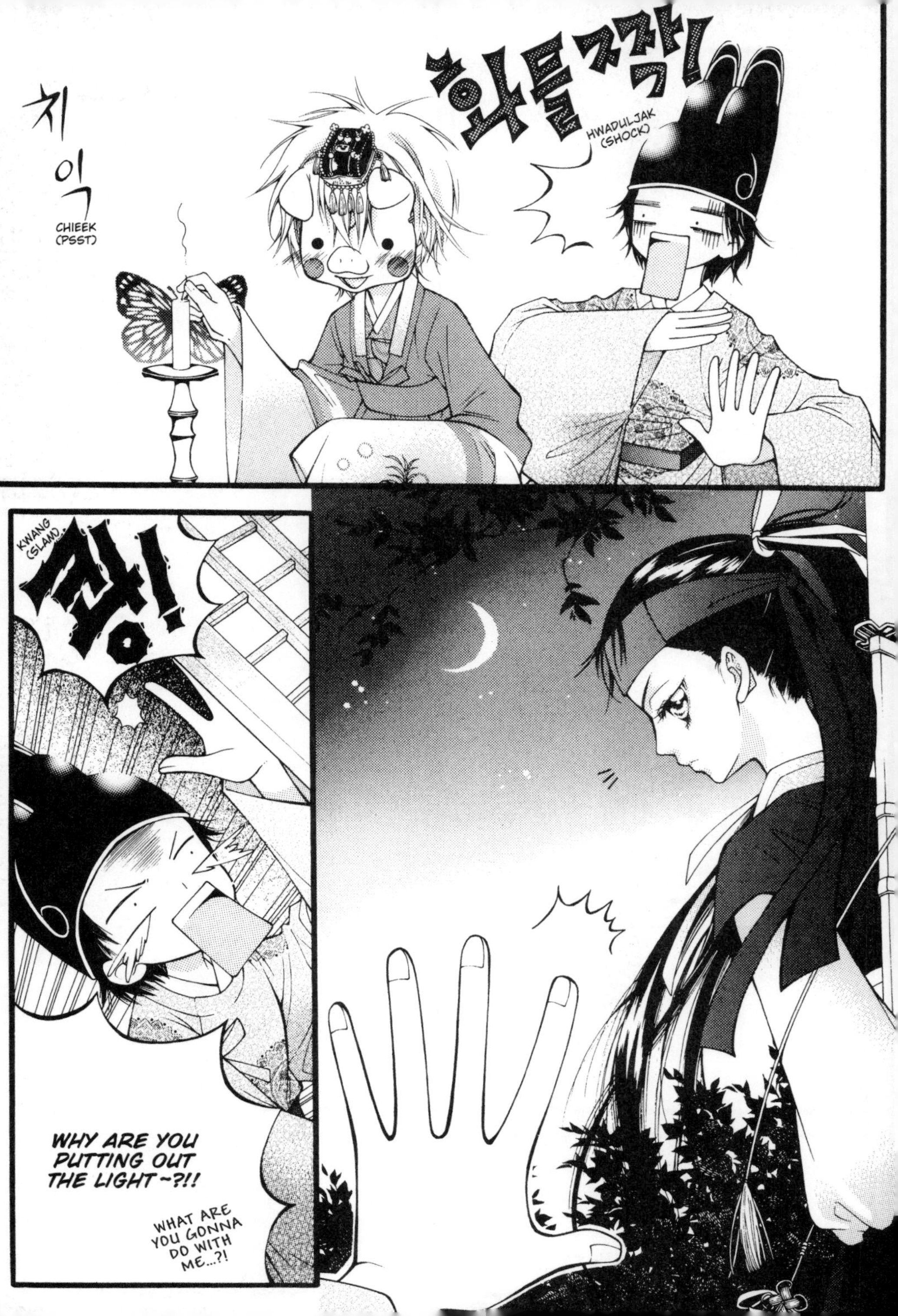

화들짝!
HWADULJAK (SHOCK)
치익
CHIEEK (PSST)
쾅!
KWANG (SLAM)
WHY ARE YOU PUTTING OUT THE LIGHT~?!!
WHAT ARE YOU GONNA DO WITH ME...?!

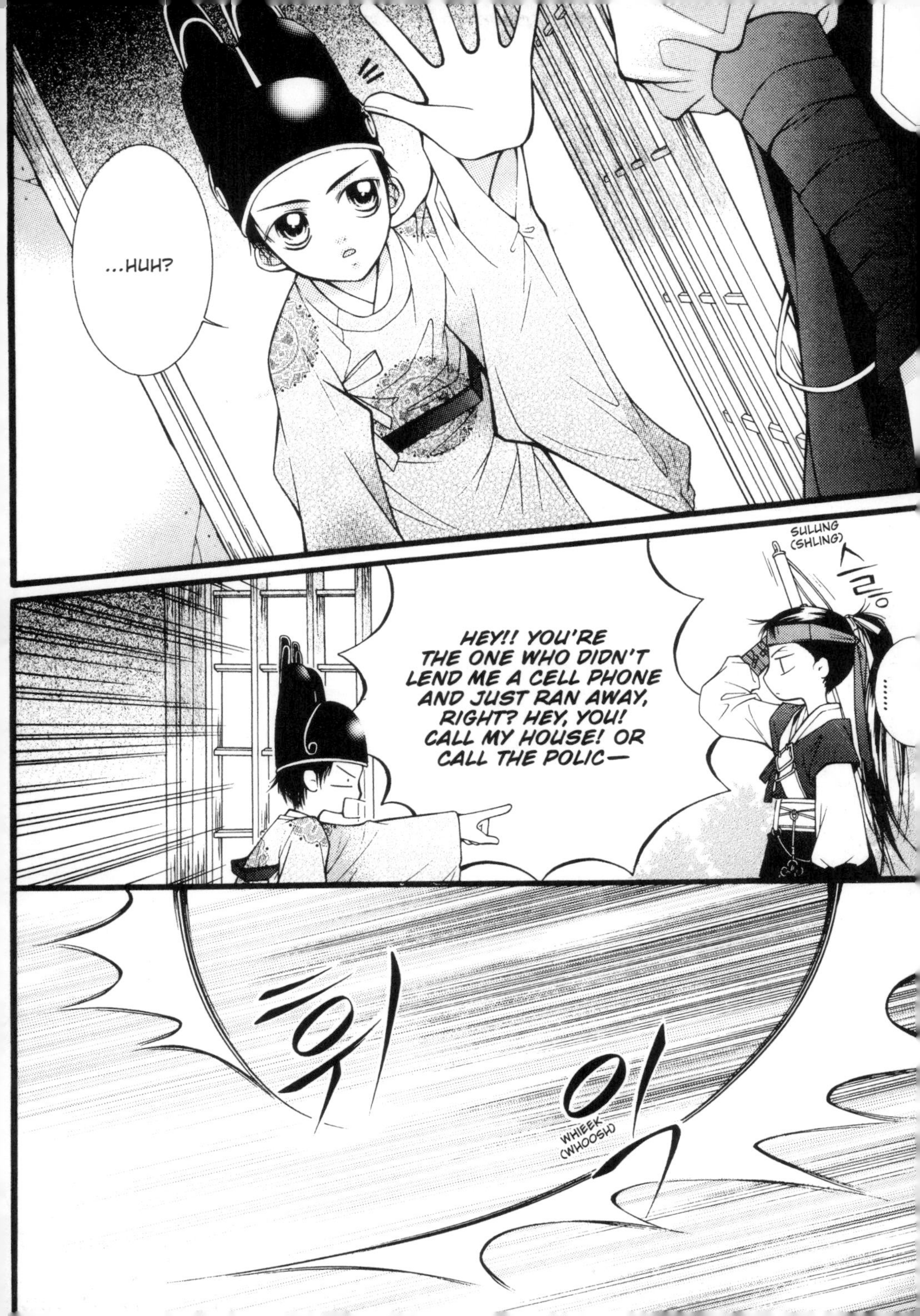
...HUH?
SULUNG (SHLING)
HEY!! YOU'RE THE ONE WHO DIDN'T LEND ME A CELL PHONE AND JUST RAN AWAY, RIGHT? HEY, YOU! CALL MY HOUSE! OR CALL THE POLIC—
......
WHIEEK (WHOOSH)

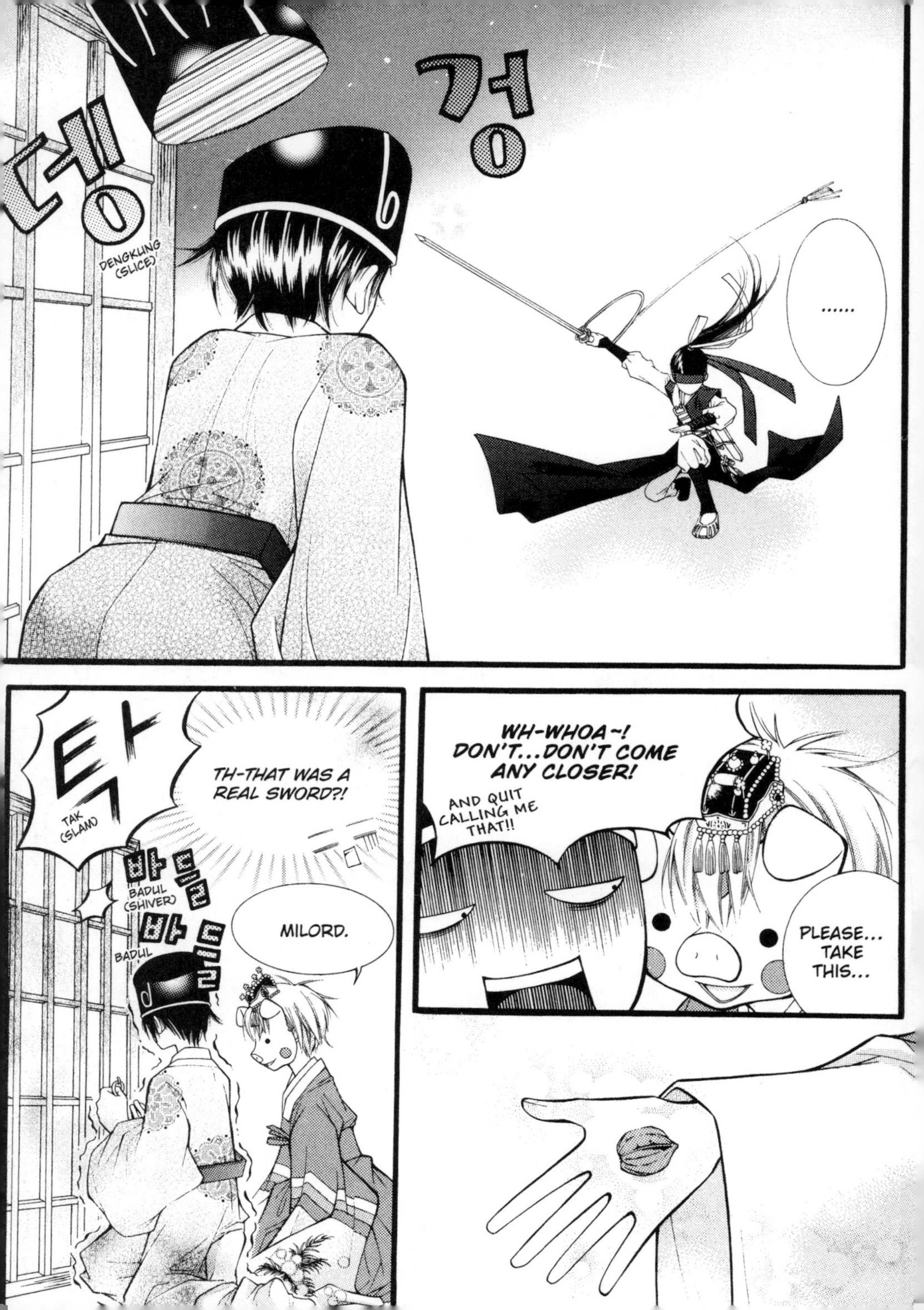
뎅
겅
DENGKUNG (SLICE)
......
탁
TAK (SLAM)
TH-THAT WAS A REAL SWORD?!
바들
BADUL (SHIVER)
바들
BADUL
MILORD.
WH-WHOA~! DON'T...DON'T COME ANY CLOSER!
AND QUIT CALLING ME THAT!!
PLEASE... TAKE THIS...

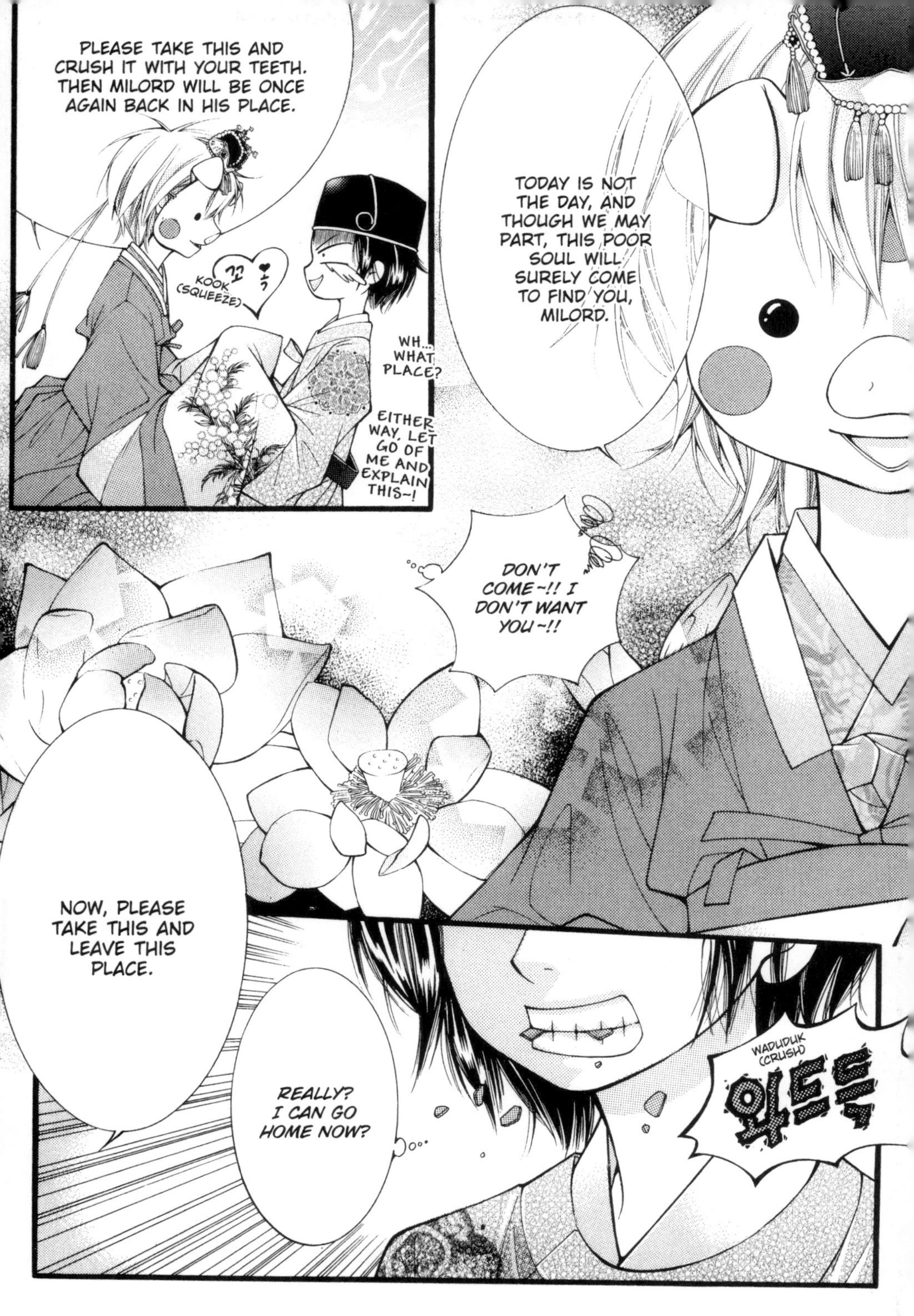
PLEASE TAKE THIS AND CRUSH IT WITH YOUR TEETH. THEN MILORD WILL BE ONCE AGAIN BACK IN HIS PLACE.
KOOK (SQUEEZE)
WH... WHAT PLACE?
EITHER WAY, LET GO OF ME AND EXPLAIN THIS~!
TODAY IS NOT THE DAY, AND THOUGH WE MAY PART, THIS POOR SOUL WILL SURELY COME TO FIND YOU, MILORD.
DON'T COME~!! I DON'T WANT YOU~!!
NOW, PLEASE TAKE THIS AND LEAVE THIS PLACE.
REALLY? I CAN GO HOME NOW?
WADUDUK (CRUSH)
와드득

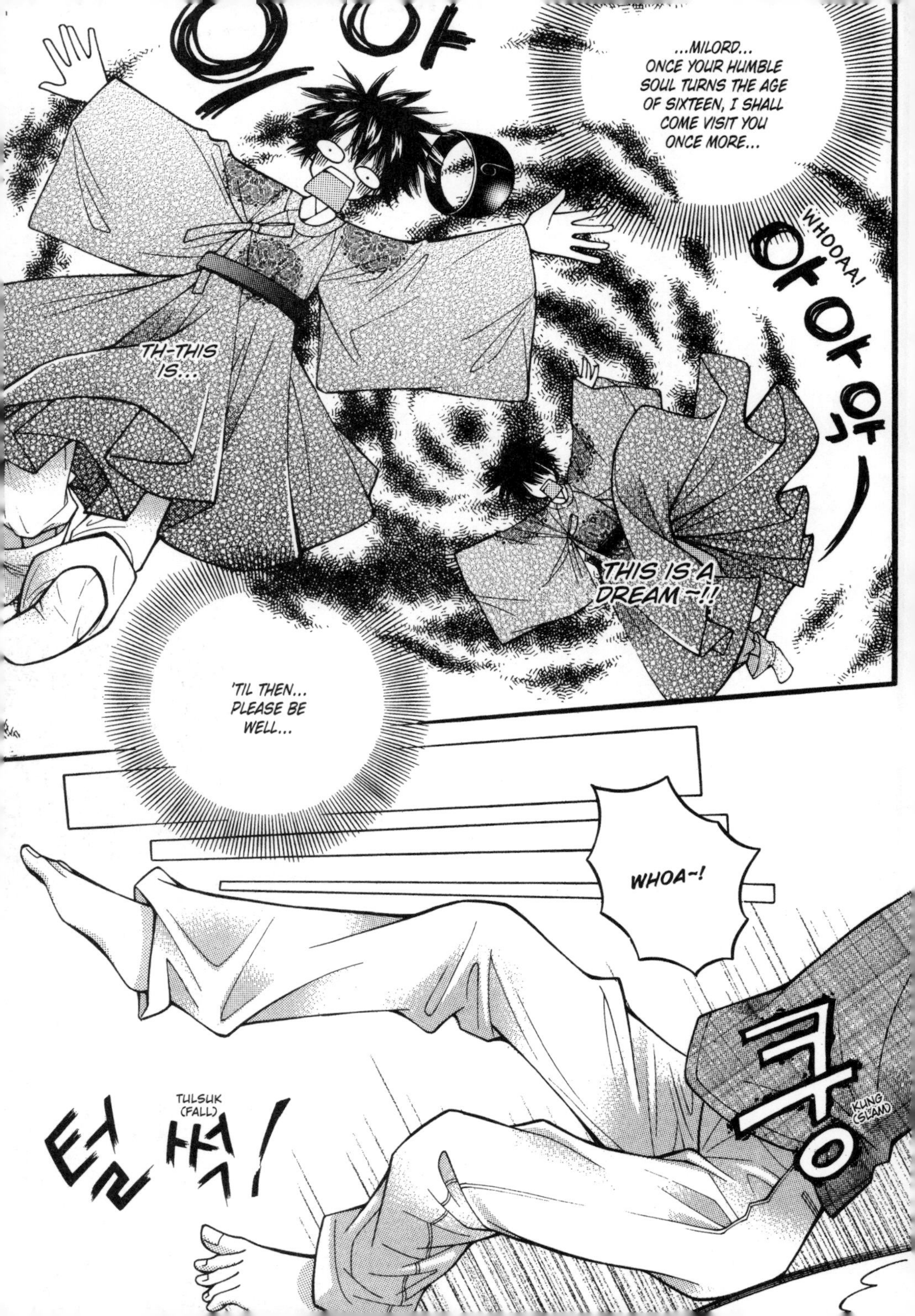
...MILORD... ONCE YOUR HUMBLE SOUL TURNS THE AGE OF SIXTEEN, I SHALL COME VISIT YOU ONCE MORE...
WHOOAA!
TH-THIS IS...
THIS IS A DREAM~!!
'TIL THEN... PLEASE BE WELL...
WHOA~!
KUNG (SLAM)
TULSUK (FALL)

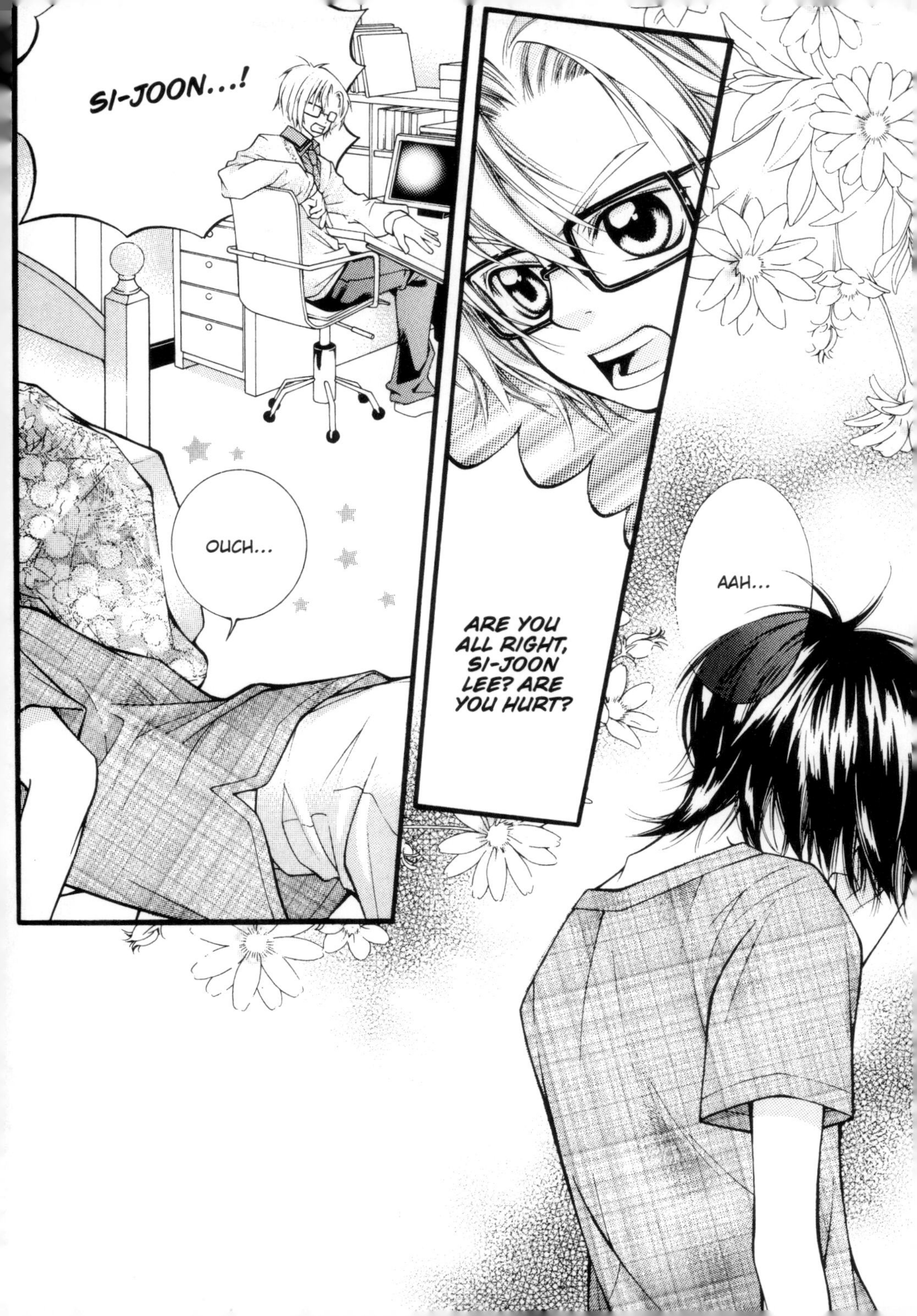
SI-JOON...!
ARE YOU ALL RIGHT, SI-JOON LEE? ARE YOU HURT?
OUCH...
AAH...

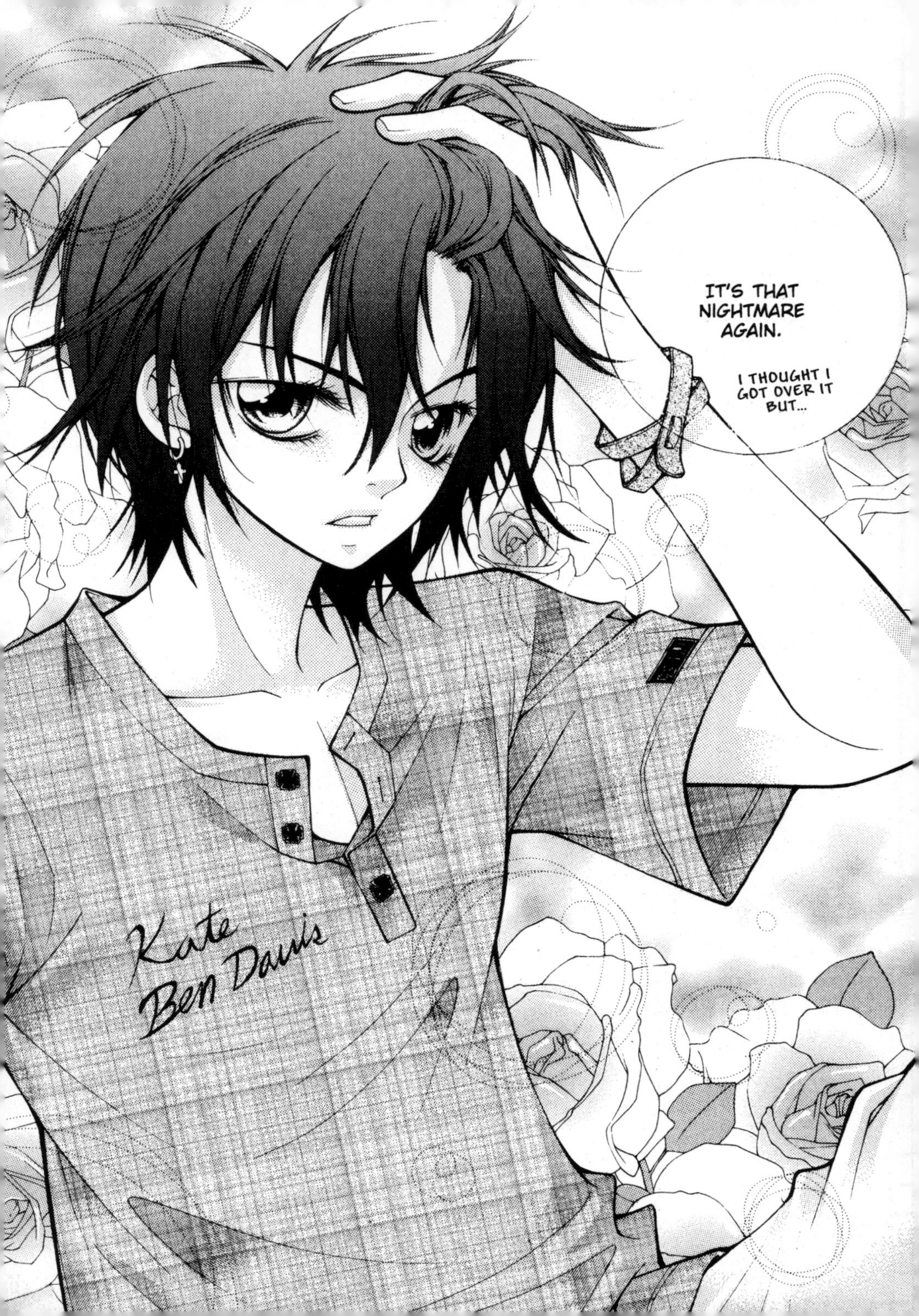
IT'S THAT NIGHTMARE AGAIN.
I THOUGHT I GOT OVER IT BUT...
Kate Ben Davis

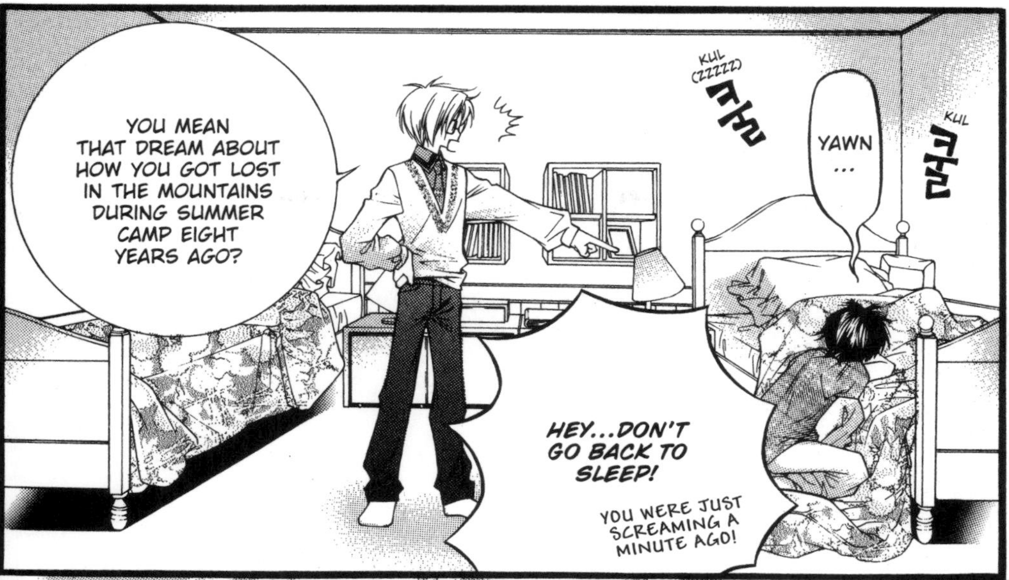
YOU MEAN THAT DREAM ABOUT HOW YOU GOT LOST IN THE MOUNTAINS DURING SUMMER CAMP EIGHT YEARS AGO?
KUL (ZZZZZ)
YAWN...
KUL
HEY...DON'T GO BACK TO SLEEP!
YOU WERE JUST SCREAMING A MINUTE AGO!

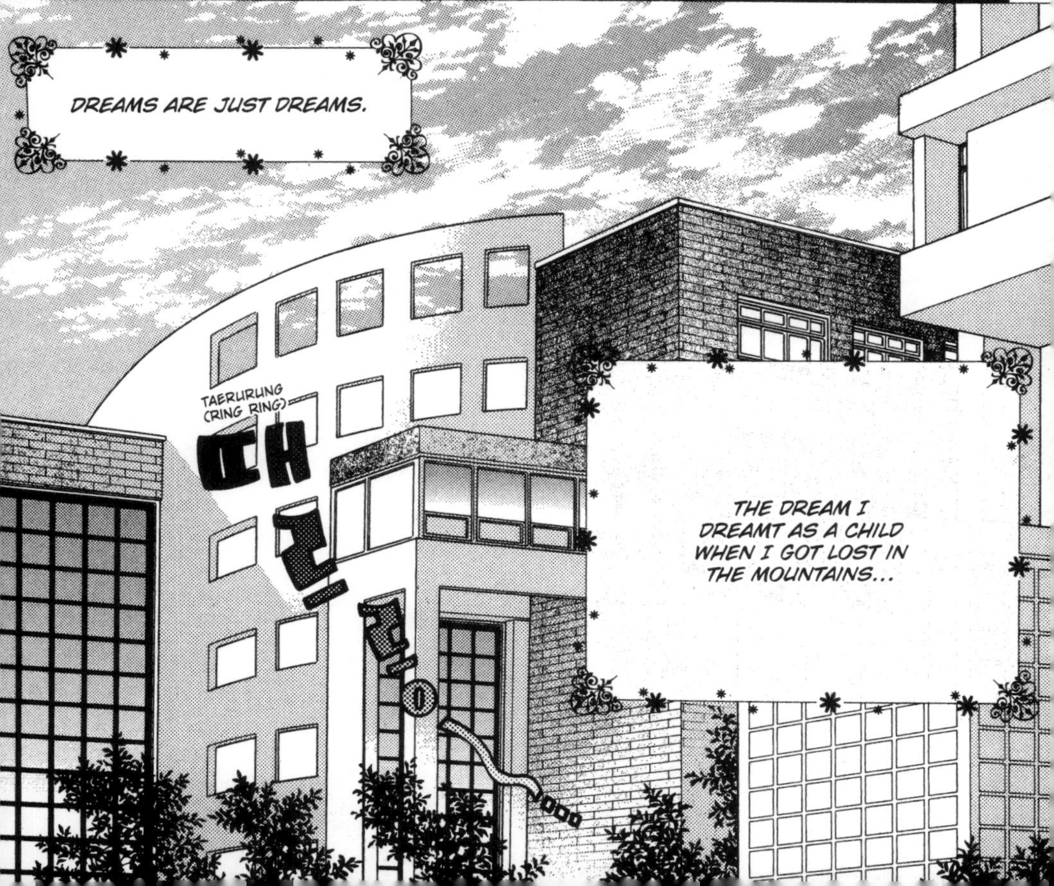
DREAMS ARE JUST DREAMS.
TAERURUNG (RING RING)
THE DREAM I DREAMT AS A CHILD WHEN I GOT LOST IN THE MOUNTAINS...

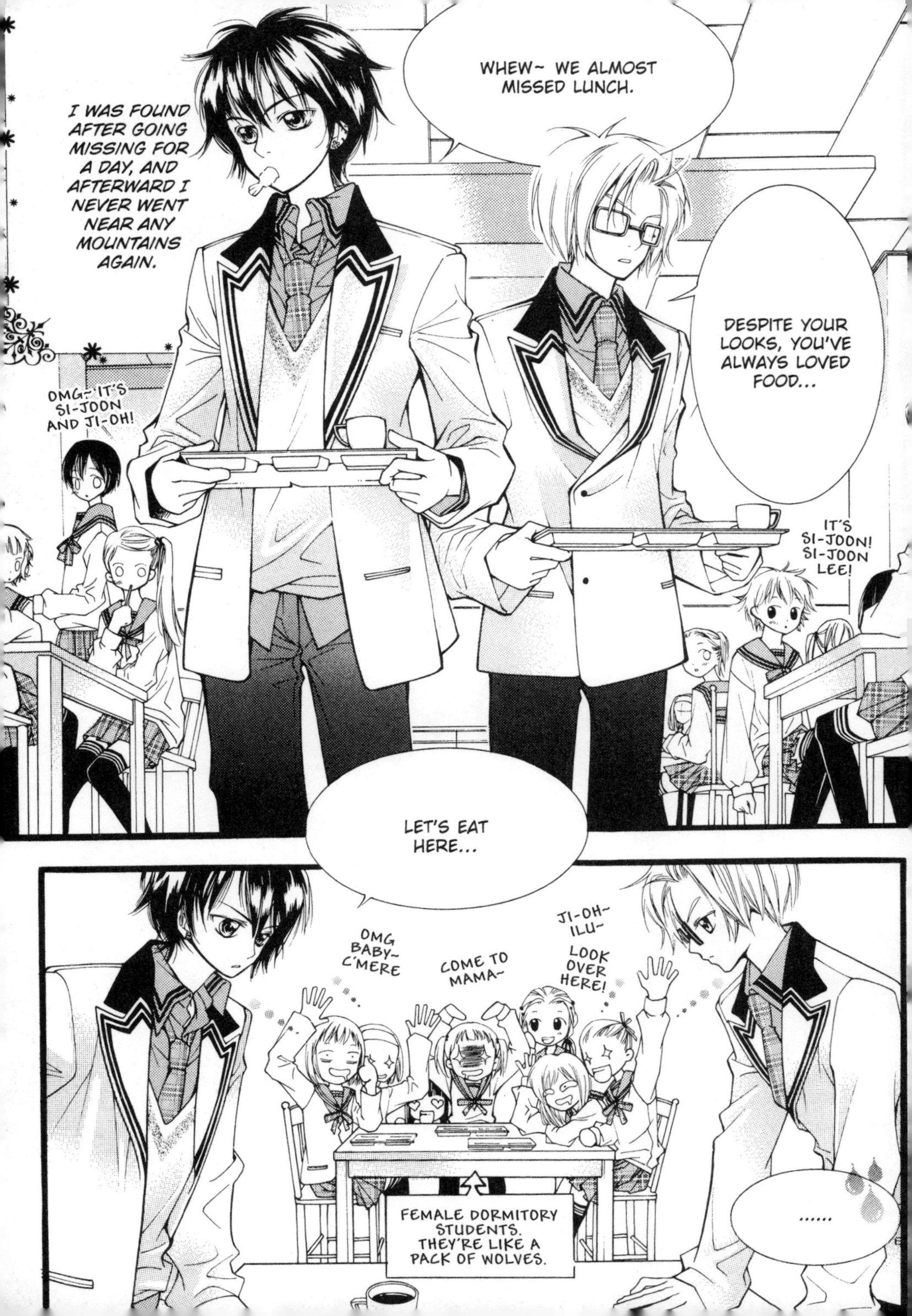

I WAS FOUND AFTER GOING MISSING FOR A DAY, AND AFTERWARD I NEVER WENT NEAR ANY MOUNTAINS AGAIN.
WHEW~ WE ALMOST MISSED LUNCH.
DESPITE YOUR LOOKS, YOU'VE ALWAYS LOVED FOOD...
OMG~ IT'S SI-JOON AND JI-OH!
IT'S SI-JOON! SI-JOON LEE!
LET'S EAT HERE...
OMG BABY~ C'MERE
COME TO MAMA~
JI-OH~ ILU~
LOOK OVER HERE!
FEMALE DORMITORY STUDENTS. THEY'RE LIKE A PACK OF WOLVES.
......

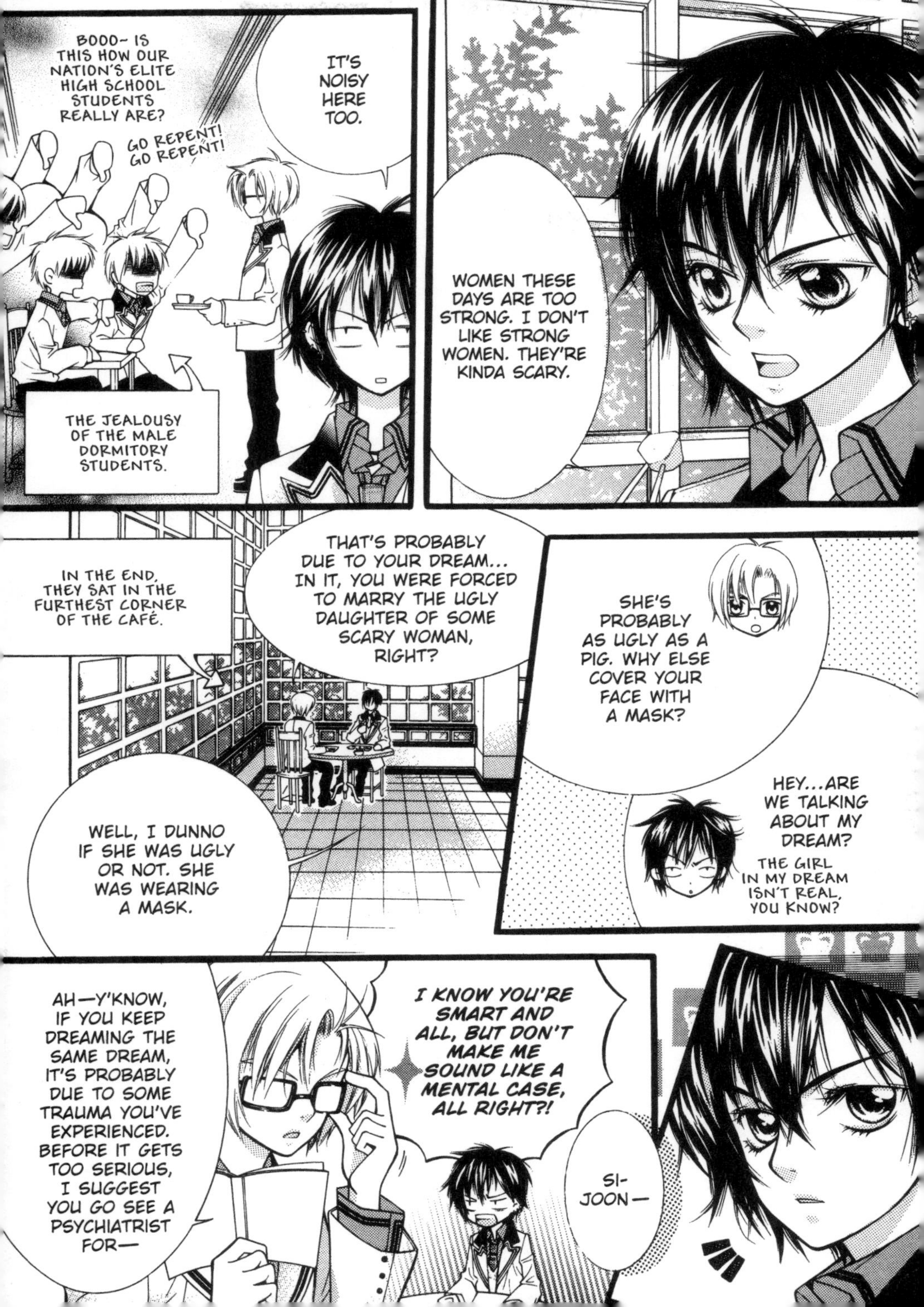
BOOO~ IS THIS HOW OUR NATION'S ELITE HIGH SCHOOL STUDENTS REALLY ARE?
GO REPENT! GO REPENT!
IT'S NOISY HERE TOO.
THE JEALOUSY OF THE MALE DORMITORY STUDENTS.
WOMEN THESE DAYS ARE TOO STRONG. I DON'T LIKE STRONG WOMEN. THEY'RE KINDA SCARY.
IN THE END, THEY SAT IN THE FURTHEST CORNER OF THE CAFÉ.
THAT'S PROBABLY DUE TO YOUR DREAM... IN IT, YOU WERE FORCED TO MARRY THE UGLY DAUGHTER OF SOME SCARY WOMAN, RIGHT?
WELL, I DUNNO IF SHE WAS UGLY OR NOT. SHE WAS WEARING A MASK.
SHE'S PROBABLY AS UGLY AS A PIG. WHY ELSE COVER YOUR FACE WITH A MASK?
HEY...ARE WE TALKING ABOUT MY DREAM?
THE GIRL IN MY DREAM ISN'T REAL, YOU KNOW?
AH—Y'KNOW, IF YOU KEEP DREAMING THE SAME DREAM, IT'S PROBABLY DUE TO SOME TRAUMA YOU'VE EXPERIENCED. BEFORE IT GETS TOO SERIOUS, I SUGGEST YOU GO SEE A PSYCHIATRIST FOR—
I KNOW YOU'RE SMART AND ALL, BUT DON'T MAKE ME SOUND LIKE A MENTAL CASE, ALL RIGHT?!
SI-JOON—

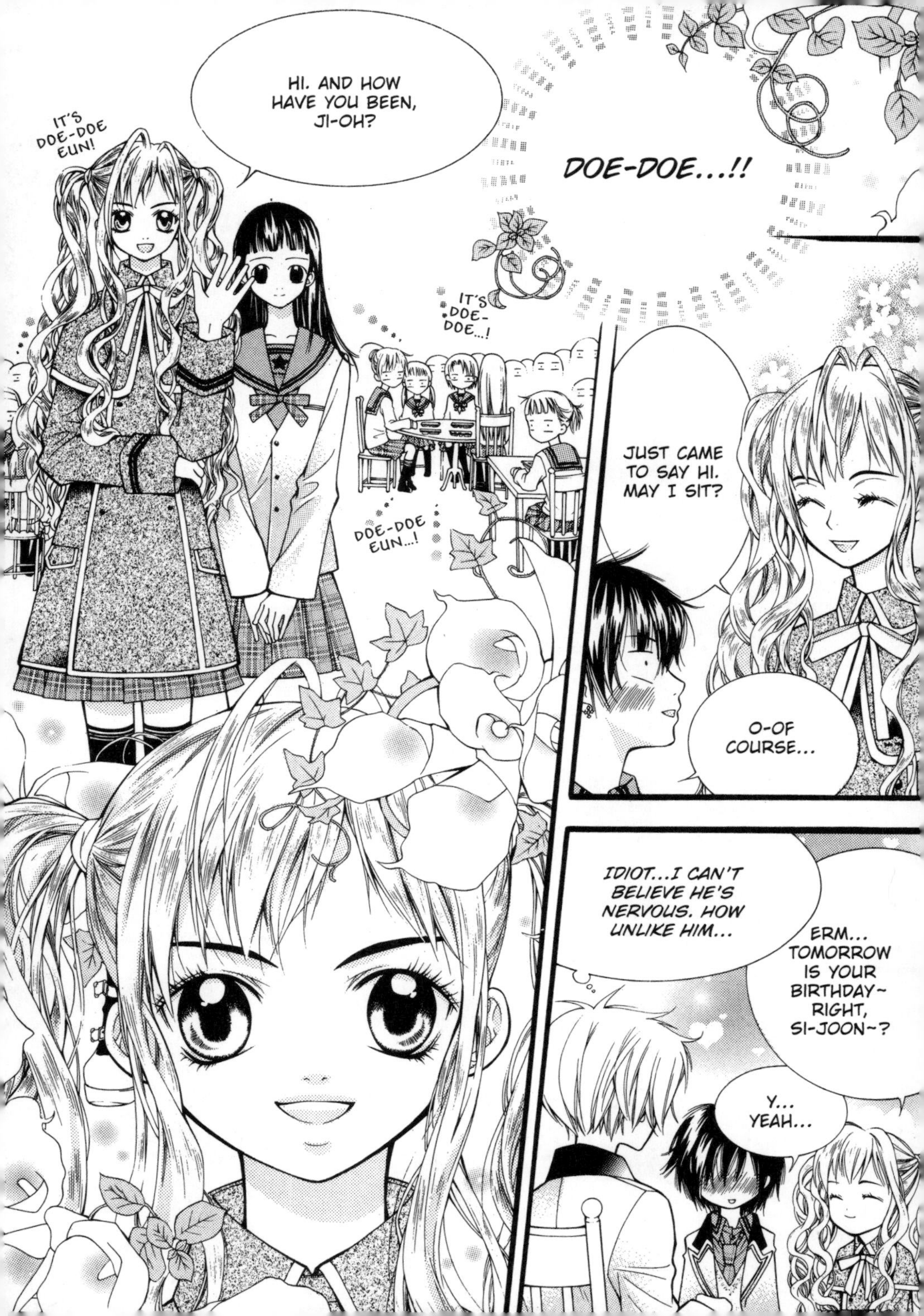
IT'S DOE-DOE EUN!
HI. AND HOW HAVE YOU BEEN, JI-OH?
DOE-DOE...!!
IT'S DOE-DOE...!
DOE-DOE EUN...!
JUST CAME TO SAY HI. MAY I SIT?
O-OF COURSE...
IDIOT...I CAN'T BELIEVE HE'S NERVOUS. HOW UNLIKE HIM...
ERM... TOMORROW IS YOUR BIRTHDAY~ RIGHT, SI-JOON~?
Y... YEAH...

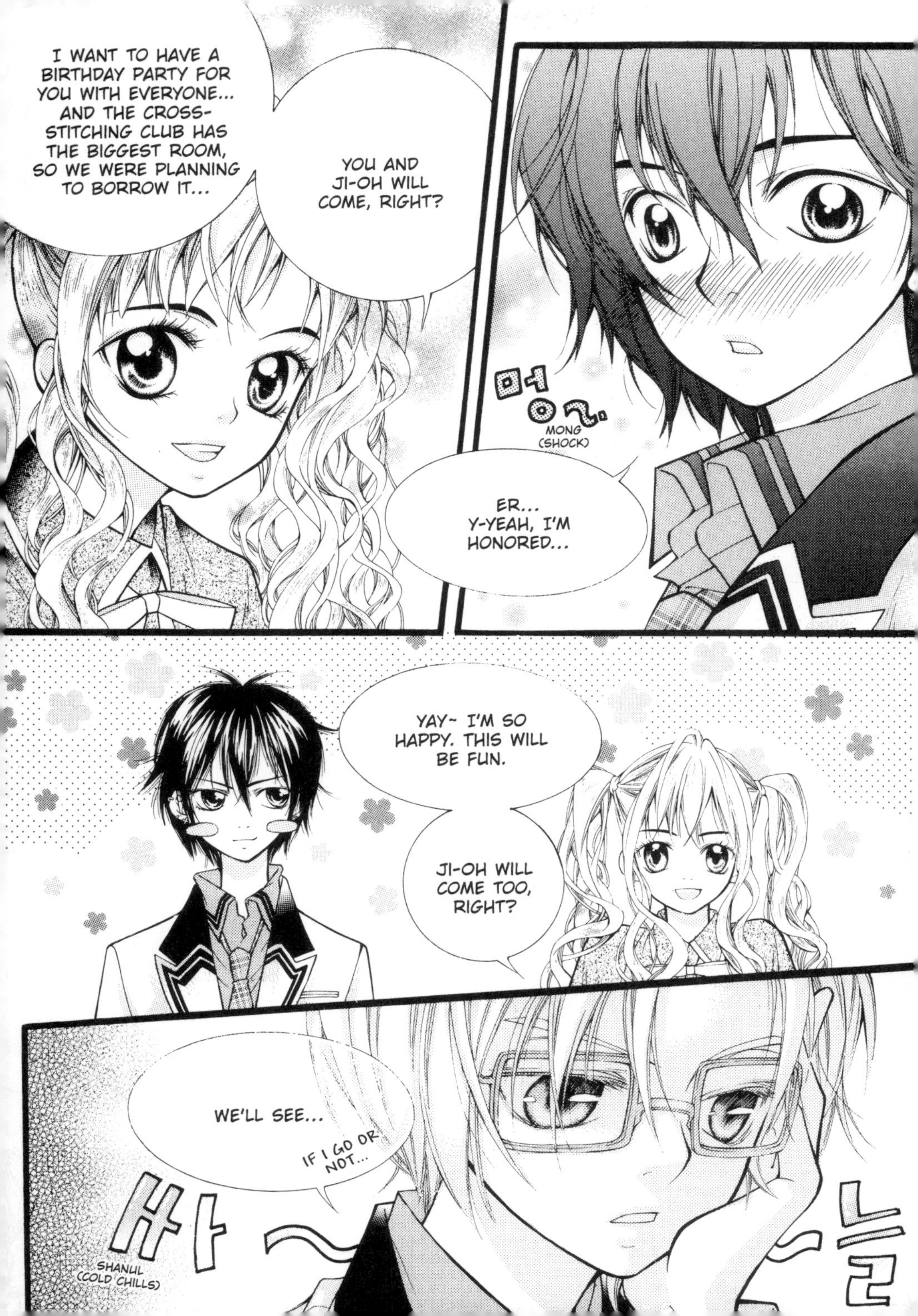
I WANT TO HAVE A BIRTHDAY PARTY FOR YOU WITH EVERYONE... AND THE CROSS-STITCHING CLUB HAS THE BIGGEST ROOM, SO WE WERE PLANNING TO BORROW IT...
YOU AND JI-OH WILL COME, RIGHT?
MONG (SHOCK)
ER... Y-YEAH, I'M HONORED...
YAY~ I'M SO HAPPY. THIS WILL BE FUN.
JI-OH WILL COME TOO, RIGHT?
WE'LL SEE...
IF I GO OR NOT...
SHANUL (COLD CHILLS)

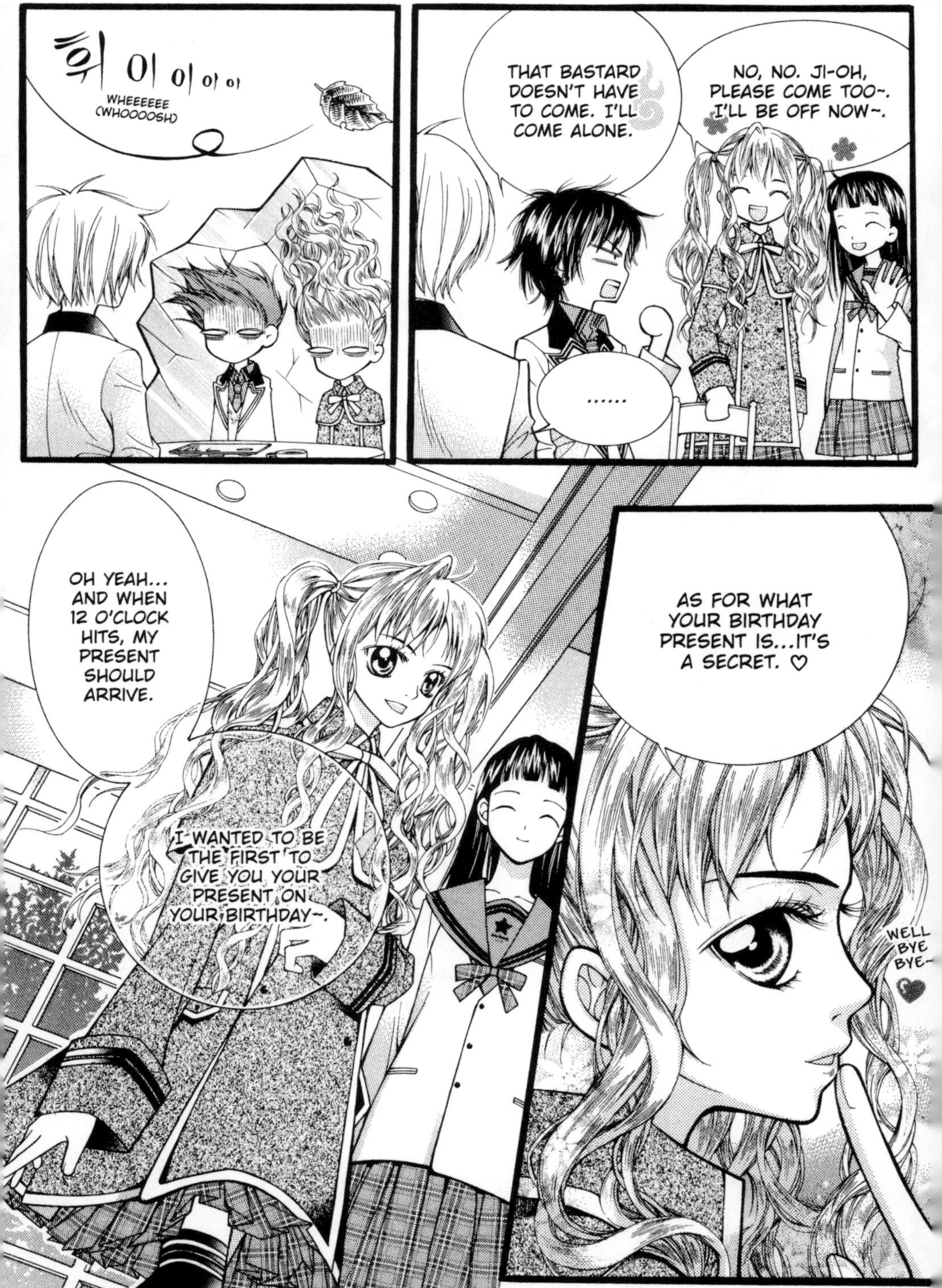
휘 이 이 이 이
WHEEEEEE (WHOOOOSH)
THAT BASTARD DOESN'T HAVE TO COME. I'LL COME ALONE.
NO, NO. JI-OH, PLEASE COME TOO~. I'LL BE OFF NOW~.
......
OH YEAH... AND WHEN 12 O'CLOCK HITS, MY PRESENT SHOULD ARRIVE.
I WANTED TO BE THE FIRST TO GIVE YOU YOUR PRESENT ON YOUR BIRTHDAY~.
AS FOR WHAT YOUR BIRTHDAY PRESENT IS...IT'S A SECRET. ♡
WELL BYE BYE~

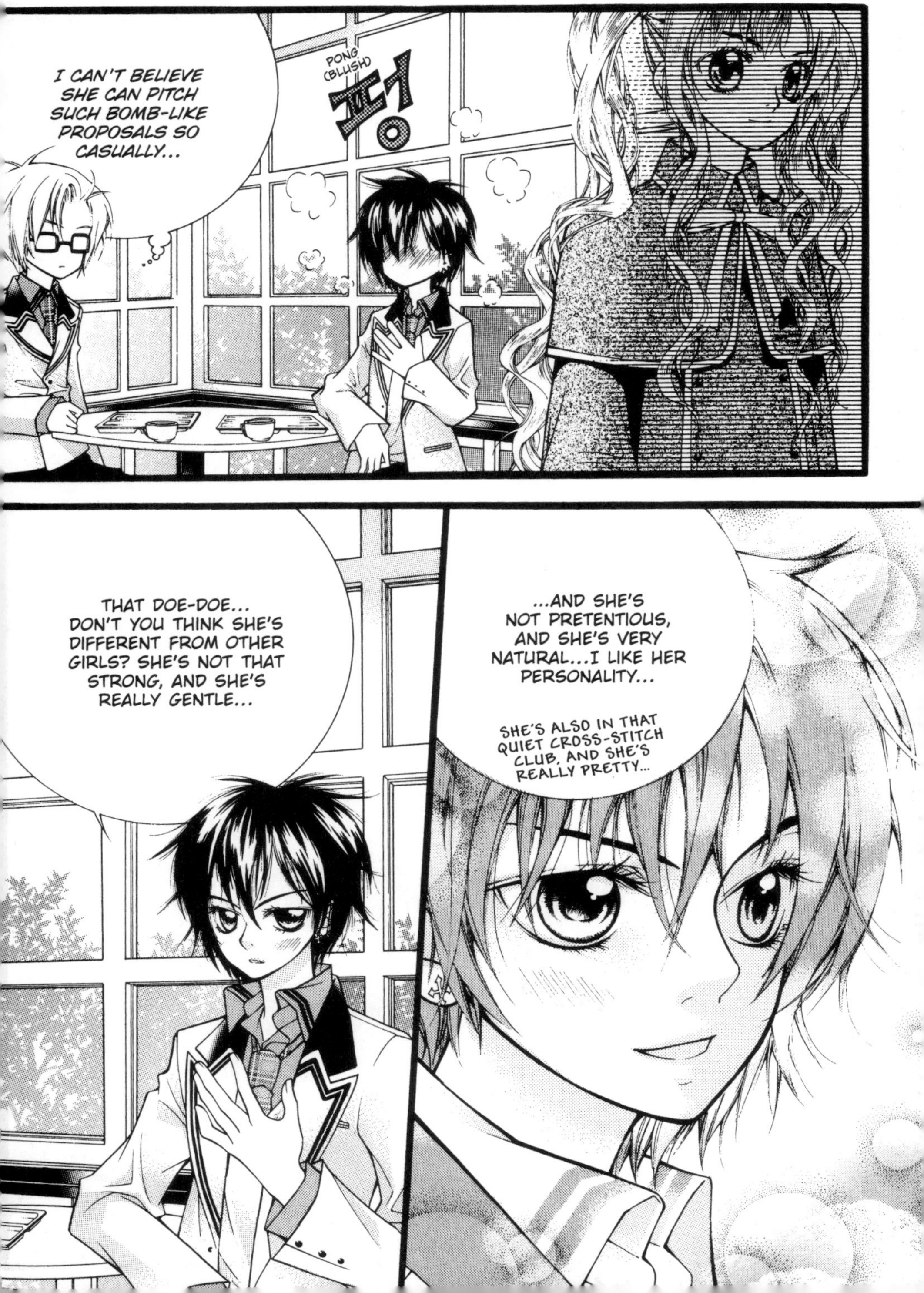
I CAN'T BELIEVE SHE CAN PITCH SUCH BOMB-LIKE PROPOSALS SO CASUALLY...
PONG (BLUSH)
THAT DOE-DOE... DON'T YOU THINK SHE'S DIFFERENT FROM OTHER GIRLS? SHE'S NOT THAT STRONG, AND SHE'S REALLY GENTLE...
...AND SHE'S NOT PRETENTIOUS, AND SHE'S VERY NATURAL...I LIKE HER PERSONALITY...
SHE'S ALSO IN THAT QUIET CROSS-STITCH CLUB, AND SHE'S REALLY PRETTY...

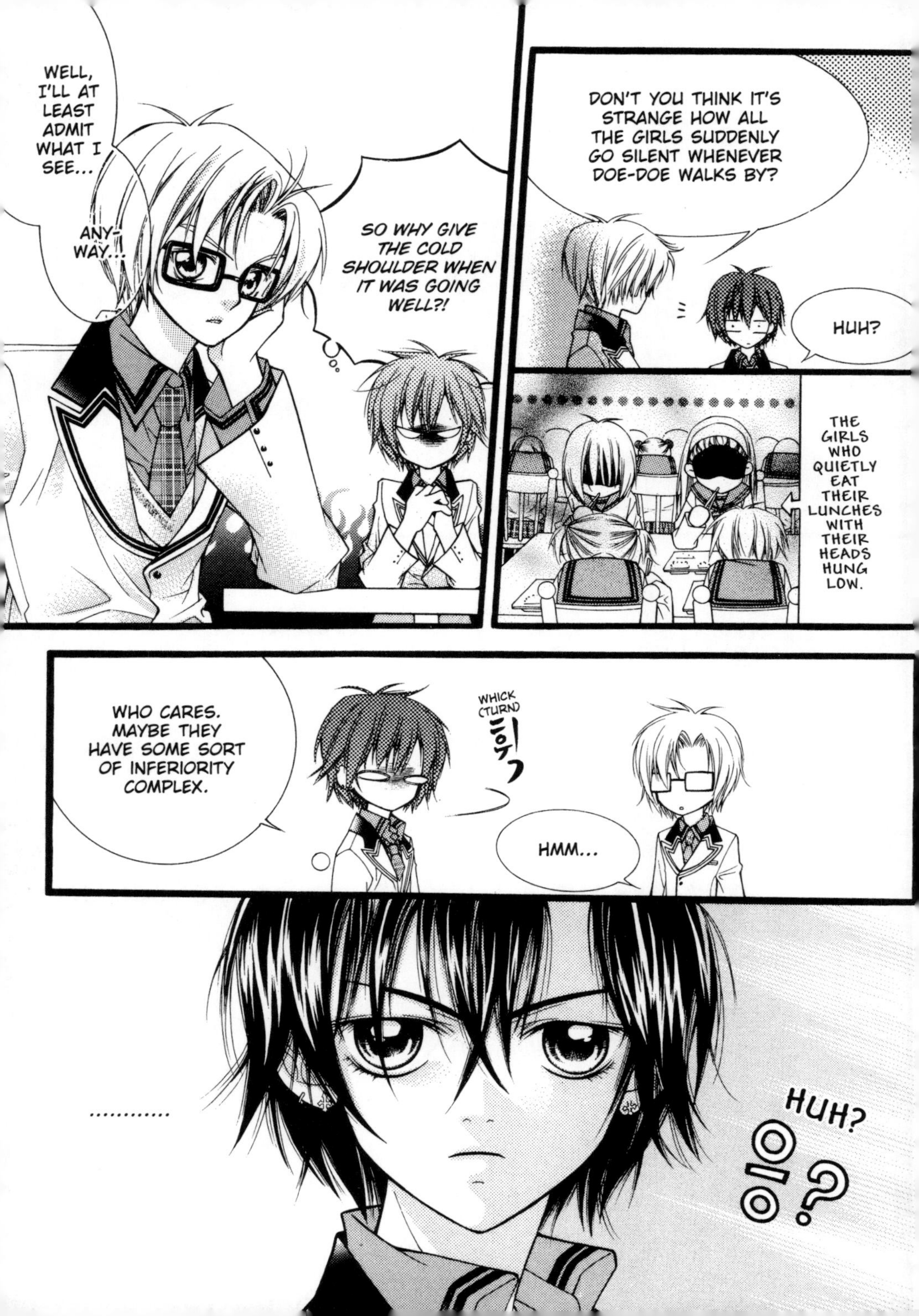
WELL, I'LL AT LEAST ADMIT WHAT I SEE...
ANY-WAY...
SO WHY GIVE THE COLD SHOULDER WHEN IT WAS GOING WELL?!
DON'T YOU THINK IT'S STRANGE HOW ALL THE GIRLS SUDDENLY GO SILENT WHENEVER DOE-DOE WALKS BY?
HUH?
THE GIRLS WHO QUIETLY EAT THEIR LUNCHES WITH THEIR HEADS HUNG LOW.
WHO CARES. MAYBE THEY HAVE SOME SORT OF INFERIORITY COMPLEX.
WHICK (TURN)
HMM...
....
HUH?
응?

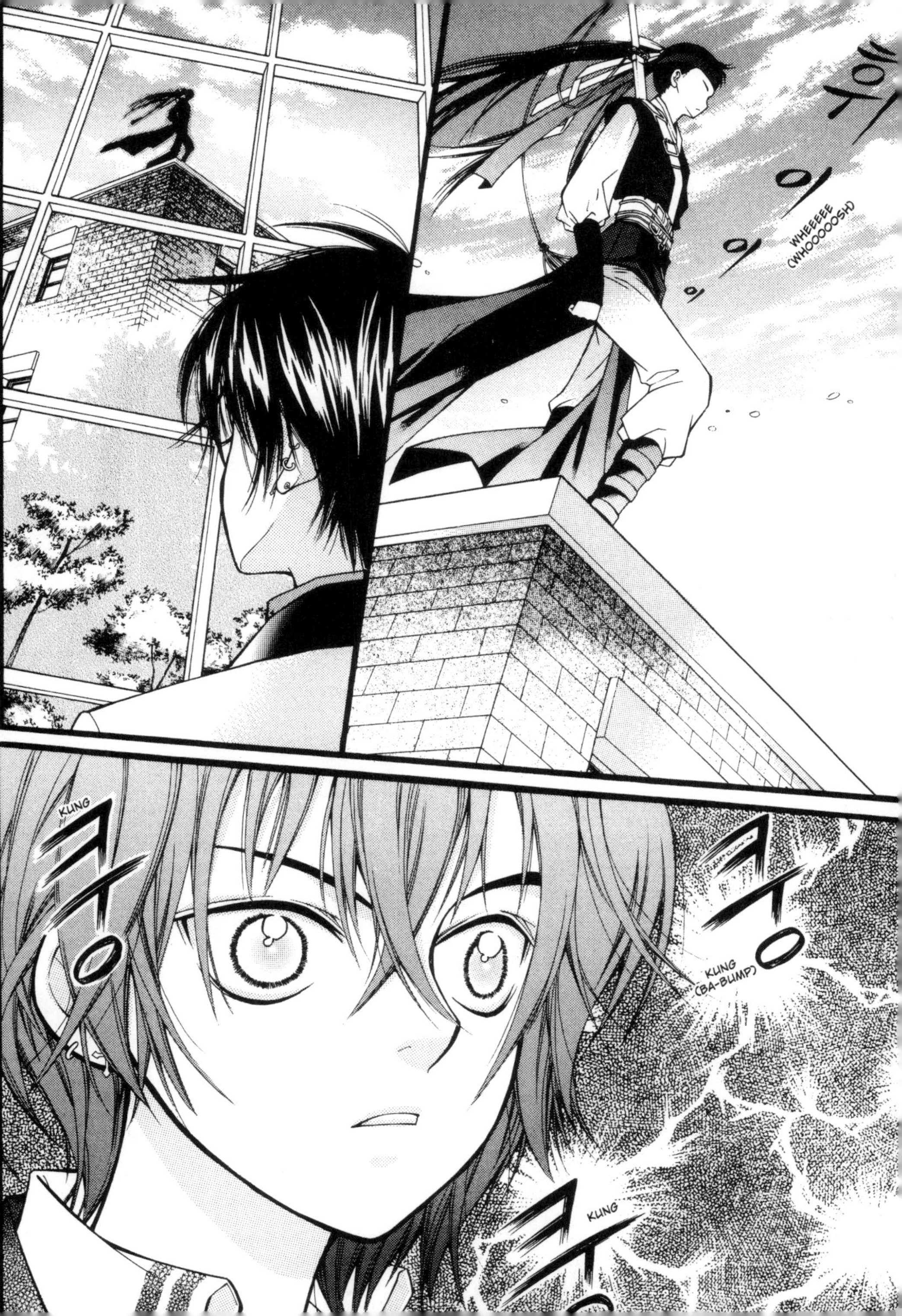

WHEEEEE (WHOOOOOSH)
KUNG
KUNG (BA-BUMP)
KUNG

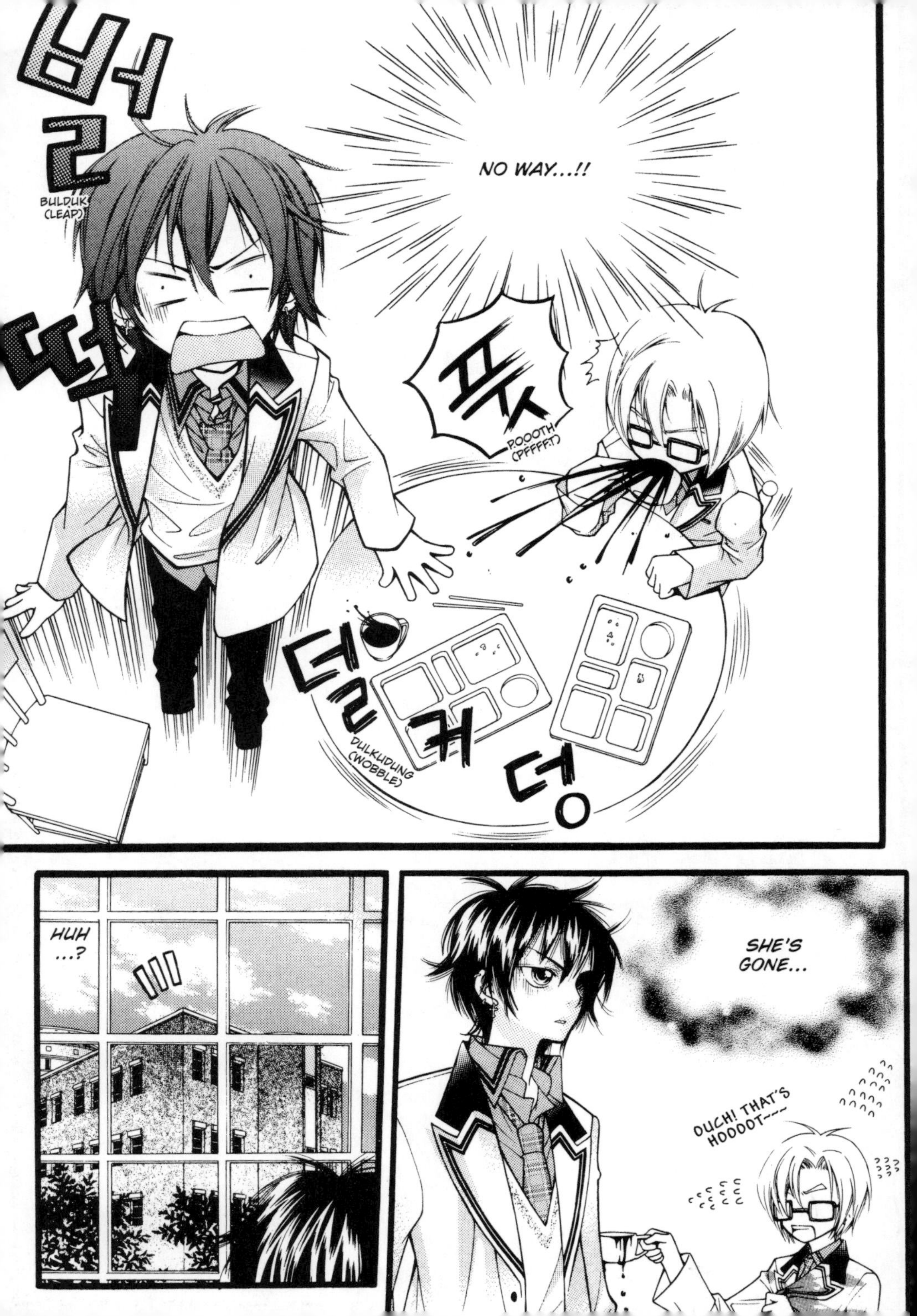
벌떡
BULDUK (LEAP)
NO WAY...!!
풋
POOOTH (PFFFFT)
덜커덩
DULKUDUNG (WOBBLE)
HUH ...?
SHE'S GONE...
OUCH! THAT'S HOOOOT~~~

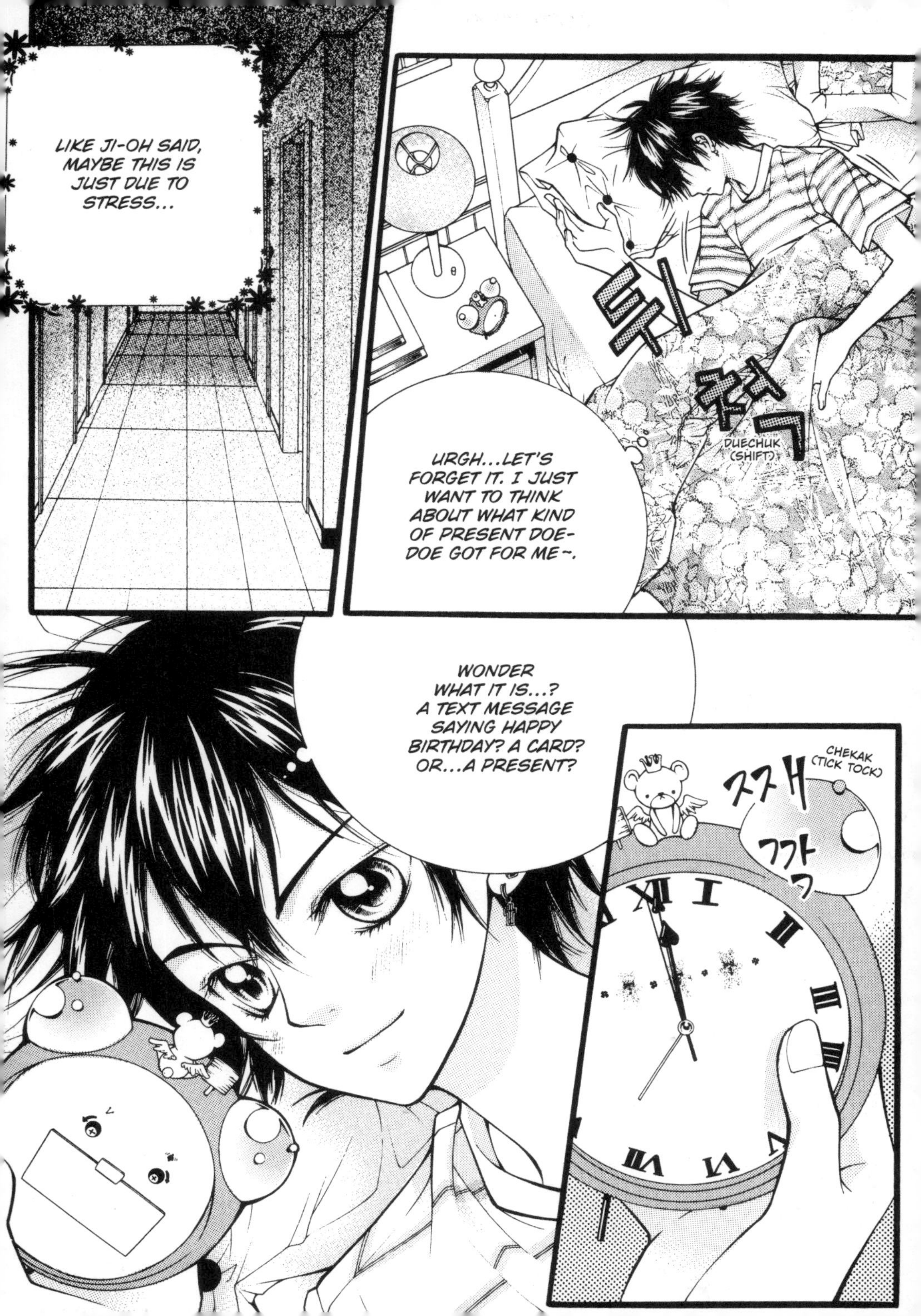
LIKE JI-OH SAID, MAYBE THIS IS JUST DUE TO STRESS...
URGH...LET'S FORGET IT. I JUST WANT TO THINK ABOUT WHAT KIND OF PRESENT DOE-DOE GOT FOR ME~.
DUECHUK (SHIFT)
WONDER WHAT IT IS...? A TEXT MESSAGE SAYING HAPPY BIRTHDAY? A CARD? OR...A PRESENT?
CHEKAK (TICK TOCK)

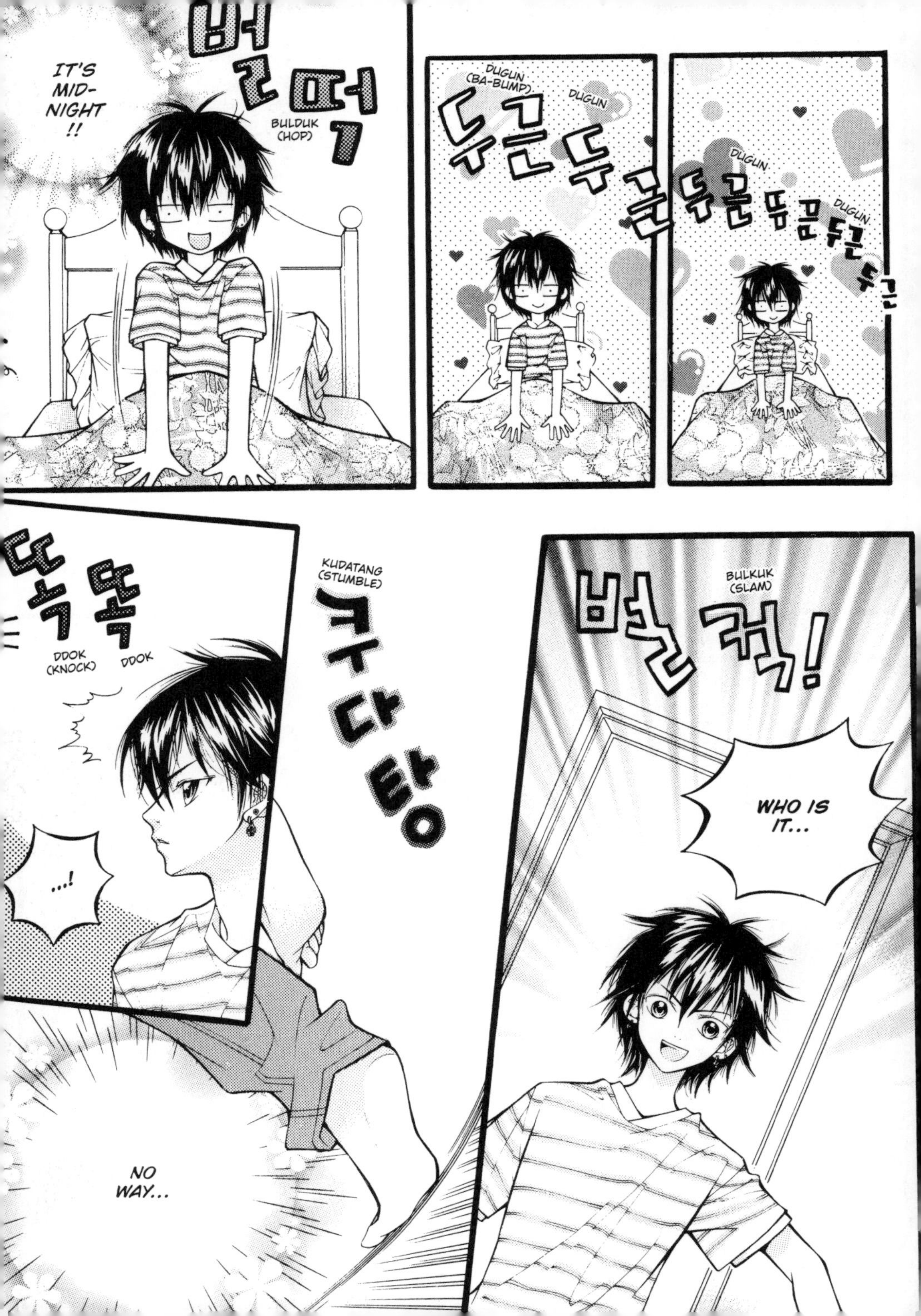
IT'S MID-NIGHT!!
벌떡
BULDUK (HOP)
두근두근
DUGUN (BA-BUMP)
DUGUN
DUGUN
DUGUN
똑똑
DDOK (KNOCK)
DDOK
...!
쿠다탕
KUDATANG (STUMBLE)
NO WAY...
벌컥!
BULKUK (SLAM)
WHO IS IT...

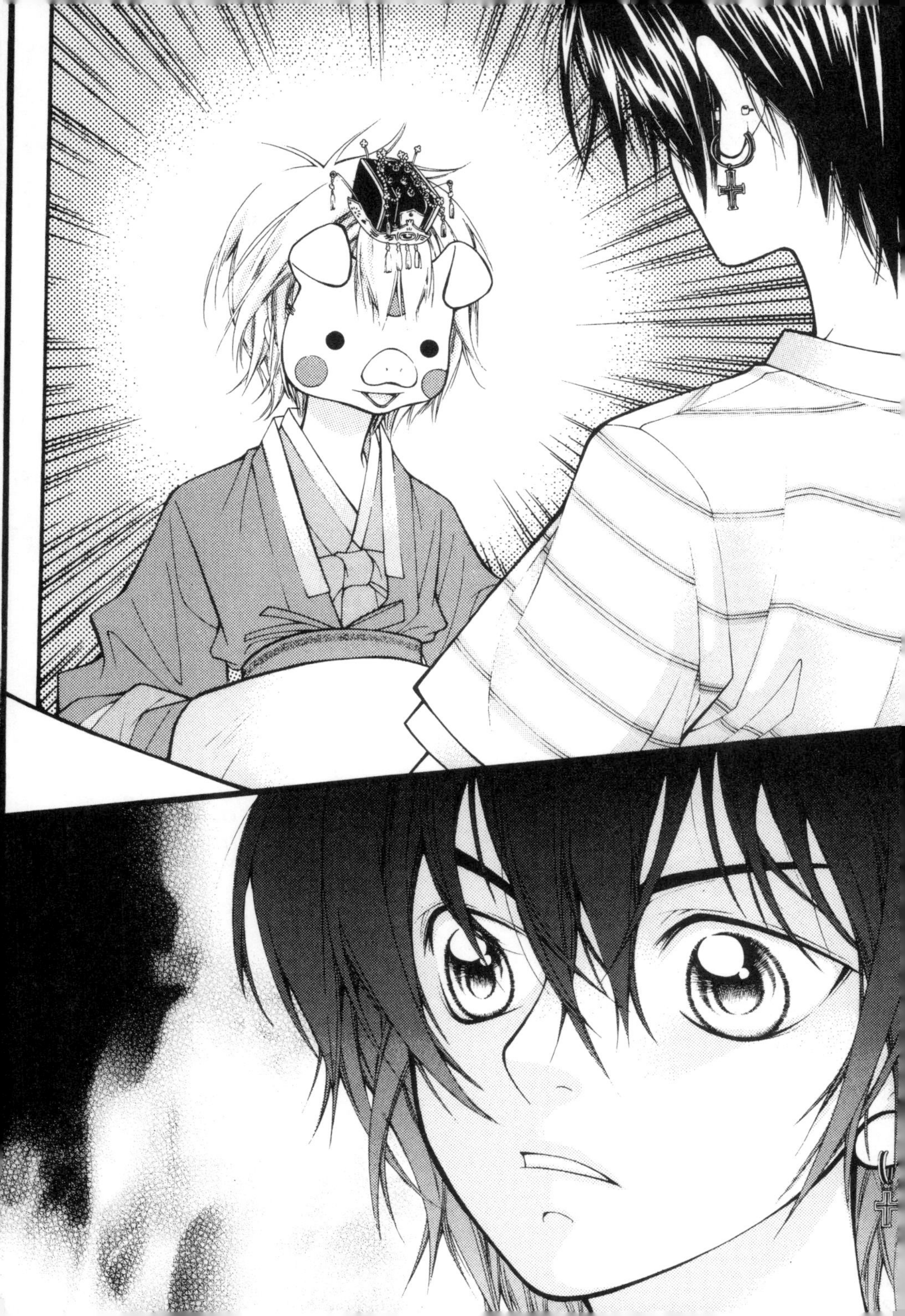

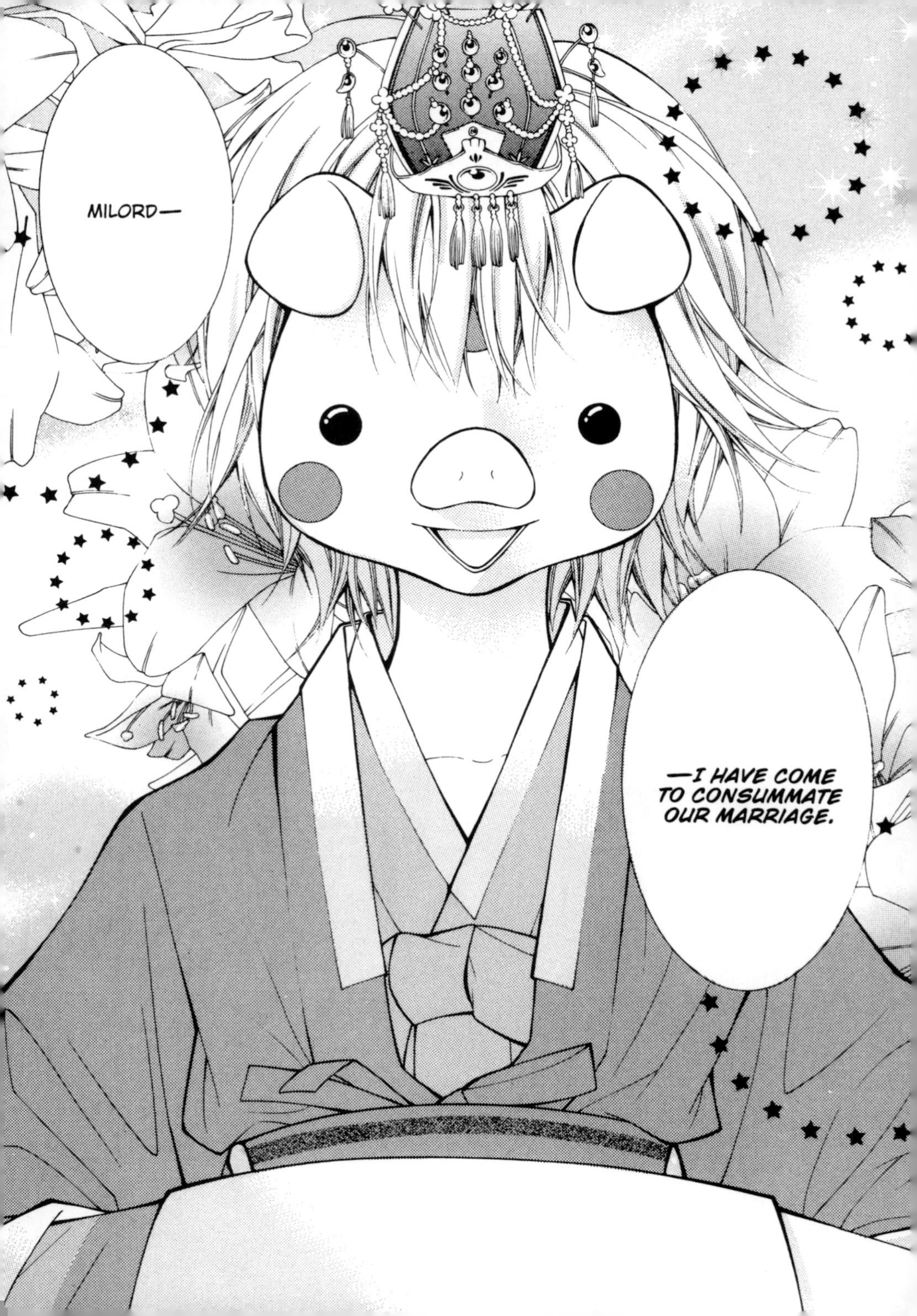
MILORD—
—I HAVE COME TO CONSUMMATE OUR MARRIAGE.

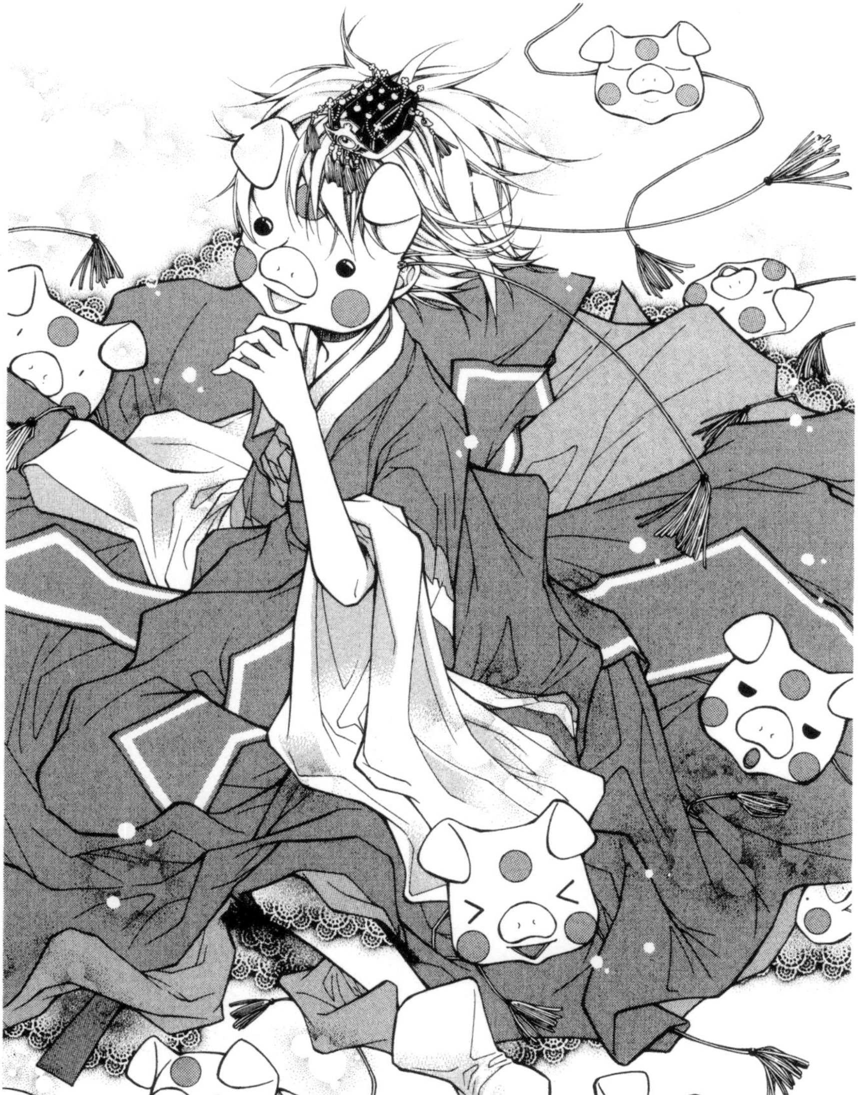

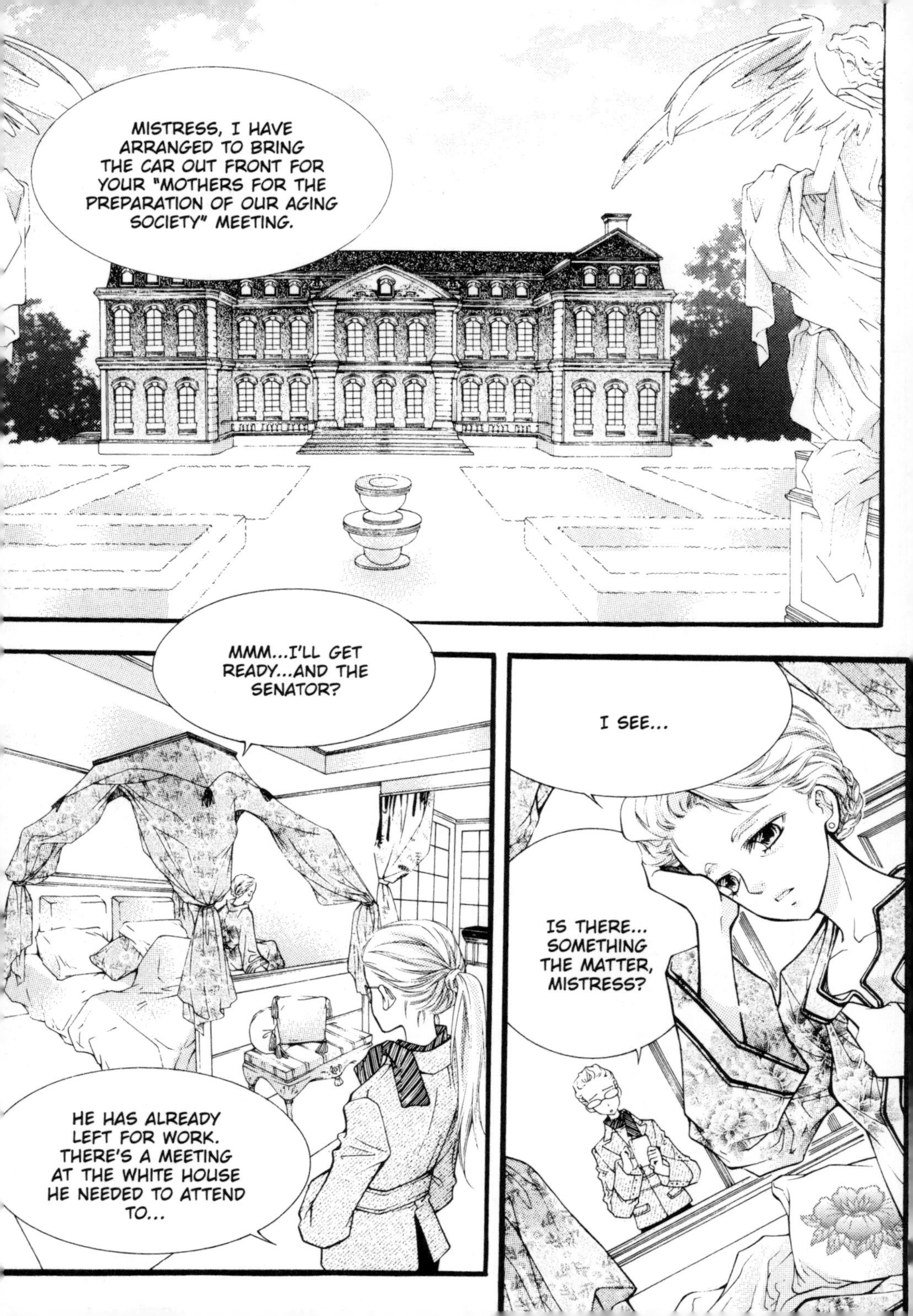
MISTRESS, I HAVE ARRANGED TO BRING THE CAR OUT FRONT FOR YOUR "MOTHERS FOR THE PREPARATION OF OUR AGING SOCIETY" MEETING.
MMM...I'LL GET READY...AND THE SENATOR?
HE HAS ALREADY LEFT FOR WORK. THERE'S A MEETING AT THE WHITE HOUSE HE NEEDED TO ATTEND TO...
I SEE...
IS THERE... SOMETHING THE MATTER, MISTRESS?

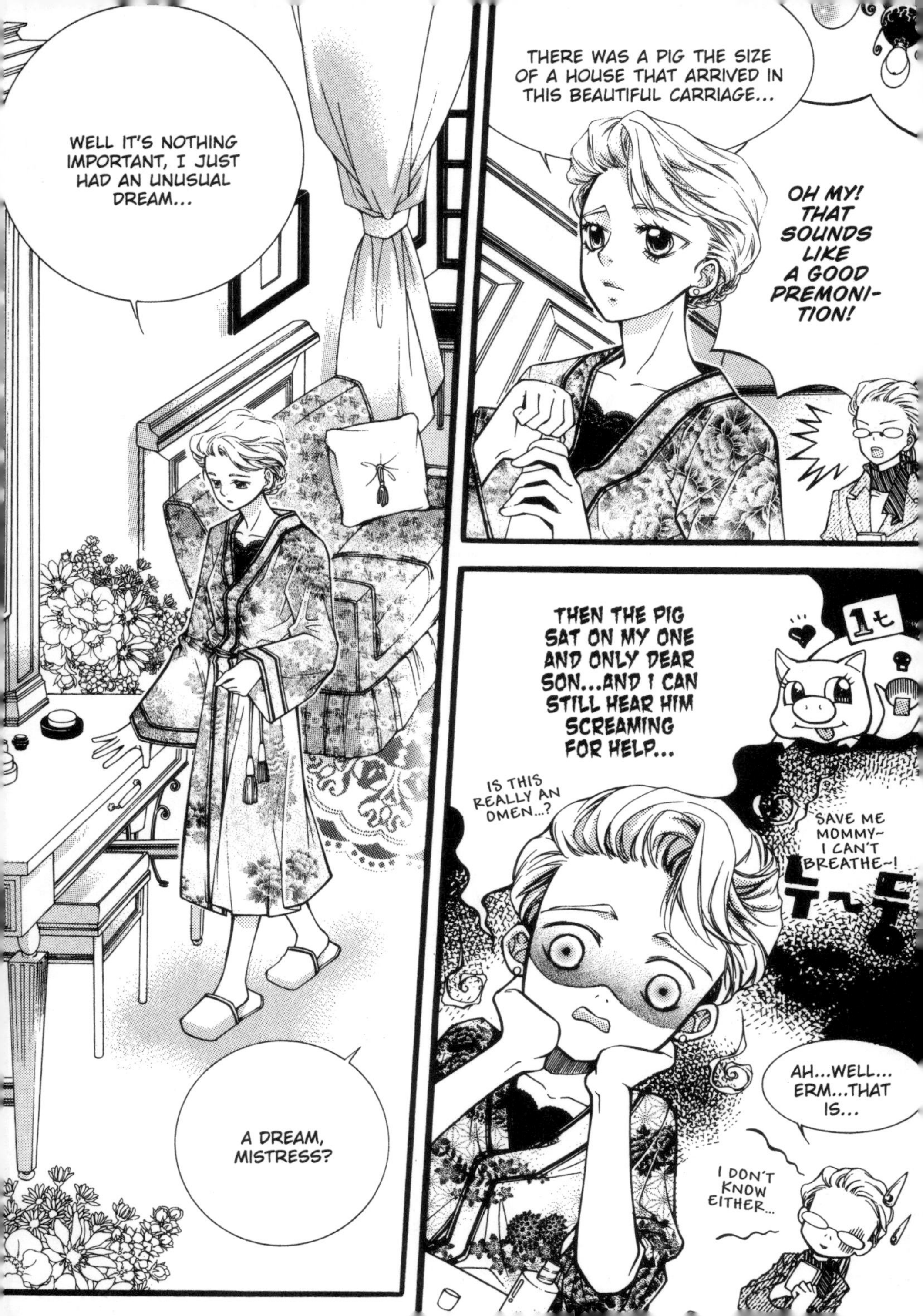
WELL IT'S NOTHING IMPORTANT, I JUST HAD AN UNUSUAL DREAM...
A DREAM, MISTRESS?
THERE WAS A PIG THE SIZE OF A HOUSE THAT ARRIVED IN THIS BEAUTIFUL CARRIAGE...
OH MY! THAT SOUNDS LIKE A GOOD PREMONI-TION!
THEN THE PIG SAT ON MY ONE AND ONLY DEAR SON...AND I CAN STILL HEAR HIM SCREAMING FOR HELP...
IS THIS REALLY AN OMEN...?
SAVE ME MOMMY~ I CAN'T BREATHE~!
AH...WELL... ERM...THAT IS...
I DON'T KNOW EITHER...

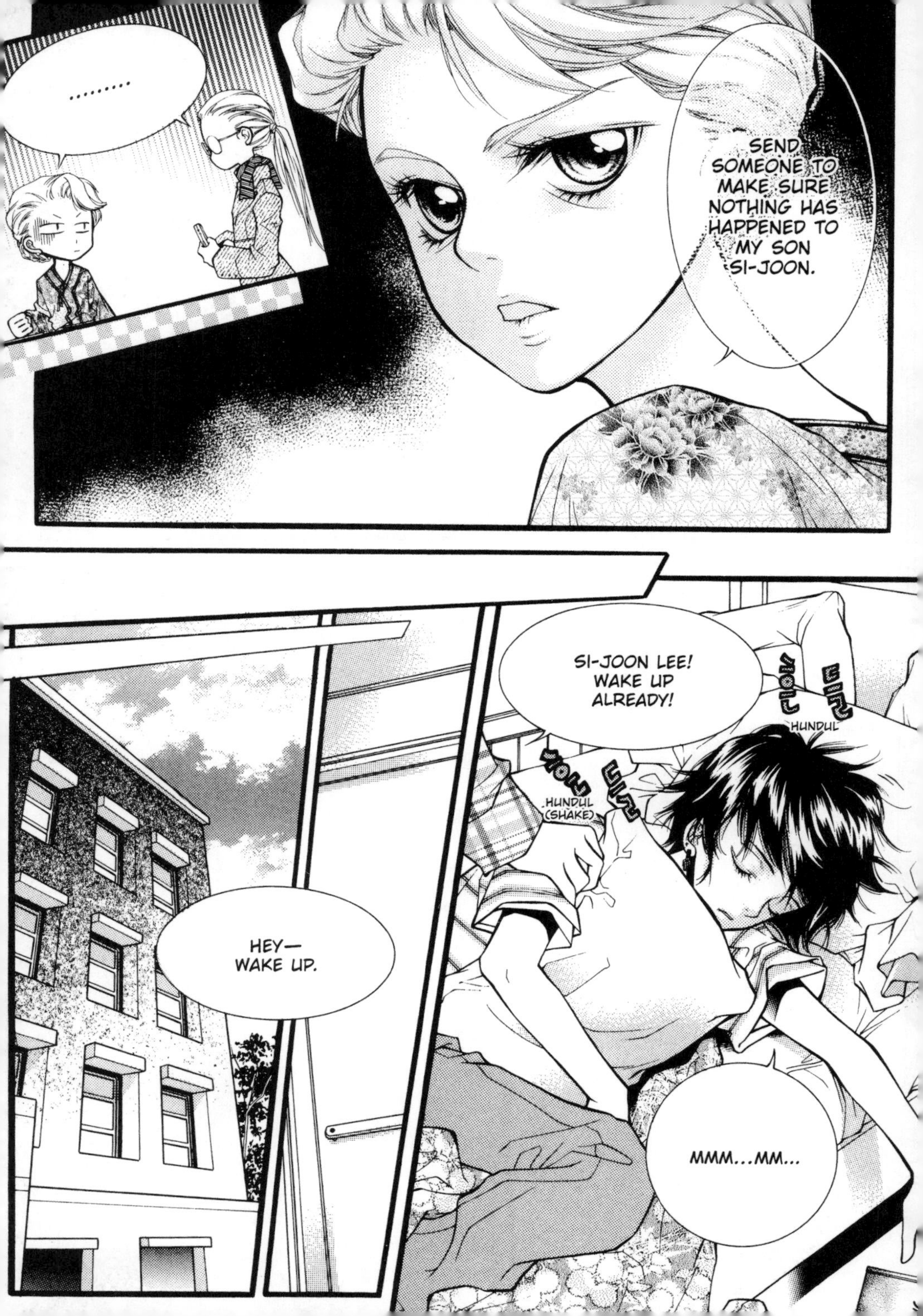
....
SEND SOMEONE TO MAKE SURE NOTHING HAS HAPPENED TO MY SON SI-JOON.
HEY— WAKE UP.
SI-JOON LEE! WAKE UP ALREADY!
HUNDUL (SHAKE)
HUNDUL
MMM...MM...

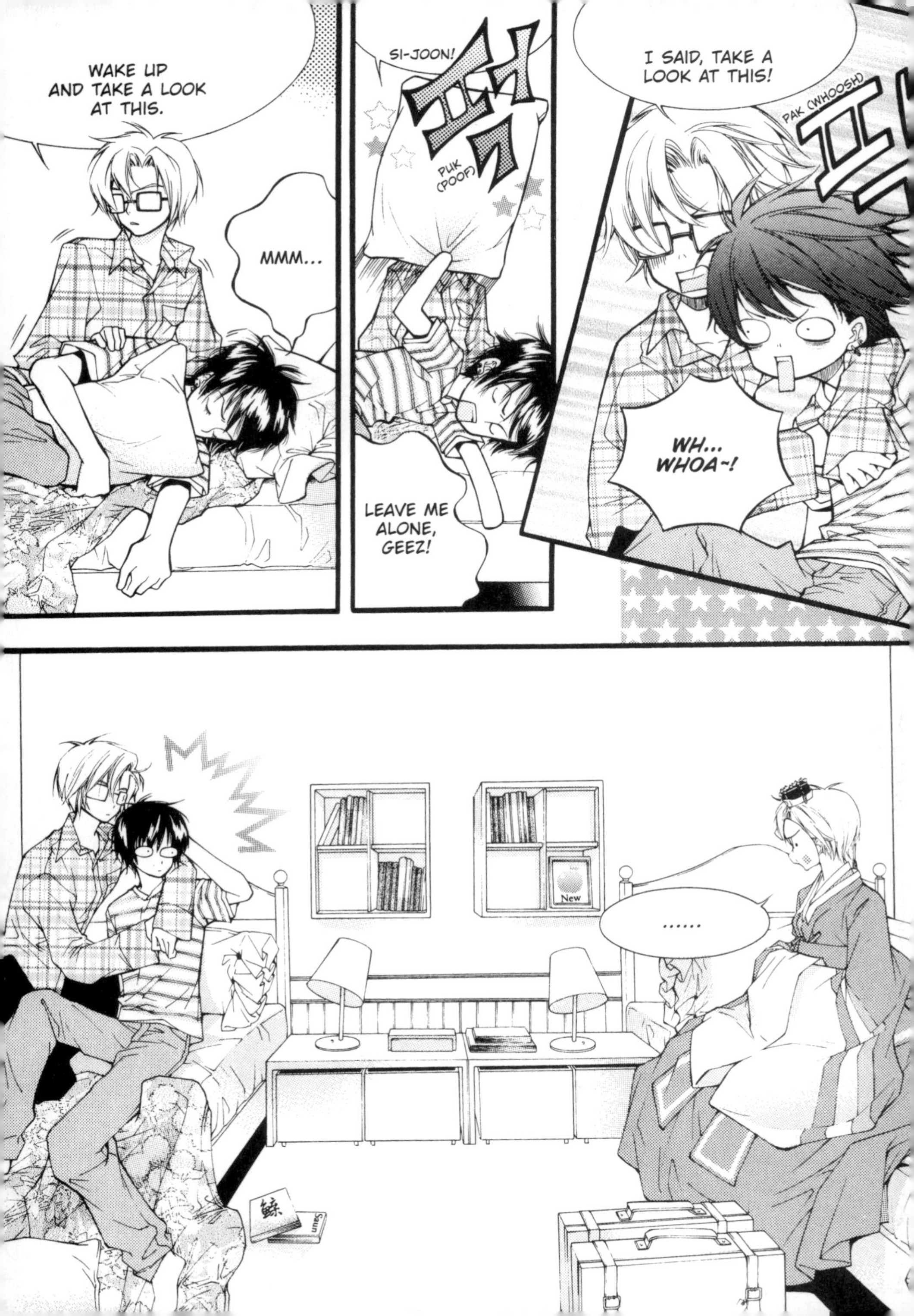
WAKE UP AND TAKE A LOOK AT THIS.
MMM...
SI-JOON!
PUK (POOF)
LEAVE ME ALONE, GEEZ!
I SAID, TAKE A LOOK AT THIS!
PAK (WHOOSH)
WH... WHOA~!
New
......

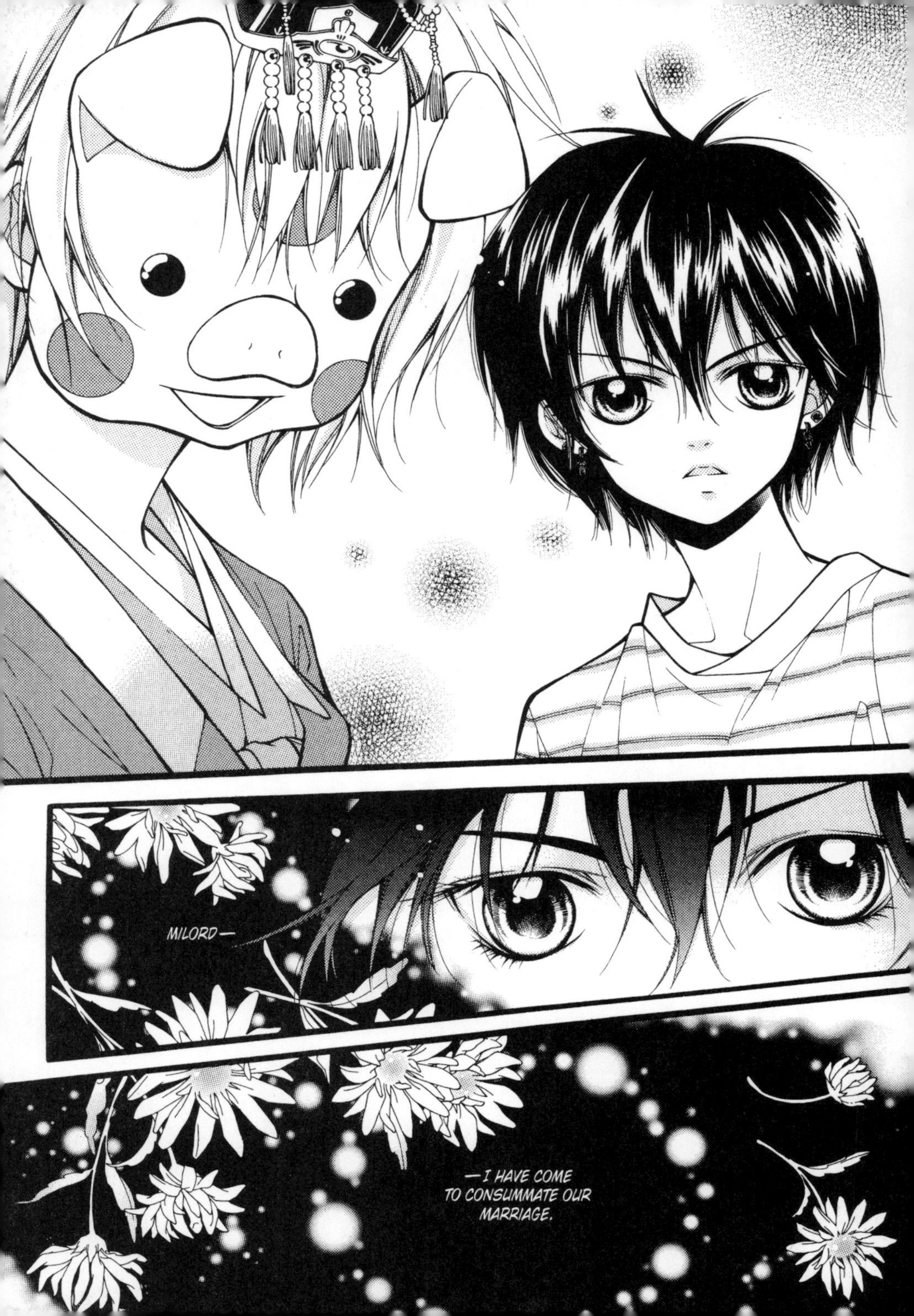
MILORD—
—I HAVE COME TO CONSUMMATE OUR MARRIAGE.

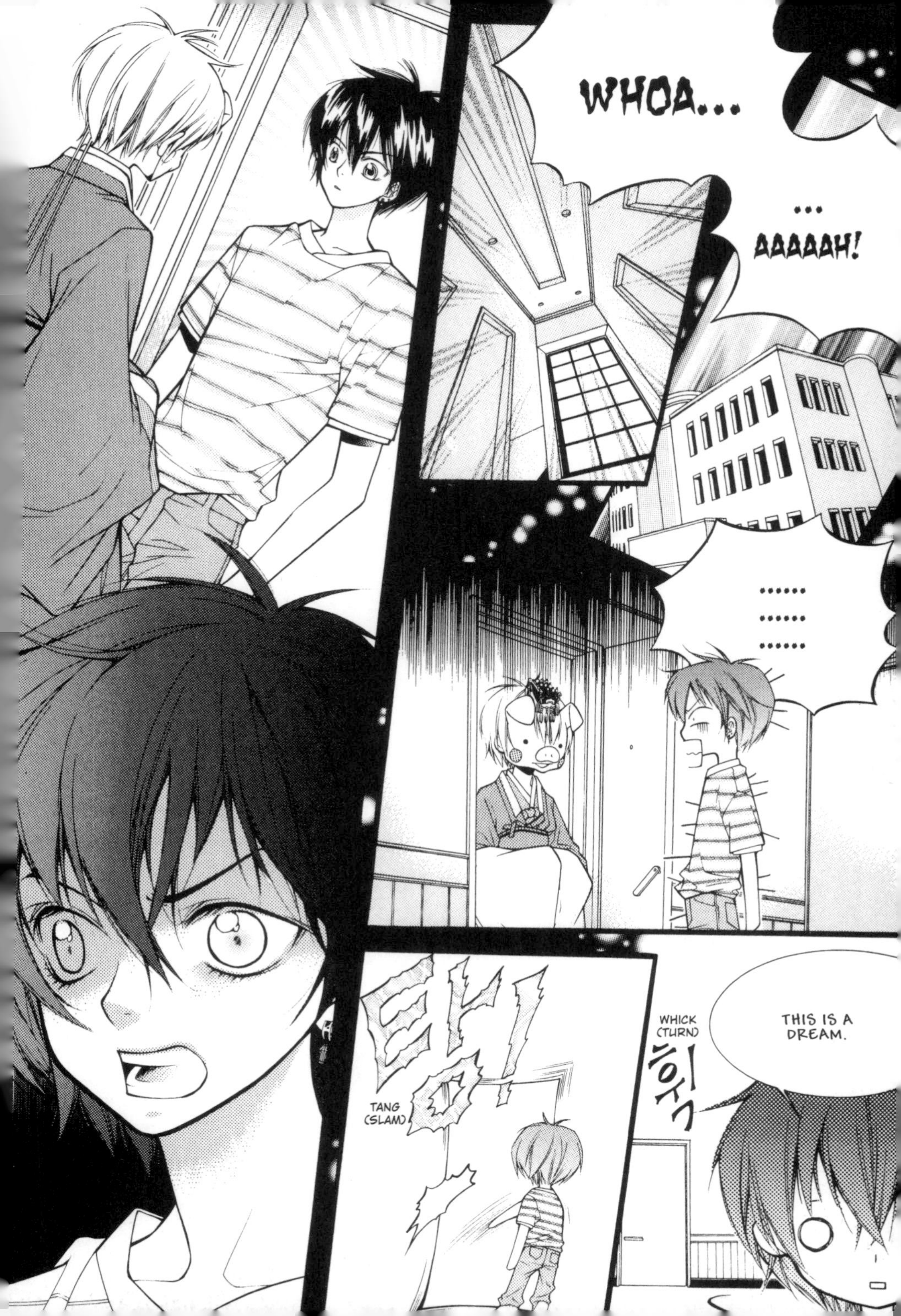
WHOA...
...
AAAAAH!
......
......
......
THIS IS A DREAM.
WHICK (TURN)
흐윽
TANG (SLAM)
탕!

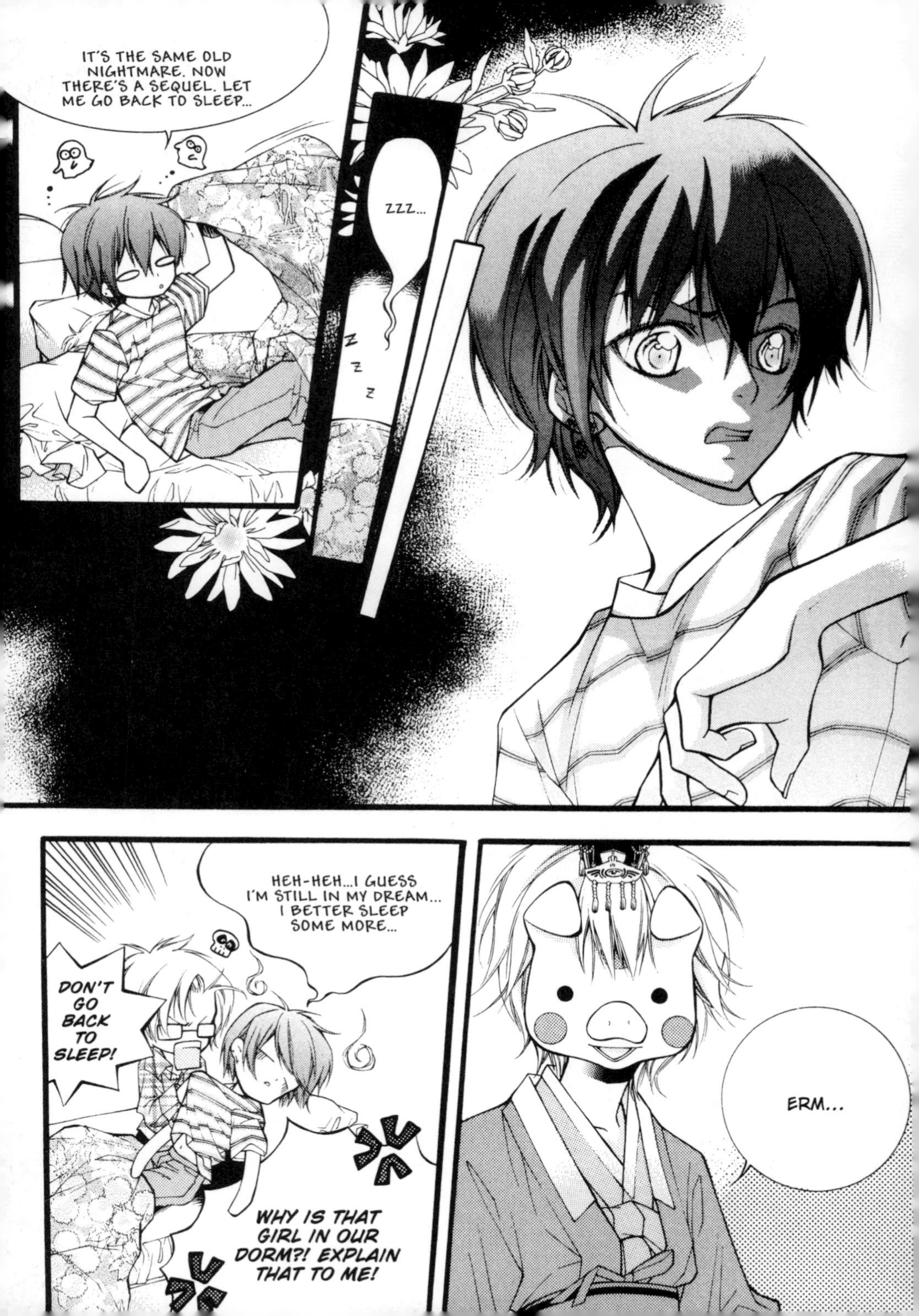
ZZZ...
Z Z Z
IT'S THE SAME OLD NIGHTMARE. NOW THERE'S A SEQUEL. LET ME GO BACK TO SLEEP...
ERM...
HEH-HEH...I GUESS I'M STILL IN MY DREAM... I BETTER SLEEP SOME MORE...
DON'T GO BACK TO SLEEP!
WHY IS THAT GIRL IN OUR DORM?! EXPLAIN THAT TO ME!

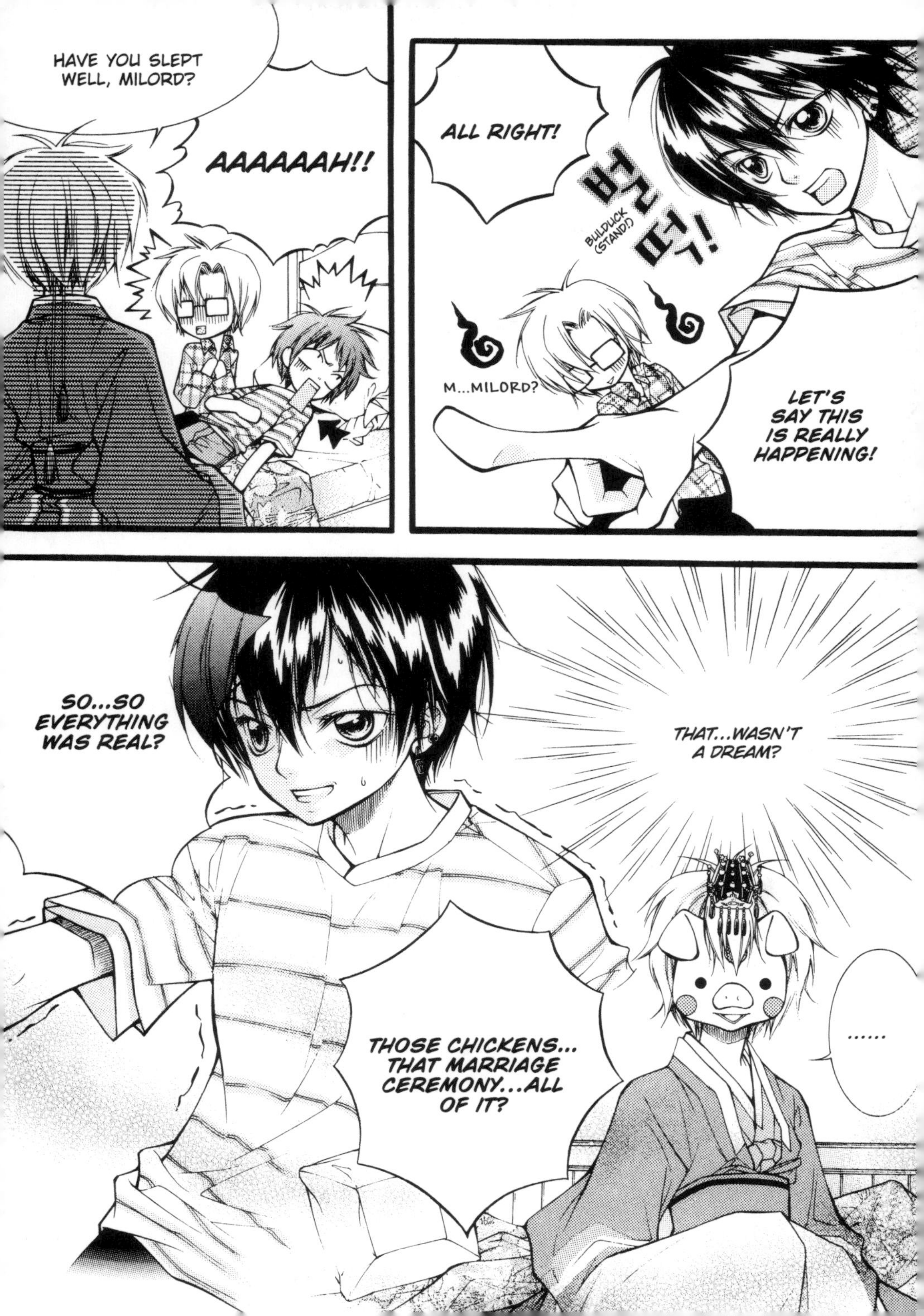
HAVE YOU SLEPT WELL, MILORD?
AAAAAAH!!
ALL RIGHT!
벌떡!
BULDUCK (STAND!)
M...MILORD?
LET'S SAY THIS IS REALLY HAPPENING!
THAT...WASN'T A DREAM?
SO...SO EVERYTHING WAS REAL?
......
THOSE CHICKENS... THAT MARRIAGE CEREMONY...ALL OF IT?

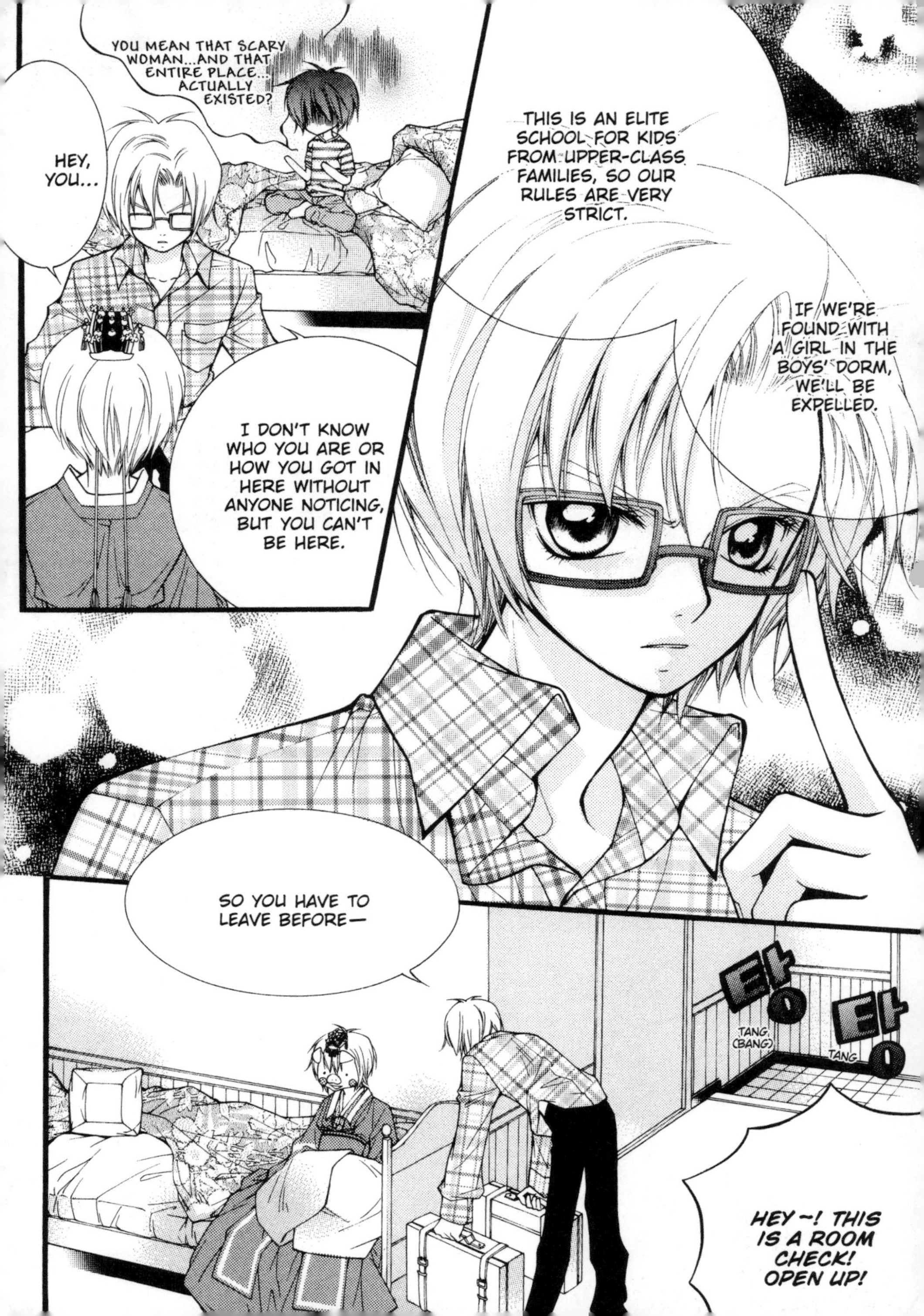

YOU MEAN THAT SCARY WOMAN...AND THAT ENTIRE PLACE... ACTUALLY EXISTED?
HEY, YOU...
I DON'T KNOW WHO YOU ARE OR HOW YOU GOT IN HERE WITHOUT ANYONE NOTICING, BUT YOU CAN'T BE HERE.
THIS IS AN ELITE SCHOOL FOR KIDS FROM UPPER-CLASS FAMILIES, SO OUR RULES ARE VERY STRICT.
IF WE'RE FOUND WITH A GIRL IN THE BOYS' DORM, WE'LL BE EXPELLED.
SO YOU HAVE TO LEAVE BEFORE—
탕
TANG (BANG)
탕
TANG
HEY~! THIS IS A ROOM CHECK! OPEN UP!

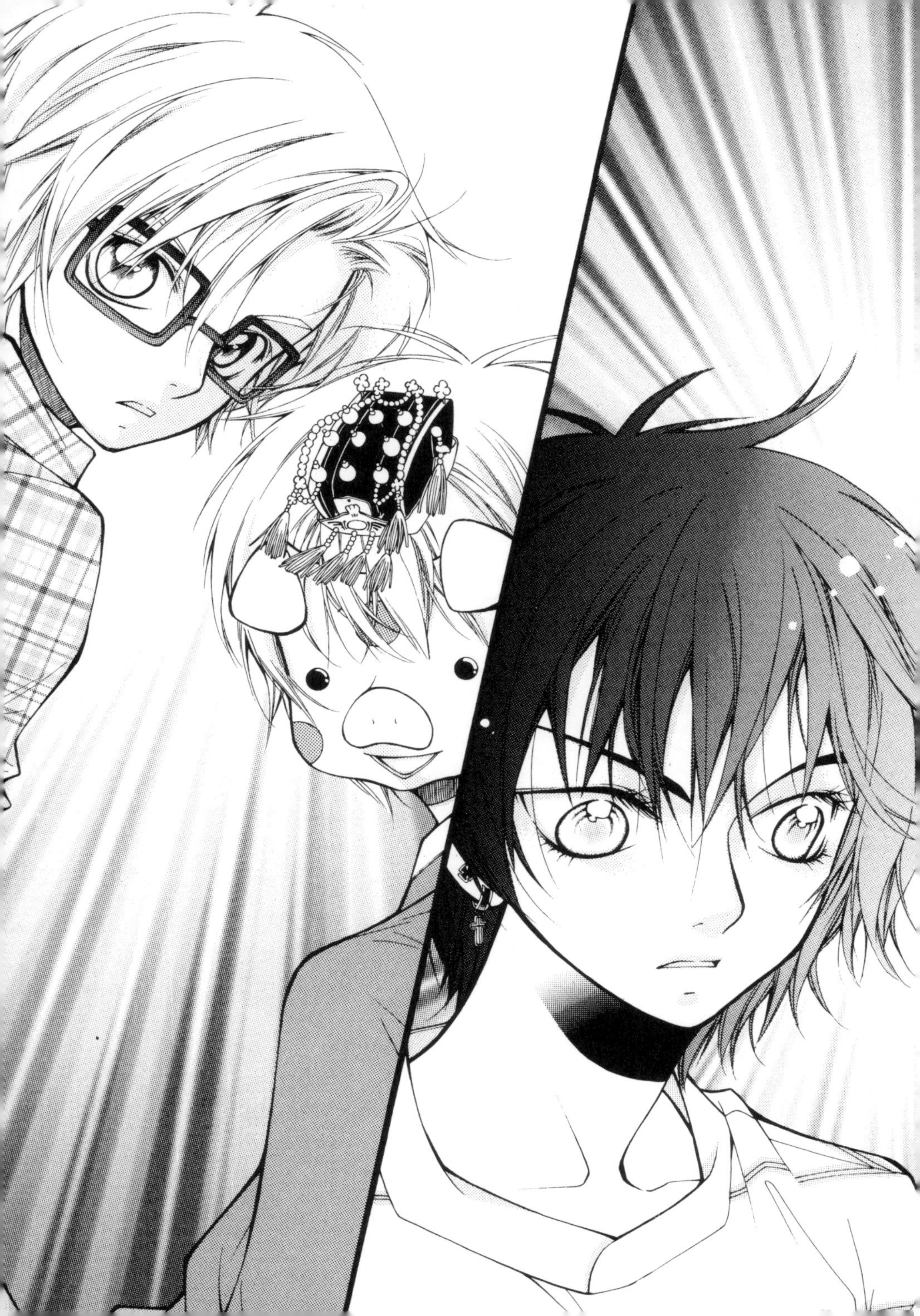

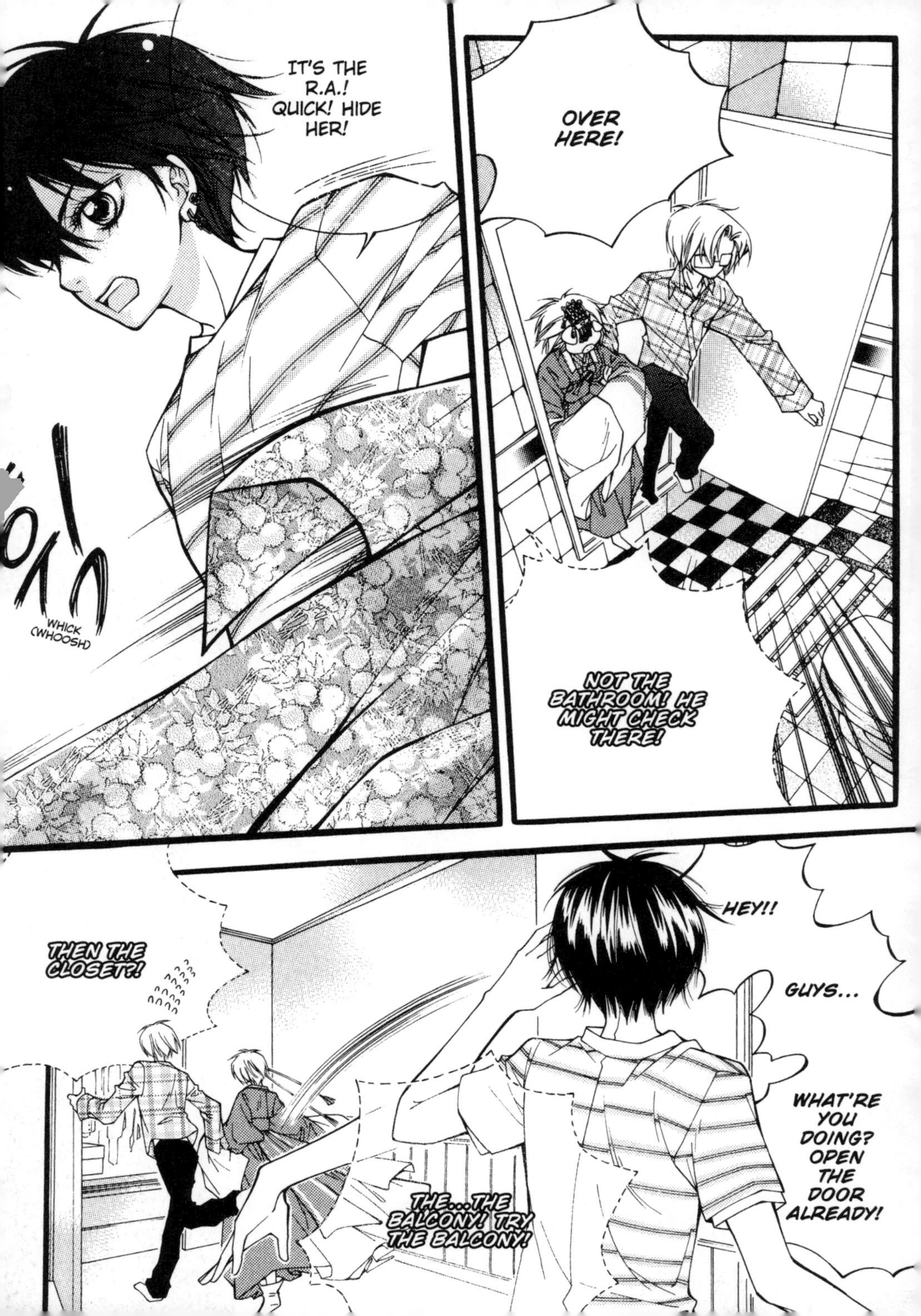
OVER HERE!
IT'S THE R.A.! QUICK! HIDE HER!
WHICK (WHOOSH)
NOT THE BATHROOM! HE MIGHT CHECK THERE!
HEY!!
GUYS...
WHAT'RE YOU DOING? OPEN THE DOOR ALREADY!
THEN THE CLOSET?!
THE...THE BALCONY! TRY THE BALCONY!

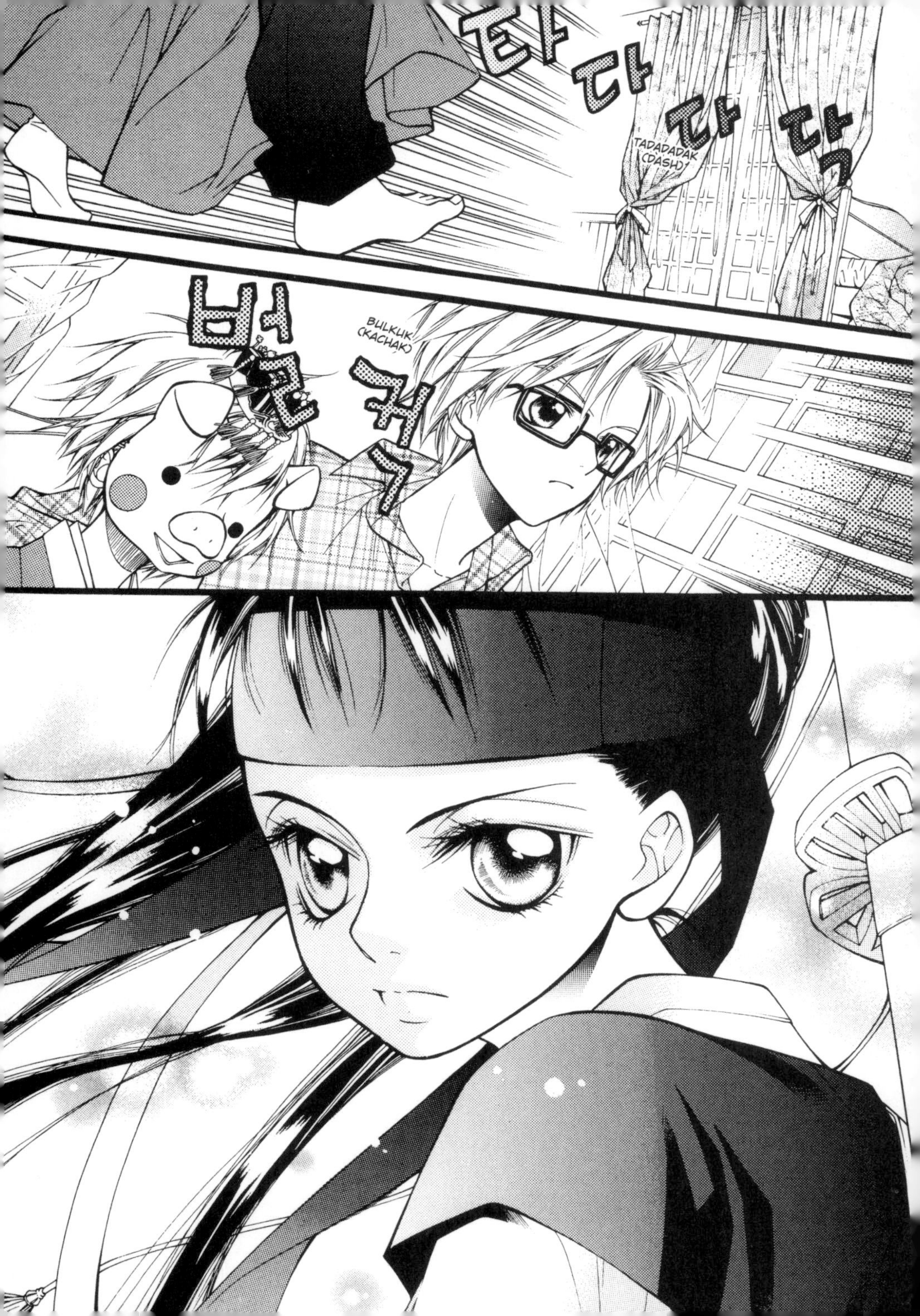
타다다닥
TADADADAK (DASH)
벌컥
BULKUK (KACHAK)

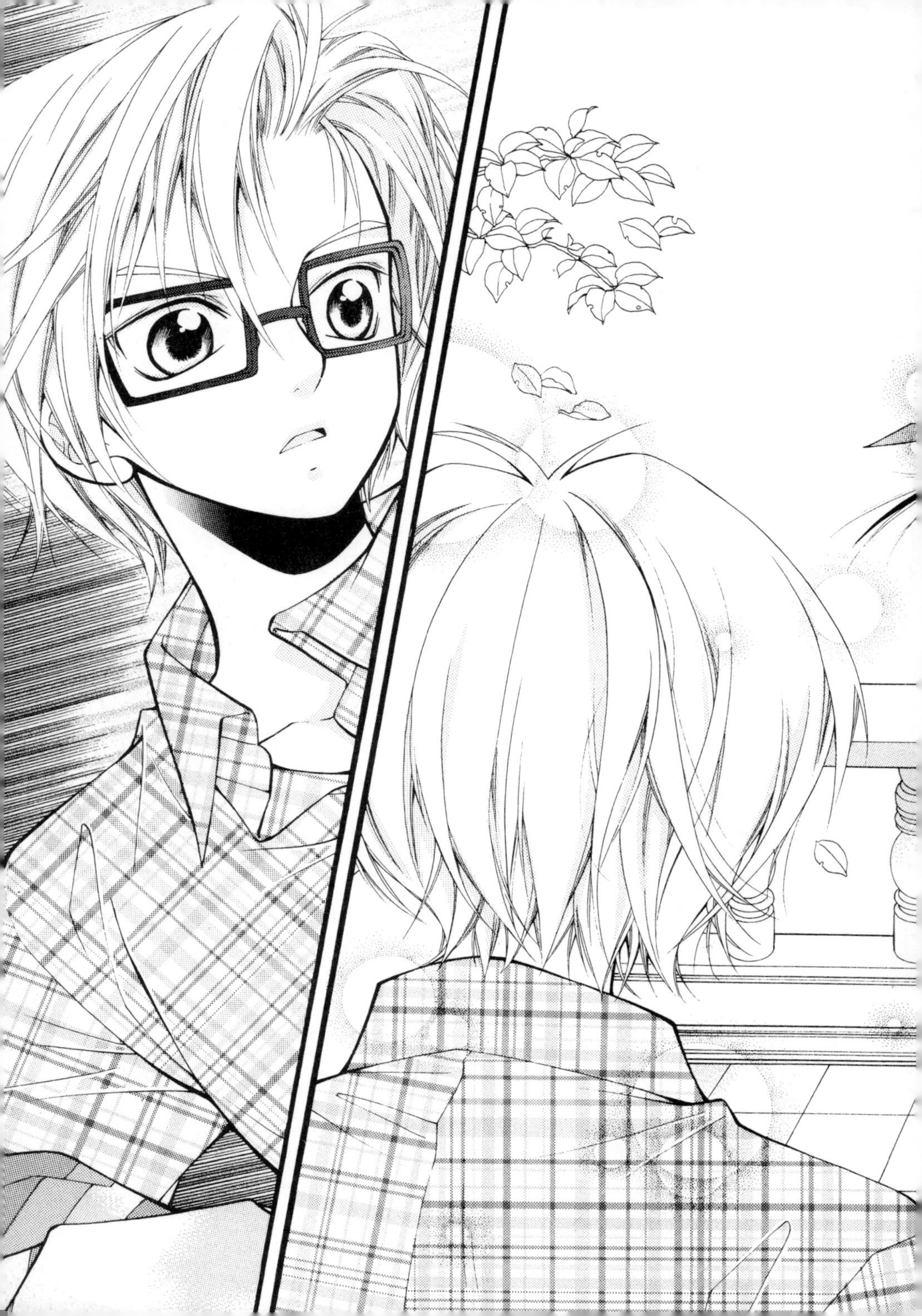

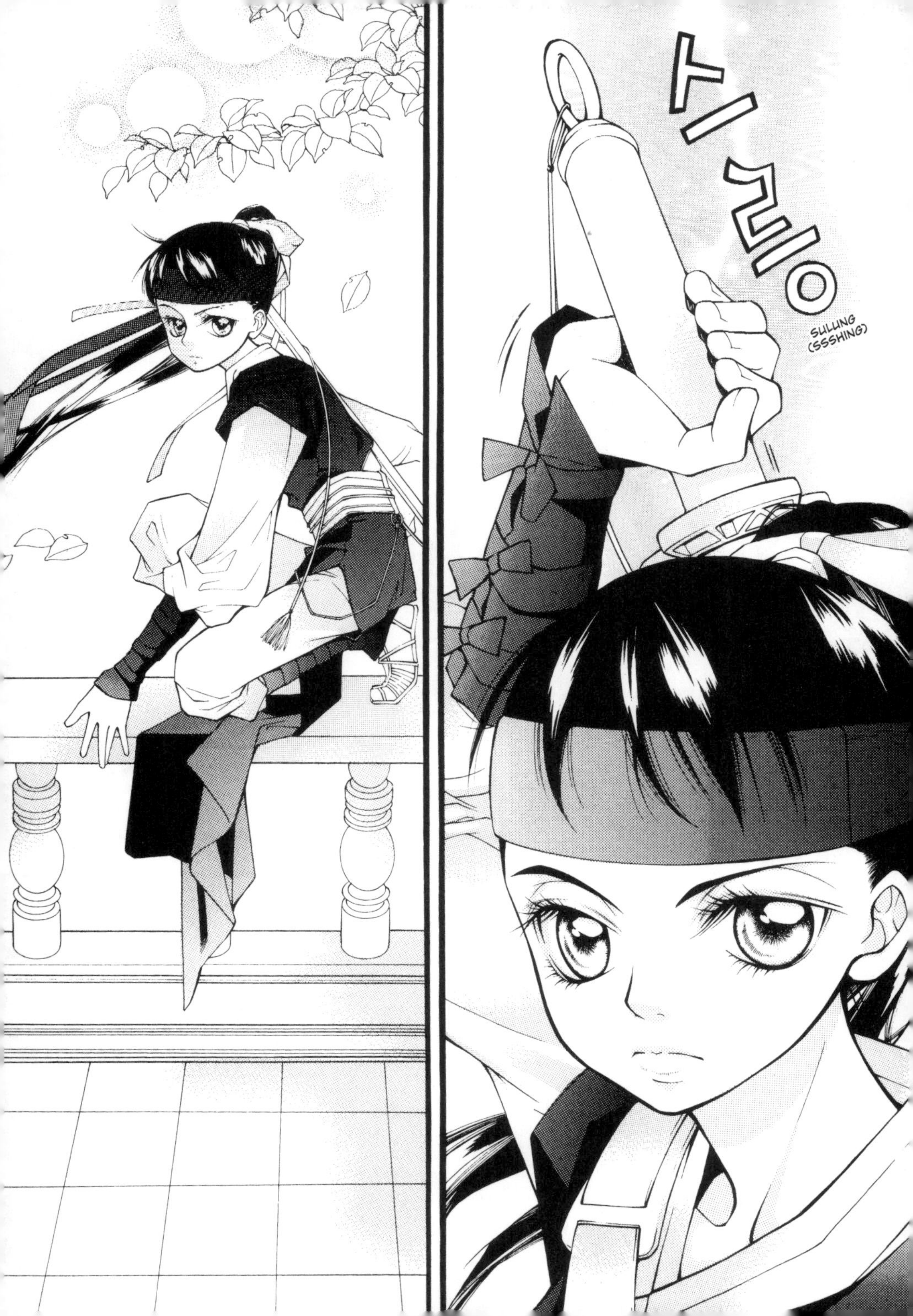
SULUNG
(SSSHING)

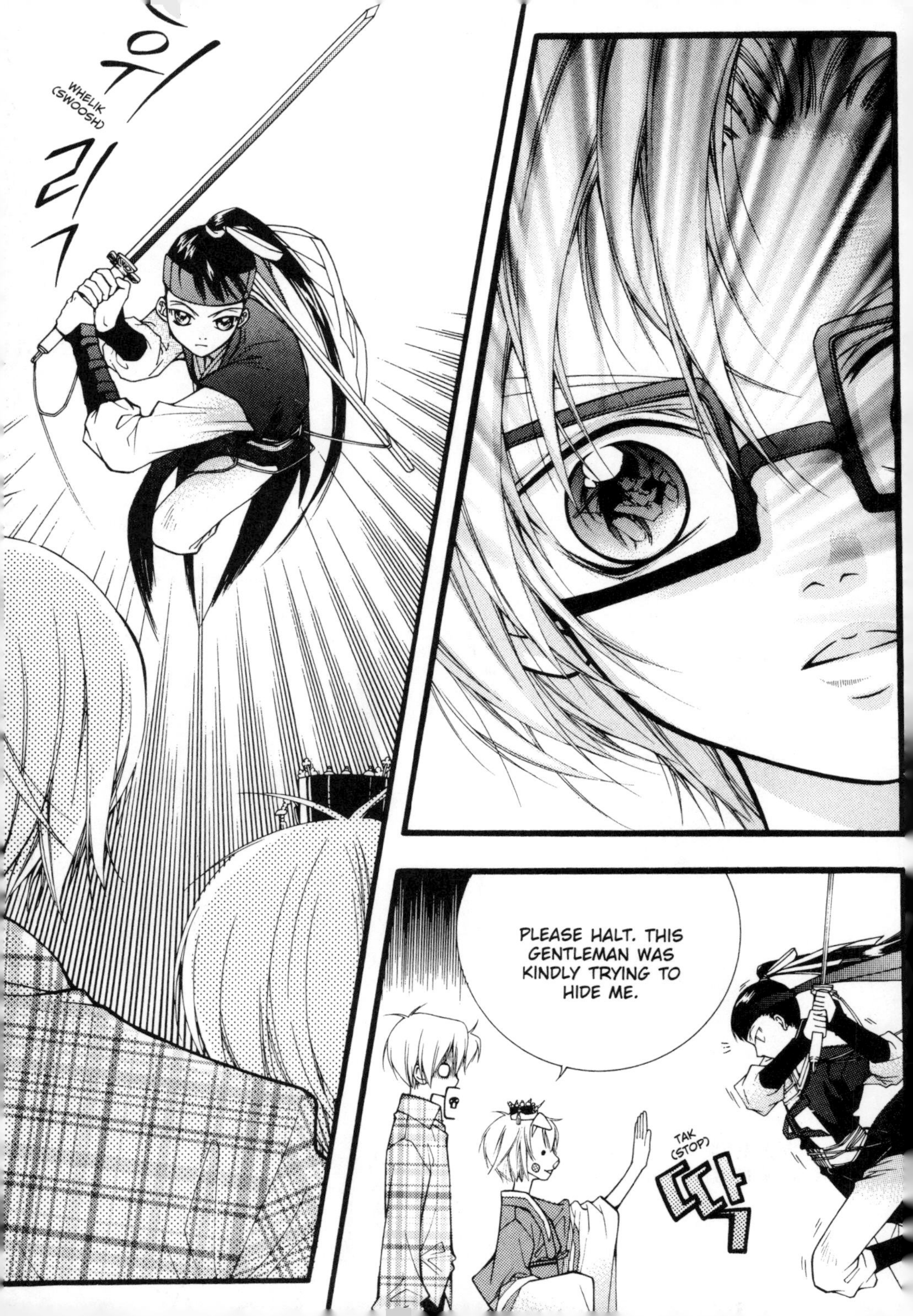

WHELIK (SWOOSH)
휘리릭
PLEASE HALT. THIS GENTLEMAN WAS KINDLY TRYING TO HIDE ME.
TAK (STOP)
딱

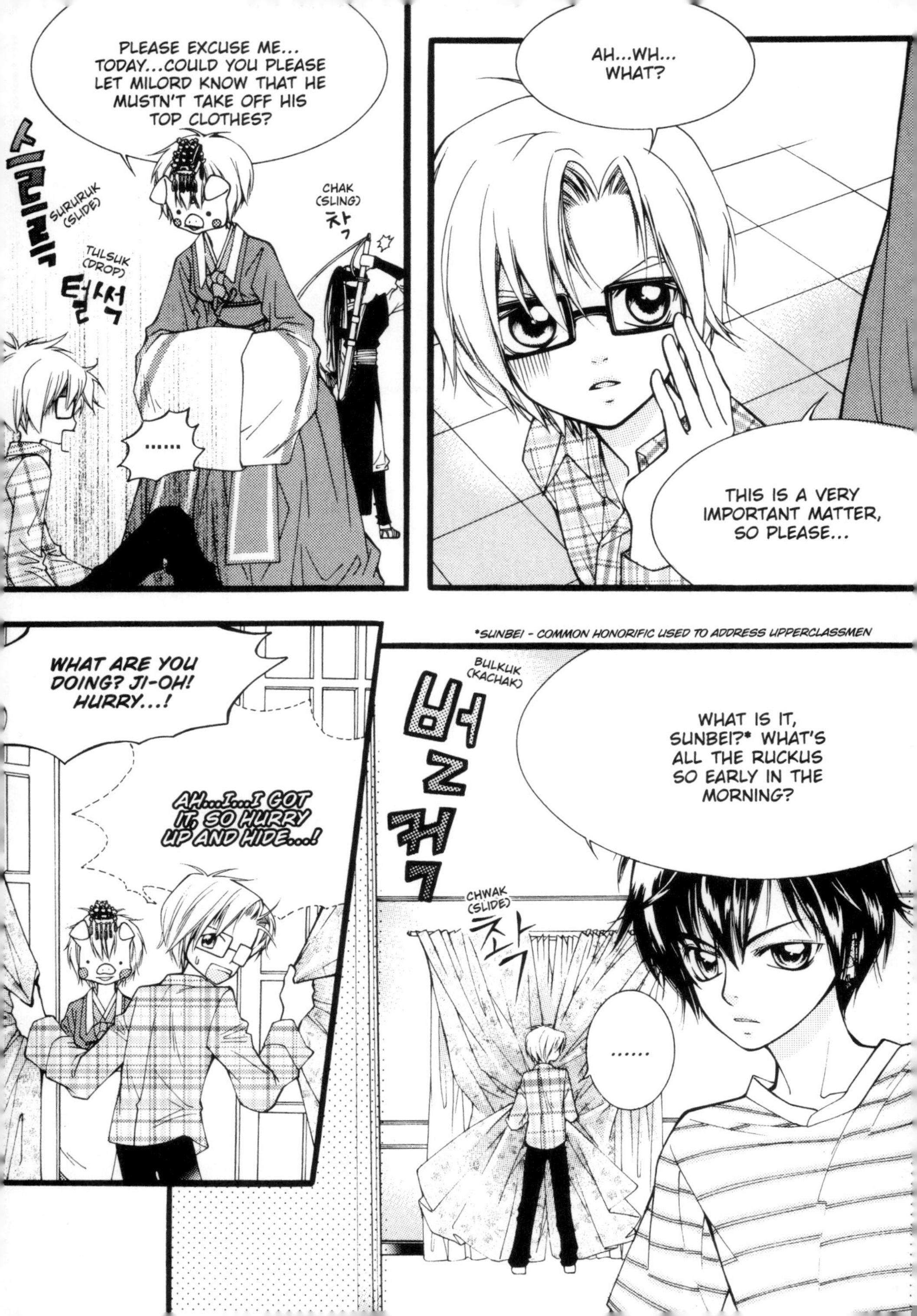
PLEASE EXCUSE ME... TODAY...COULD YOU PLEASE LET MILORD KNOW THAT HE MUSTN'T TAKE OFF HIS TOP CLOTHES?
SURURUK (SLIDE)
TULSUK (DROP)
털썩
CHAK (SLING)
착
......
AH...WH... WHAT?
THIS IS A VERY IMPORTANT MATTER, SO PLEASE...
WHAT ARE YOU DOING? JI-OH! HURRY...!
AH...I...I GOT IT, SO HURRY UP AND HIDE...!
BULKUK (KACHAK)
WHAT IS IT, SUNBEI?* WHAT'S ALL THE RUCKUS SO EARLY IN THE MORNING?
CHWAK (SLIDE)
......
*SUNBEI - COMMON HONORIFIC USED TO ADDRESS UPPERCLASSMEN

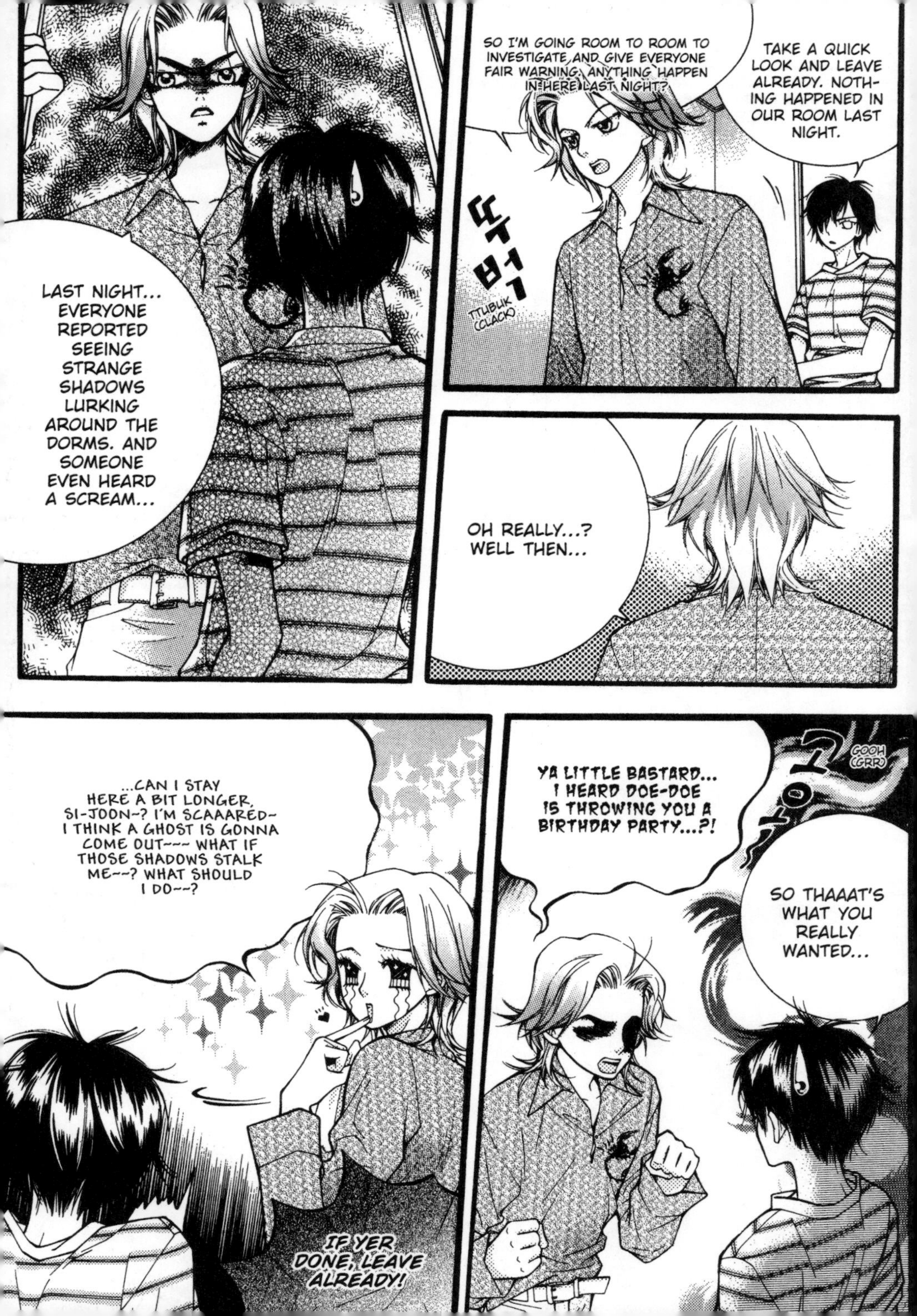
LAST NIGHT... EVERYONE REPORTED SEEING STRANGE SHADOWS LURKING AROUND THE DORMS. AND SOMEONE EVEN HEARD A SCREAM...
SO I'M GOING ROOM TO ROOM TO INVESTIGATE AND GIVE EVERYONE FAIR WARNING. ANYTHING HAPPEN IN HERE LAST NIGHT?
TTUBUK (CLACK)
TAKE A QUICK LOOK AND LEAVE ALREADY. NOTHING HAPPENED IN OUR ROOM LAST NIGHT.
OH REALLY...? WELL THEN...
...CAN I STAY HERE A BIT LONGER, SI-JOON~? I'M SCAAARED~ I THINK A GHOST IS GONNA COME OUT~~~ WHAT IF THOSE SHADOWS STALK ME~~? WHAT SHOULD I DO~~?
IF YER DONE, LEAVE ALREADY!
YA LITTLE BASTARD... I HEARD DOE-DOE IS THROWING YOU A BIRTHDAY PARTY...?!
GOOH (GRR)
SO THAAAT'S WHAT YOU REALLY WANTED...

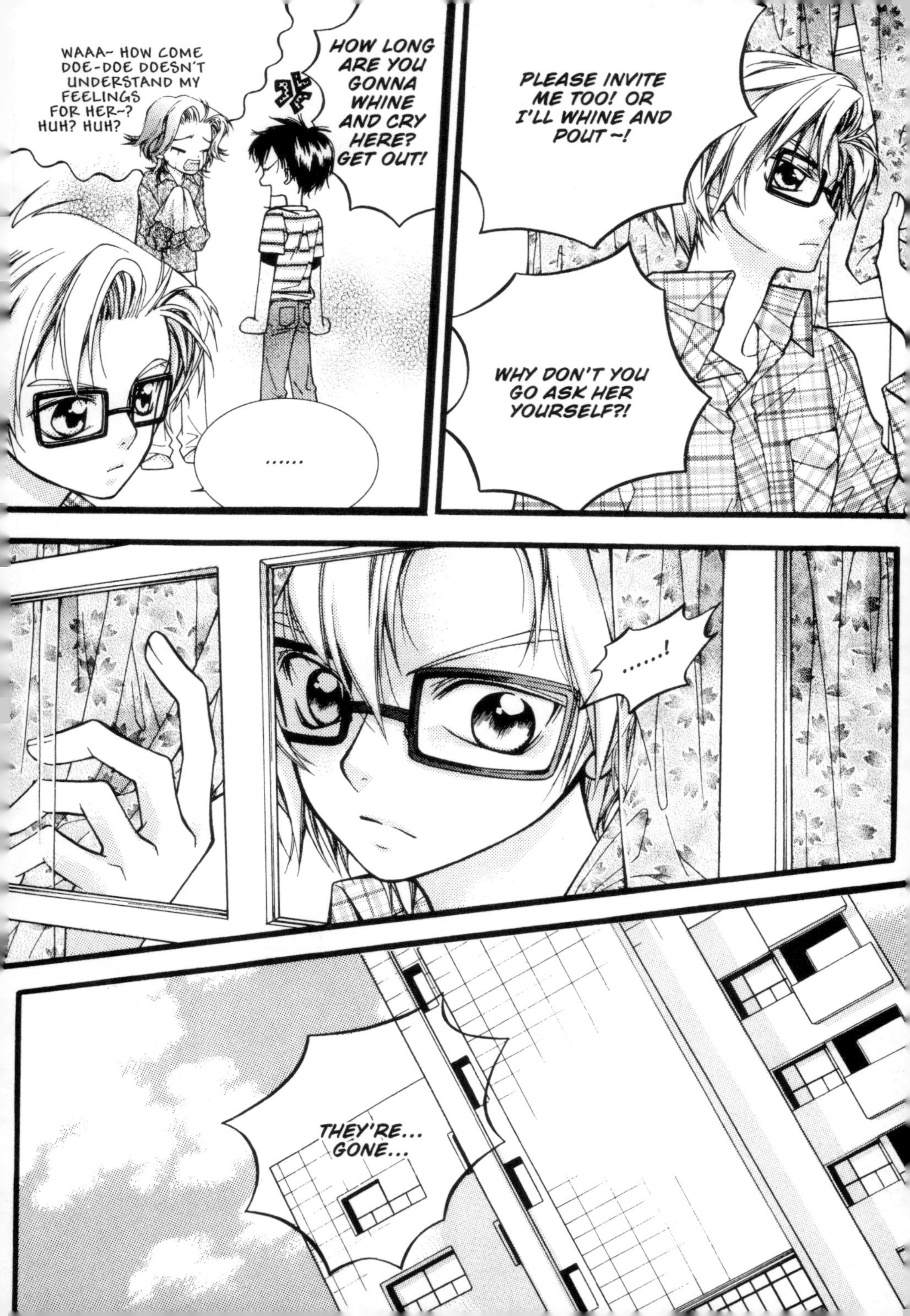
WAAA~ HOW COME DOE-DOE DOESN'T UNDERSTAND MY FEELINGS FOR HER~? HUH? HUH?
HOW LONG ARE YOU GONNA WHINE AND CRY HERE? GET OUT!
......
PLEASE INVITE ME TOO! OR I'LL WHINE AND POUT ~!
WHY DON'T YOU GO ASK HER YOURSELF?!
......!
THEY'RE... GONE...

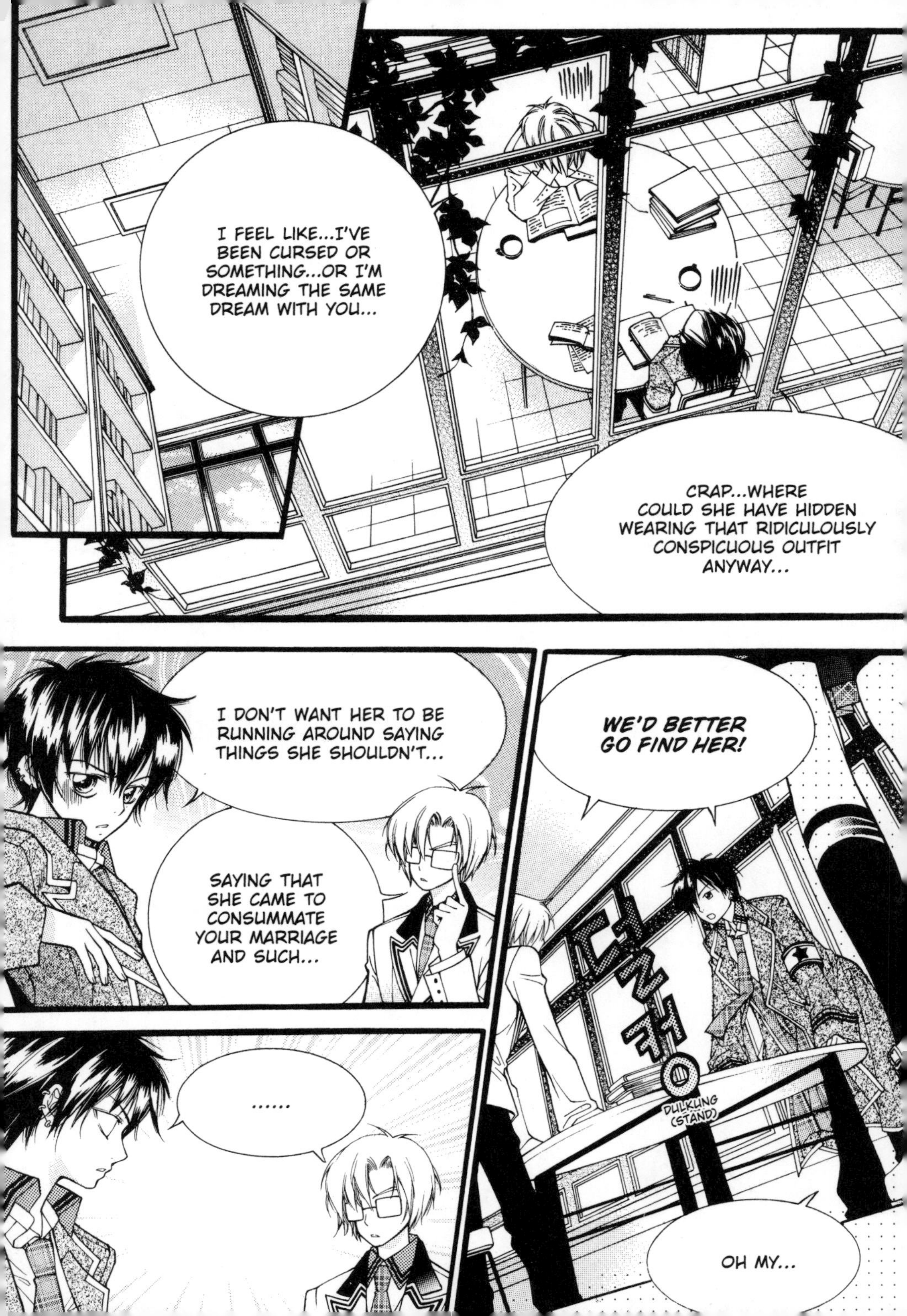

I FEEL LIKE...I'VE BEEN CURSED OR SOMETHING...OR I'M DREAMING THE SAME DREAM WITH YOU...
CRAP...WHERE COULD SHE HAVE HIDDEN WEARING THAT RIDICULOUSLY CONSPICUOUS OUTFIT ANYWAY...
I DON'T WANT HER TO BE RUNNING AROUND SAYING THINGS SHE SHOULDN'T...
SAYING THAT SHE CAME TO CONSUMMATE YOUR MARRIAGE AND SUCH...
......
WE'D BETTER GO FIND HER!
DULKUNG (STAND)
OH MY...

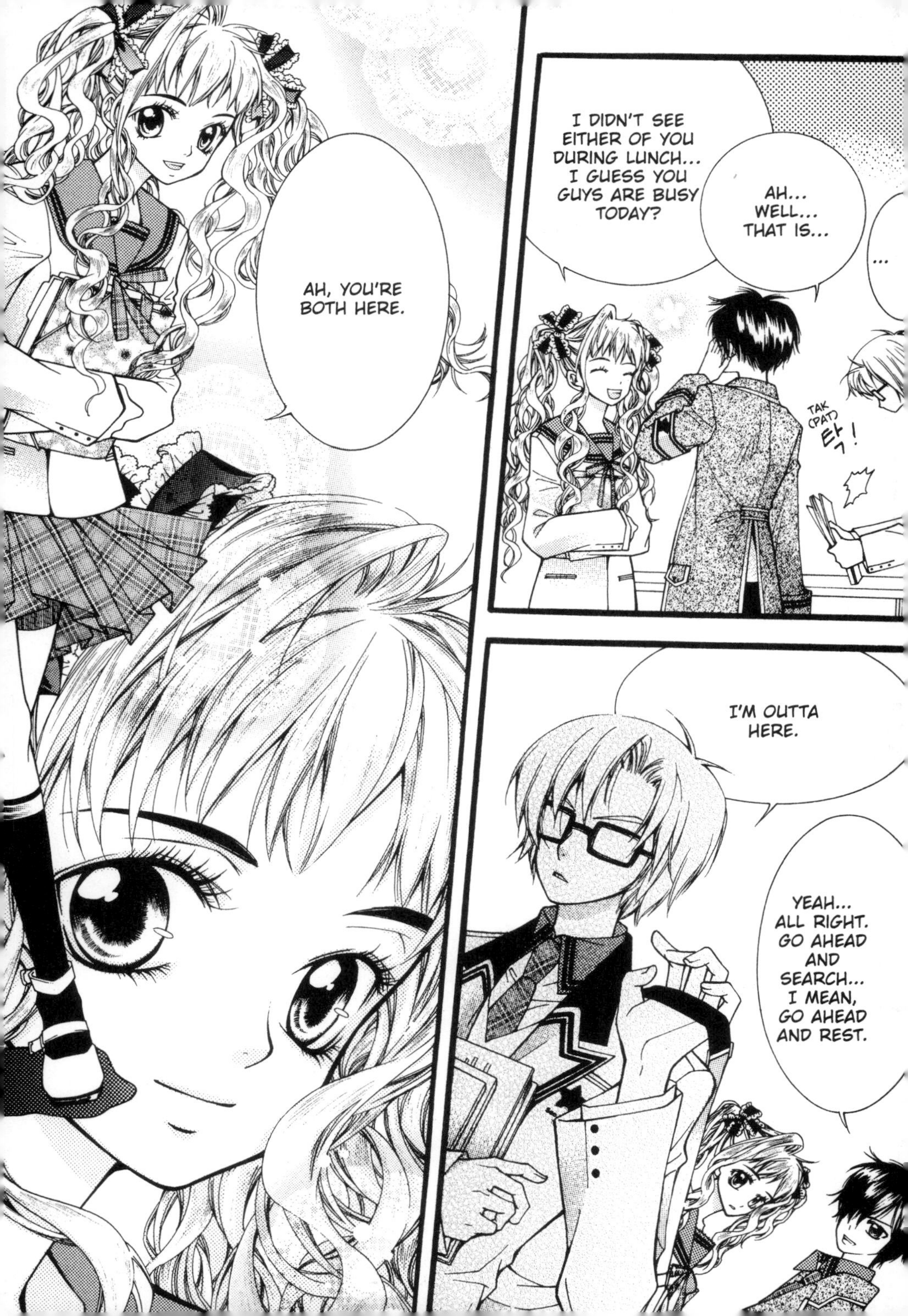
AH, YOU'RE BOTH HERE.
I DIDN'T SEE EITHER OF YOU DURING LUNCH... I GUESS YOU GUYS ARE BUSY TODAY?
AH... WELL... THAT IS...
...
TAK (PAT) 탁!
I'M OUTTA HERE.
YEAH... ALL RIGHT. GO AHEAD AND SEARCH... I MEAN, GO AHEAD AND REST.

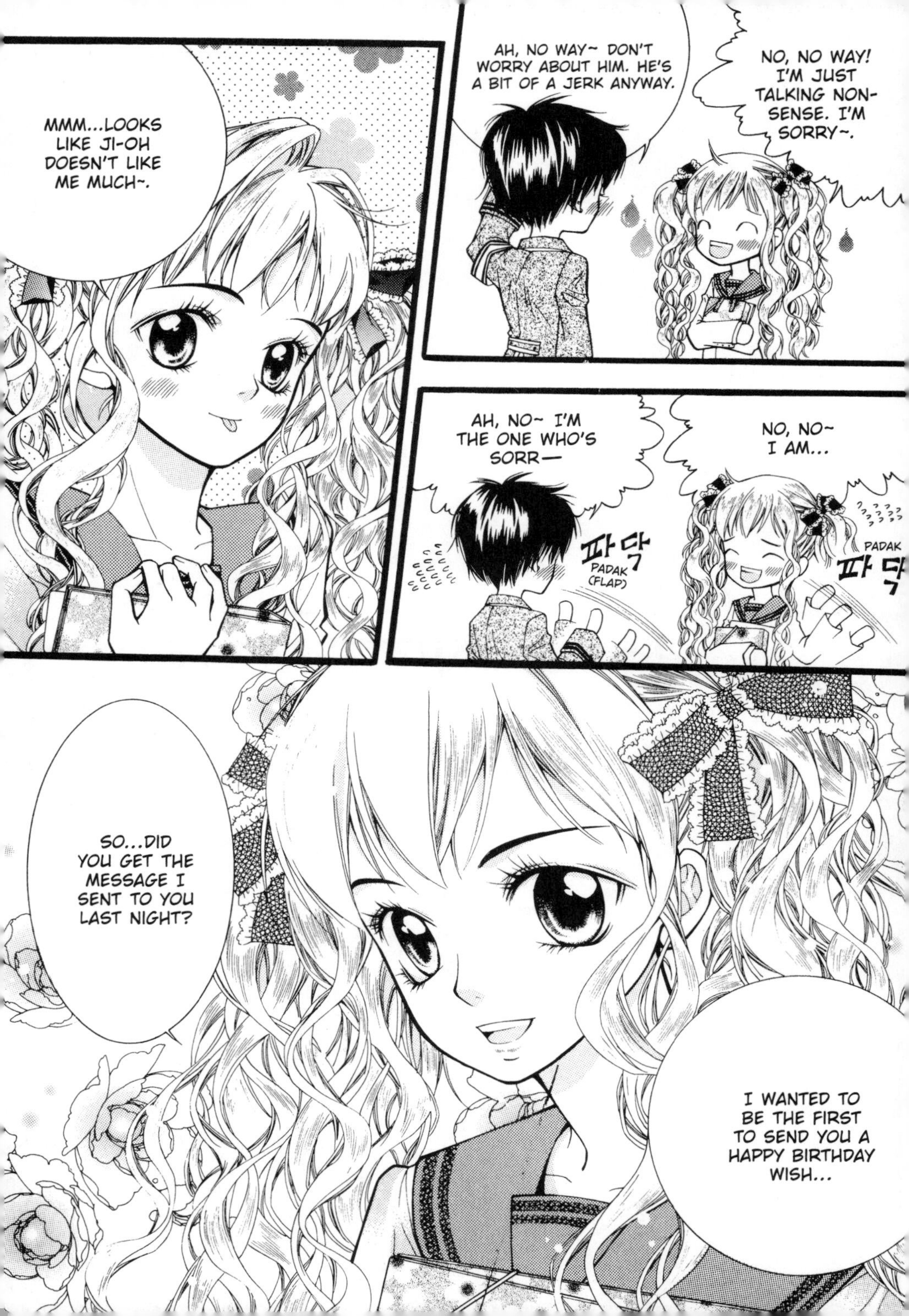
MMM...LOOKS LIKE JI-OH DOESN'T LIKE ME MUCH~.
AH, NO WAY~ DON'T WORRY ABOUT HIM. HE'S A BIT OF A JERK ANYWAY.
NO, NO WAY! I'M JUST TALKING NON-SENSE. I'M SORRY~.
AH, NO~ I'M THE ONE WHO'S SORR—
NO, NO~ I AM...
파닥
PADAK (FLAP)
PADAK
파닥
SO...DID YOU GET THE MESSAGE I SENT TO YOU LAST NIGHT?
I WANTED TO BE THE FIRST TO SEND YOU A HAPPY BIRTHDAY WISH...

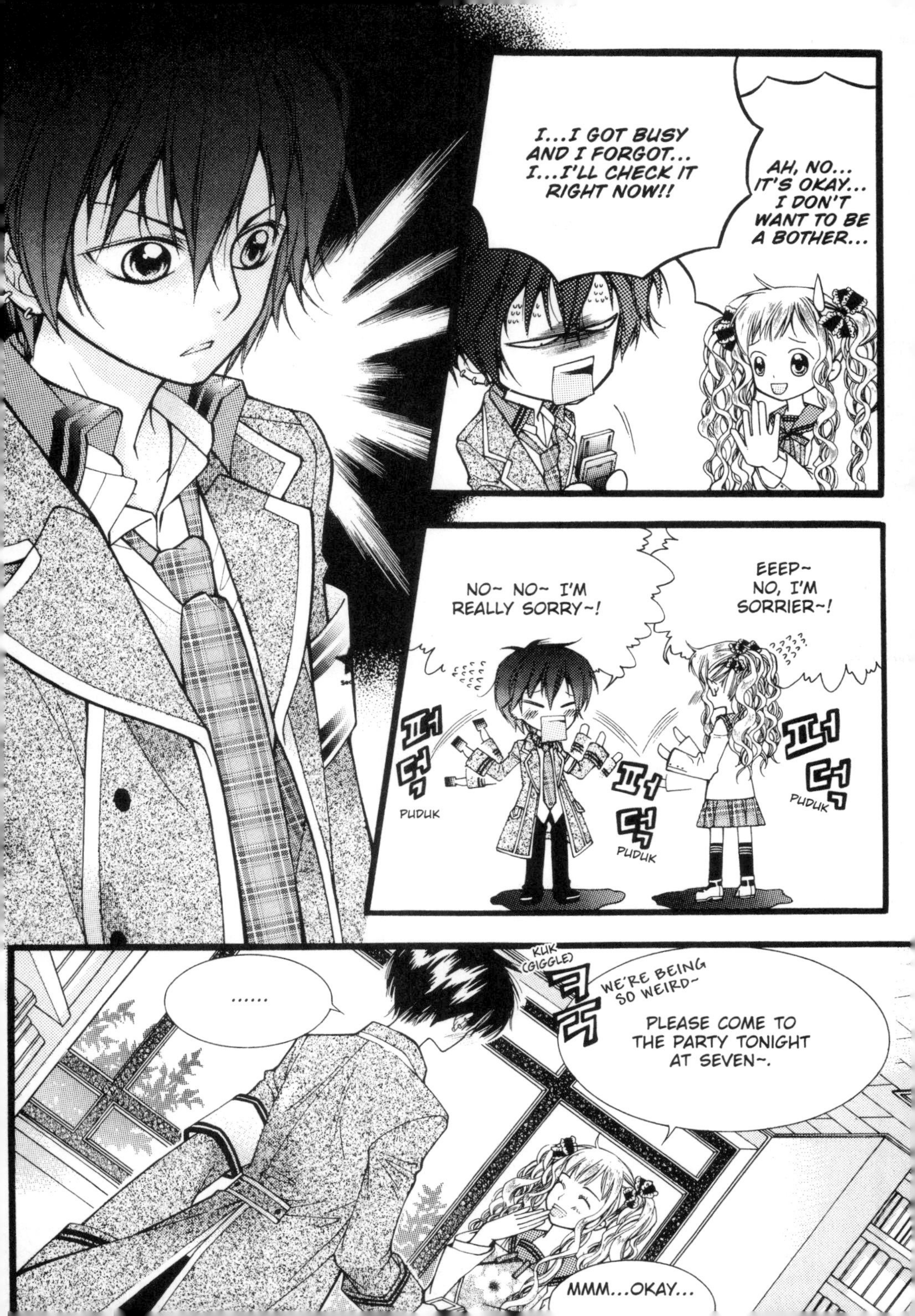
I...I GOT BUSY AND I FORGOT... I...I'LL CHECK IT RIGHT NOW!!
AH, NO... IT'S OKAY... I DON'T WANT TO BE A BOTHER...
NO~ NO~ I'M REALLY SORRY~!
EEEP~ NO, I'M SORRIER~!
PUDUK
PUDUK
PUDUK
......
KUK (GIGGLE)
WE'RE BEING SO WEIRD~
PLEASE COME TO THE PARTY TONIGHT AT SEVEN~.
MMM...OKAY...

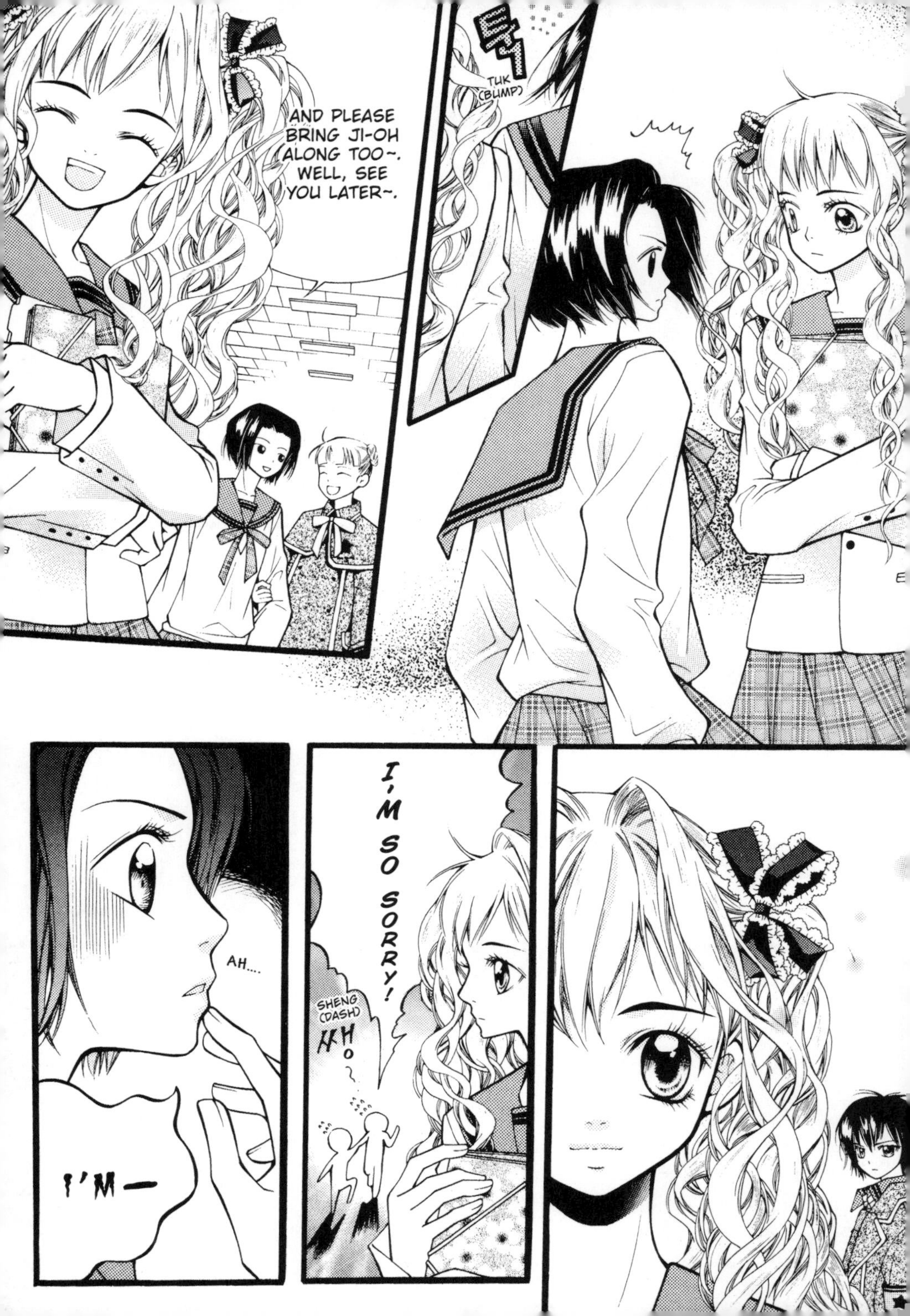
AND PLEASE BRING JI-OH ALONG TOO~. WELL, SEE YOU LATER~.
TUK (BUMP)
AH....
I'M—
I'M SO SORRY!
SHENG (DASH)

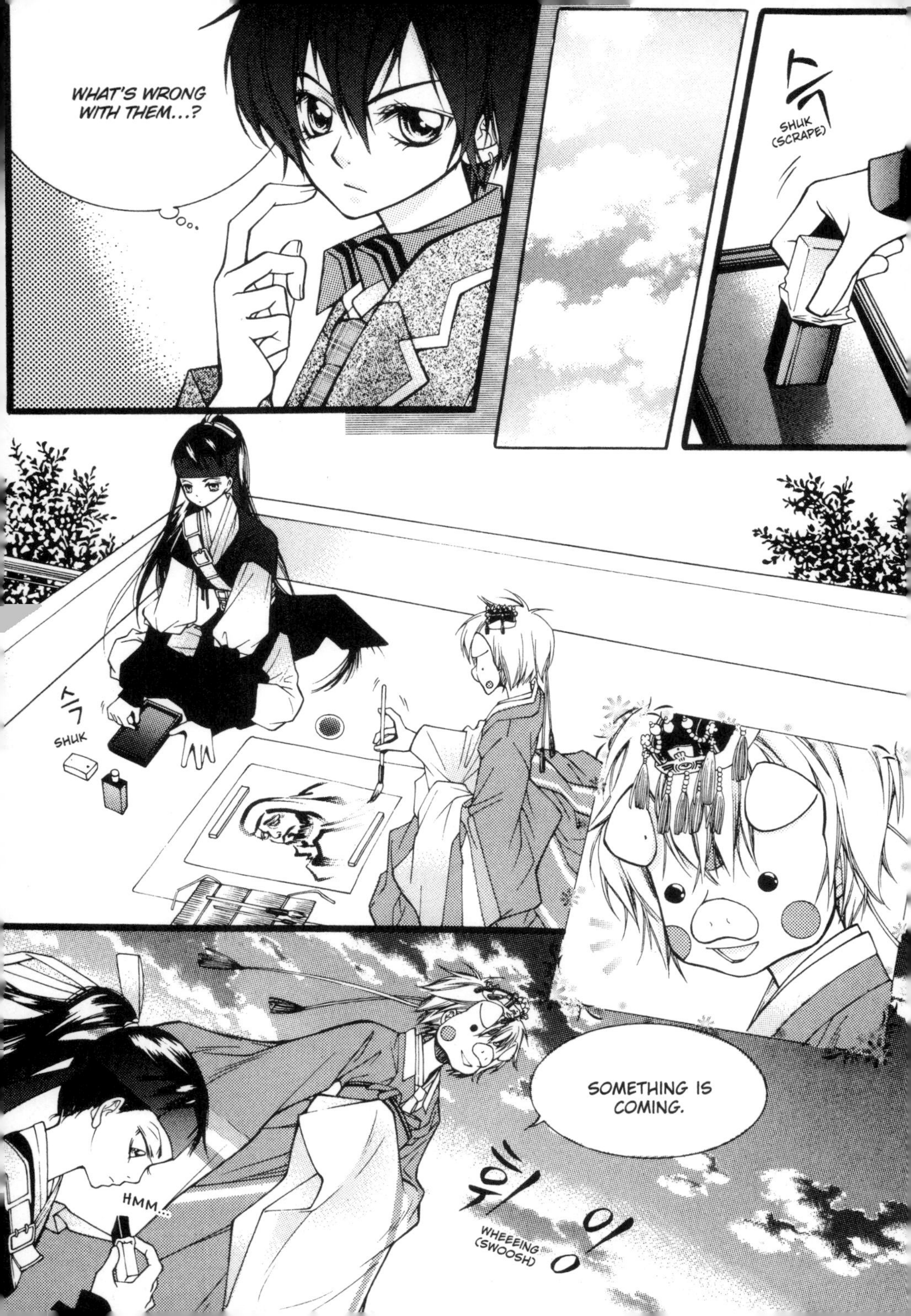
WHAT'S WRONG WITH THEM...?
SHUK (SCRAPE)
SHUK
SOMETHING IS COMING.
HMM...
WHEEEING (SWOOSH)

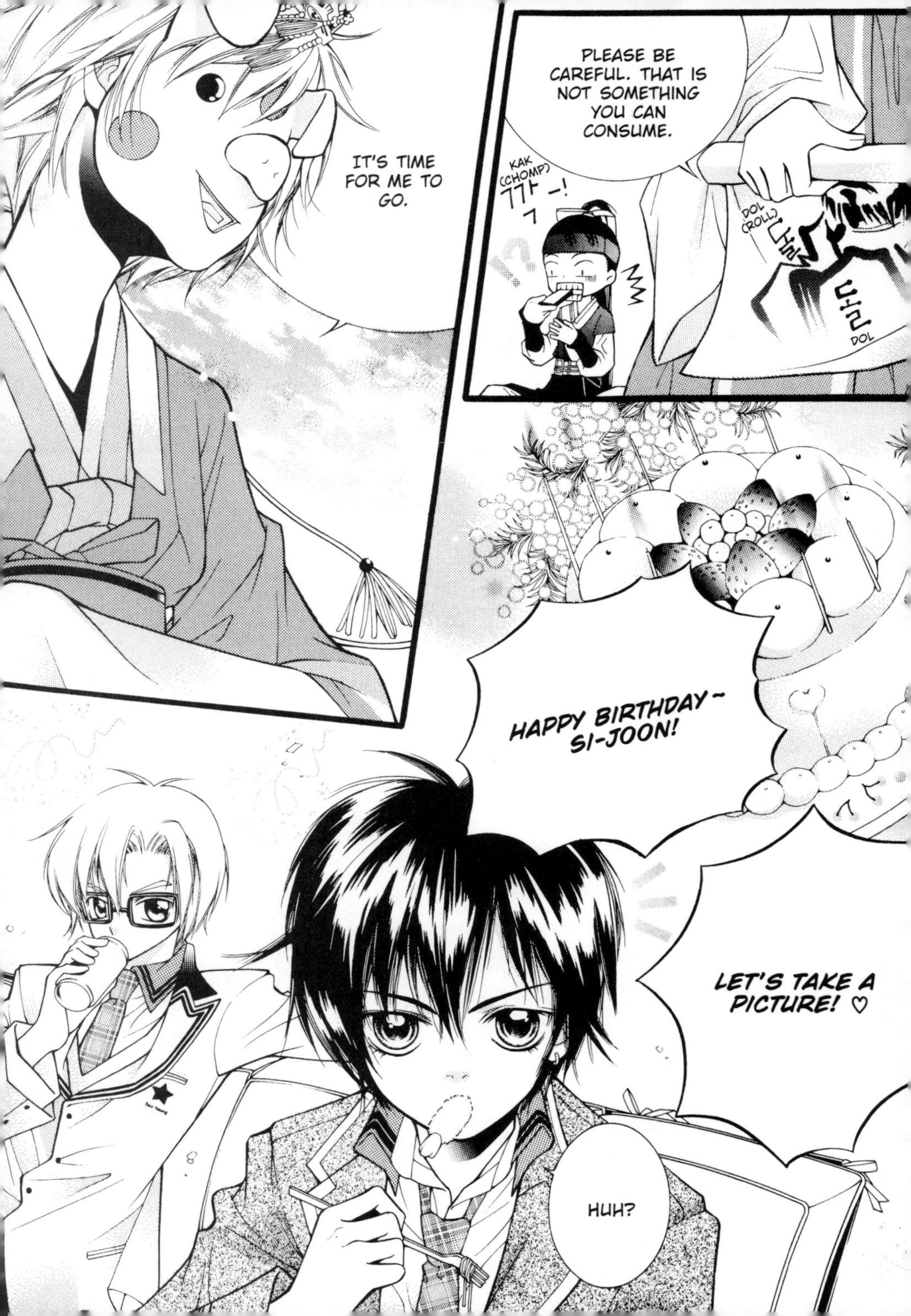

IT'S TIME FOR ME TO GO.
PLEASE BE CAREFUL. THAT IS NOT SOMETHING YOU CAN CONSUME.
KAK (CHOMP)
DOL (ROLL)
DOL
HAPPY BIRTHDAY~ SI-JOON!
LET'S TAKE A PICTURE! ♡
HUH?

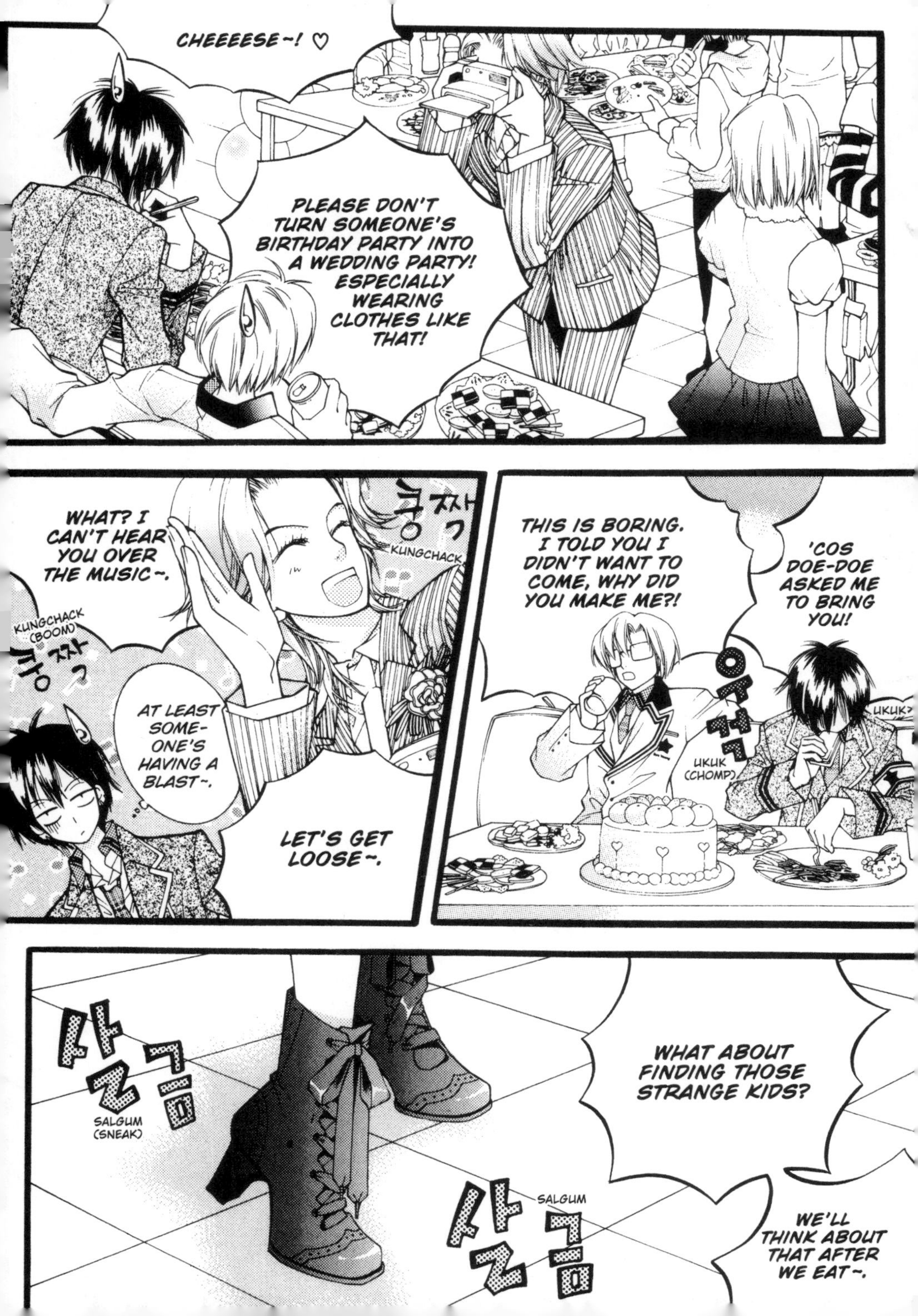
CHEEEEESE~! ♡
PLEASE DON'T TURN SOMEONE'S BIRTHDAY PARTY INTO A WEDDING PARTY! ESPECIALLY WEARING CLOTHES LIKE THAT!
쿵짝
KUNGCHACK
WHAT? I CAN'T HEAR YOU OVER THE MUSIC~.
KUNGCHACK (BOOM)
쿵짝
AT LEAST SOME-ONE'S HAVING A BLAST~.
LET'S GET LOOSE~.
THIS IS BORING. I TOLD YOU I DIDN'T WANT TO COME, WHY DID YOU MAKE ME?!
'COS DOE-DOE ASKED ME TO BRING YOU!
우걱
UKUK (CHOMP)
UKUK
살금
SALGUM (SNEAK)
WHAT ABOUT FINDING THOSE STRANGE KIDS?
살금
SALGUM
WE'LL THINK ABOUT THAT AFTER WE EAT~.

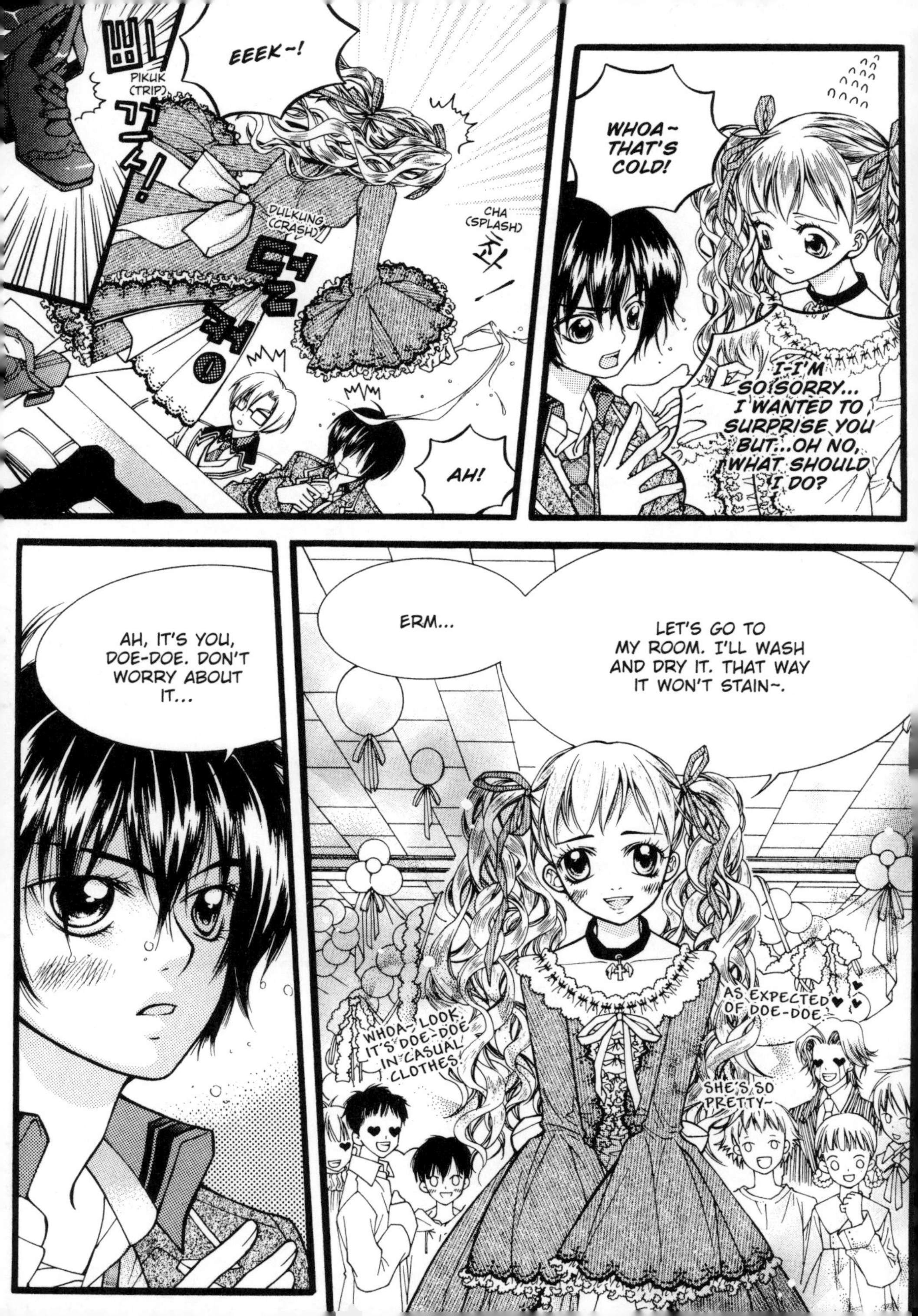
PIKUK (TRIP)
EEEK~!
DULKUNG (CRASH)
CHA (SPLASH)
AH!
WHOA~ THAT'S COLD!
I-I'M SO SORRY... I WANTED TO SURPRISE YOU BUT...OH NO, WHAT SHOULD I DO?
AH, IT'S YOU, DOE-DOE. DON'T WORRY ABOUT IT...
ERM...
LET'S GO TO MY ROOM. I'LL WASH AND DRY IT. THAT WAY IT WON'T STAIN~.
WHOA, LOOK. IT'S DOE-DOE IN CASUAL CLOTHES.
AS EXPECTED OF DOE-DOE.
SHE'S SO PRETTY~

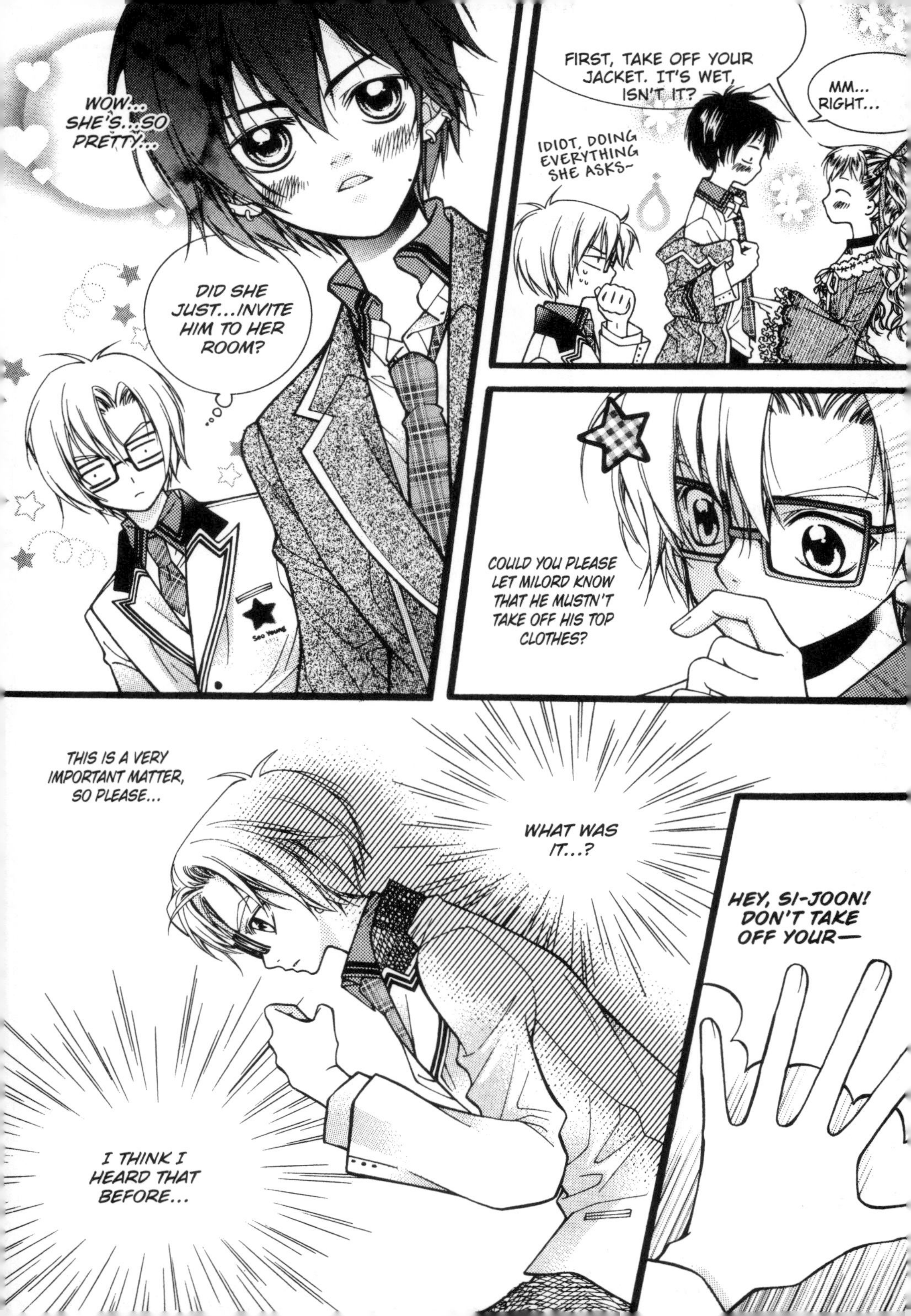
WOW... SHE'S...SO PRETTY...
DID SHE JUST...INVITE HIM TO HER ROOM?
Seo Young
FIRST, TAKE OFF YOUR JACKET. IT'S WET, ISN'T IT?
MM... RIGHT...
IDIOT, DOING EVERYTHING SHE ASKS~
COULD YOU PLEASE LET MILORD KNOW THAT HE MUSTN'T TAKE OFF HIS TOP CLOTHES?
THIS IS A VERY IMPORTANT MATTER, SO PLEASE...
WHAT WAS IT...?
I THINK I HEARD THAT BEFORE...
HEY, SI-JOON! DON'T TAKE OFF YOUR—

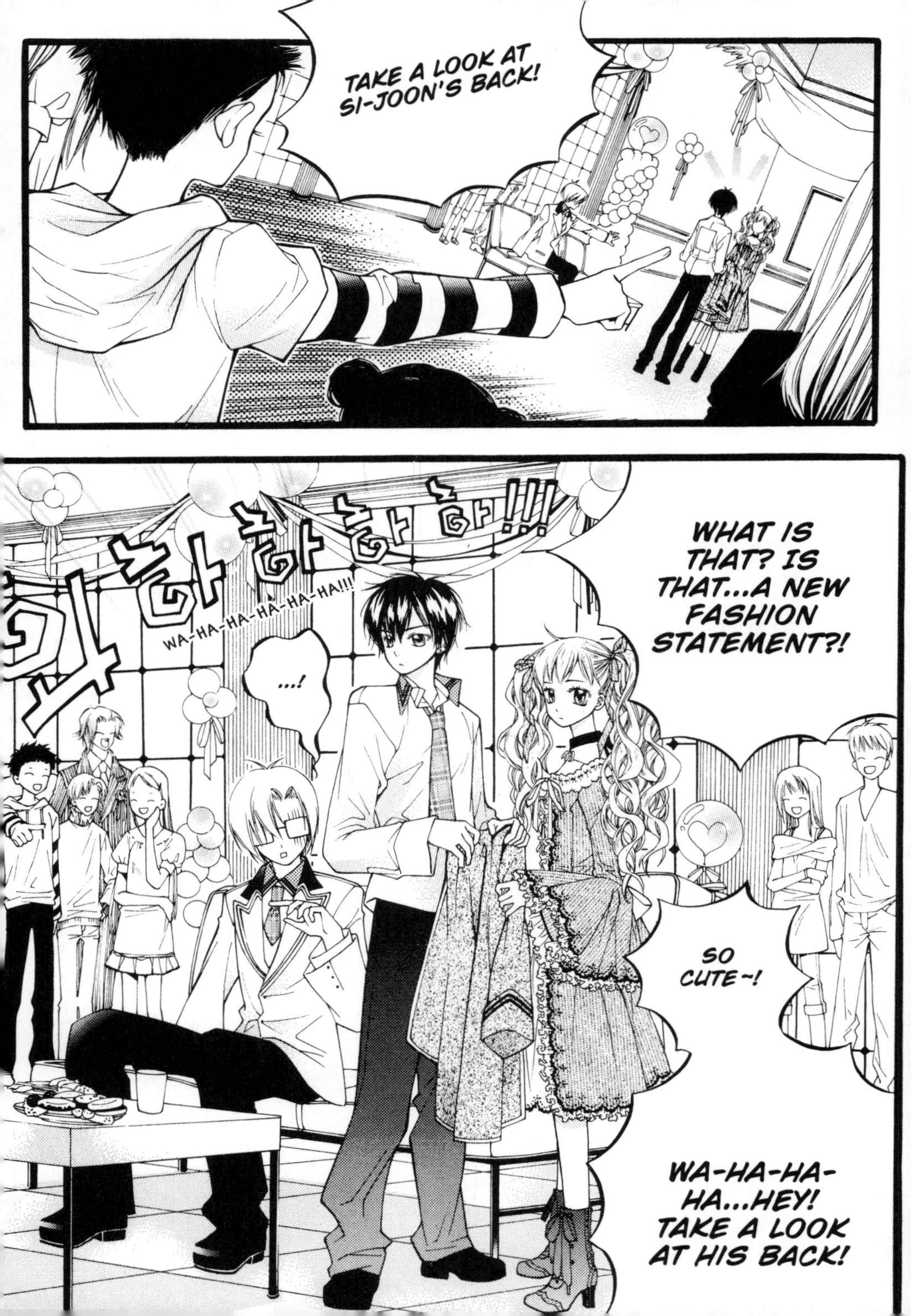
TAKE A LOOK AT SI-JOON'S BACK!
WHAT IS THAT? IS THAT...A NEW FASHION STATEMENT?!
SO CUTE~!
WA-HA-HA-HA...HEY! TAKE A LOOK AT HIS BACK!
...!
WA-HA-HA-HA-HA-HA!!!

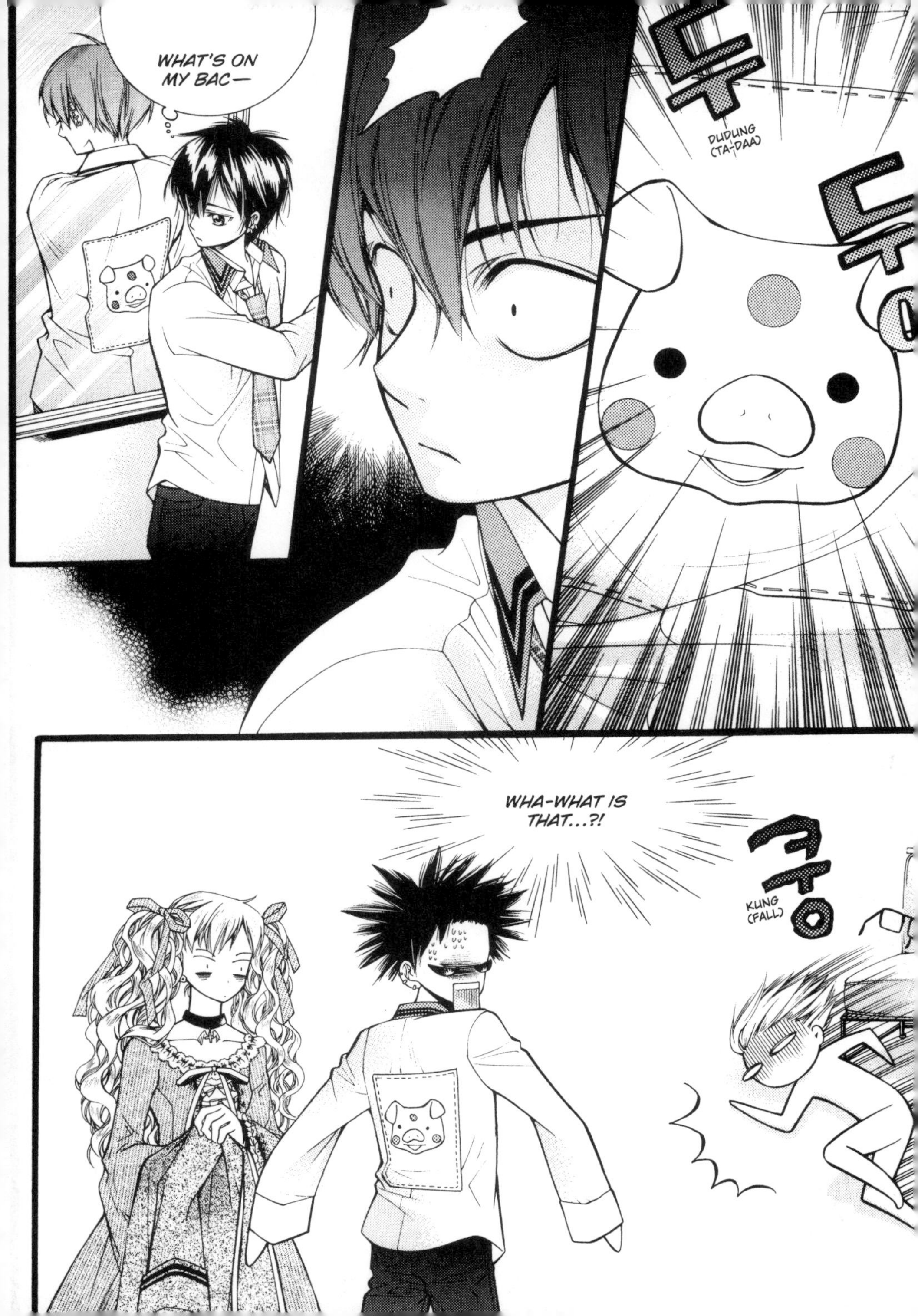
WHAT'S ON MY BAC—
두둥
DUDUNG (TA-DAA)
WHA-WHAT IS THAT...?!
쿵
KUNG (FALL)

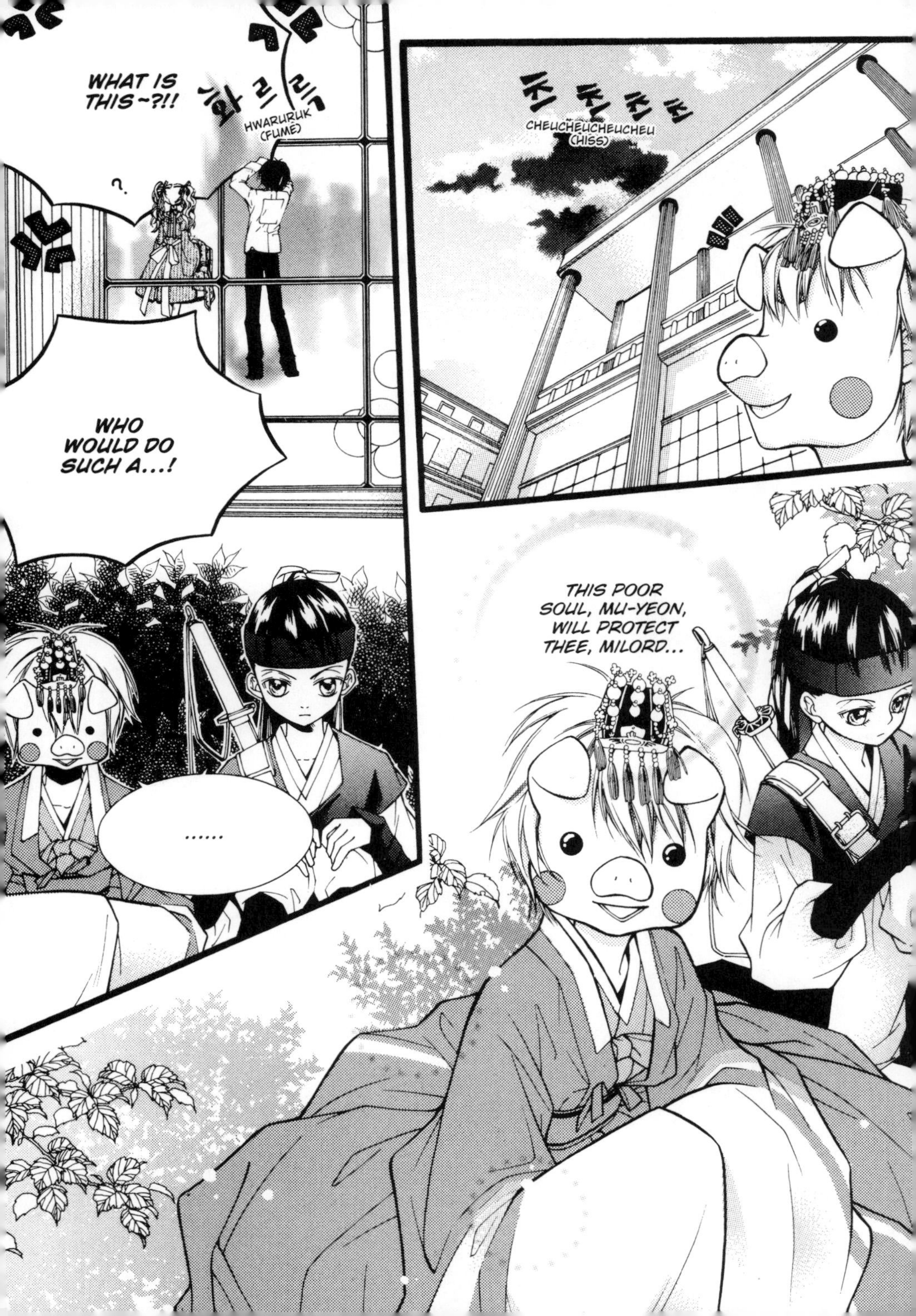

WHAT IS THIS~?!!
화르륵
HWARURUK (FUME)
WHO WOULD DO SUCH A...!
츠츠츠츠
CHEUCHEUCHEUCHEU (HISS)
......
THIS POOR SOUL, MU-YEON, WILL PROTECT THEE, MILORD...

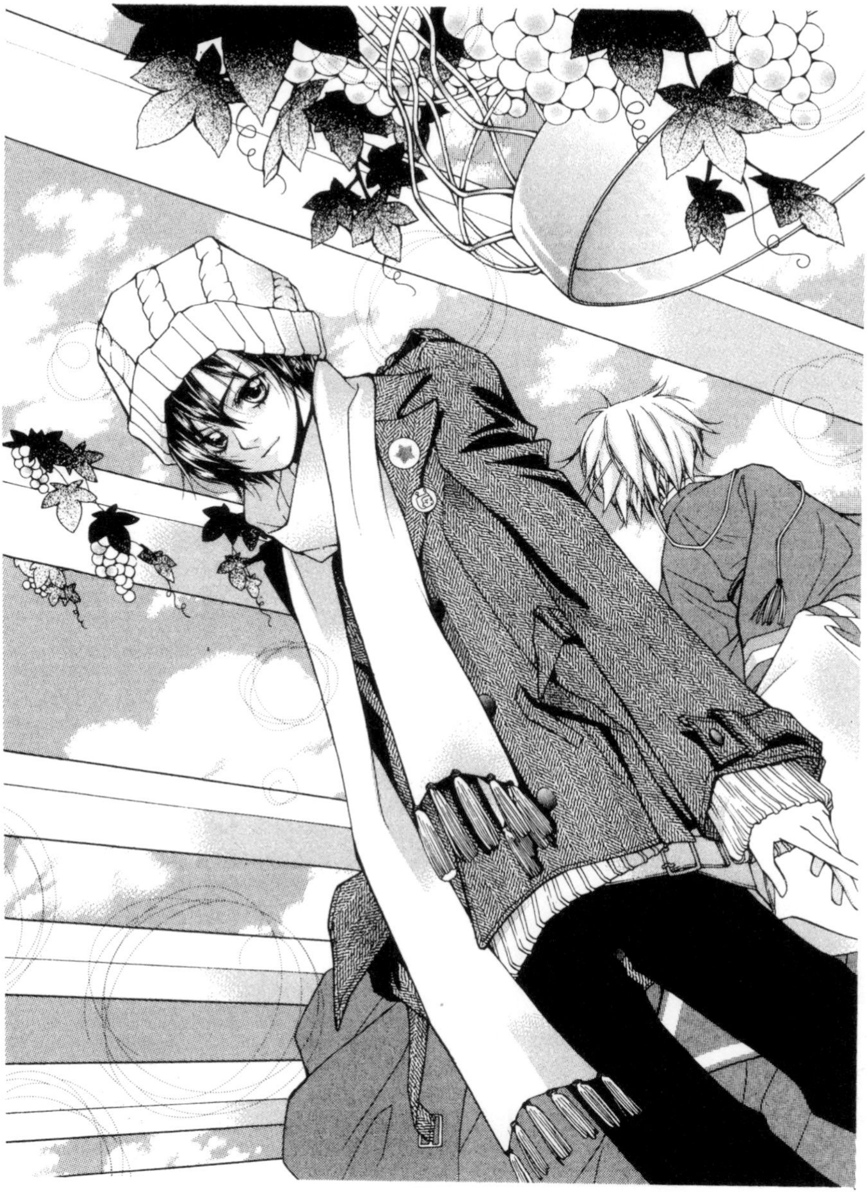

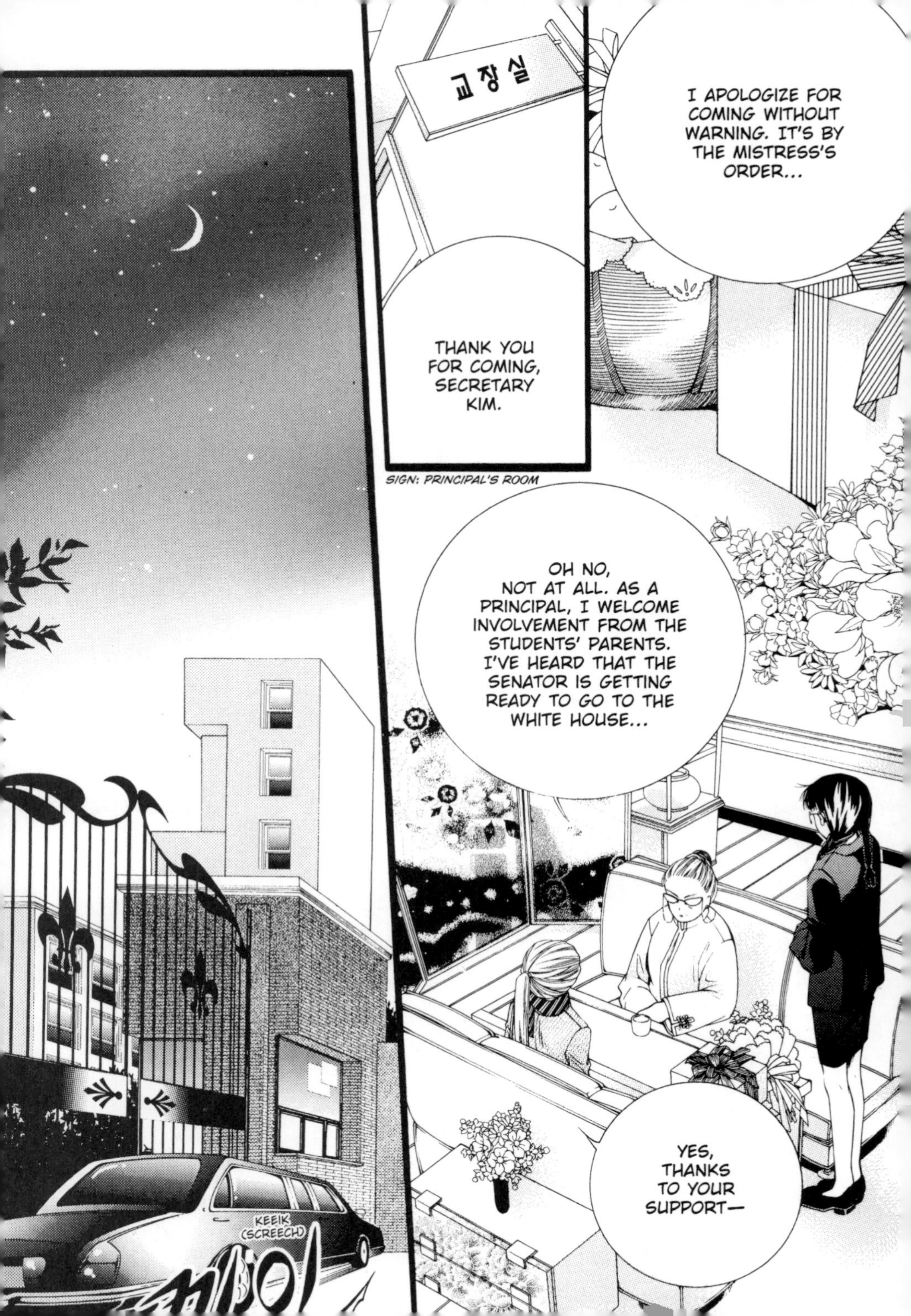
KEEIK (SCREECH)
교장실
THANK YOU FOR COMING, SECRETARY KIM.
I APOLOGIZE FOR COMING WITHOUT WARNING. IT'S BY THE MISTRESS'S ORDER...
SIGN: PRINCIPAL'S ROOM
OH NO, NOT AT ALL. AS A PRINCIPAL, I WELCOME INVOLVEMENT FROM THE STUDENTS' PARENTS. I'VE HEARD THAT THE SENATOR IS GETTING READY TO GO TO THE WHITE HOUSE...
YES, THANKS TO YOUR SUPPORT—

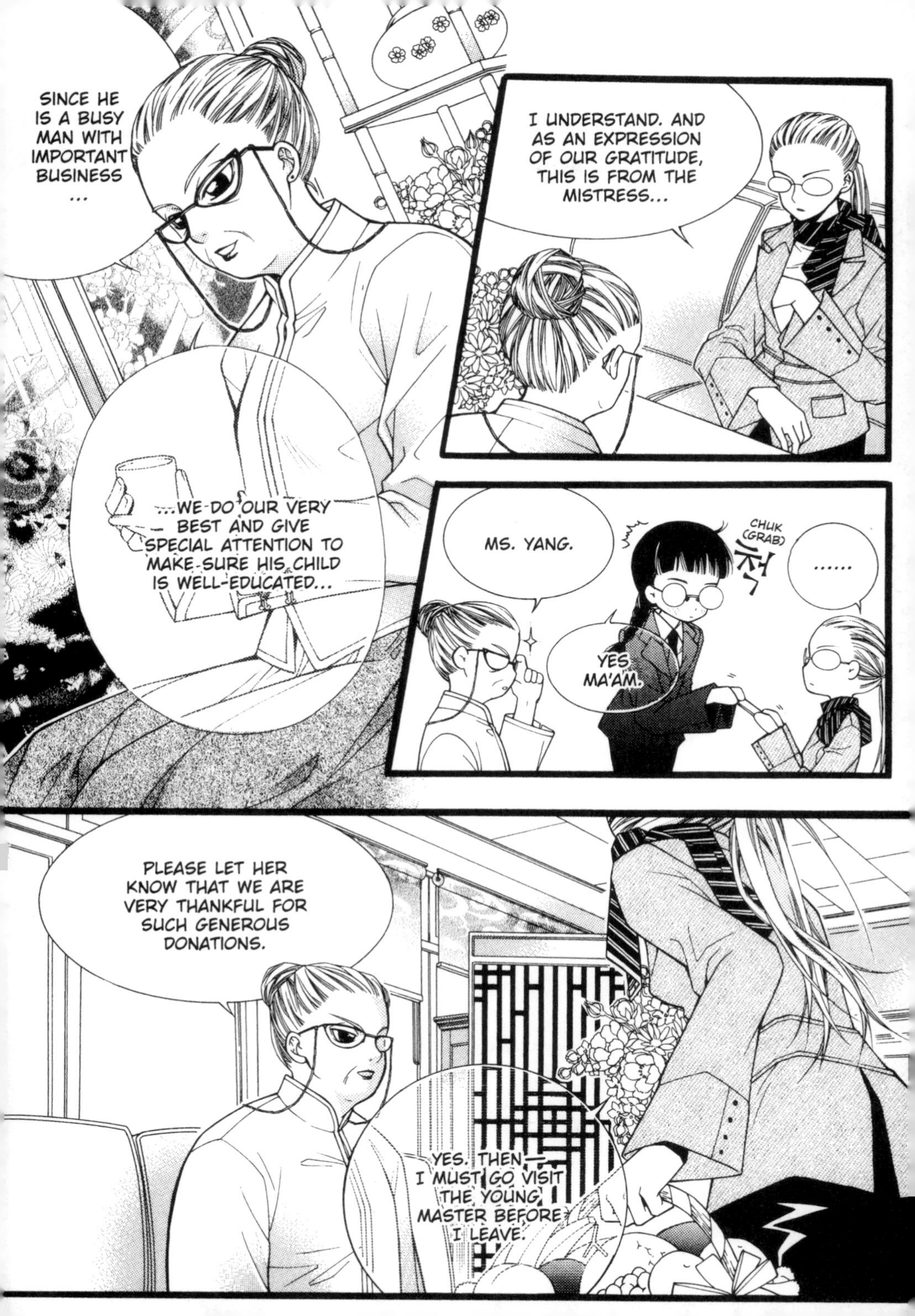
SINCE HE IS A BUSY MAN WITH IMPORTANT BUSINESS ...
...WE DO OUR VERY BEST AND GIVE SPECIAL ATTENTION TO MAKE SURE HIS CHILD IS WELL-EDUCATED...
I UNDERSTAND. AND AS AN EXPRESSION OF OUR GRATITUDE, THIS IS FROM THE MISTRESS...
MS. YANG.
YES MA'AM.
CHUK (GRAB)
척
......
PLEASE LET HER KNOW THAT WE ARE VERY THANKFUL FOR SUCH GENEROUS DONATIONS.
YES. THEN— I MUST GO VISIT THE YOUNG MASTER BEFORE I LEAVE.

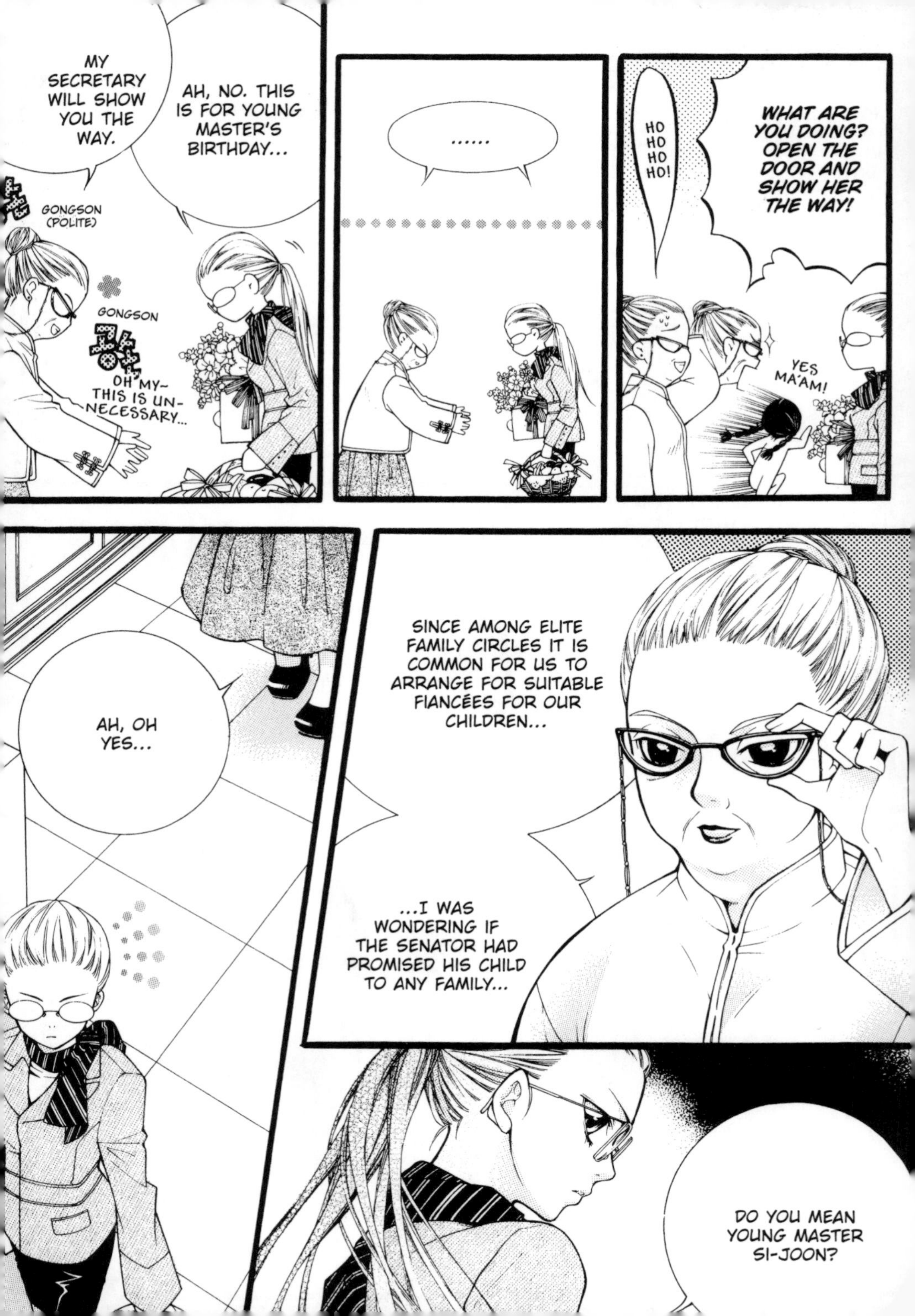
AH, NO. THIS IS FOR YOUNG MASTER'S BIRTHDAY...
MY SECRETARY WILL SHOW YOU THE WAY.
GONGSON (POLITE)
GONGSON
OH MY~ THIS IS UN-NECESSARY...
......
WHAT ARE YOU DOING? OPEN THE DOOR AND SHOW HER THE WAY!
HO HO HO HO!
YES MA'AM!
AH, OH YES...
SINCE AMONG ELITE FAMILY CIRCLES IT IS COMMON FOR US TO ARRANGE FOR SUITABLE FIANCÉES FOR OUR CHILDREN...
...I WAS WONDERING IF THE SENATOR HAD PROMISED HIS CHILD TO ANY FAMILY...
DO YOU MEAN YOUNG MASTER SI-JOON?

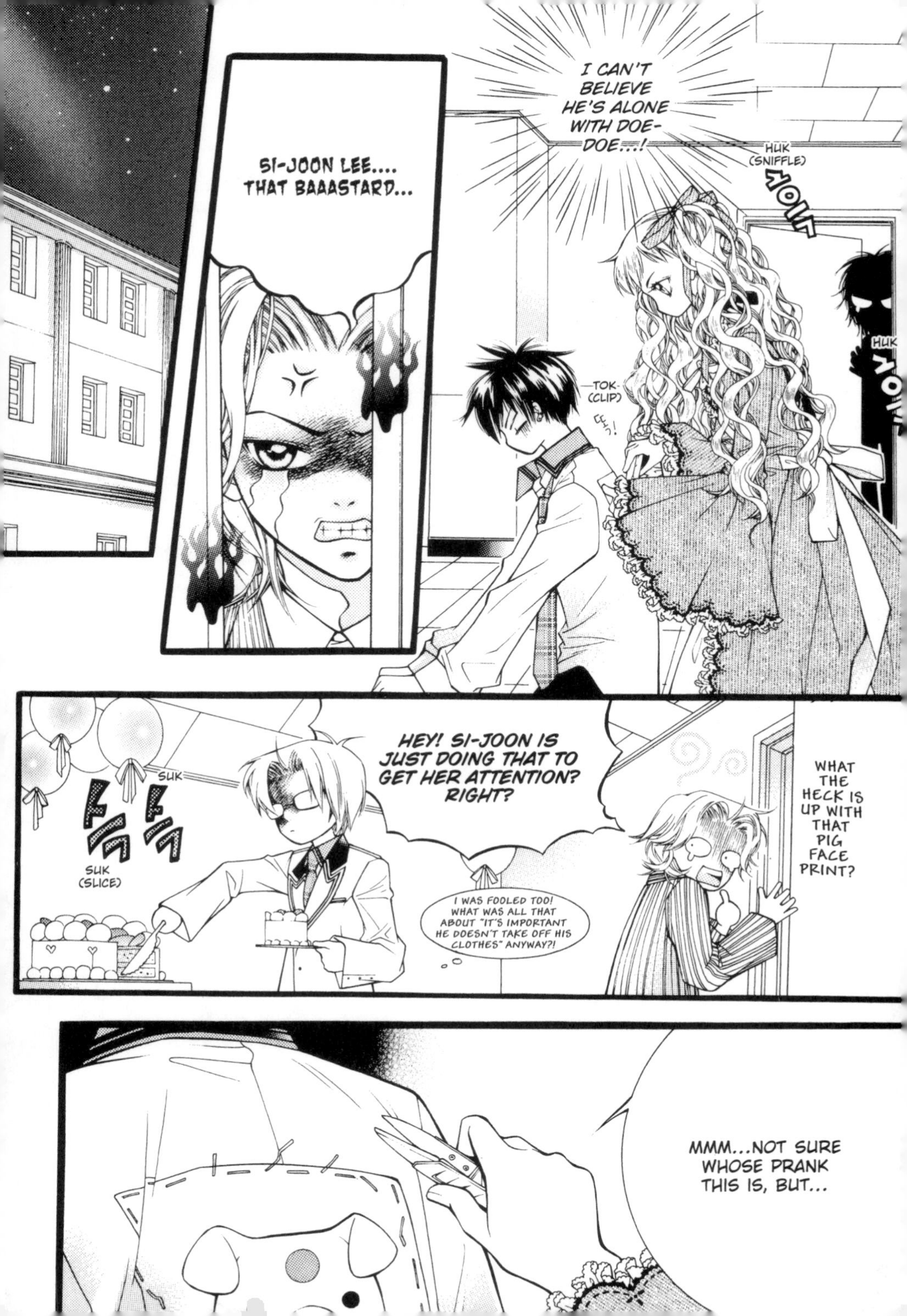
SI-JOON LEE.... THAT BAAASTARD...
I CAN'T BELIEVE HE'S ALONE WITH DOE-DOE...!
HUK (SNIFFLE)
HUK
TOK (CLIP)
SUK
SUK (SLICE)
HEY! SI-JOON IS JUST DOING THAT TO GET HER ATTENTION? RIGHT?
I WAS FOOLED TOO! WHAT WAS ALL THAT ABOUT "IT'S IMPORTANT HE DOESN'T TAKE OFF HIS CLOTHES" ANYWAY?!
WHAT THE HECK IS UP WITH THAT PIG FACE PRINT?
MMM...NOT SURE WHOSE PRANK THIS IS, BUT...

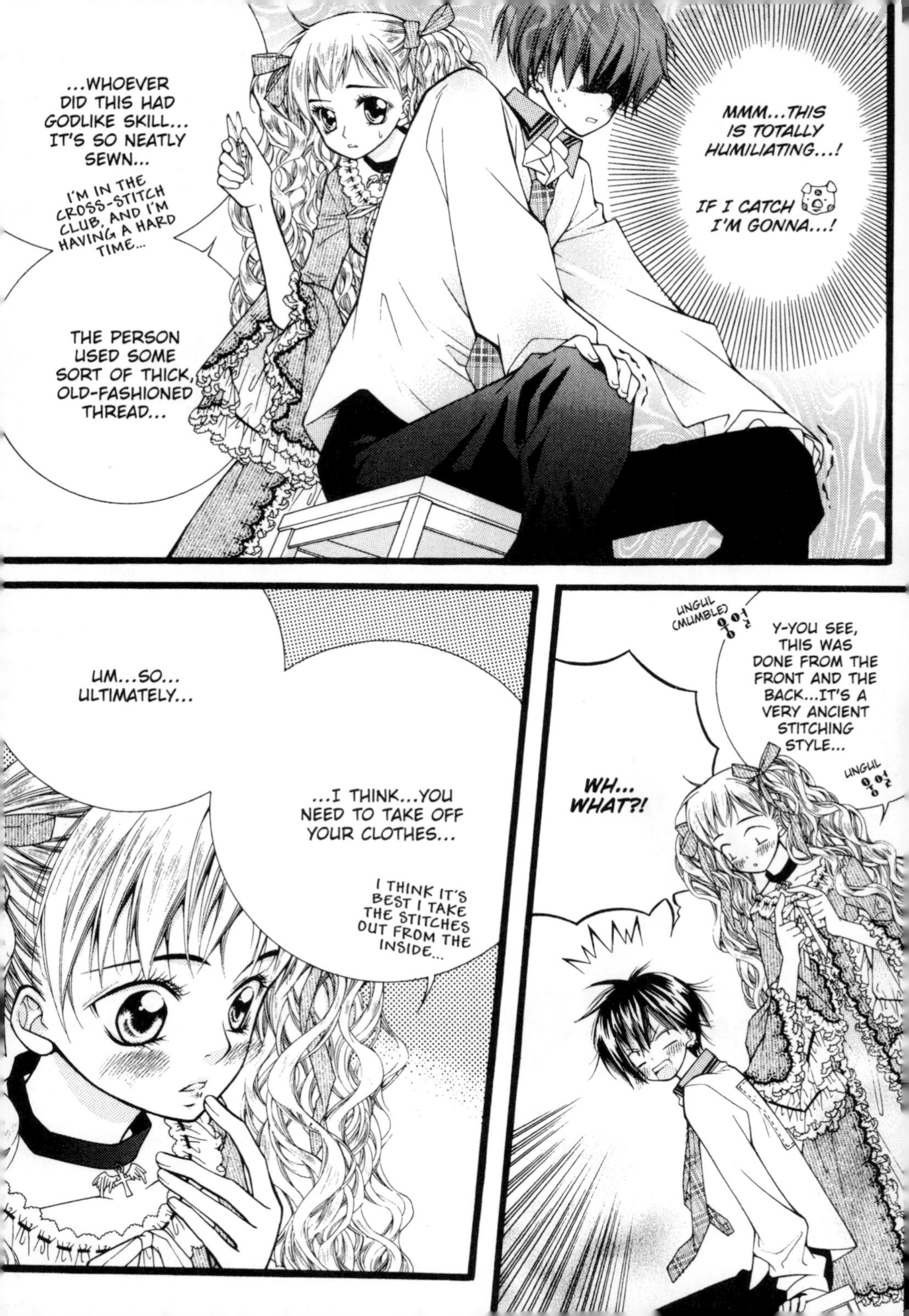
MMM...THIS IS TOTALLY HUMILIATING...!
IF I CATCH I'M GONNA...!
...WHOEVER DID THIS HAD GODLIKE SKILL... IT'S SO NEATLY SEWN...
I'M IN THE CROSS-STITCH CLUB, AND I'M HAVING A HARD TIME...
THE PERSON USED SOME SORT OF THICK, OLD-FASHIONED THREAD...
UNGUL (MUMBLE)
Y-YOU SEE, THIS WAS DONE FROM THE FRONT AND THE BACK...IT'S A VERY ANCIENT STITCHING STYLE...
UNGUL
WH... WHAT?!
UM...SO... ULTIMATELY...
...I THINK...YOU NEED TO TAKE OFF YOUR CLOTHES...
I THINK IT'S BEST I TAKE THE STITCHES OUT FROM THE INSIDE...

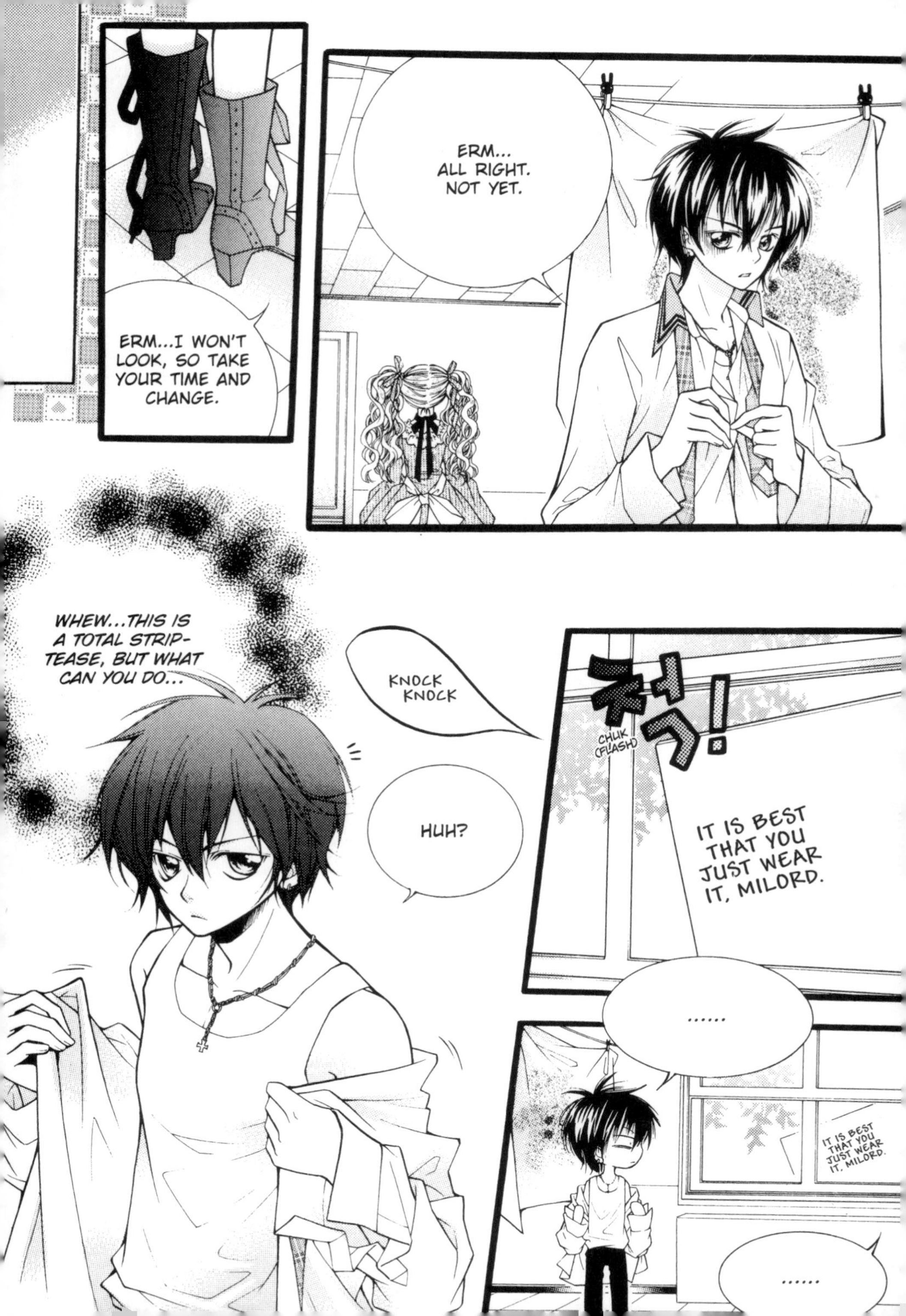
ERM...I WON'T LOOK, SO TAKE YOUR TIME AND CHANGE.
ERM... ALL RIGHT. NOT YET.
WHEW...THIS IS A TOTAL STRIP-TEASE, BUT WHAT CAN YOU DO...
KNOCK KNOCK
HUH?
척!
CHUK (FLASH)
IT IS BEST THAT YOU JUST WEAR IT, MILORD.
......
IT IS BEST THAT YOU JUST WEAR IT, MILORD.
......

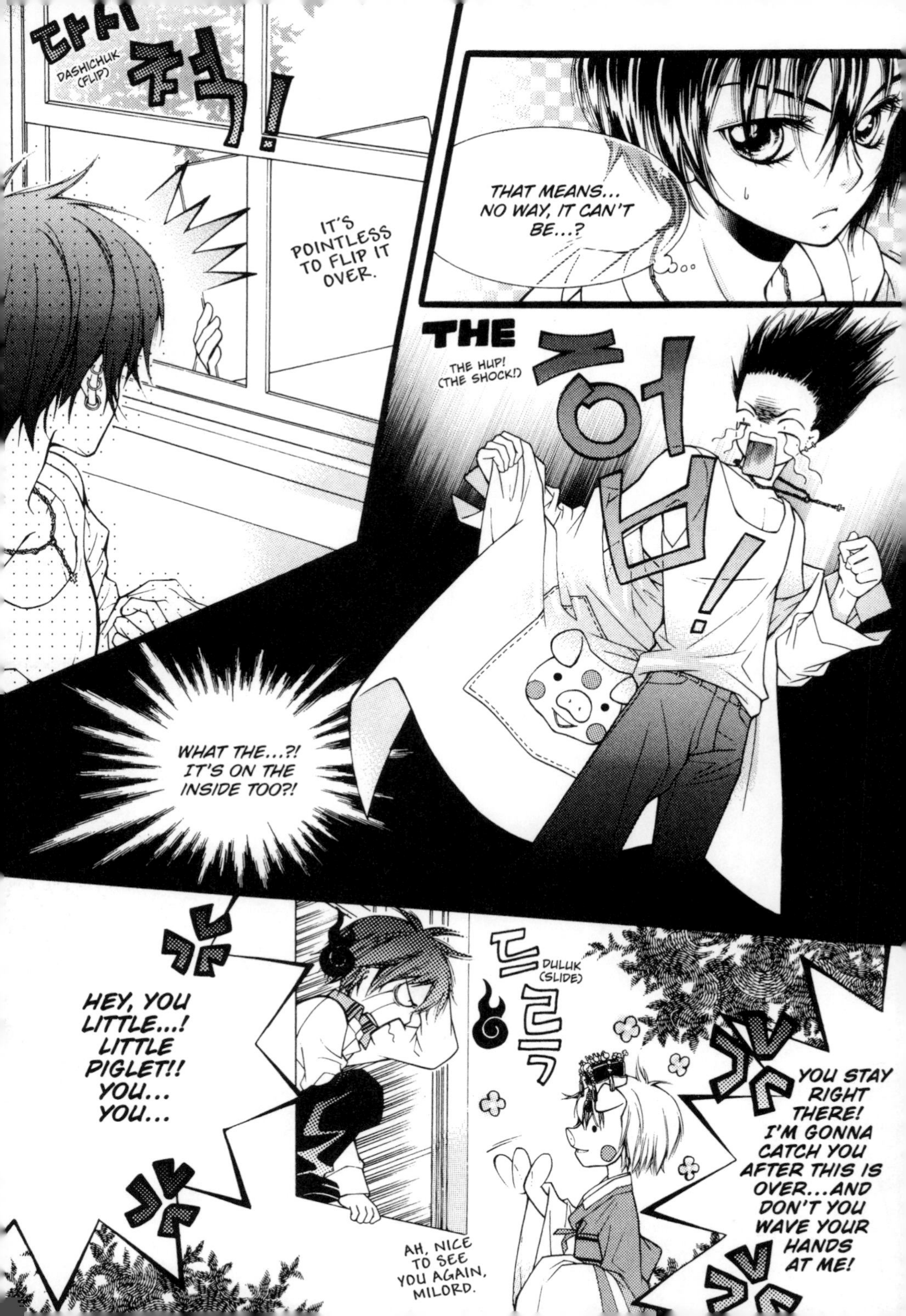

다시 춰!
DASHICHUK (FLIP)
IT'S POINTLESS TO FLIP IT OVER.
THAT MEANS... NO WAY, IT CAN'T BE...?
THE 헉!
THE HUP! (THE SHOCK!)
WHAT THE...?! IT'S ON THE INSIDE TOO?!
HEY, YOU LITTLE...! LITTLE PIGLET!! YOU... YOU...
드르륵
DULUK (SLIDE)
AH, NICE TO SEE YOU AGAIN, MILORD.
YOU STAY RIGHT THERE! I'M GONNA CATCH YOU AFTER THIS IS OVER...AND DON'T YOU WAVE YOUR HANDS AT ME!

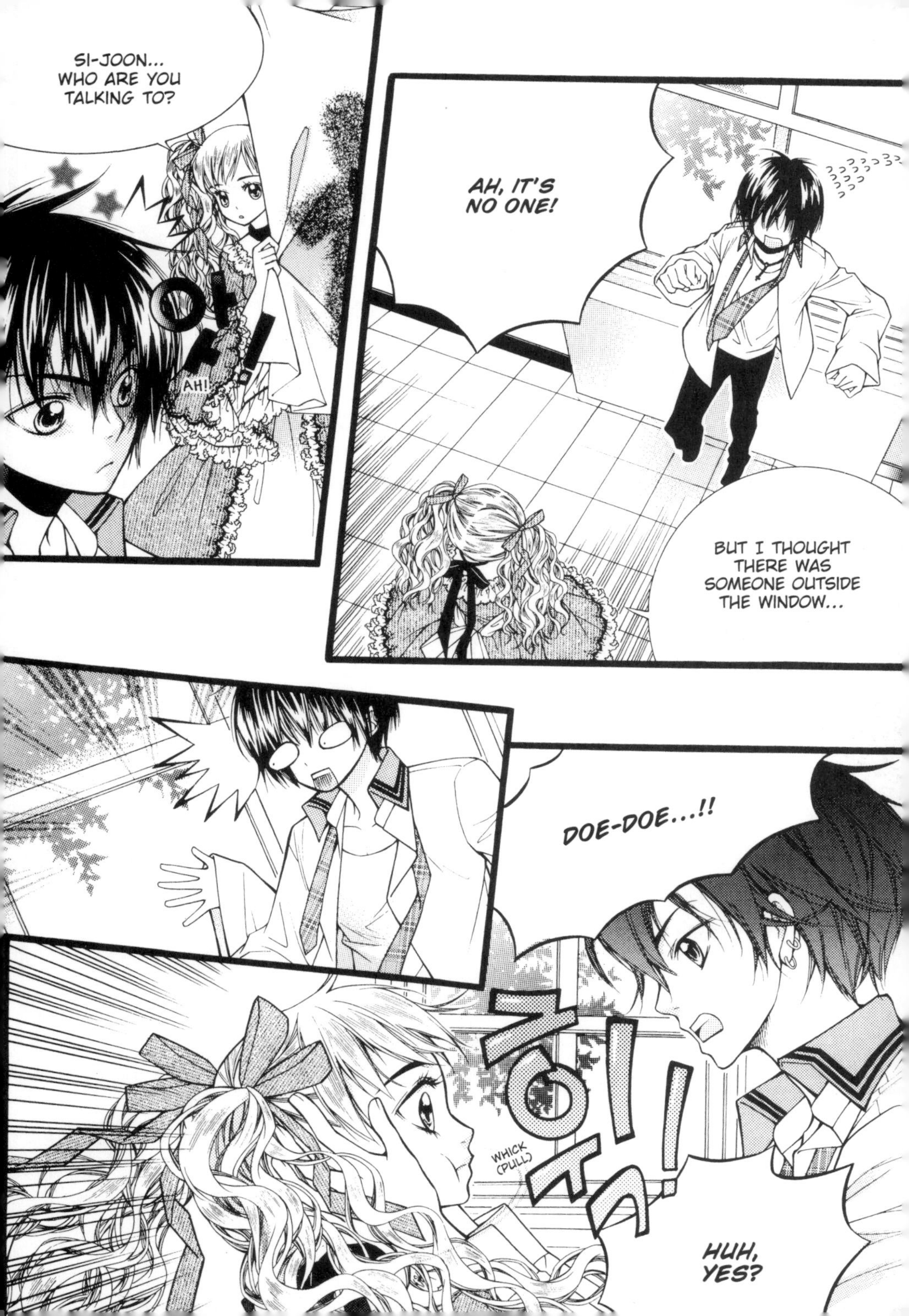

SI-JOON... WHO ARE YOU TALKING TO?
AH!
AH, IT'S NO ONE!
BUT I THOUGHT THERE WAS SOMEONE OUTSIDE THE WINDOW...
DOE-DOE...!!
WHICK (PULL)
HUH, YES?

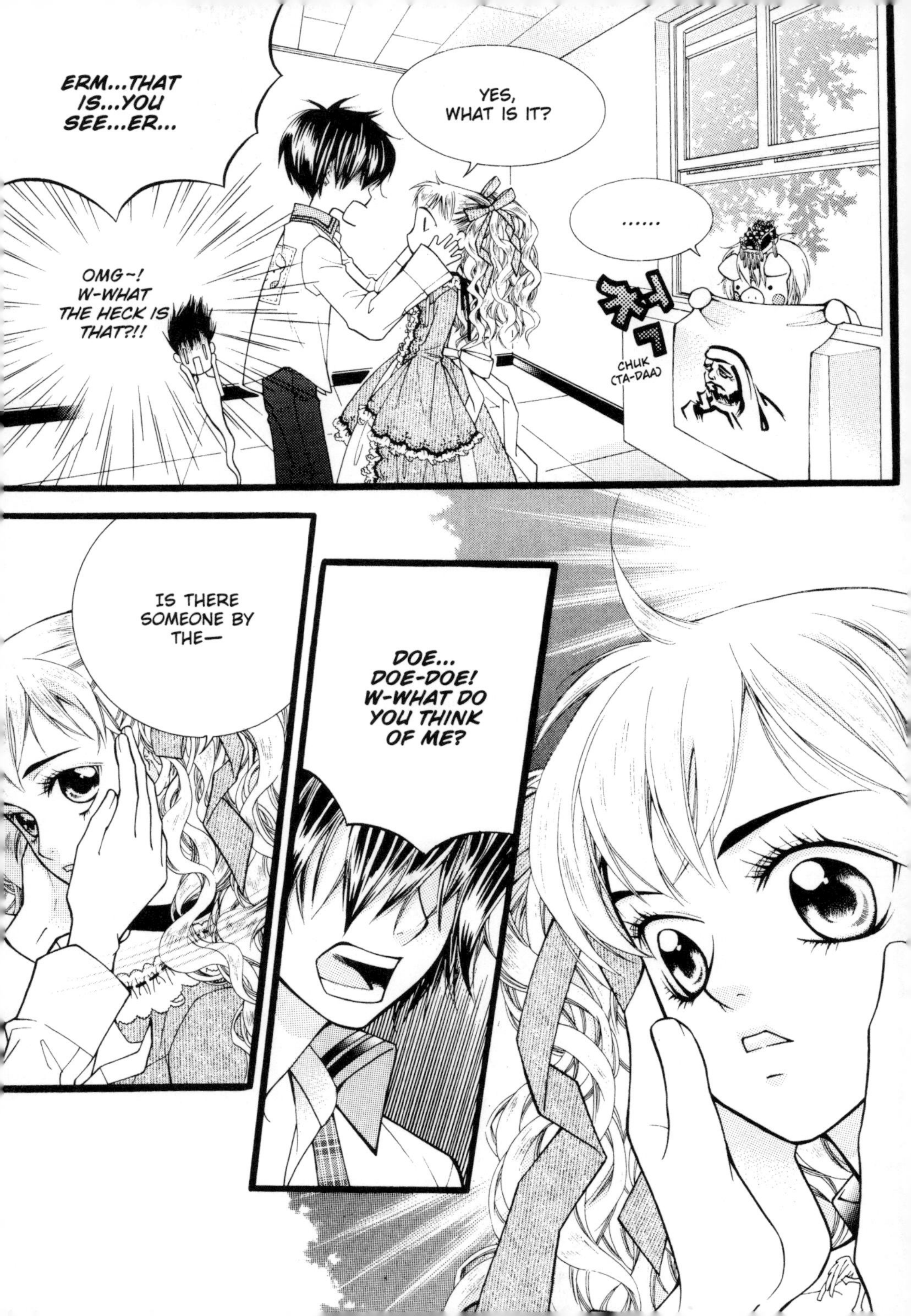
ERM...THAT IS...YOU SEE...ER...
YES, WHAT IS IT?
OMG~! W-WHAT THE HECK IS THAT?!!
......
CHUK (TA-DAA)
IS THERE SOMEONE BY THE—
DOE... DOE-DOE! W-WHAT DO YOU THINK OF ME?

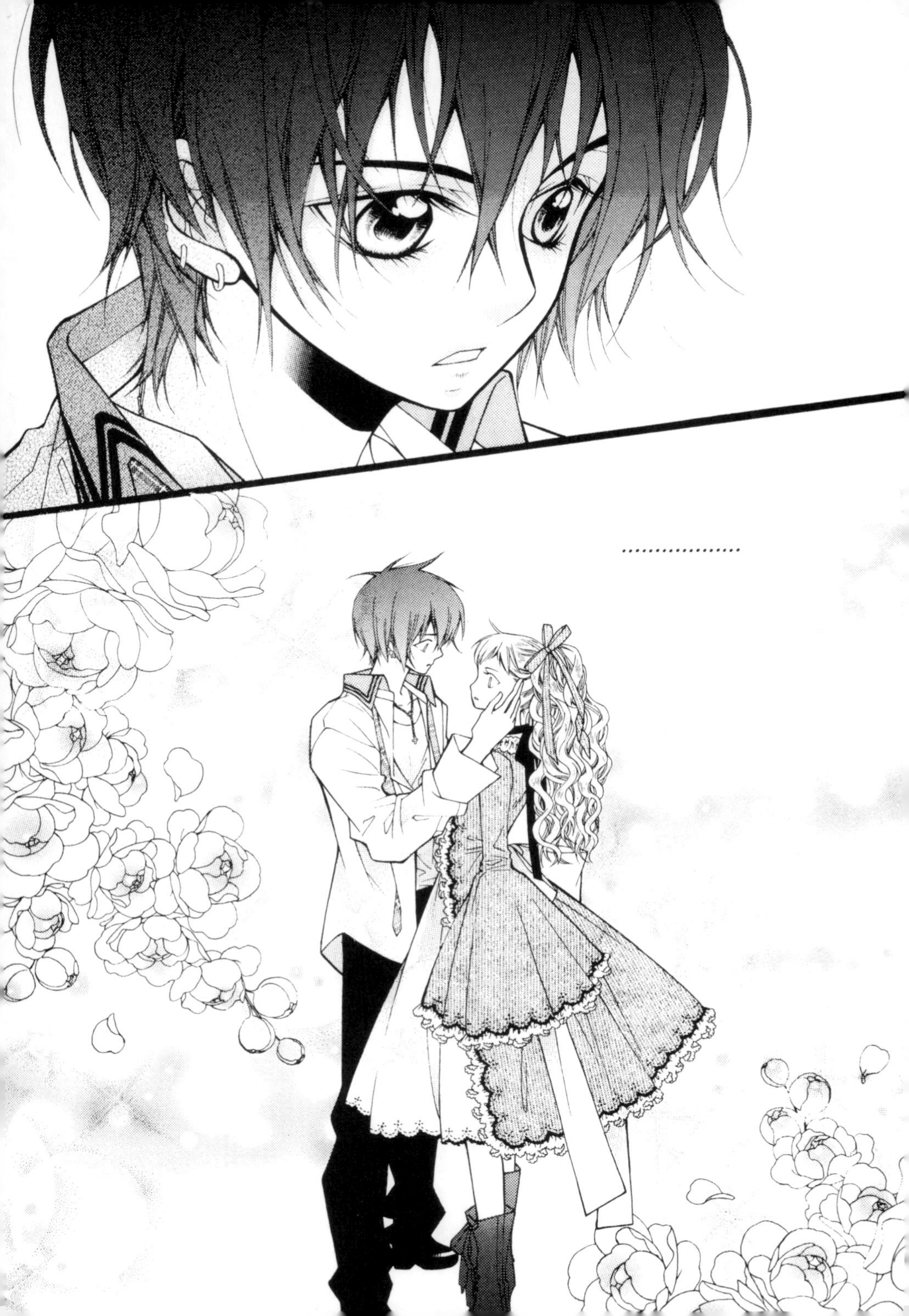
....

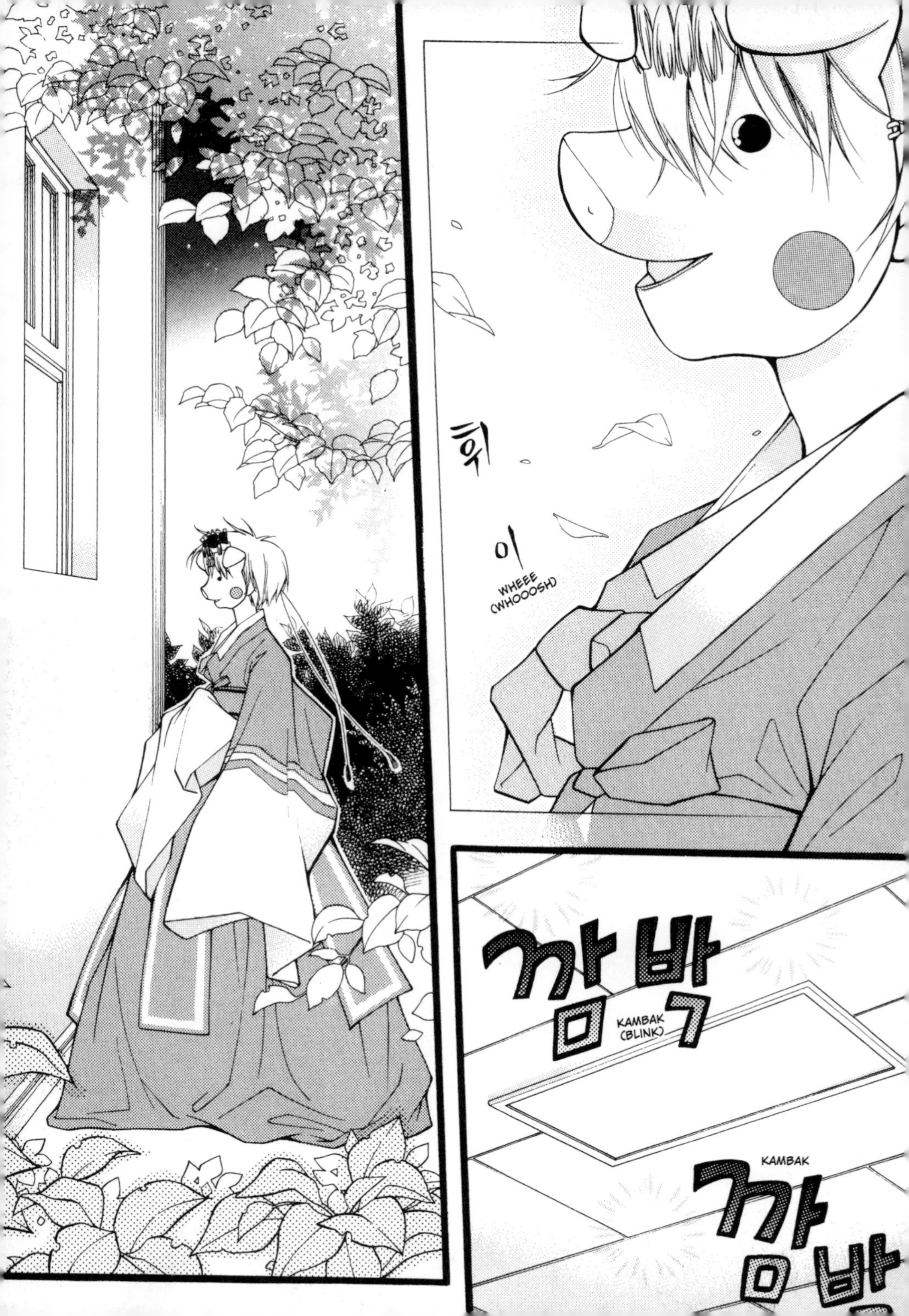

휘이
WHEEE (WHOOOSH)
깜박
KAMBAK (BLINK)
깜박
KAMBAK

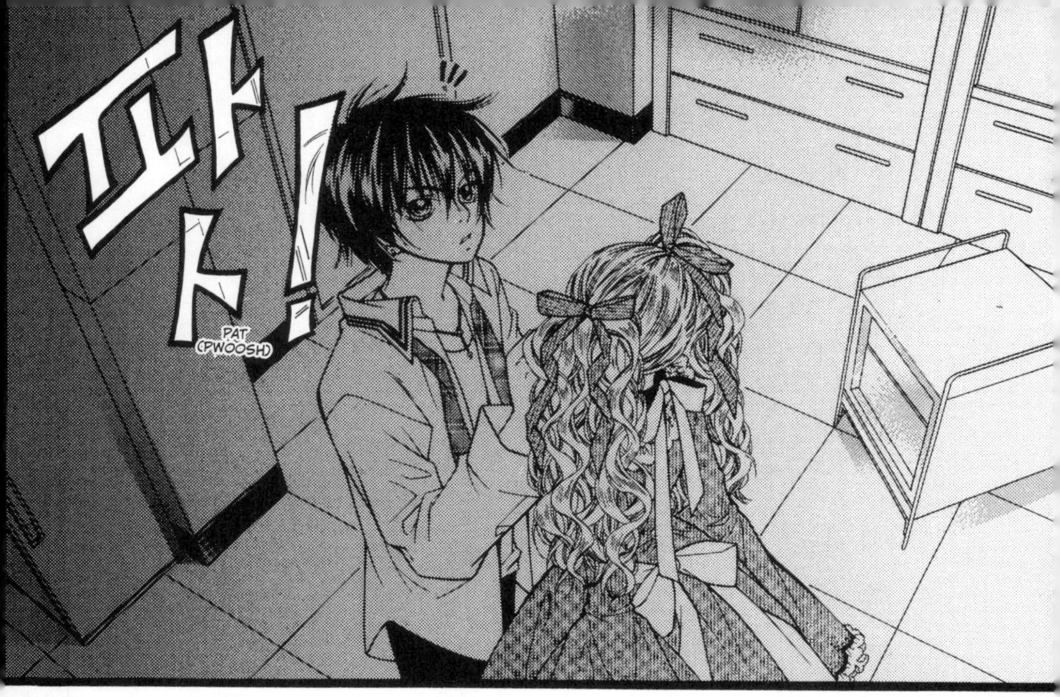

PAT
(PWOOSH)

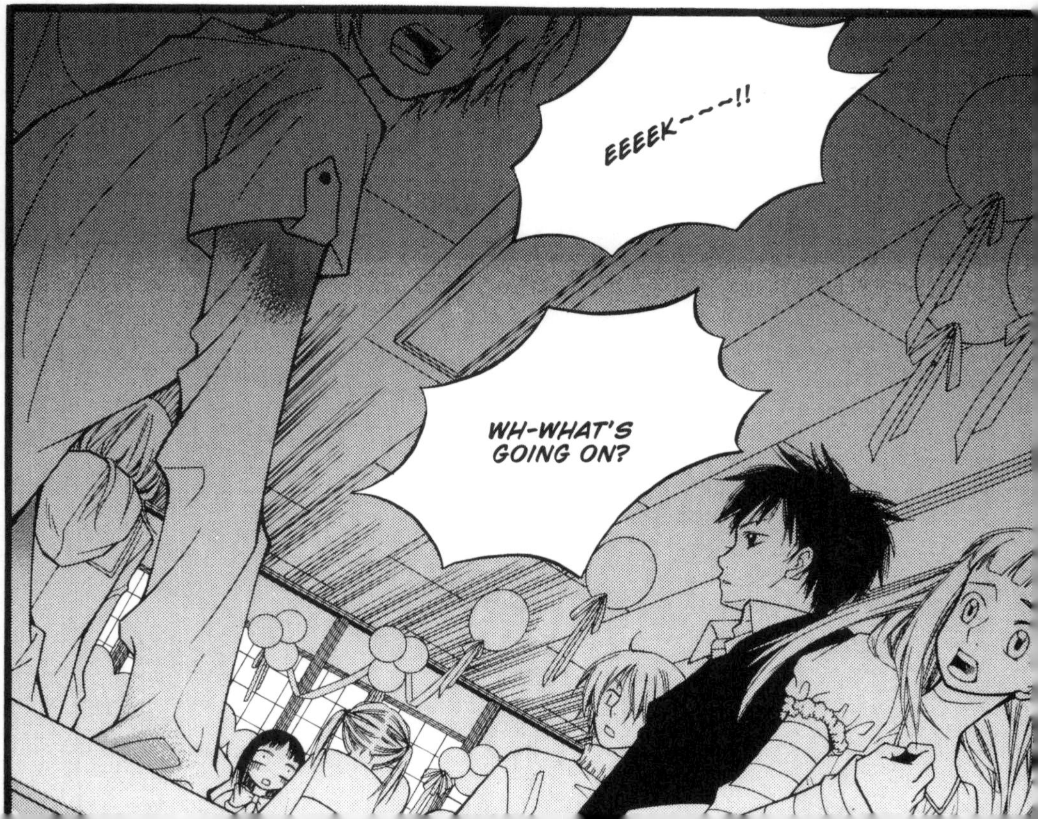

EEEEK---!!
WH-WHAT'S GOING ON?

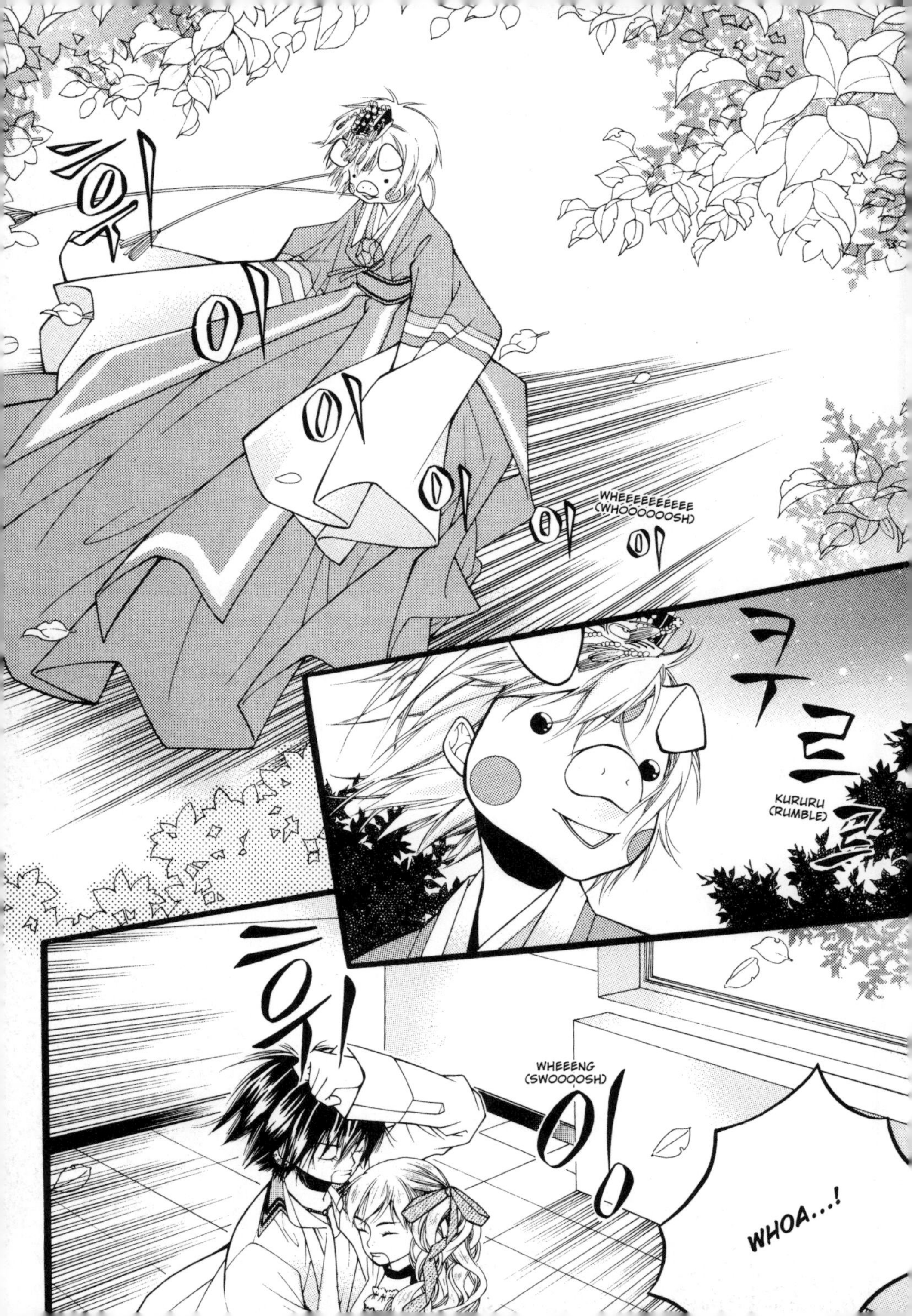
WHEEEEEEEEEE (WHOOOOOOSH)
KURURU (RUMBLE)
WHEEENG (SWOOOOSH)
WHOA...!

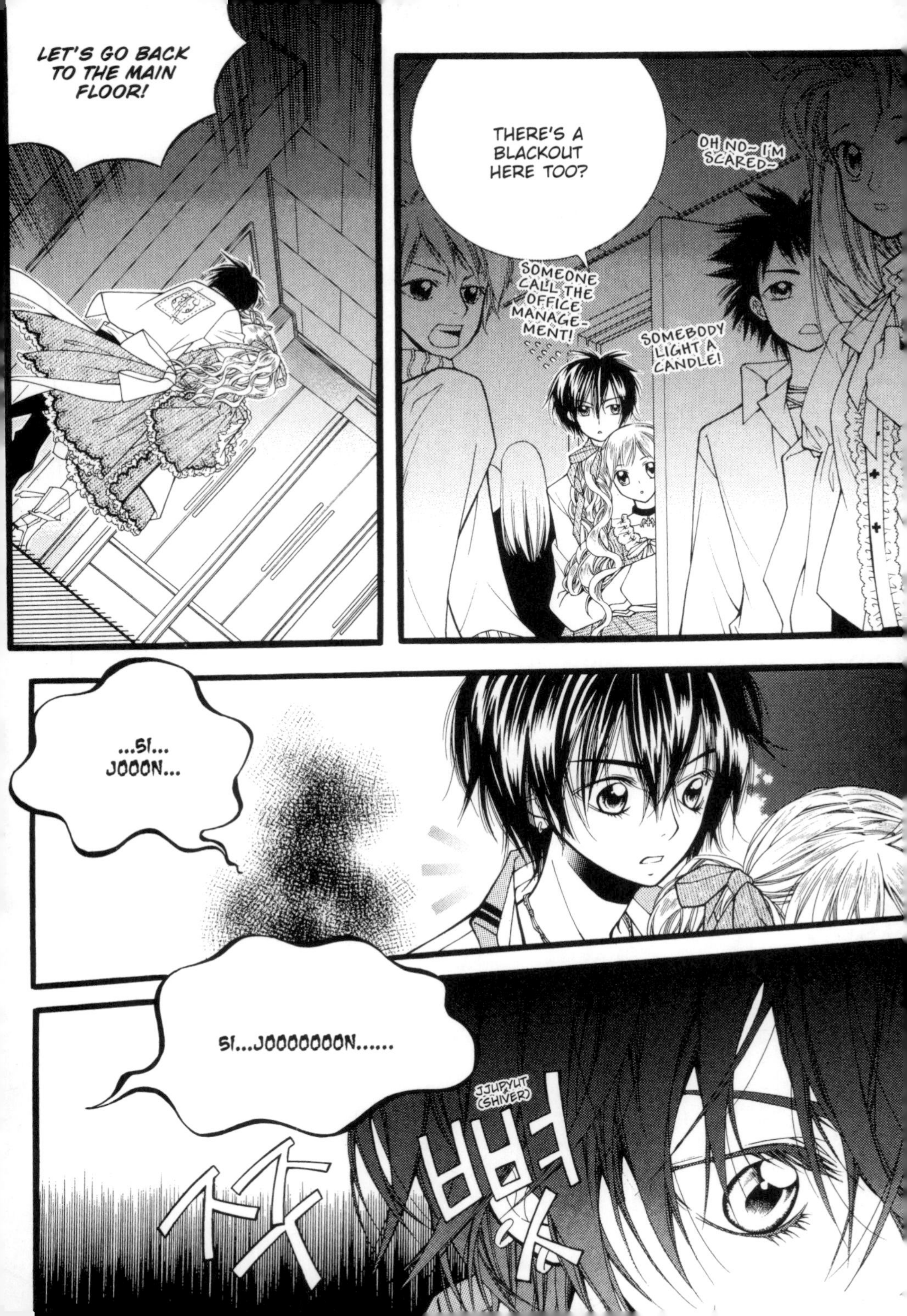
LET'S GO BACK TO THE MAIN FLOOR!
THERE'S A BLACKOUT HERE TOO?
SOMEONE CALL THE OFFICE MANAGE-MENT!
OH NO~ I'M SCARED~
SOMEBODY LIGHT A CANDLE!
...SI... JOOON...
SI...JOOOOOOON......
JJUPYUT (SHIVER)

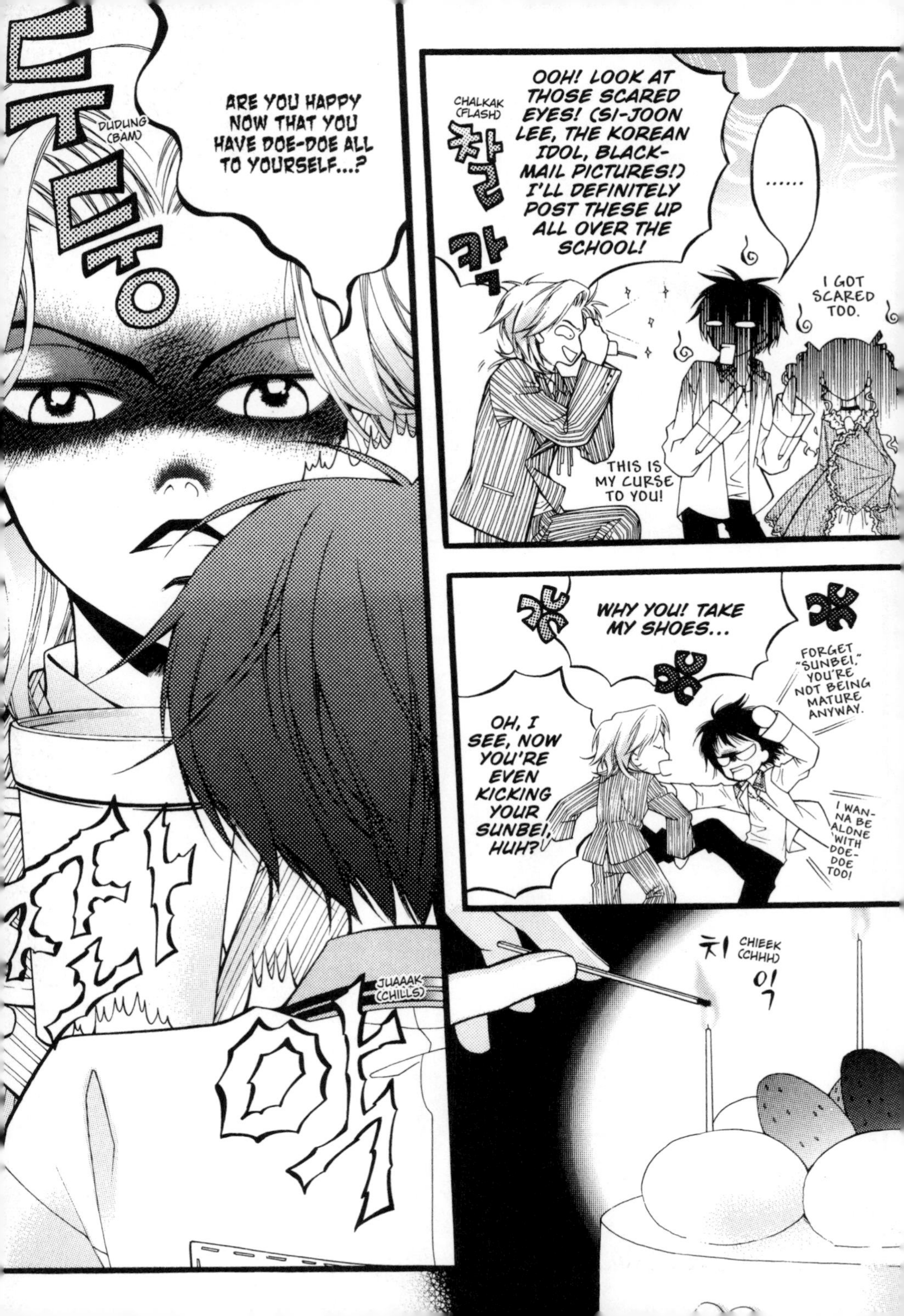

DUDUNG (BAM)
ARE YOU HAPPY NOW THAT YOU HAVE DOE-DOE ALL TO YOURSELF...?
JUAAAK (CHILLS)
CHALKAK (FLASH)
OOH! LOOK AT THOSE SCARED EYES! (SI-JOON LEE, THE KOREAN IDOL, BLACK-MAIL PICTURES!) I'LL DEFINITELY POST THESE UP ALL OVER THE SCHOOL!
......
I GOT SCARED TOO.
THIS IS MY CURSE TO YOU!
WHY YOU! TAKE MY SHOES...
FORGET "SUNBEI." YOU'RE NOT BEING MATURE ANYWAY.
OH, I SEE, NOW YOU'RE EVEN KICKING YOUR SUNBEI, HUH?
I WAN-NA BE ALONE WITH DOE-DOE TOO!
치익
CHIEEK (CHHH)

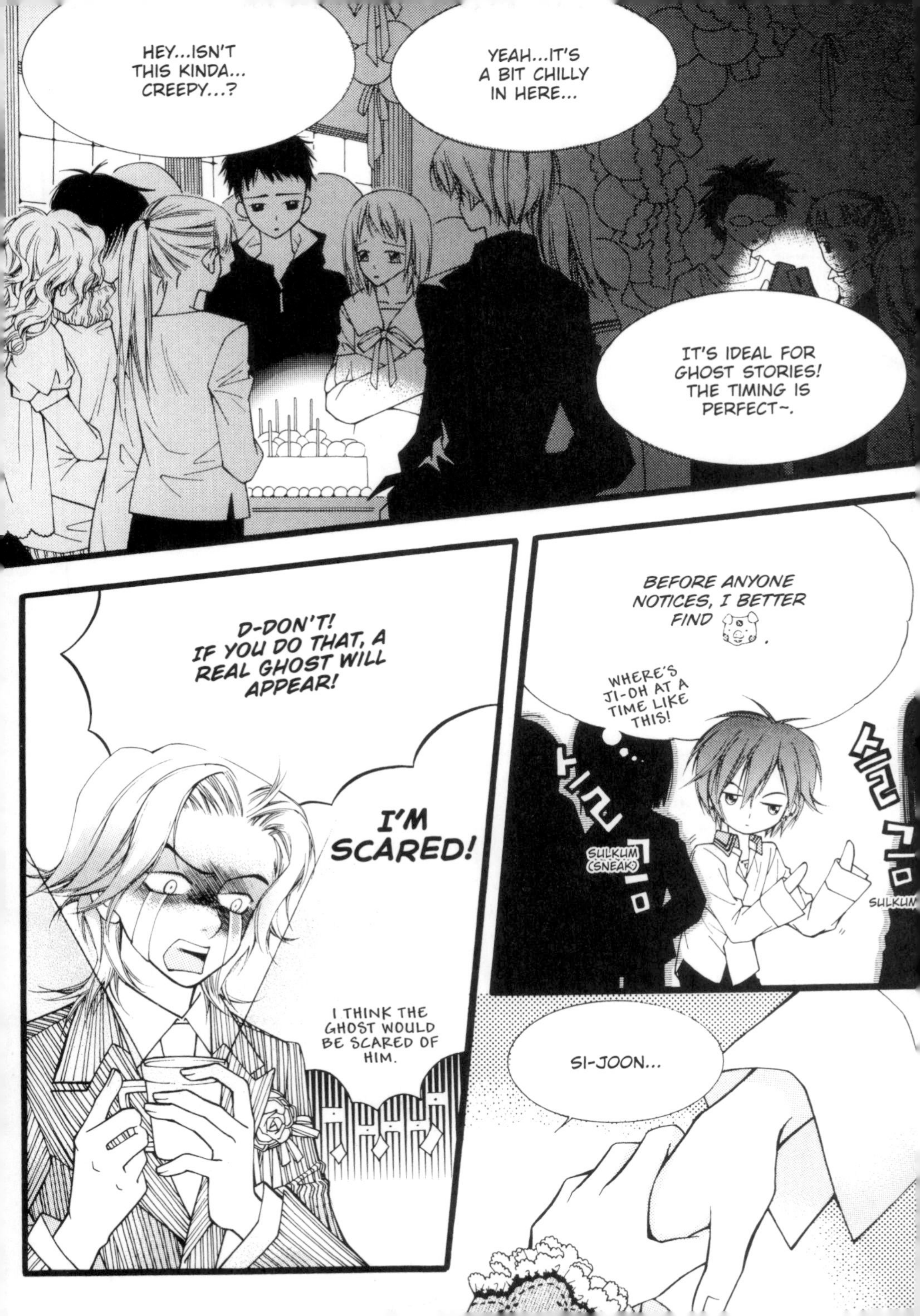

HEY...ISN'T THIS KINDA... CREEPY...?
YEAH...IT'S A BIT CHILLY IN HERE...
IT'S IDEAL FOR GHOST STORIES! THE TIMING IS PERFECT~.
D-DON'T! IF YOU DO THAT, A REAL GHOST WILL APPEAR!
I'M SCARED!
I THINK THE GHOST WOULD BE SCARED OF HIM.
BEFORE ANYONE NOTICES, I BETTER FIND .
WHERE'S JI-OH AT A TIME LIKE THIS!
SULKUM (SNEAK)
SULKUM
SI-JOON...

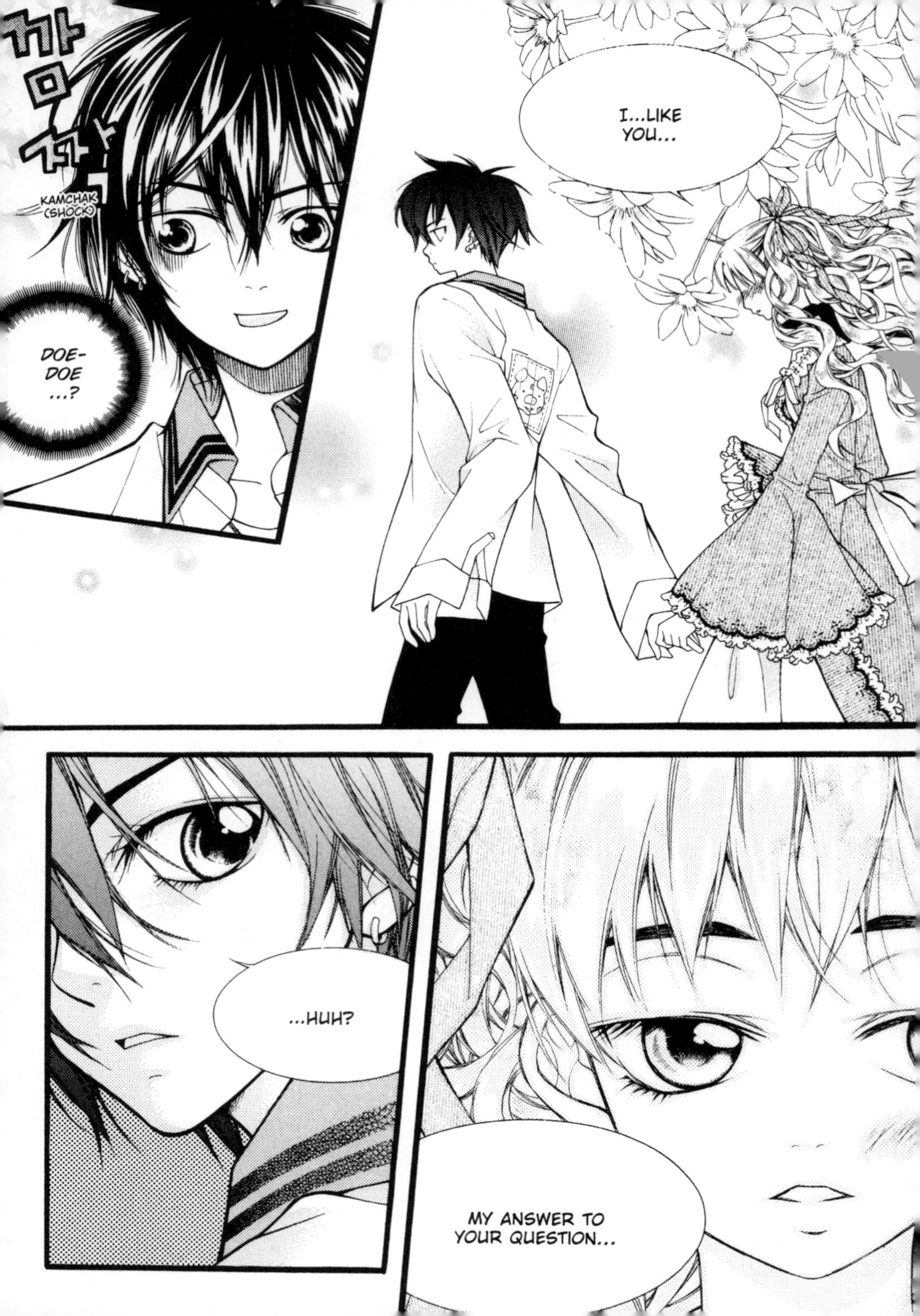
KAMCHAK (SHOCK)
DOE-DOE ...?
I...LIKE YOU...
...HUH?
MY ANSWER TO YOUR QUESTION...

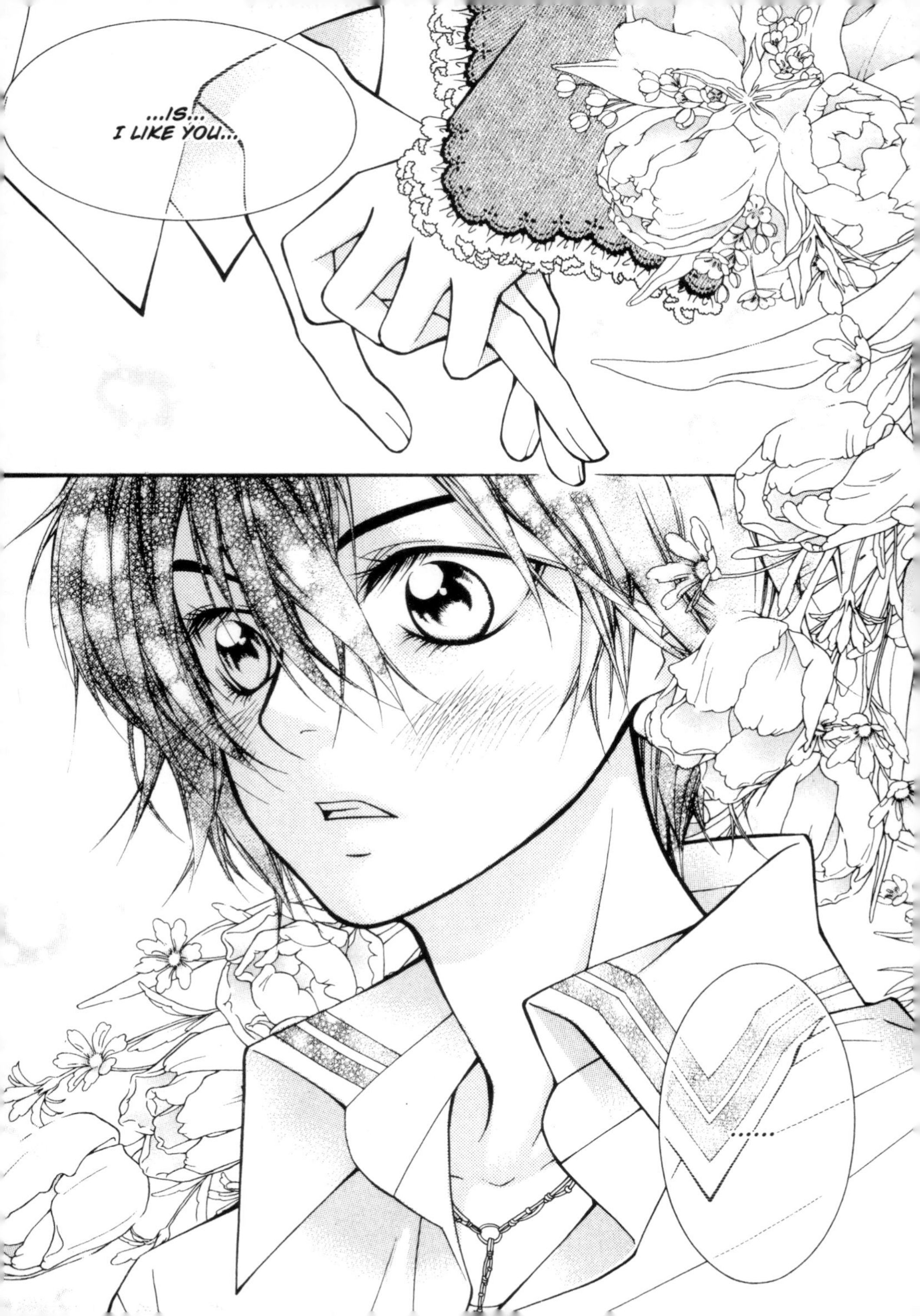
...IS... I LIKE YOU...
......

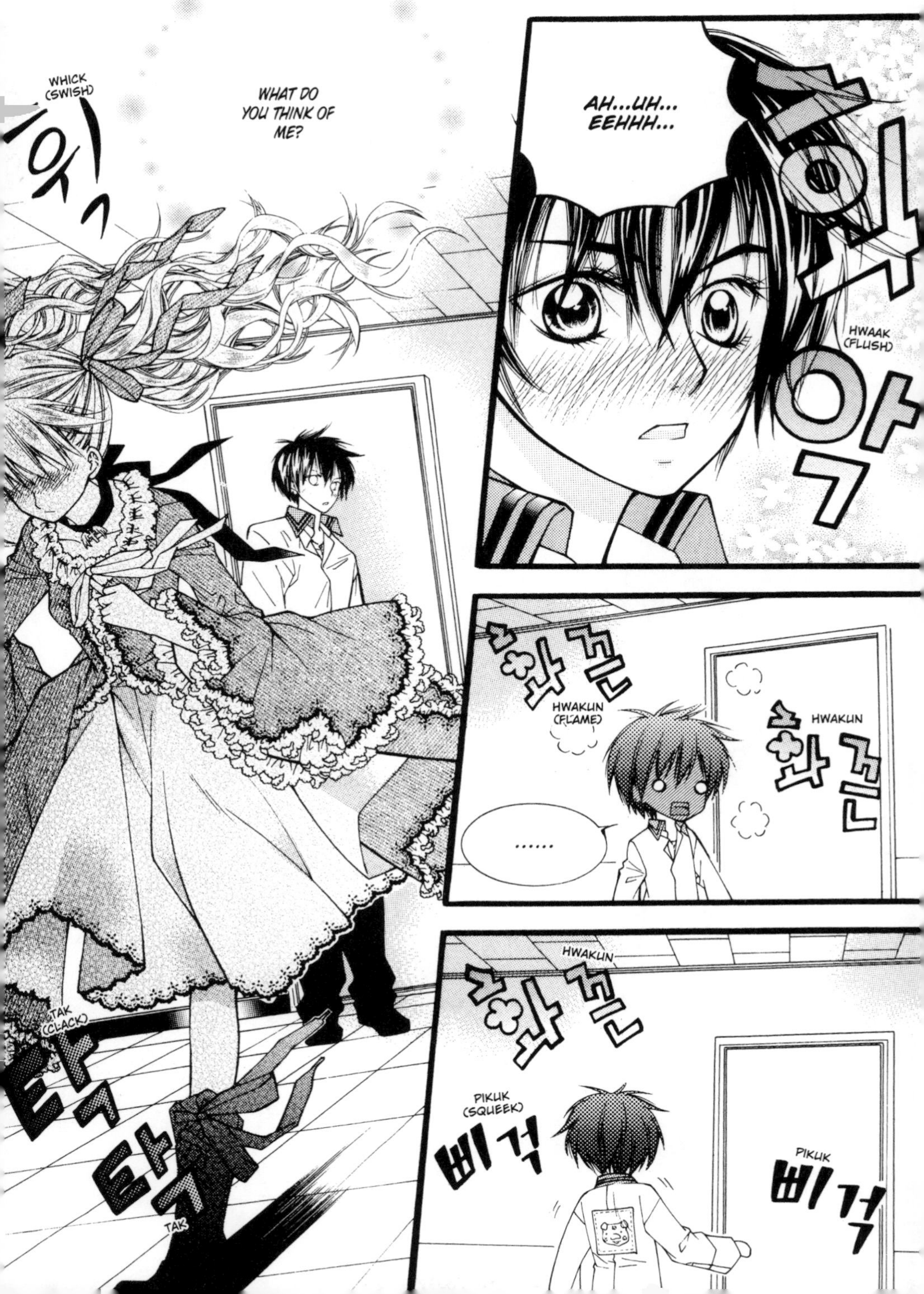
WHICK (SWISH)
WHAT DO YOU THINK OF ME?
TAK (CLACK)
TAK
AH...UH... EEHHH...
HWAAK (FLUSH)
HWAKUN (FLAME)
HWAKUN
......
HWAKUN
PIKUK (SQUEEK)
PIKUK

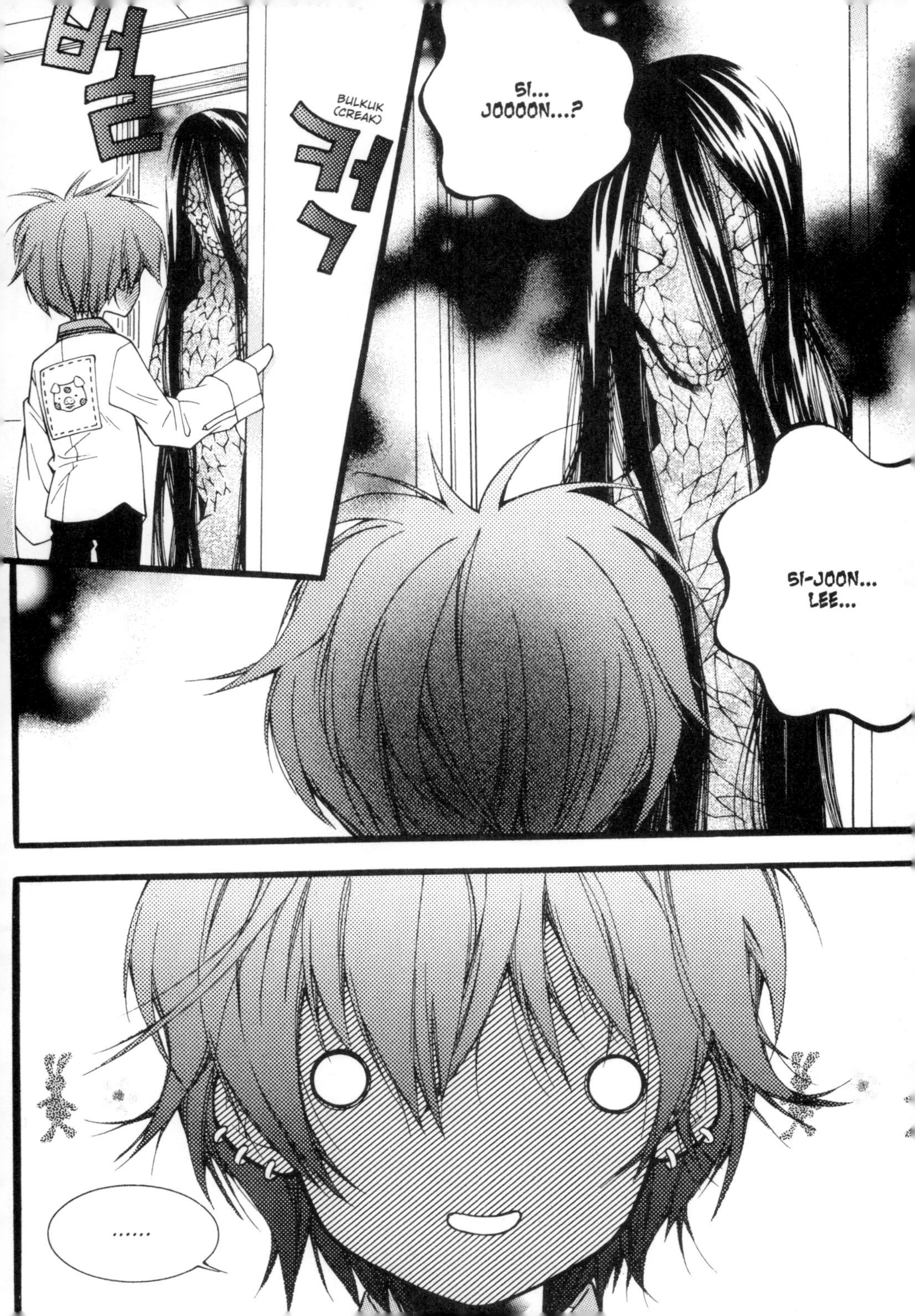
벌컥
BULKUK (CREAK)
SI... JOOOON...?
SI-JOON... LEE...
......

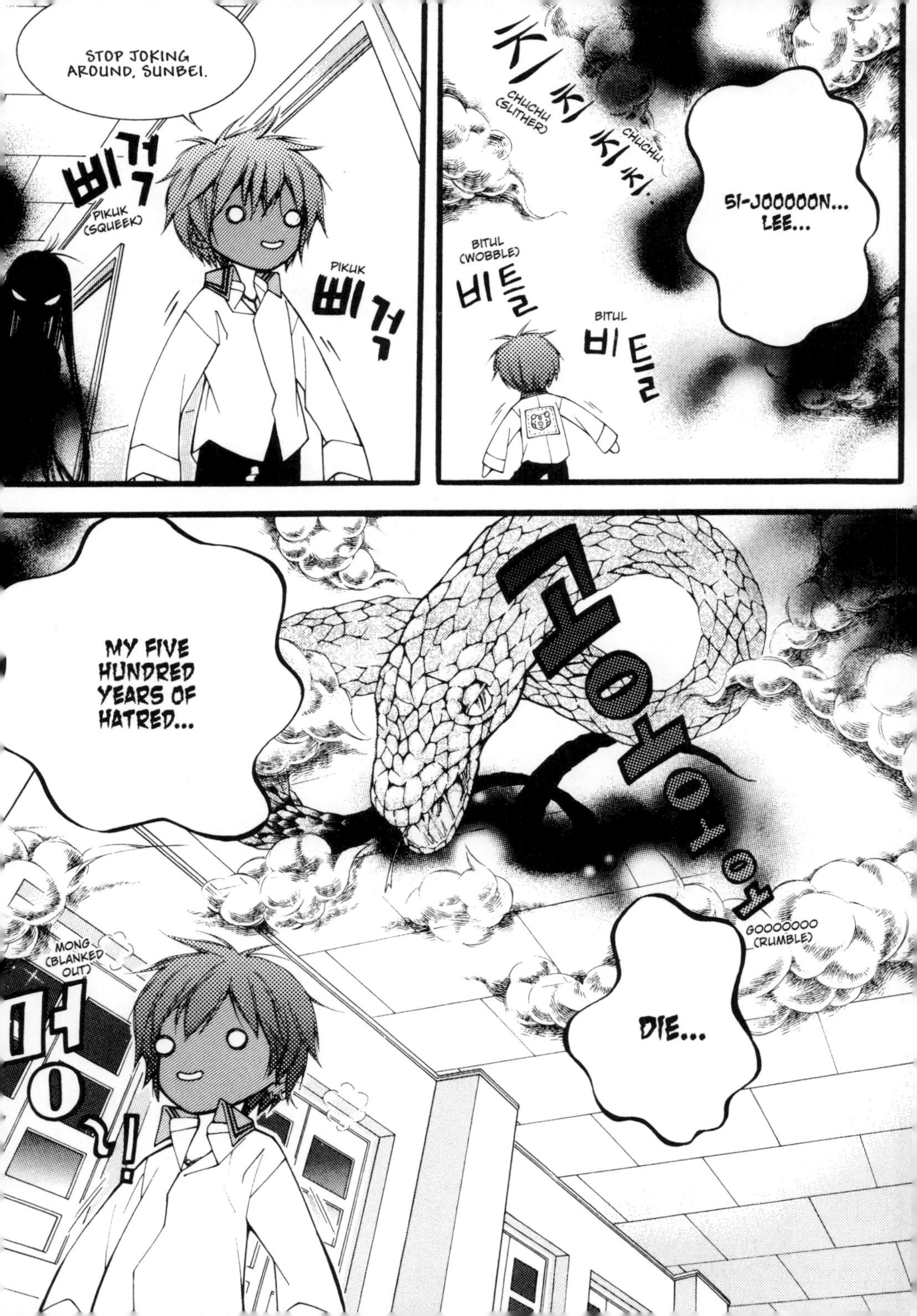
STOP JOKING AROUND, SUNBEI.
삐걱
PIKUK (SQUEEK)
PIKUK
삐걱
치치치치
CHUCHU (SLITHER)
CHUCHU
SI-JOOOOON... LEE...
BITUL (WOBBLE)
비틀
BITUL
비틀
MY FIVE HUNDRED YEARS OF HATRED...
고오오오오
GOOOOOOO (RUMBLE)
DIE...
MONG (BLANKED OUT)
멍~!

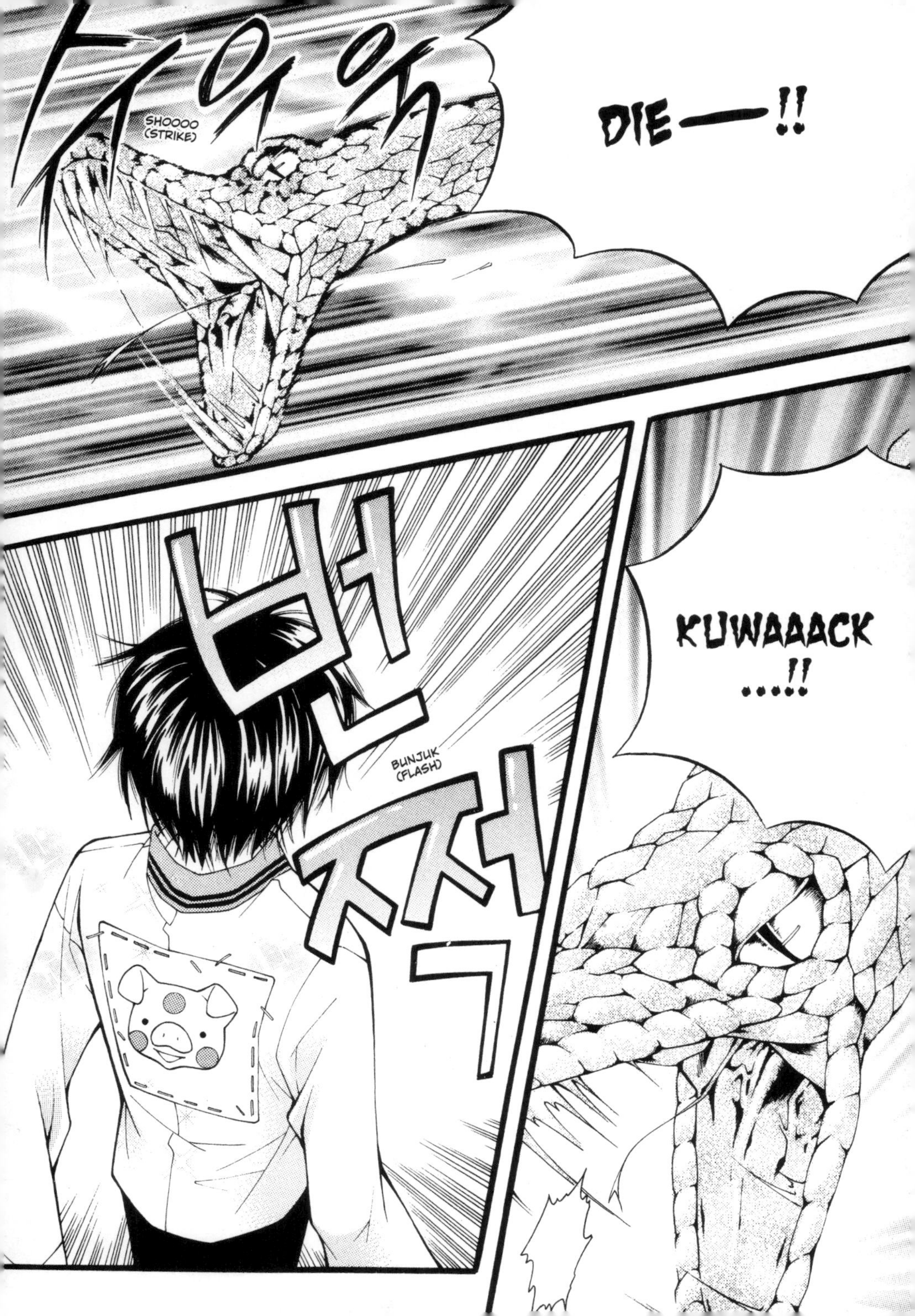
DIE—!!
쇠아악
SHOOOO (STRIKE)
KUWAAACK ....!!
번쩍
BUNJUK (FLASH)

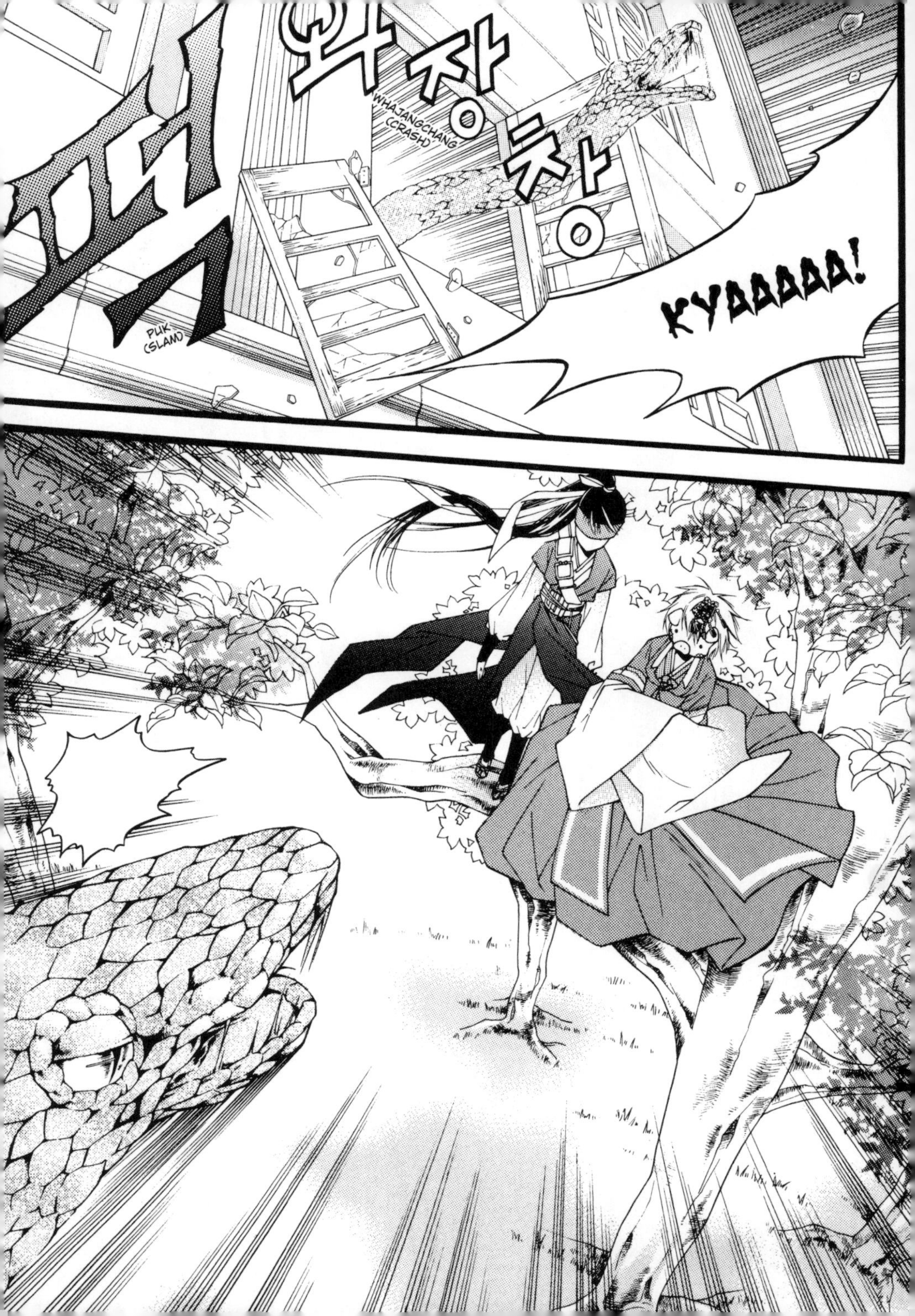
퍽
PUK (SLAM)
와장창
WHAJANGCHANG (CRASH)
KYAAAAA!

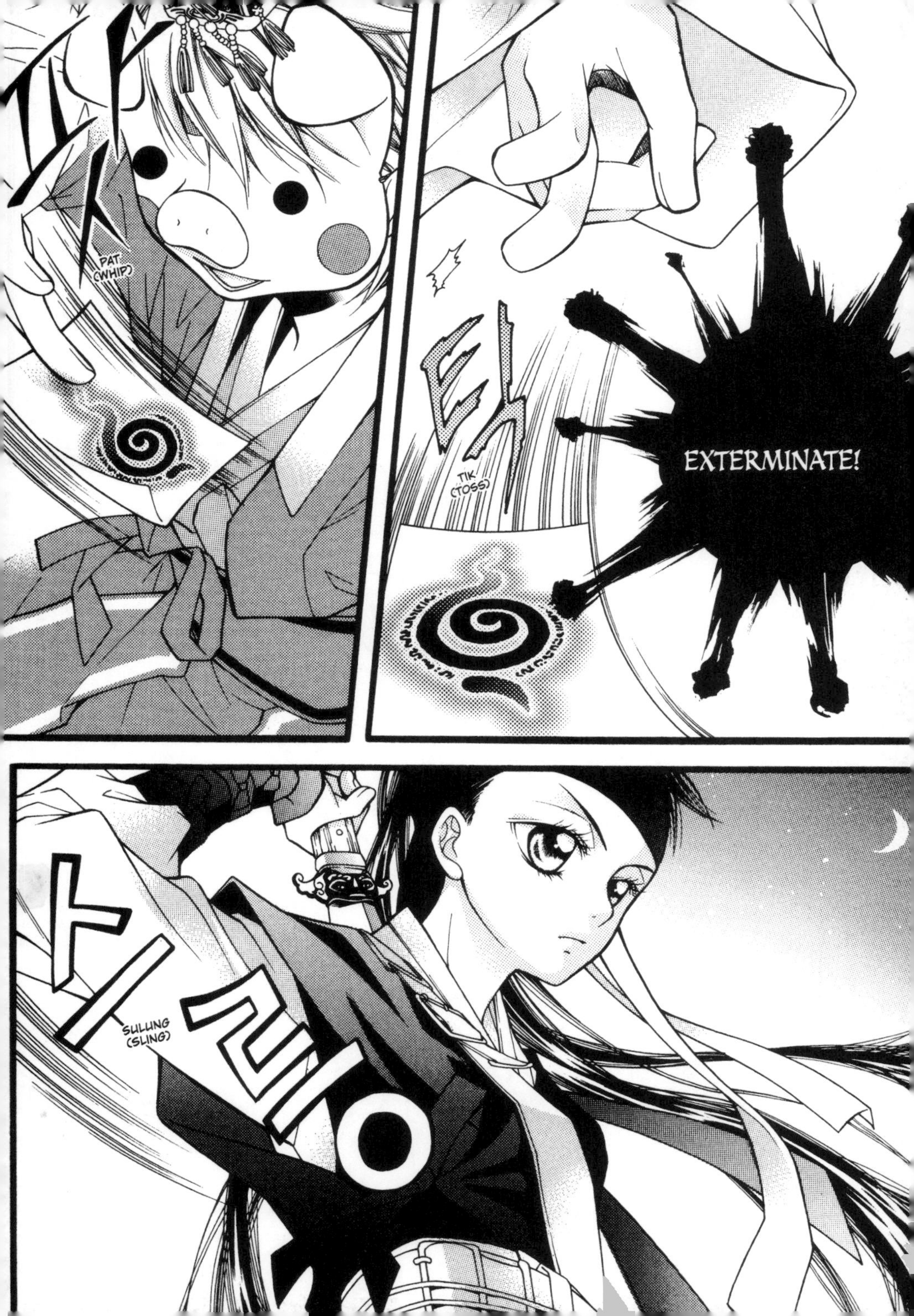
EXTERMINATE!
TIK (TOSS)
PAT (WHIP)
SULUNG (SLING)

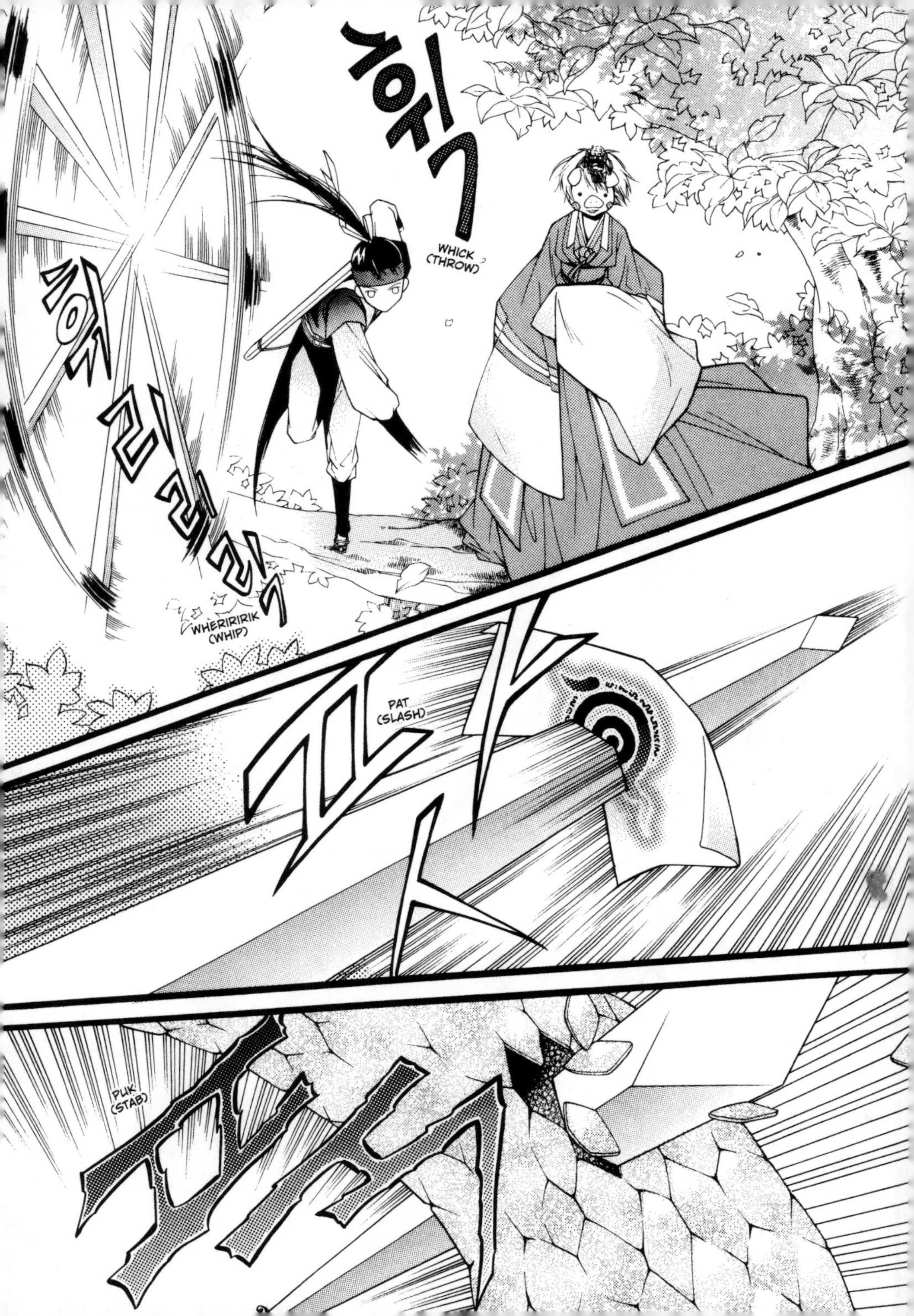
WHERIRIRIK (WHIP)
WHICK (THROW)
PAT (SLASH)
PUK (STAB)

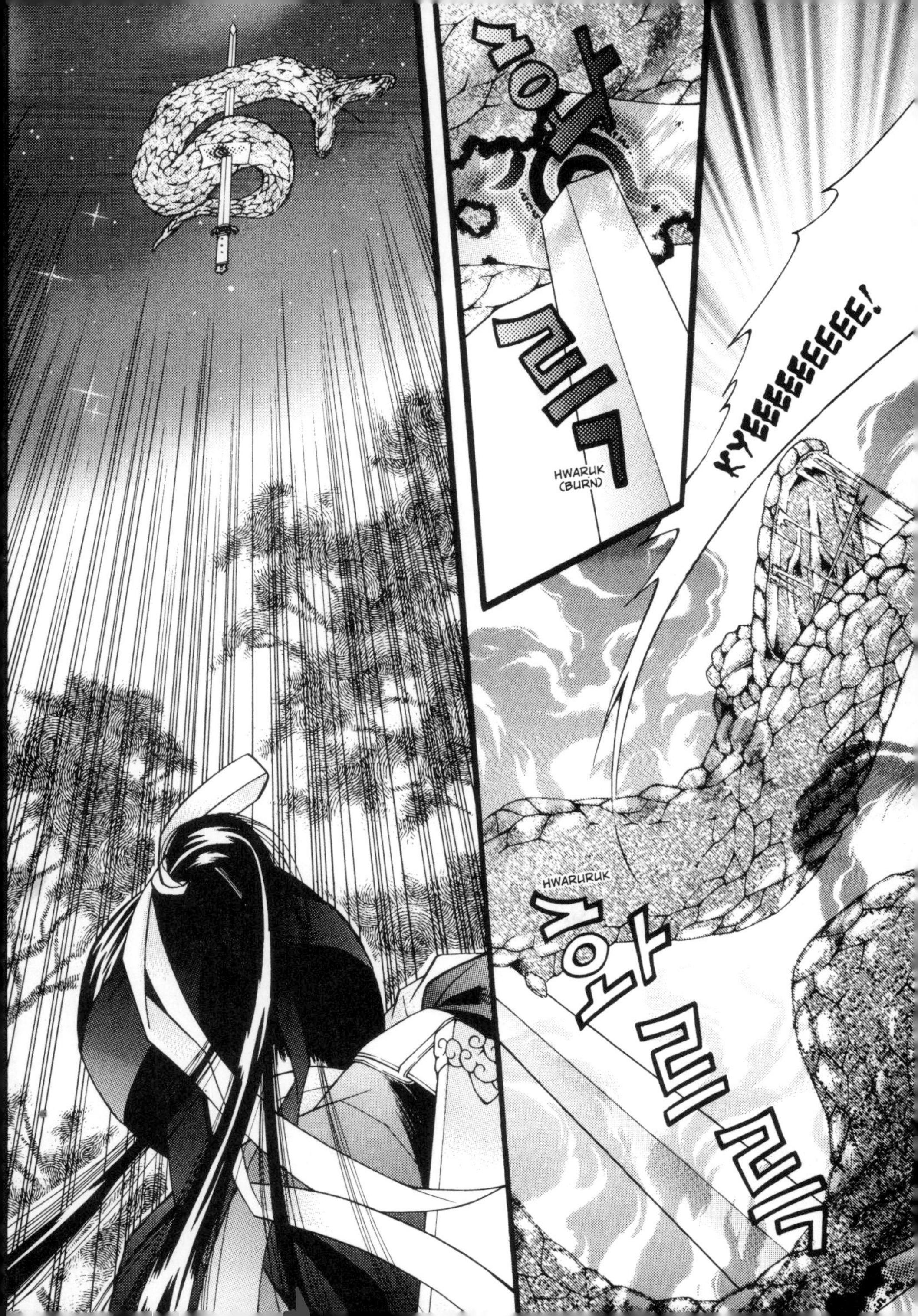
HWARUK
(BURN)
KYEEEEEEEEEE!
HWARURUK

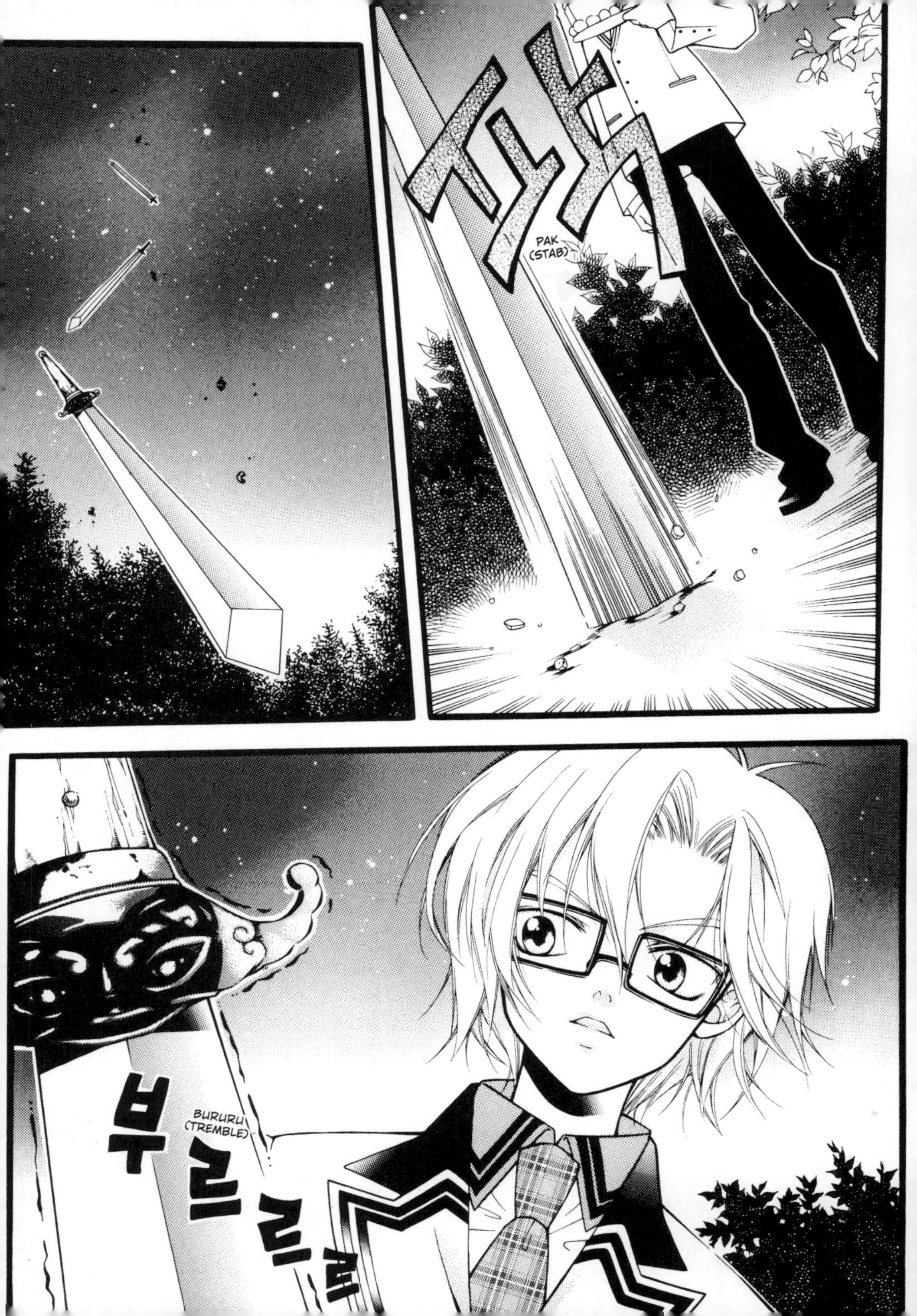
PAK (STAB)
BURURU (TREMBLE)
부르르

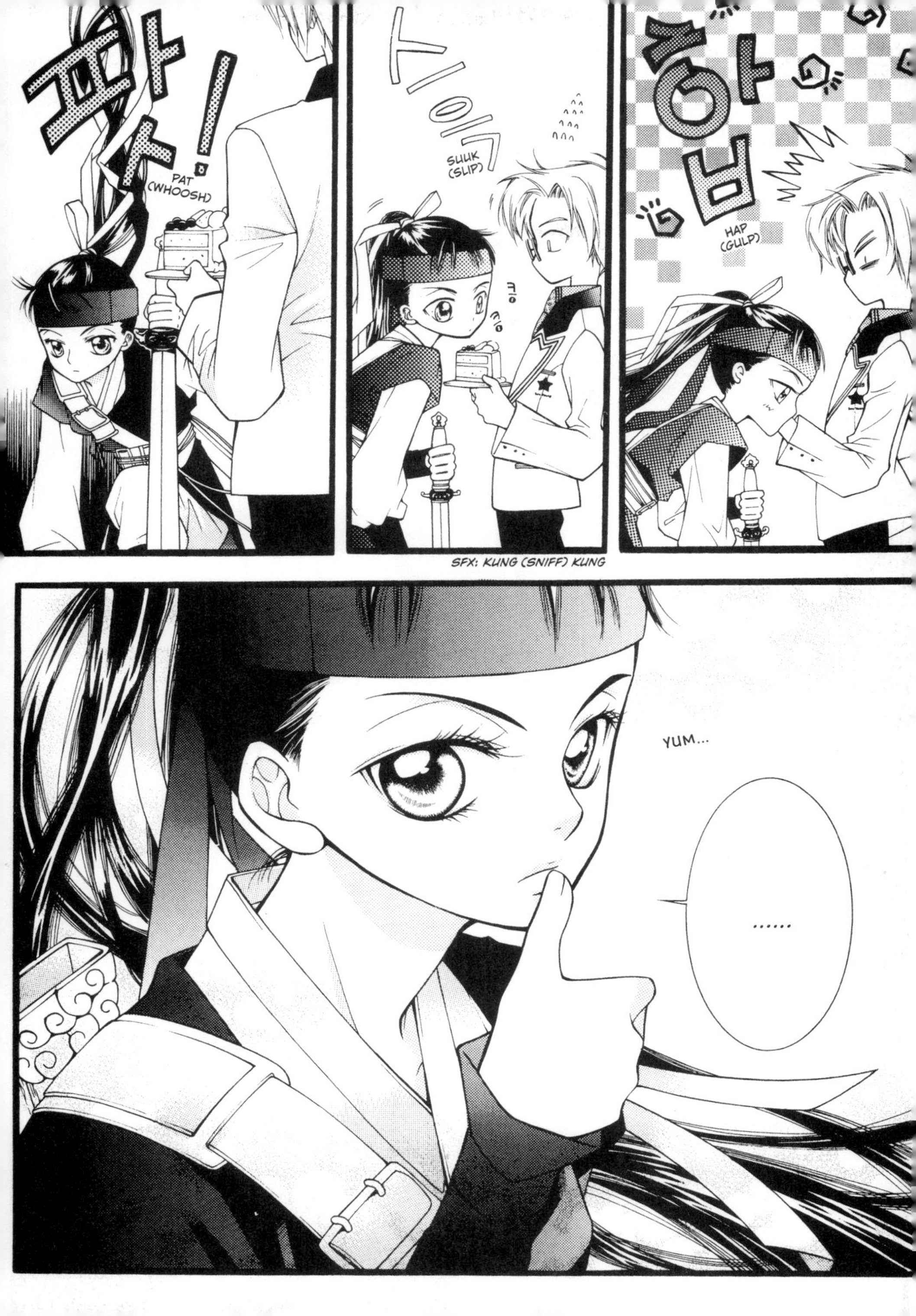
팟!
PAT (WHOOSH)
스이윽
SUUK (SLIP)
킁
킁
SFX: KUNG (SNIFF) KUNG
합
HAP (GULP)
YUM...
......

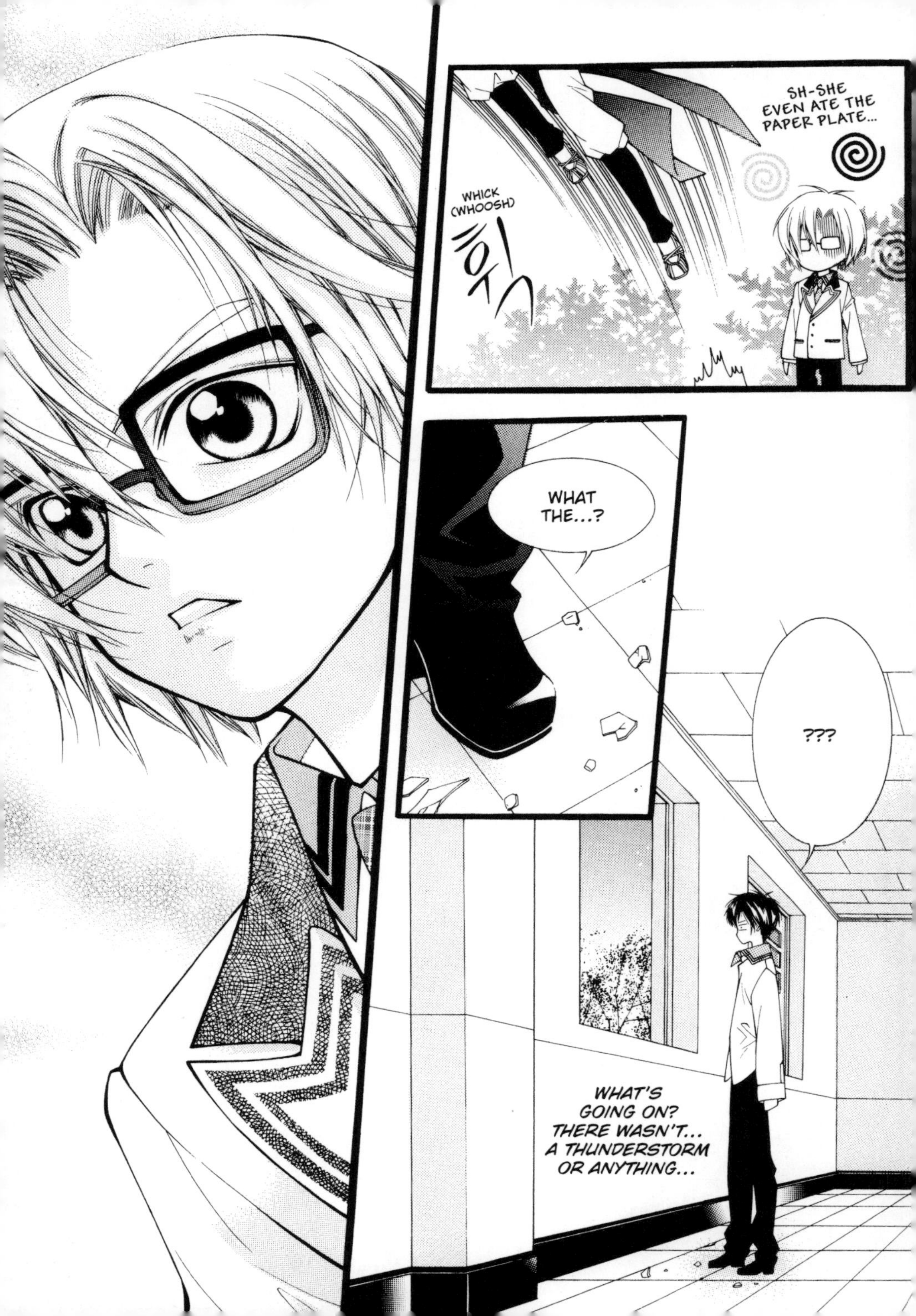

SH-SHE EVEN ATE THE PAPER PLATE...
WHICK (WHOOSH)
휘익
WHAT THE...?
???
WHAT'S GOING ON? THERE WASN'T... A THUNDERSTORM OR ANYTHING...

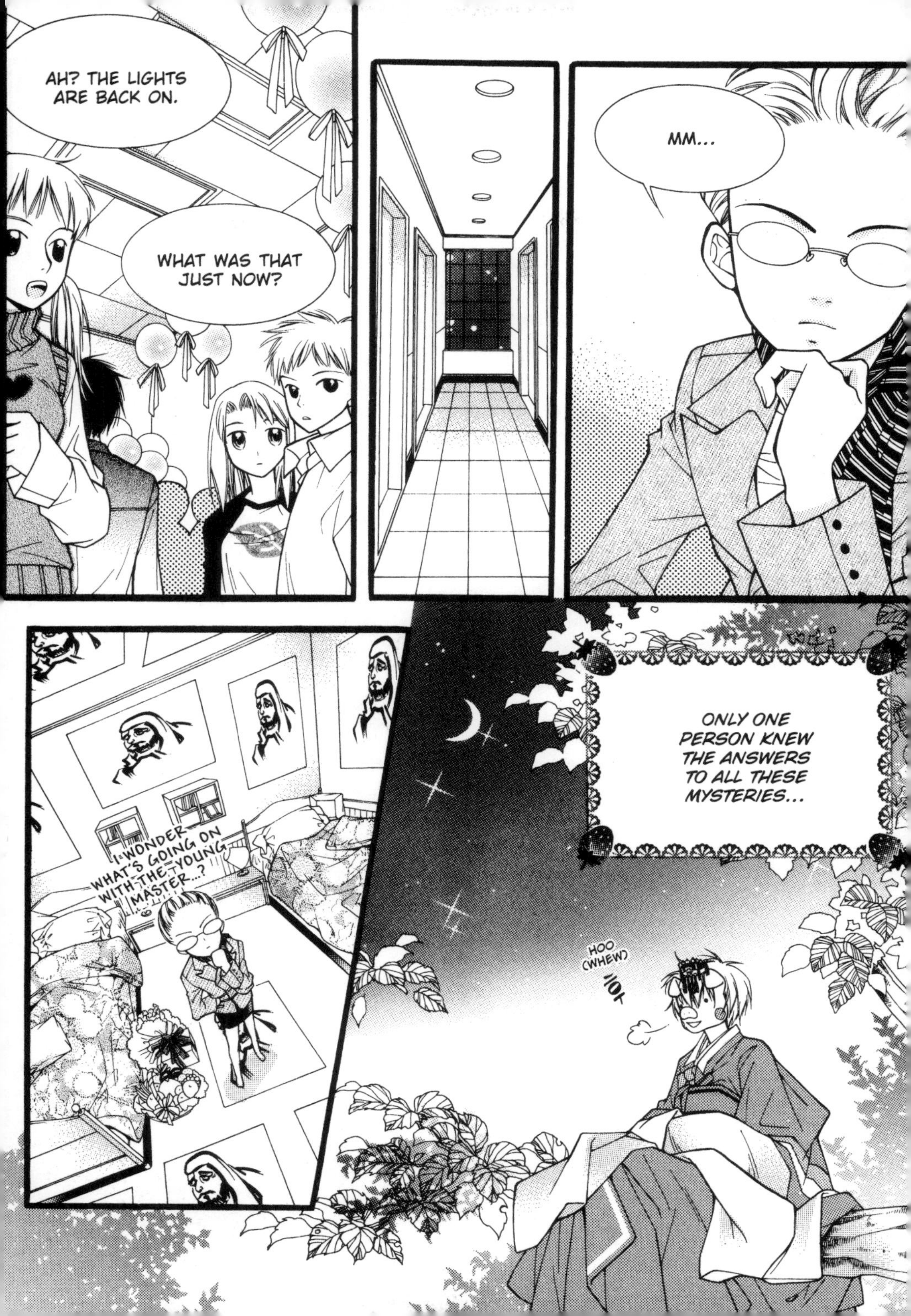
AH? THE LIGHTS ARE BACK ON.
WHAT WAS THAT JUST NOW?
MM...
I WONDER WHAT'S GOING ON WITH THE YOUNG MASTER...?
ONLY ONE PERSON KNEW THE ANSWERS TO ALL THESE MYSTERIES...
HOO (WHEW)

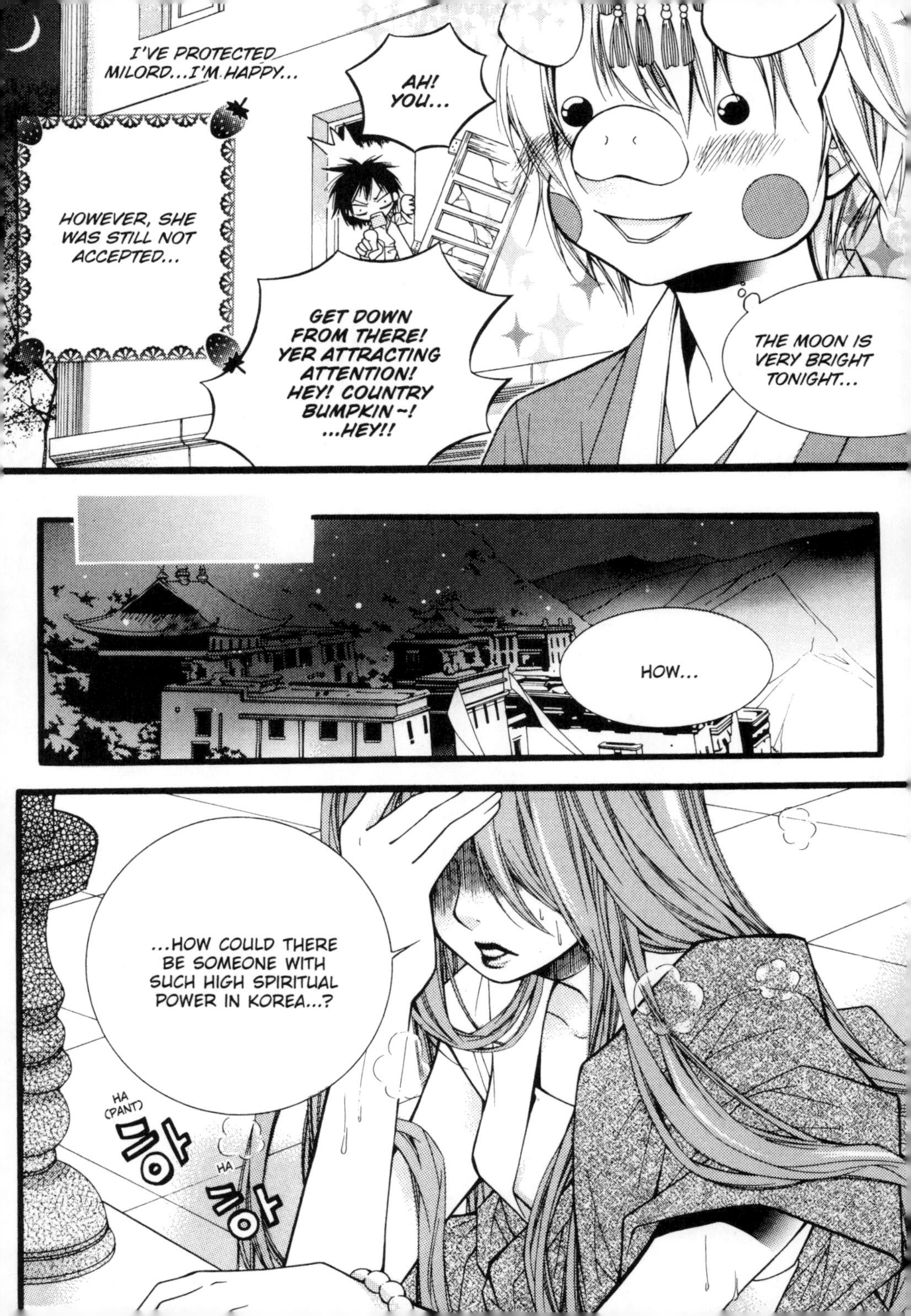
THE MOON IS VERY BRIGHT TONIGHT...
AH! YOU...
I'VE PROTECTED MILORD...I'M HAPPY...
HOWEVER, SHE WAS STILL NOT ACCEPTED...
GET DOWN FROM THERE! YER ATTRACTING ATTENTION! HEY! COUNTRY BUMPKIN~! ...HEY!!
HOW...
...HOW COULD THERE BE SOMEONE WITH SUCH HIGH SPIRITUAL POWER IN KOREA...?
HA (PANT)
하아
HA
하아

SEEMS LIKE WE KEEP GETTING NEW CHARACTERS EVERY CHAPTER.

YES, MILORD.

HELLO~!

OMG! YOU HAVE NO EYES!

HE-HE-~!

FOR NOW...

DON'T RUN AWAY~~!

IT'S A GHOST!

JUST 'COS YOU ADD FLOWERS AND BUBBLES IN YER HAIR DOESN'T MEAN YER PRETTY!

DUDADADAK (DASH)

HULCHUK (SNIFFLE)

HULCHUK

WAIT A SEC. NOW THAT I THINK ABOUT IT...SHE ALSO DOESN'T HAVE...!

...?
!
UGH!!!
두둥
DUDUNG (TA-DAA)
MILORD~ ♥
UK (UGH)
UK
......

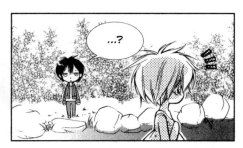

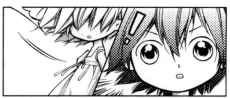

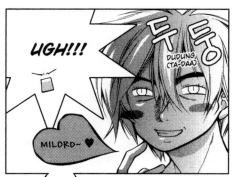

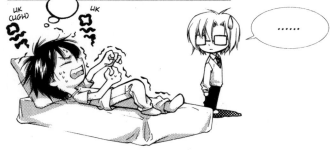

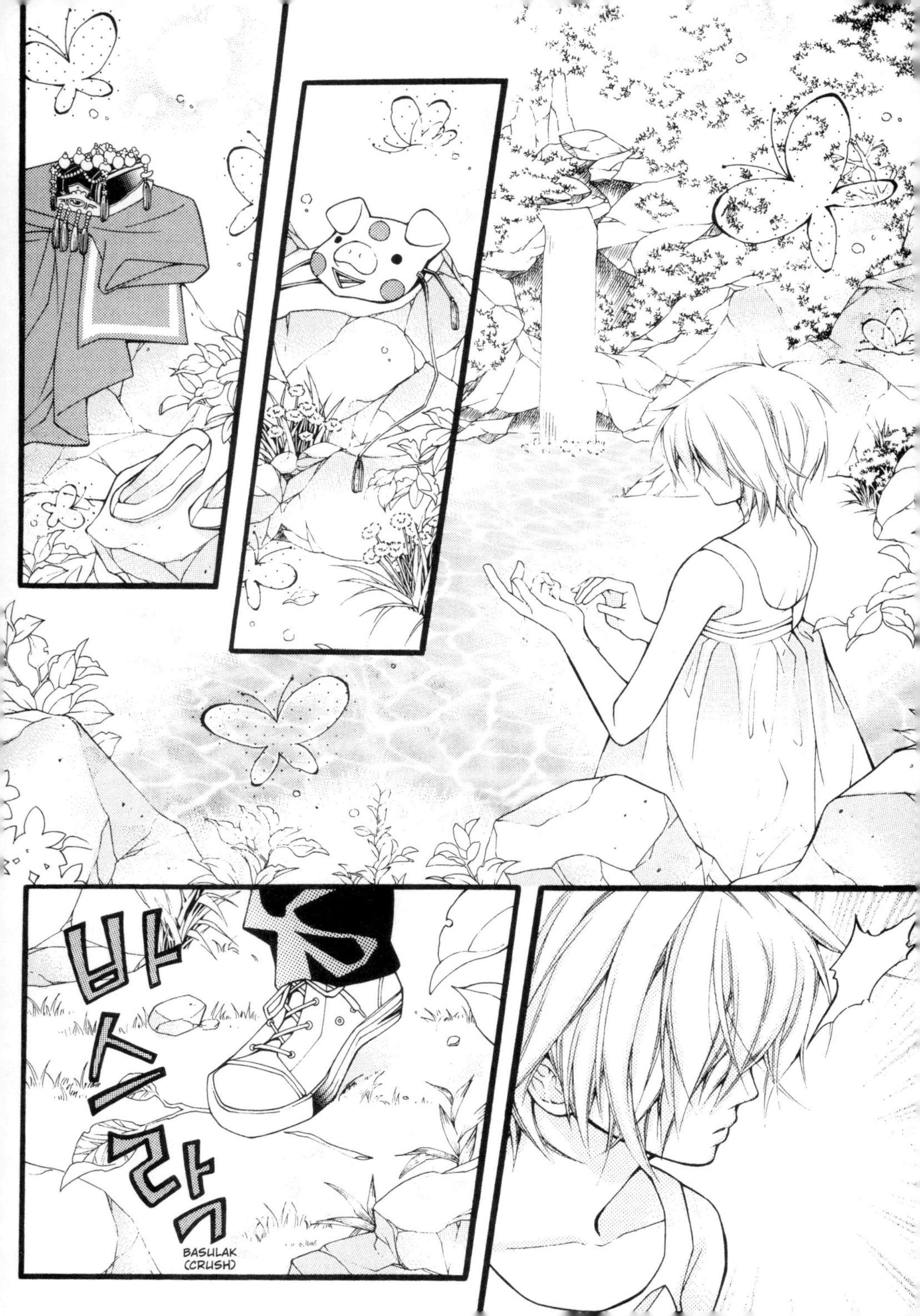
바스락
BASULAK
(CRUSH)

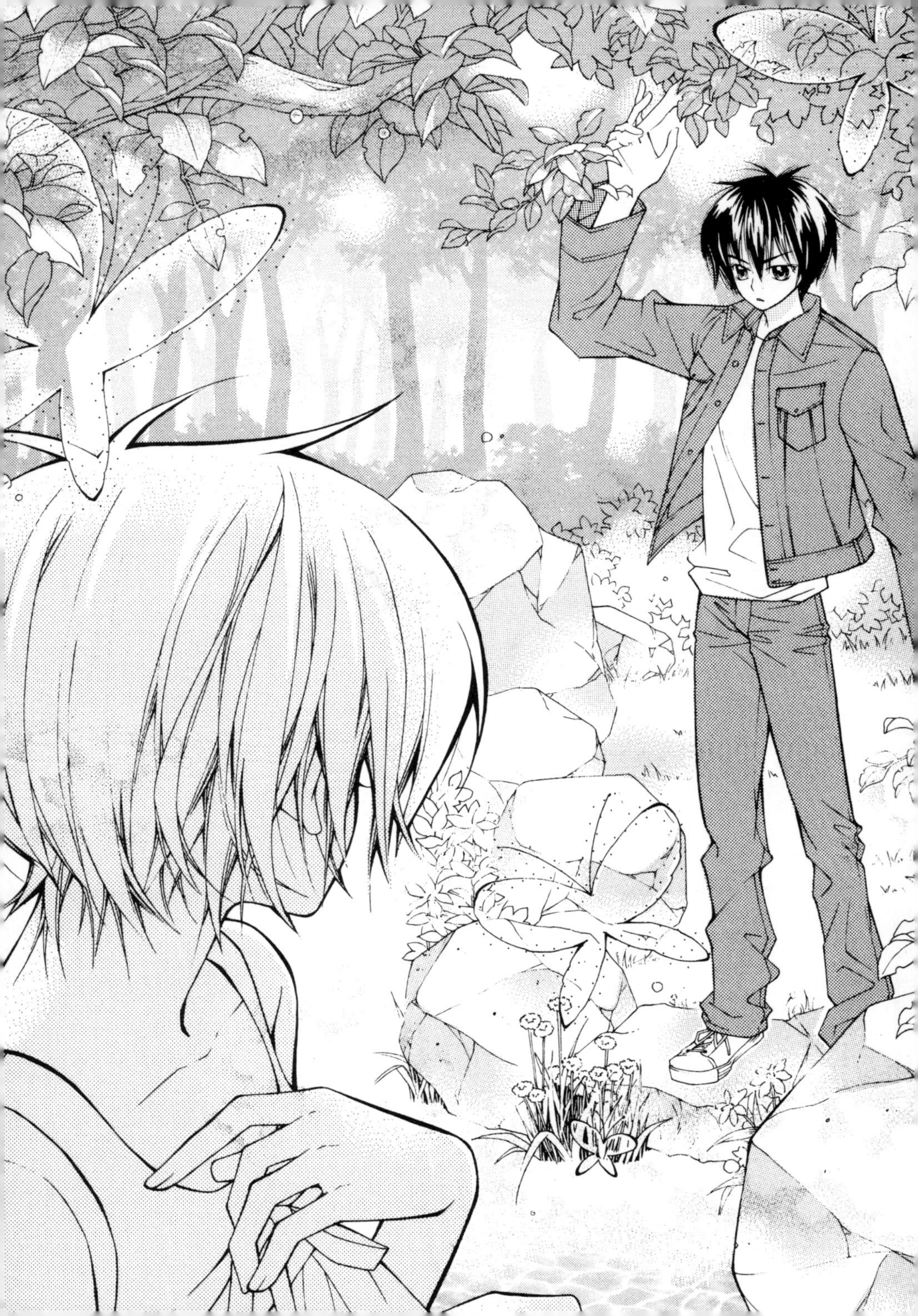

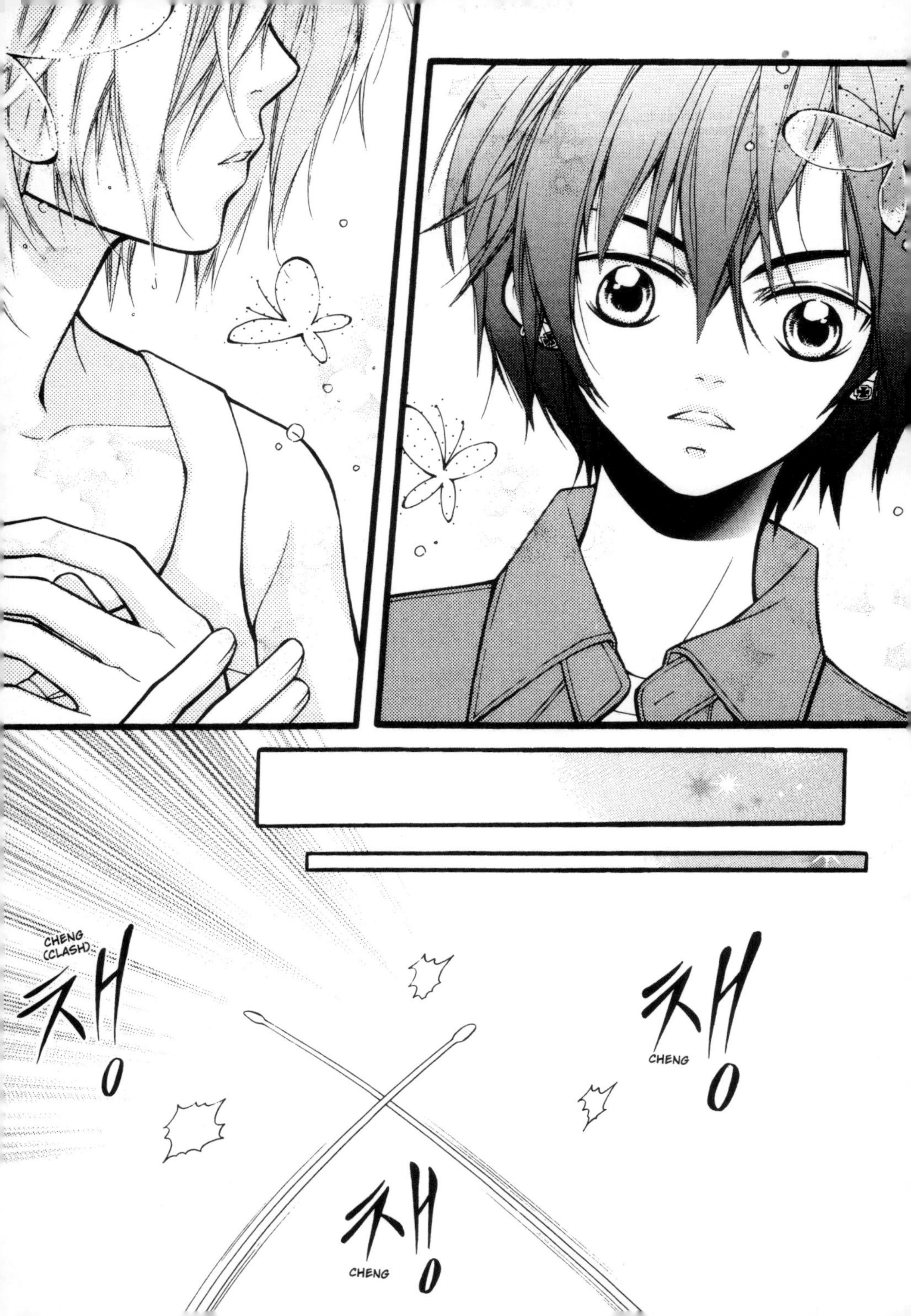

재앵
CHENG
재앵
CHENG (CLASH)
재앵
CHENG

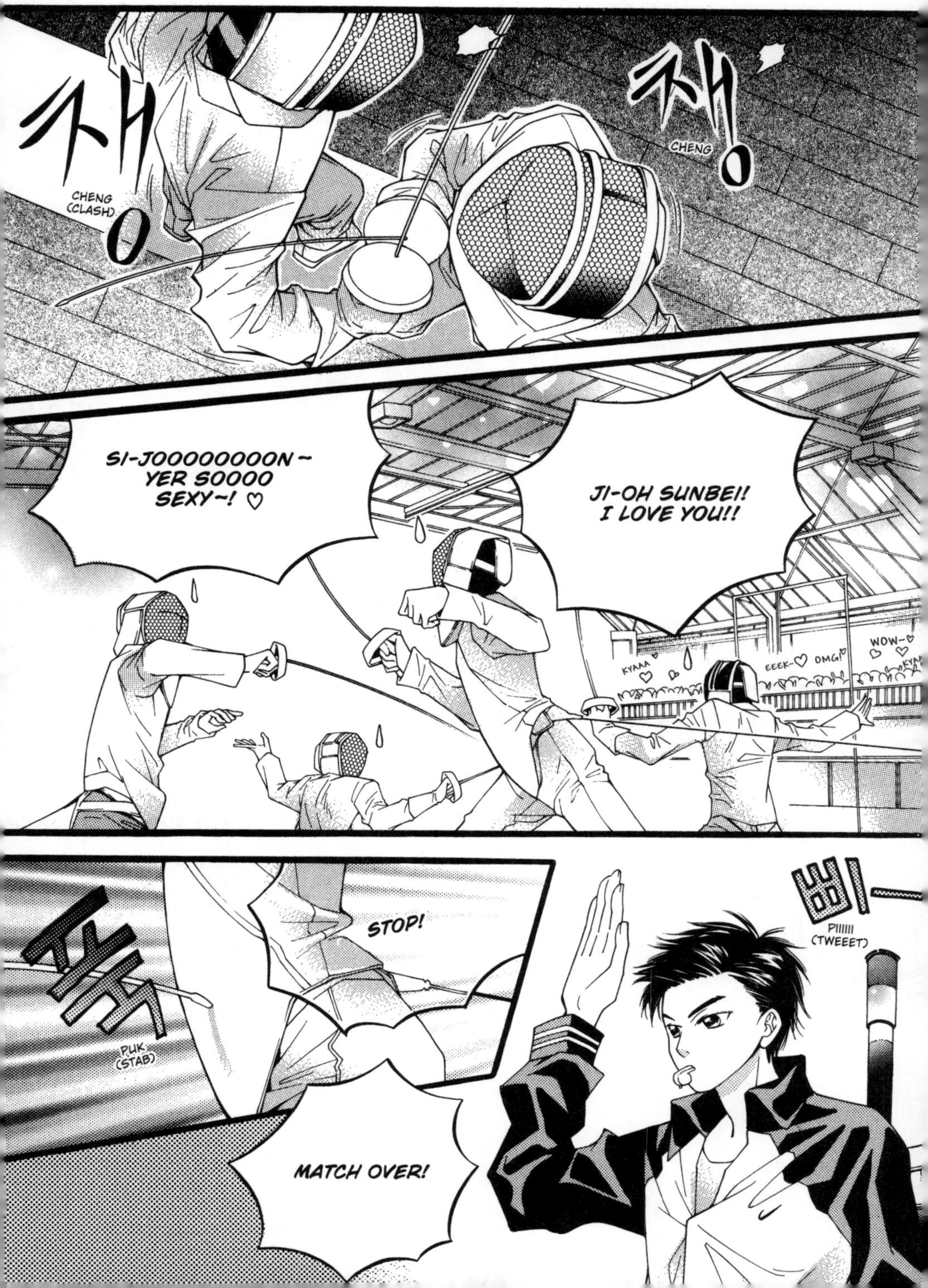

챙
CHENG (CLASH)
챙!
CHENG
SI-JOOOOOOOON~ YER SOOOO SEXY~! ♡
JI-OH SUNBEI! I LOVE YOU!!
KYAAA
EEEK-♡
OMG!♡
WOW~♡
STOP!
푹
PUK (STAB)
삑
PIIIIII (TWEEET)
MATCH OVER!

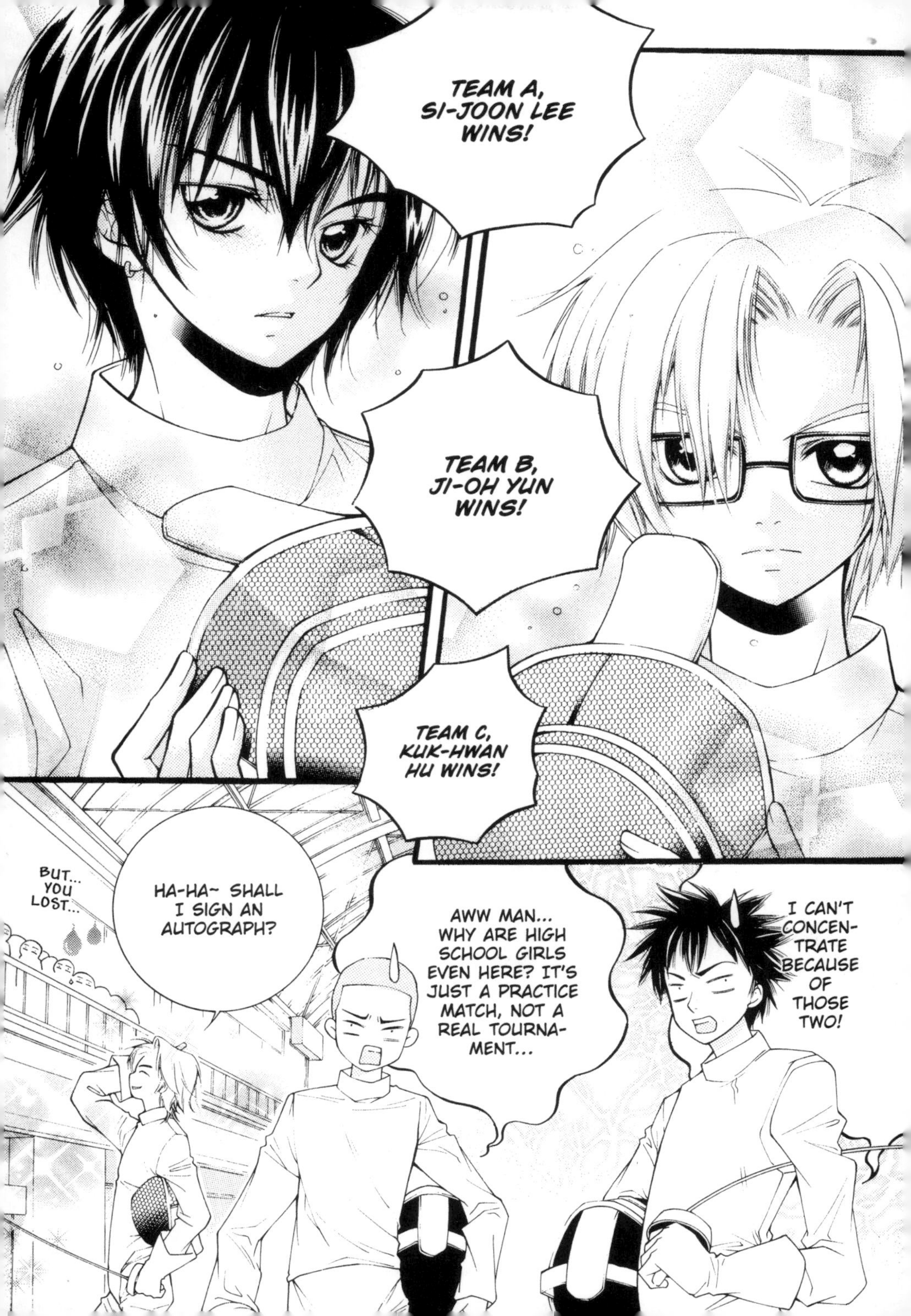
TEAM A, SI-JOON LEE WINS!
TEAM B, JI-OH YUN WINS!
TEAM C, KUK-HWAN HU WINS!
BUT... YOU LOST...
HA-HA~ SHALL I SIGN AN AUTOGRAPH?
AWW MAN... WHY ARE HIGH SCHOOL GIRLS EVEN HERE? IT'S JUST A PRACTICE MATCH, NOT A REAL TOURNA-MENT...
I CAN'T CONCEN-TRATE BECAUSE OF THOSE TWO!

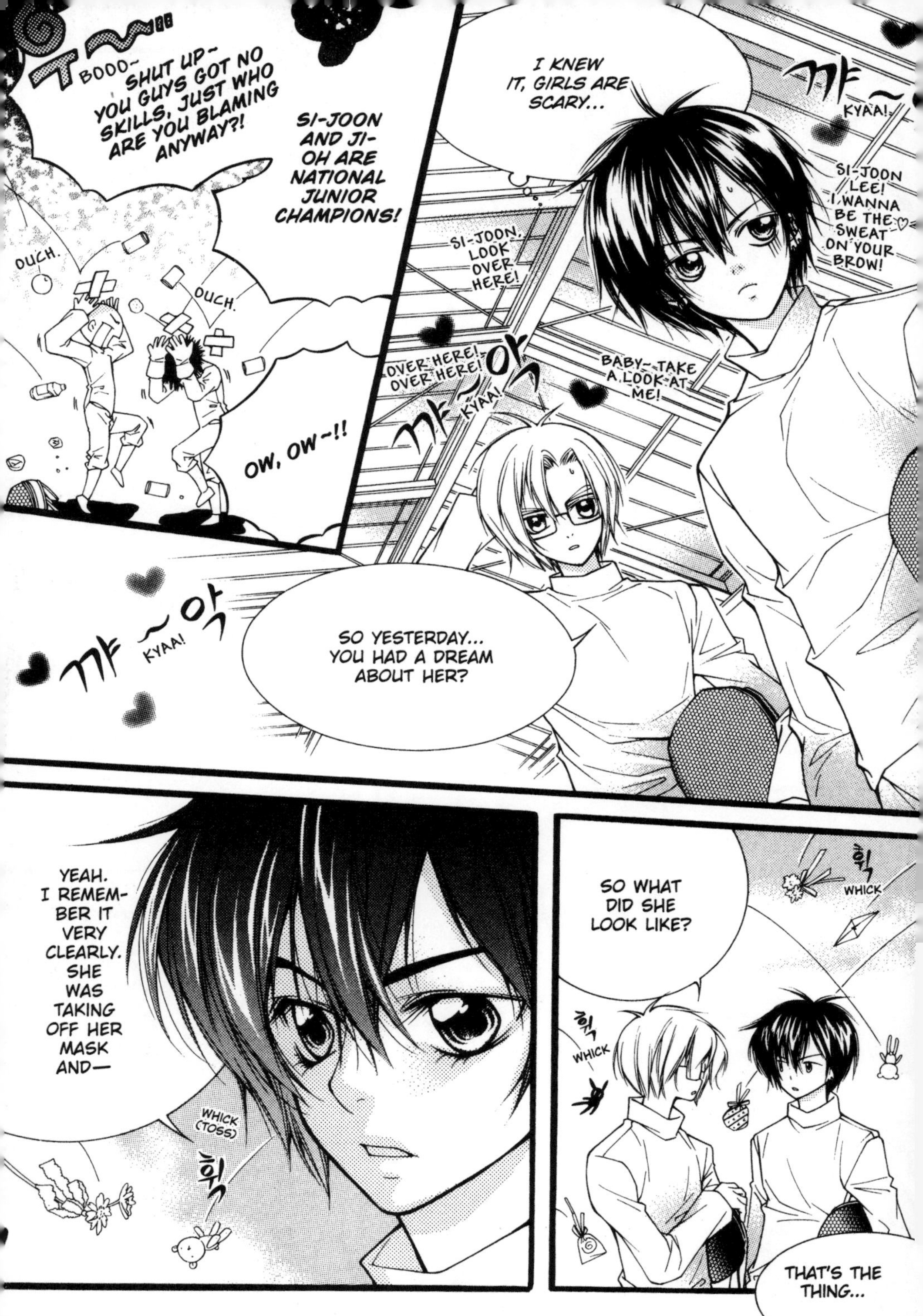
BOOO~
SHUT UP~ YOU GUYS GOT NO SKILLS, JUST WHO ARE YOU BLAMING ANYWAY?!
SI-JOON AND JI-OH ARE NATIONAL JUNIOR CHAMPIONS!
OUCH.
OUCH.
OW, OW~!!
I KNEW IT, GIRLS ARE SCARY...
까~
KYAA!
SI-JOON LEE! I WANNA BE THE ♡ SWEAT ON YOUR BROW!
SI-JOON, LOOK OVER HERE!
OVER HERE! OVER HERE!
까~악
KYAA!
BABY~ TAKE A LOOK AT ME!
까~악
KYAA!
SO YESTERDAY... YOU HAD A DREAM ABOUT HER?
YEAH. I REMEMBER IT VERY CLEARLY. SHE WAS TAKING OFF HER MASK AND—
WHICK (TOSS)
휙
SO WHAT DID SHE LOOK LIKE?
휙
WHICK
휙
WHICK
THAT'S THE THING...

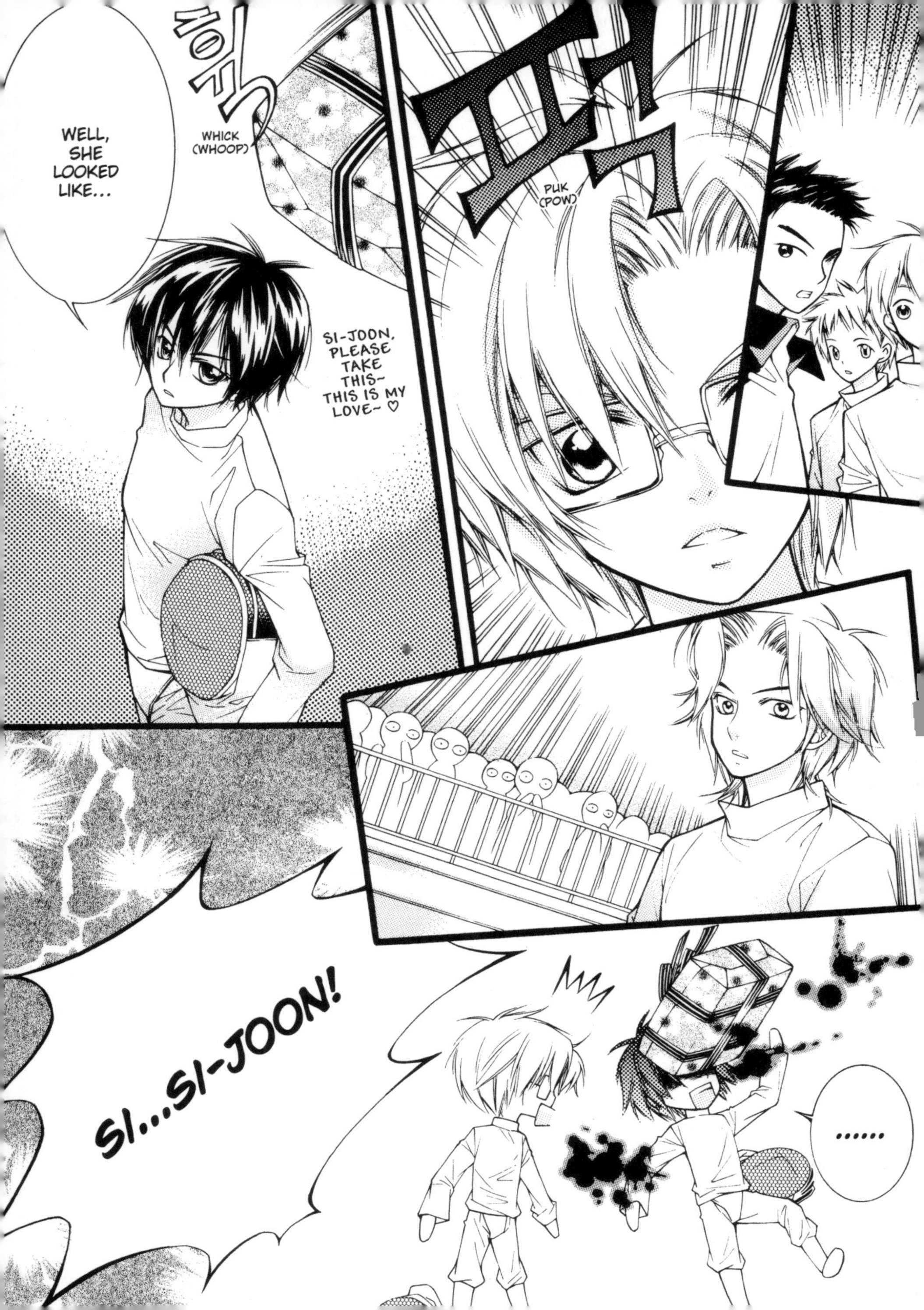

WELL, SHE LOOKED LIKE...
SI-JOON, PLEASE TAKE THIS~ THIS IS MY LOVE~ ♡
휘익
WHICK (WHOOP)
퍽
PUK (POW)
SI...SI-JOON!
......

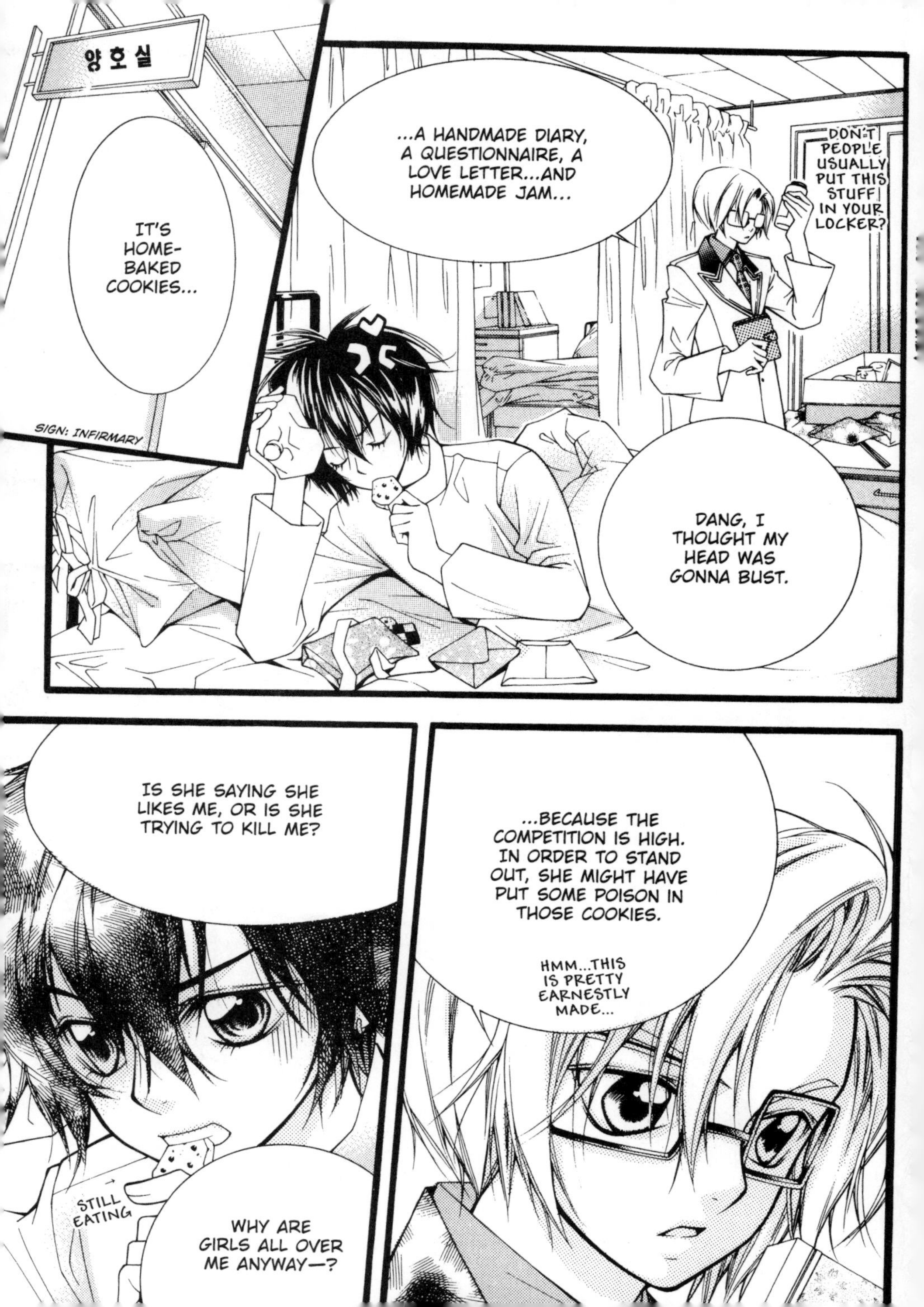

양호실
SIGN: INFIRMARY
IT'S HOME-BAKED COOKIES...
...A HANDMADE DIARY, A QUESTIONNAIRE, A LOVE LETTER...AND HOMEMADE JAM...
DON'T PEOPLE USUALLY PUT THIS STUFF IN YOUR LOCKER?
DANG, I THOUGHT MY HEAD WAS GONNA BUST.
IS SHE SAYING SHE LIKES ME, OR IS SHE TRYING TO KILL ME?
STILL EATING
WHY ARE GIRLS ALL OVER ME ANYWAY—?
...BECAUSE THE COMPETITION IS HIGH. IN ORDER TO STAND OUT, SHE MIGHT HAVE PUT SOME POISON IN THOSE COOKIES.
HMM...THIS IS PRETTY EARNESTLY MADE...

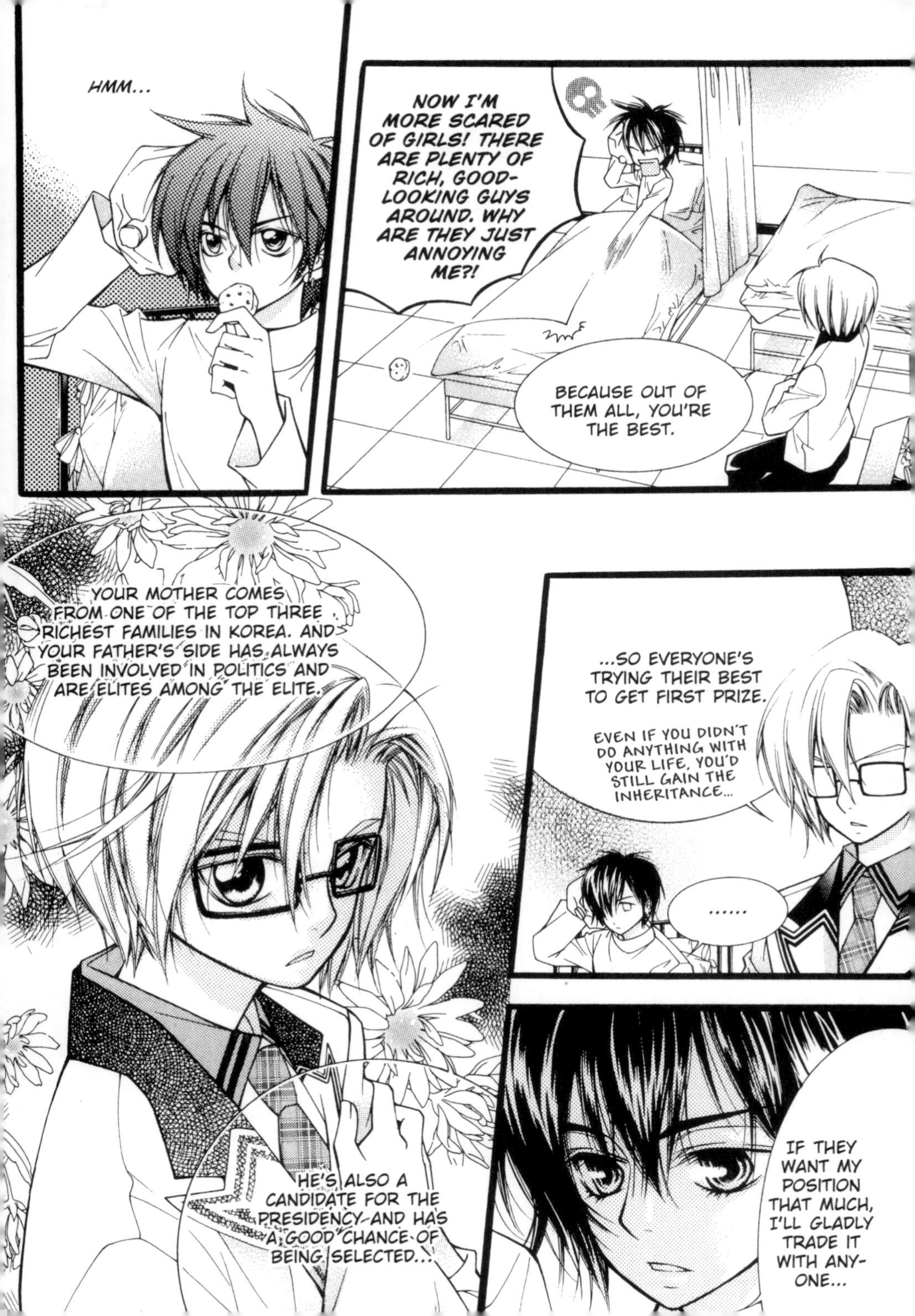
HMM...
NOW I'M MORE SCARED OF GIRLS! THERE ARE PLENTY OF RICH, GOOD-LOOKING GUYS AROUND. WHY ARE THEY JUST ANNOYING ME?!
BECAUSE OUT OF THEM ALL, YOU'RE THE BEST.
YOUR MOTHER COMES FROM ONE OF THE TOP THREE RICHEST FAMILIES IN KOREA. AND YOUR FATHER'S SIDE HAS ALWAYS BEEN INVOLVED IN POLITICS AND ARE ELITES AMONG THE ELITE.
...SO EVERYONE'S TRYING THEIR BEST TO GET FIRST PRIZE.
EVEN IF YOU DIDN'T DO ANYTHING WITH YOUR LIFE, YOU'D STILL GAIN THE INHERITANCE...
......
HE'S ALSO A CANDIDATE FOR THE PRESIDENCY AND HAS A GOOD CHANCE OF BEING SELECTED...
IF THEY WANT MY POSITION THAT MUCH, I'LL GLADLY TRADE IT WITH ANY-ONE...

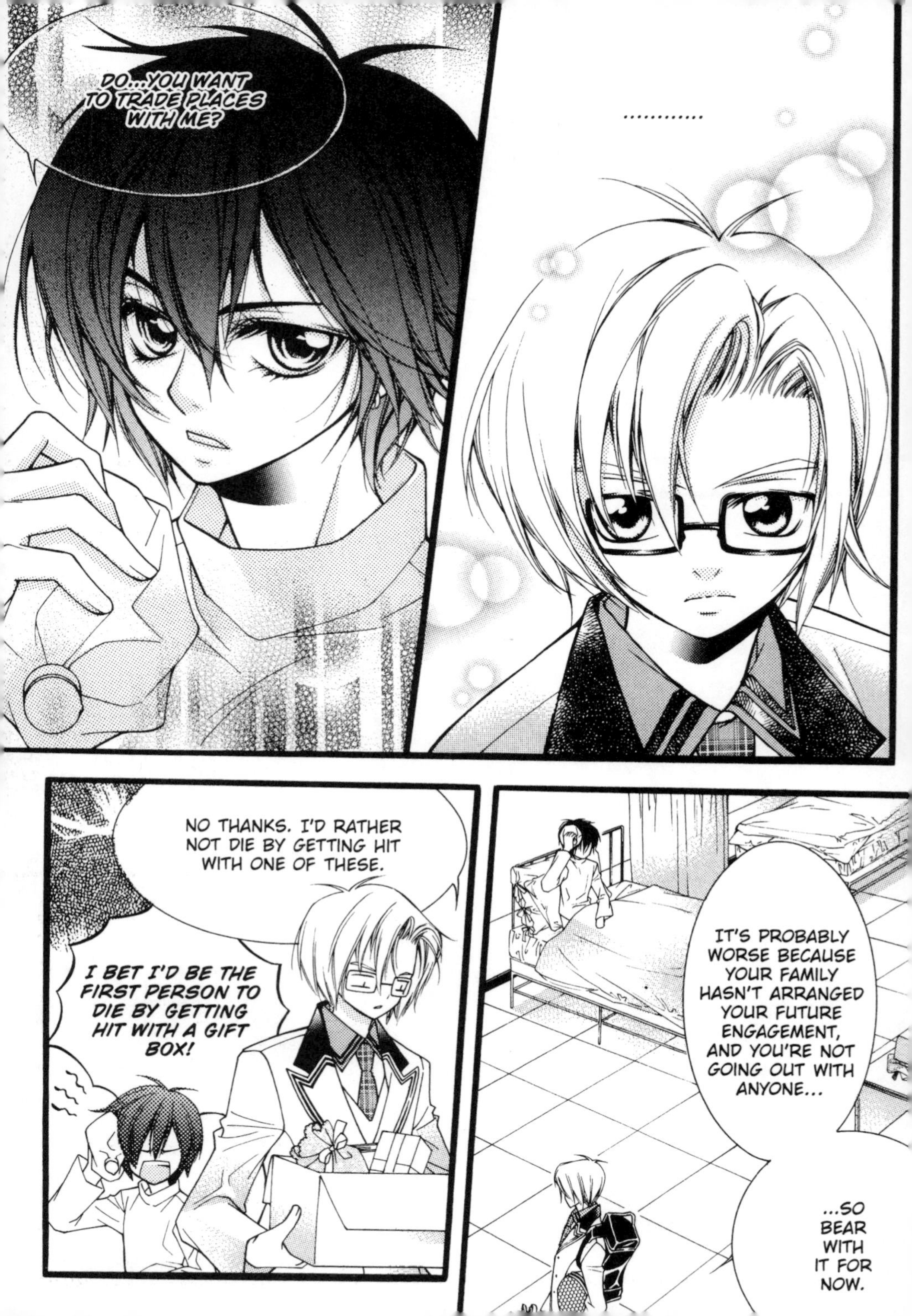

....
DO...YOU WANT TO TRADE PLACES WITH ME?
IT'S PROBABLY WORSE BECAUSE YOUR FAMILY HASN'T ARRANGED YOUR FUTURE ENGAGEMENT, AND YOU'RE NOT GOING OUT WITH ANYONE...
...SO BEAR WITH IT FOR NOW.
NO THANKS. I'D RATHER NOT DIE BY GETTING HIT WITH ONE OF THESE.
I BET I'D BE THE FIRST PERSON TO DIE BY GETTING HIT WITH A GIFT BOX!

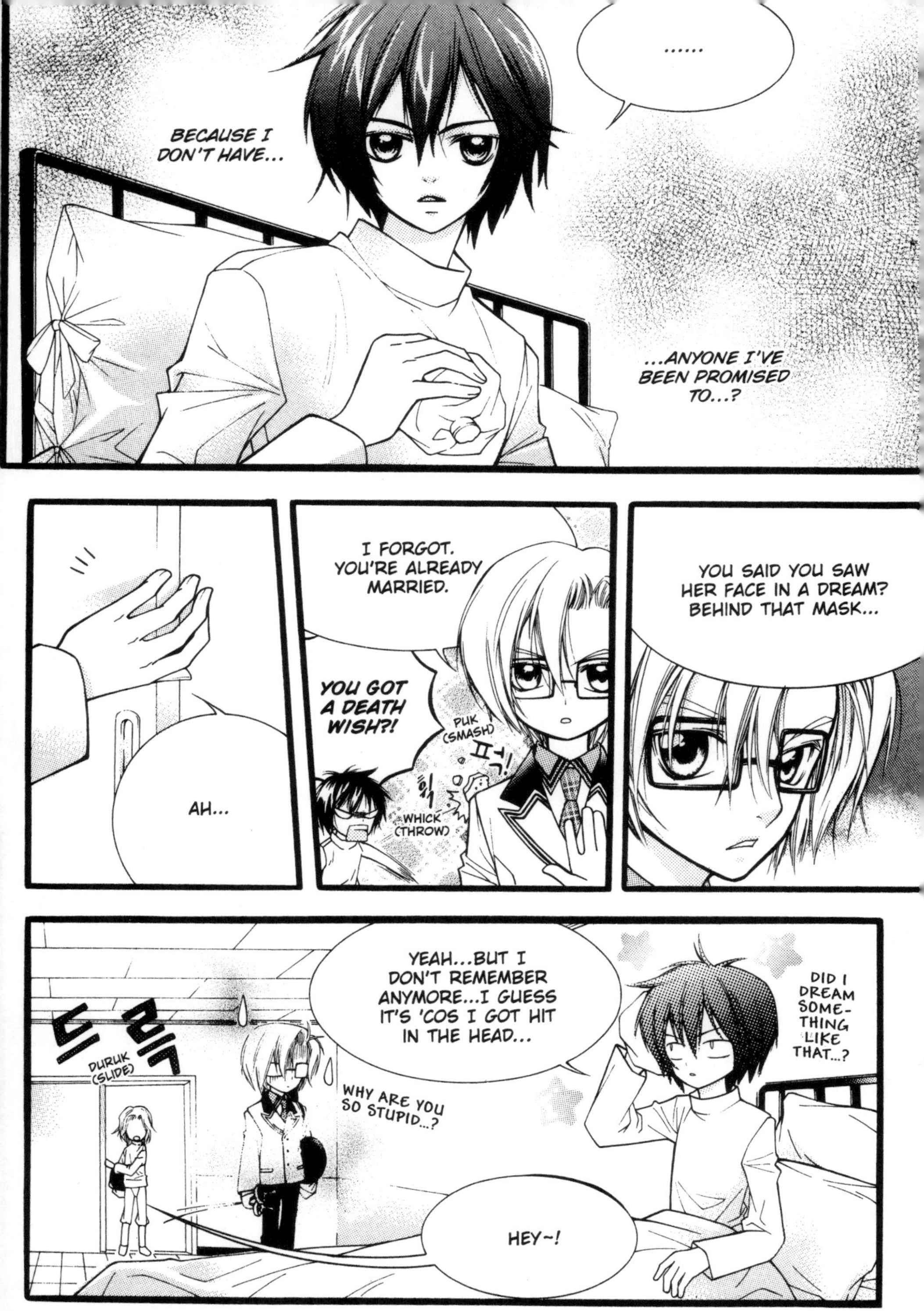
BECAUSE I DON'T HAVE...
......
...ANYONE I'VE BEEN PROMISED TO...?
AH...
I FORGOT. YOU'RE ALREADY MARRIED.
YOU GOT A DEATH WISH?!
PUK (SMASH)
WHICK (THROW)
YOU SAID YOU SAW HER FACE IN A DREAM? BEHIND THAT MASK...
DID I DREAM SOMETHING LIKE THAT...?
YEAH...BUT I DON'T REMEMBER ANYMORE...I GUESS IT'S 'COS I GOT HIT IN THE HEAD...
WHY ARE YOU SO STUPID...?
DURUK (SLIDE)
HEY~!

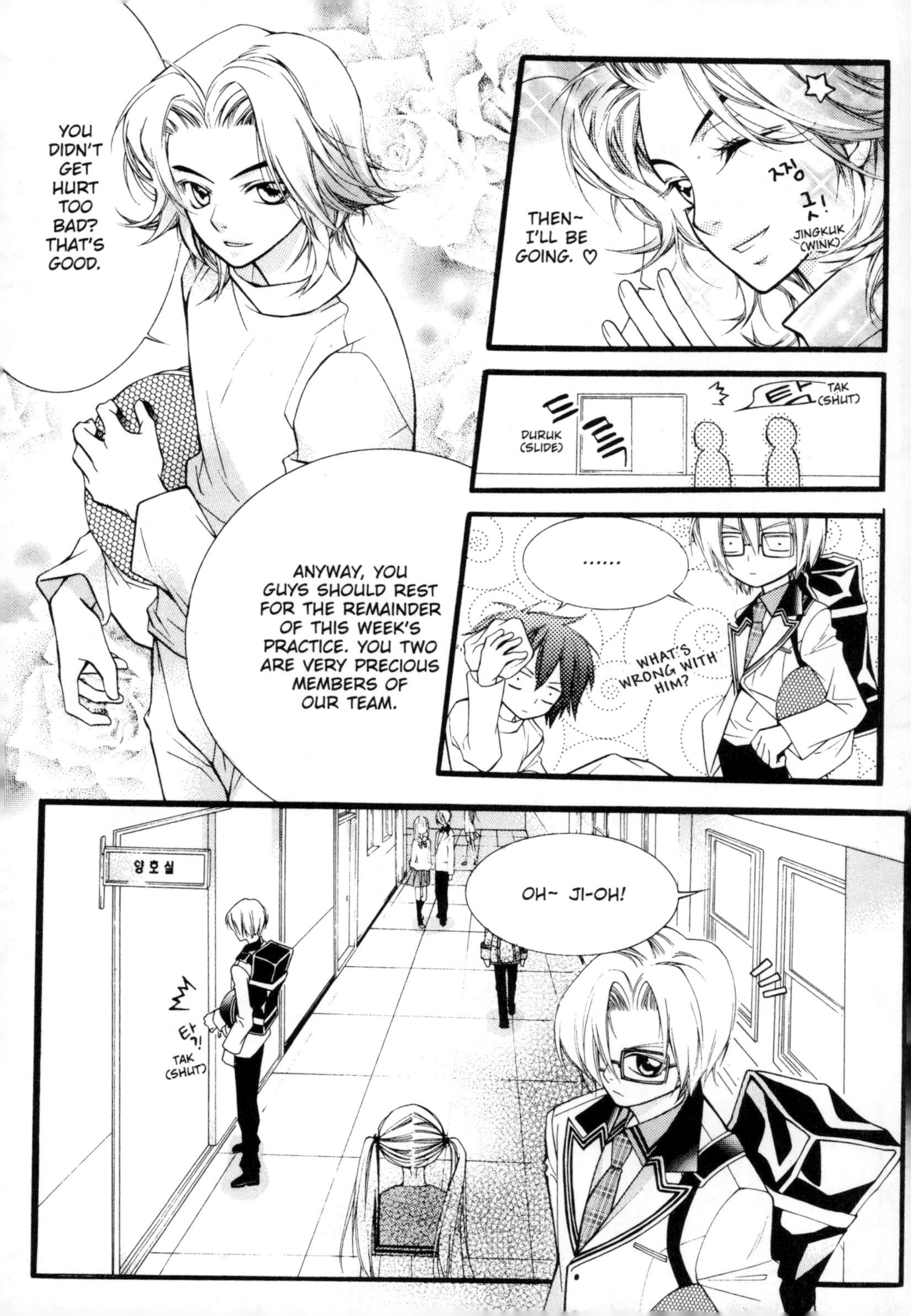

YOU DIDN'T GET HURT TOO BAD? THAT'S GOOD.
THEN~ I'LL BE GOING. ♡
JINGKUK (WINK)
ANYWAY, YOU GUYS SHOULD REST FOR THE REMAINDER OF THIS WEEK'S PRACTICE. YOU TWO ARE VERY PRECIOUS MEMBERS OF OUR TEAM.
DURUK (SLIDE)
TAK (SHUT)
......
WHAT'S WRONG WITH HIM?
양호실
탁!
TAK (SHUT)
OH~ JI-OH!

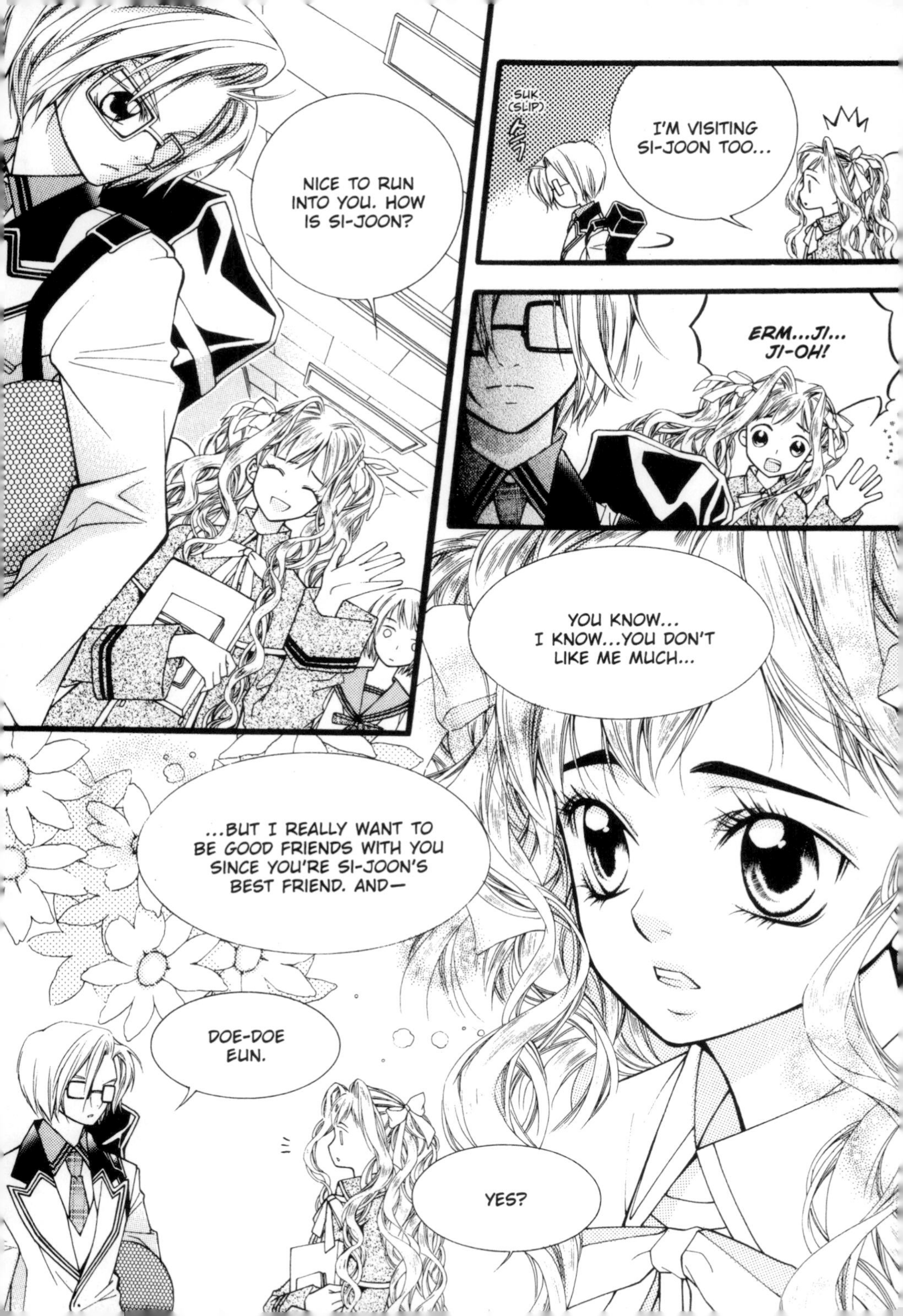
NICE TO RUN INTO YOU. HOW IS SI-JOON?
SUK (SLIP)
I'M VISITING SI-JOON TOO...
ERM...JI... JI-OH!
YOU KNOW... I KNOW...YOU DON'T LIKE ME MUCH...
...BUT I REALLY WANT TO BE GOOD FRIENDS WITH YOU SINCE YOU'RE SI-JOON'S BEST FRIEND. AND—
DOE-DOE EUN.
YES?

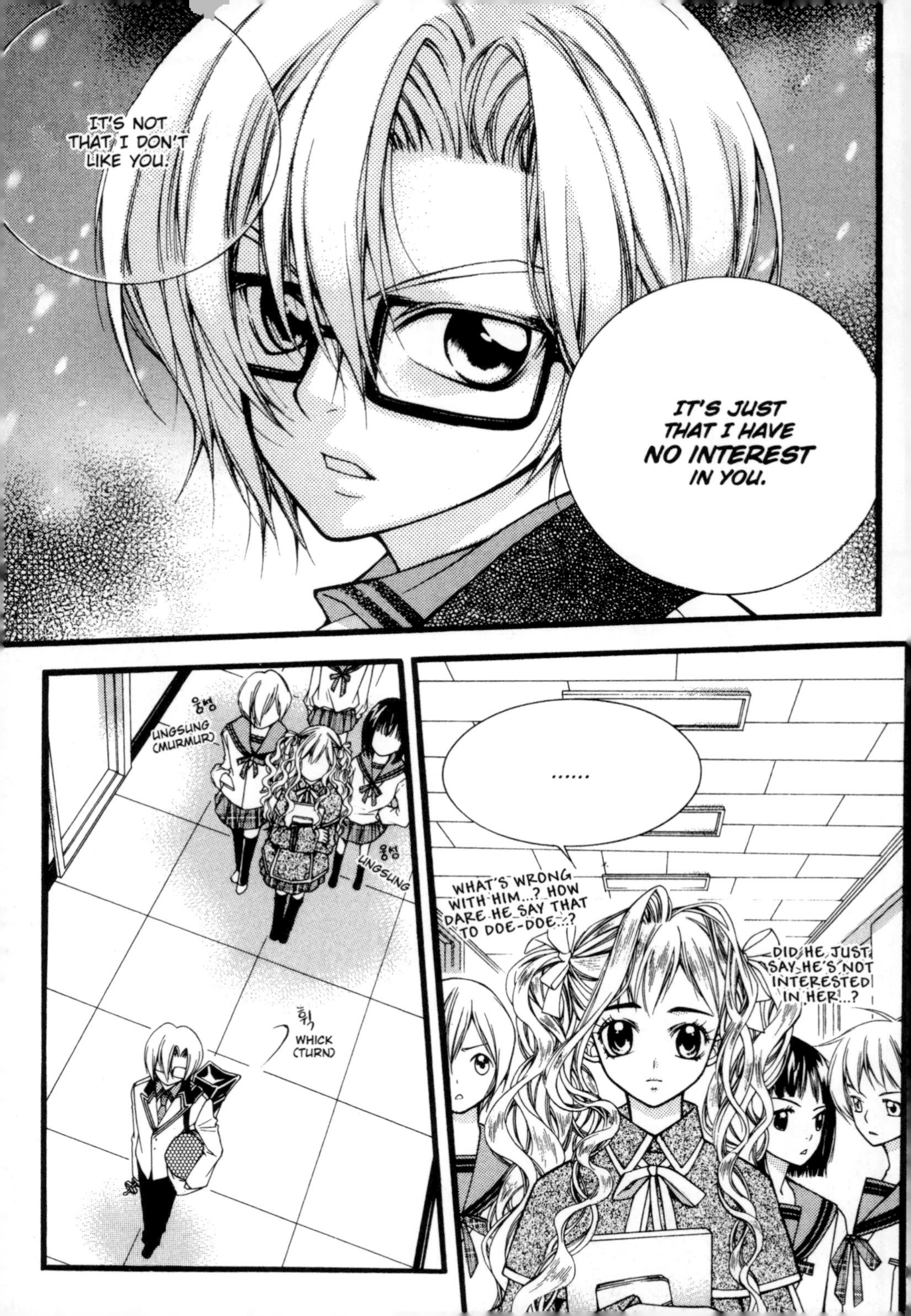
IT'S NOT THAT I DON'T LIKE YOU.
IT'S JUST THAT I HAVE NO INTEREST IN YOU.
......
웅성
UNGSUNG (MURMUR)
웅성
UNGSUNG
훽
WHICK (TURN)
WHAT'S WRONG WITH HIM...? HOW DARE HE SAY THAT TO DOE-DOE...?
DID HE JUST SAY HE'S NOT INTERESTED IN HER...?

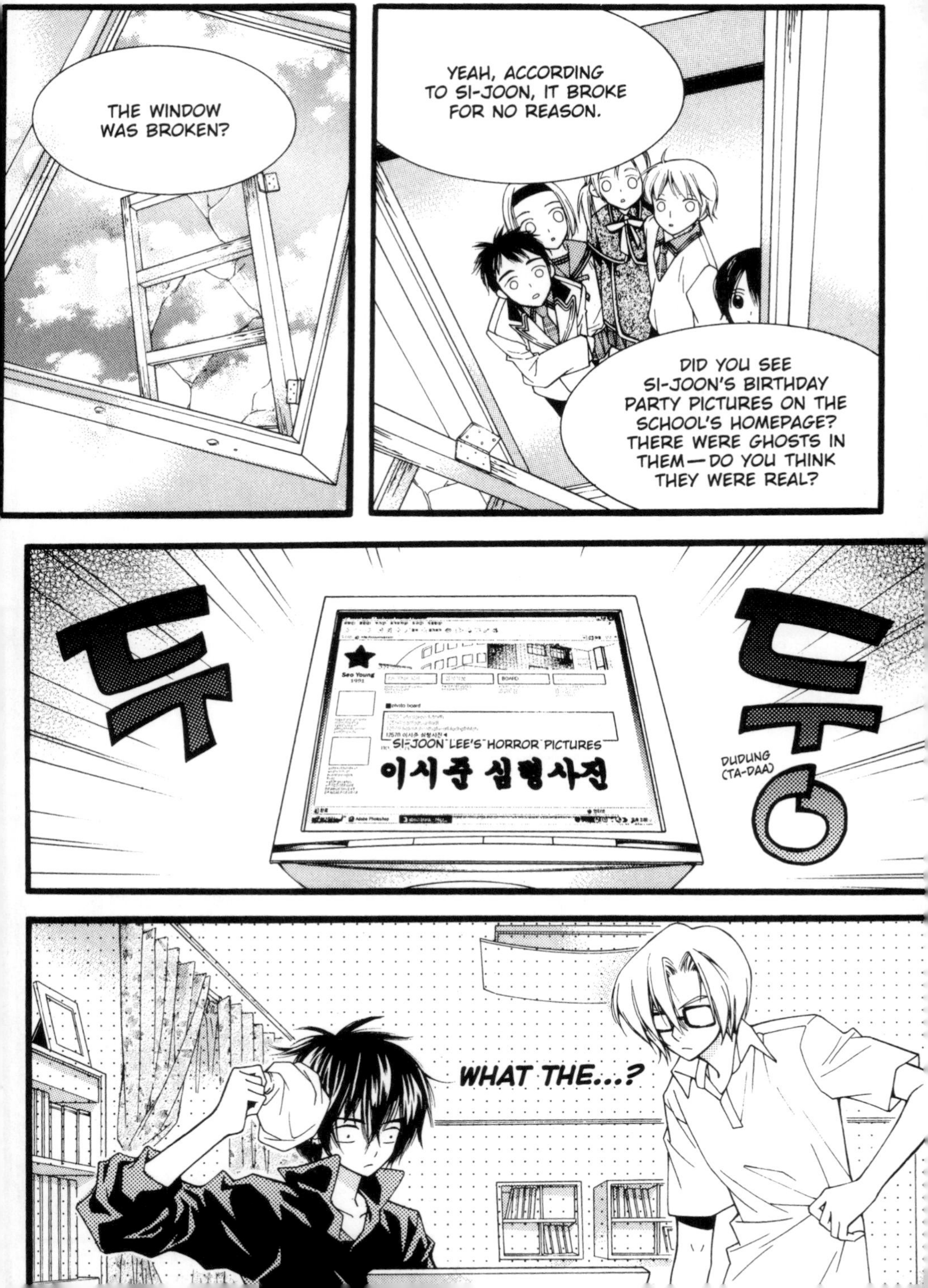
THE WINDOW WAS BROKEN?
YEAH, ACCORDING TO SI-JOON, IT BROKE FOR NO REASON.
DID YOU SEE SI-JOON'S BIRTHDAY PARTY PICTURES ON THE SCHOOL'S HOMEPAGE? THERE WERE GHOSTS IN THEM—DO YOU THINK THEY WERE REAL?
두
Seo Young
BOARD
photo board
SI-JOON LEE'S HORROR PICTURES
이시준 심령사진
둥
DUDUNG (TA-DAA)
WHAT THE...?

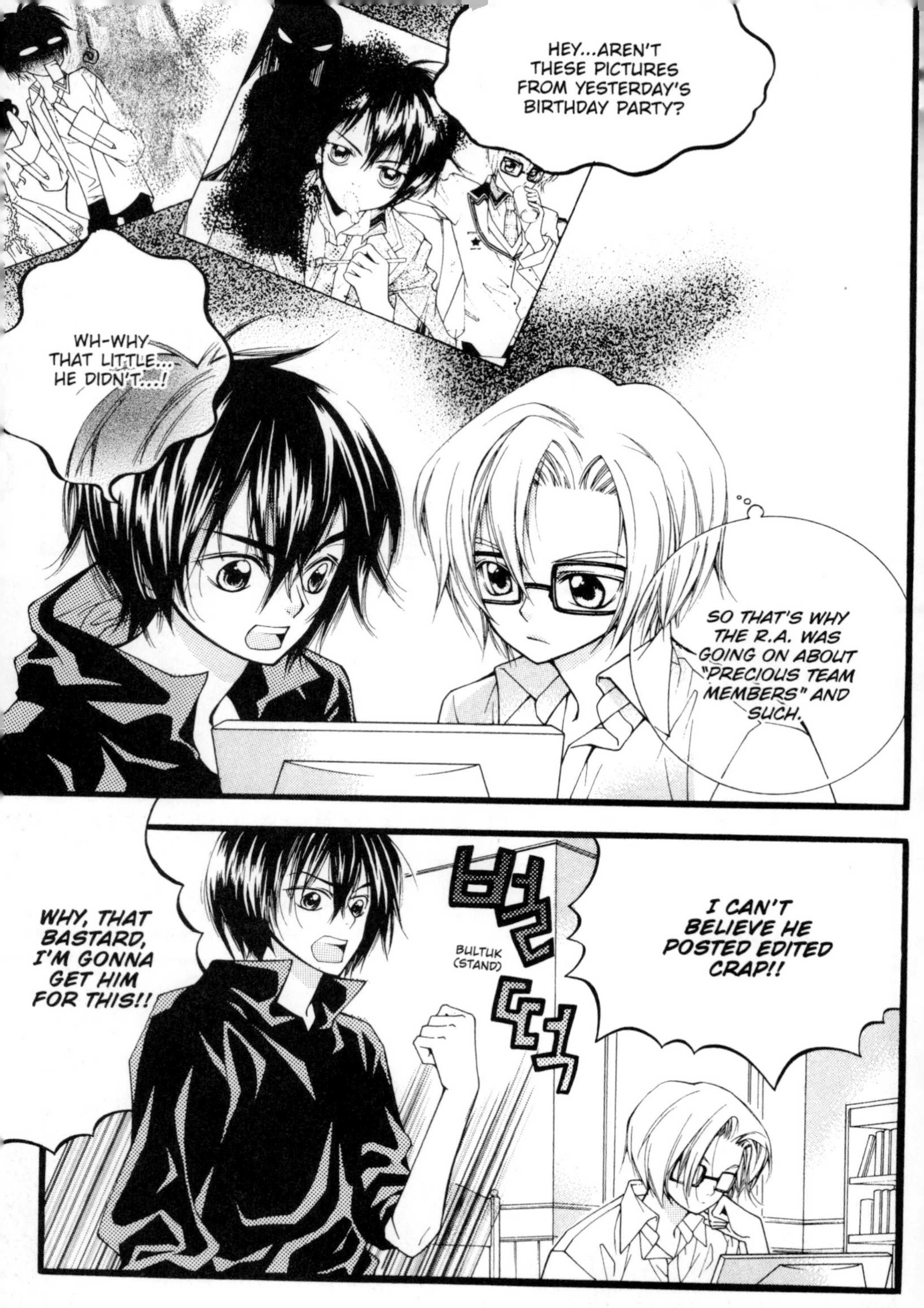
HEY...AREN'T THESE PICTURES FROM YESTERDAY'S BIRTHDAY PARTY?
WH-WHY THAT LITTLE... HE DIDN'T...!
SO THAT'S WHY THE R.A. WAS GOING ON ABOUT "PRECIOUS TEAM MEMBERS" AND SUCH.
WHY, THAT BASTARD, I'M GONNA GET HIM FOR THIS!!
벌떡
BULTUK (STAND)
I CAN'T BELIEVE HE POSTED EDITED CRAP!!

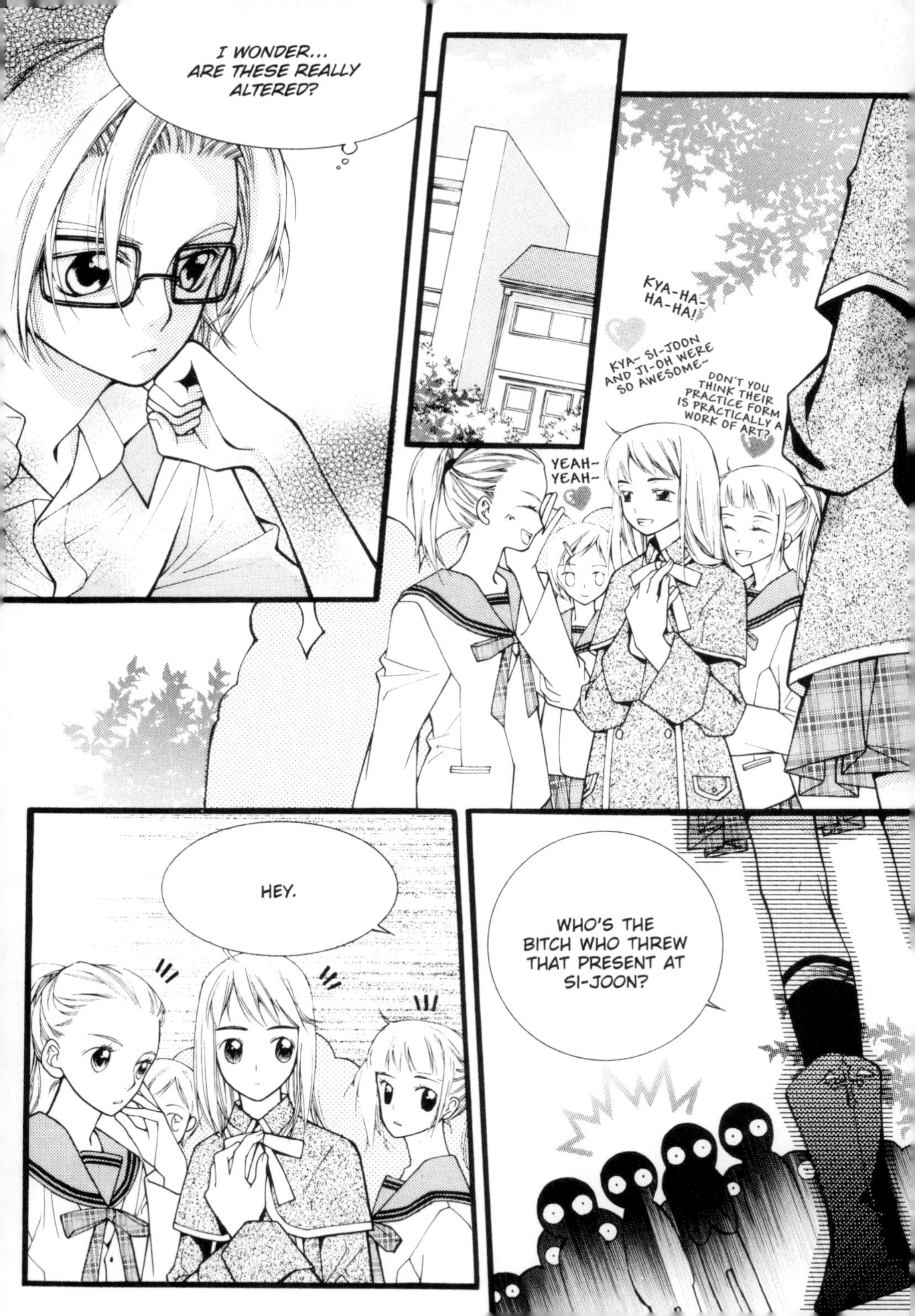

I WONDER... ARE THESE REALLY ALTERED?
KYA-HA-HA-HA!
KYA~ SI-JOON AND JI-OH WERE SO AWESOME~
DON'T YOU THINK THEIR PRACTICE FORM IS PRACTICALLY A WORK OF ART?
YEAH-YEAH-
HEY.
WHO'S THE BITCH WHO THREW THAT PRESENT AT SI-JOON?

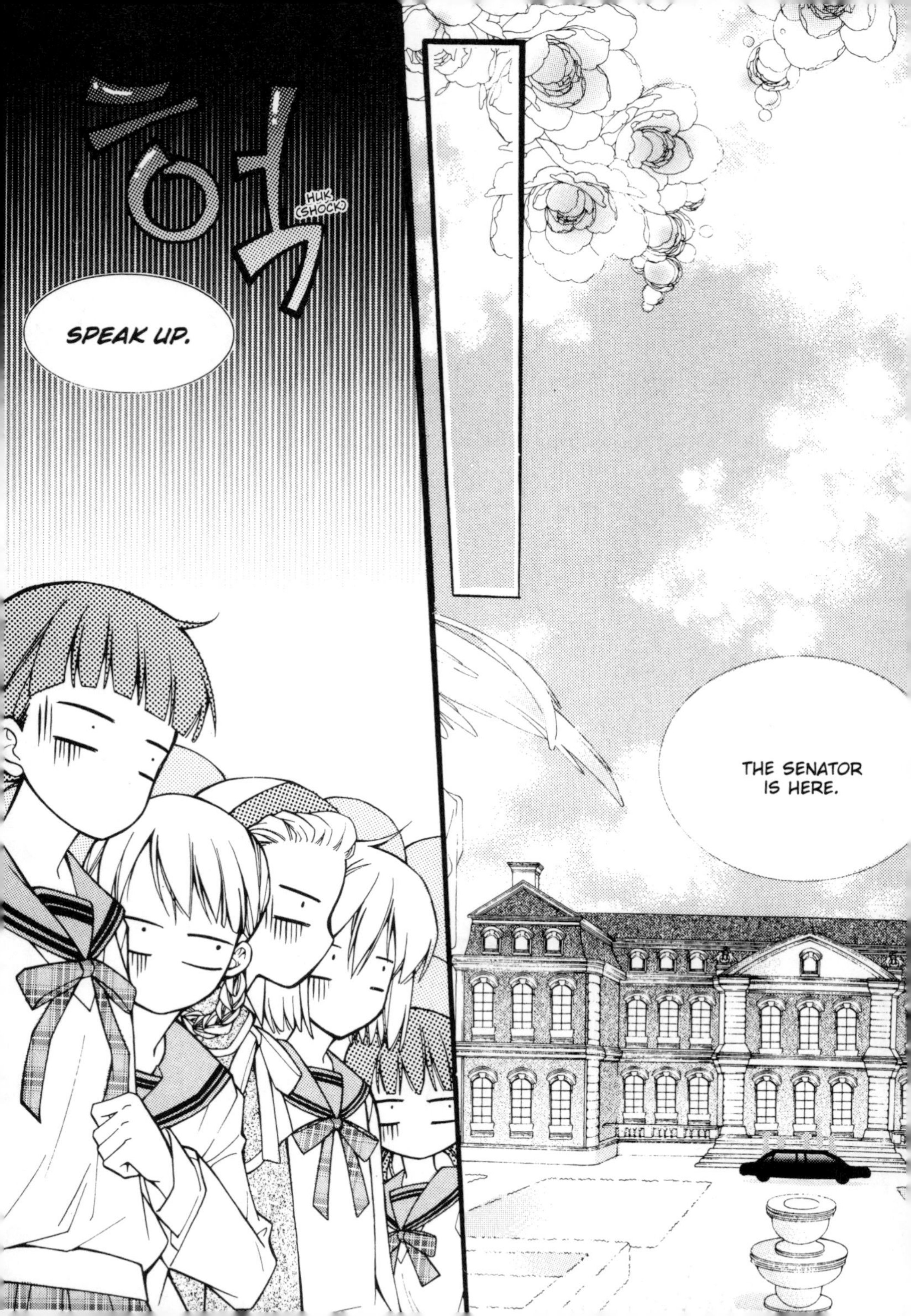

THE SENATOR IS HERE.
HUK (SHOCK)
SPEAK UP.

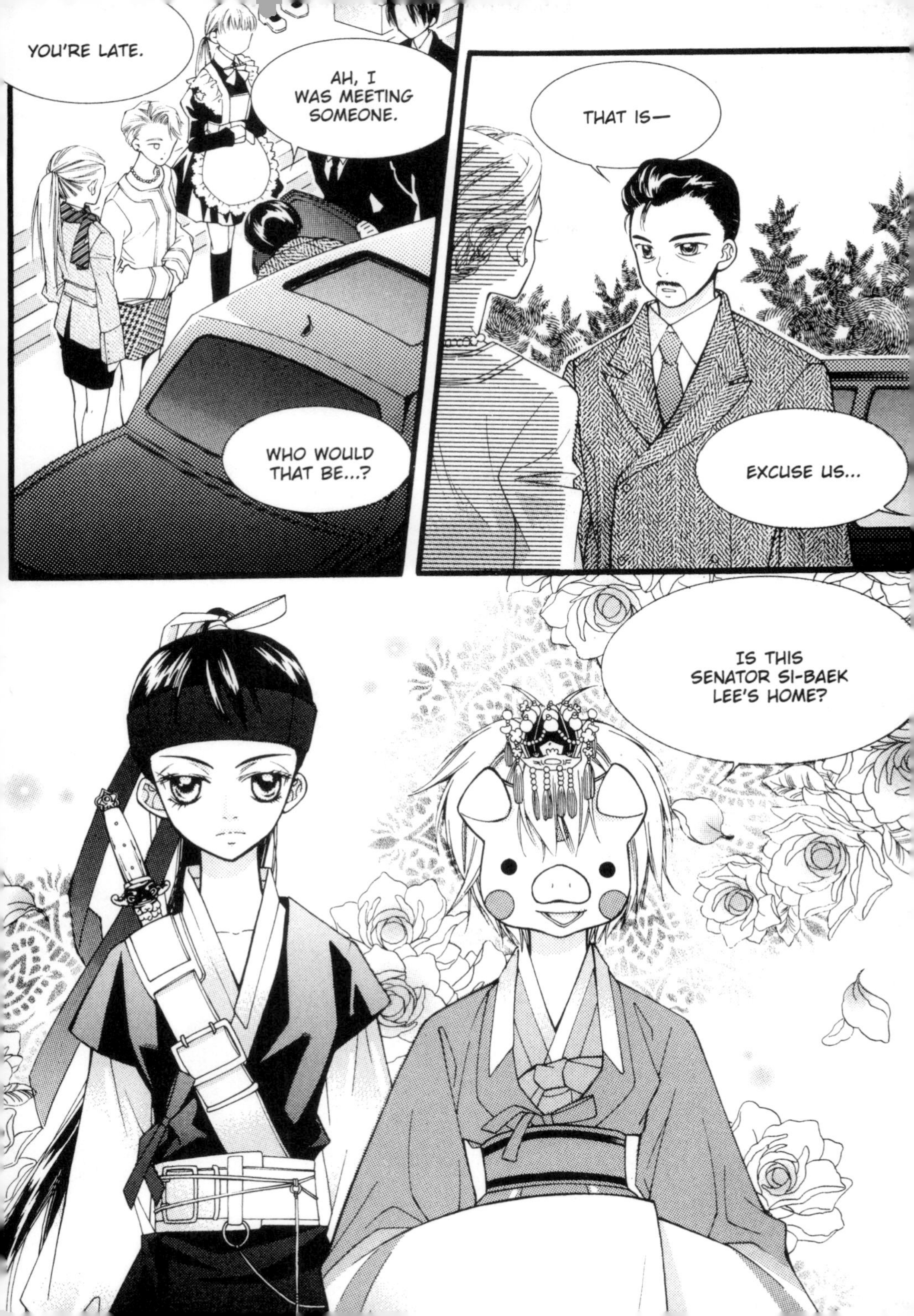
YOU'RE LATE.
AH, I WAS MEETING SOMEONE.
WHO WOULD THAT BE...?
THAT IS—
EXCUSE US...
IS THIS SENATOR SI-BAEK LEE'S HOME?

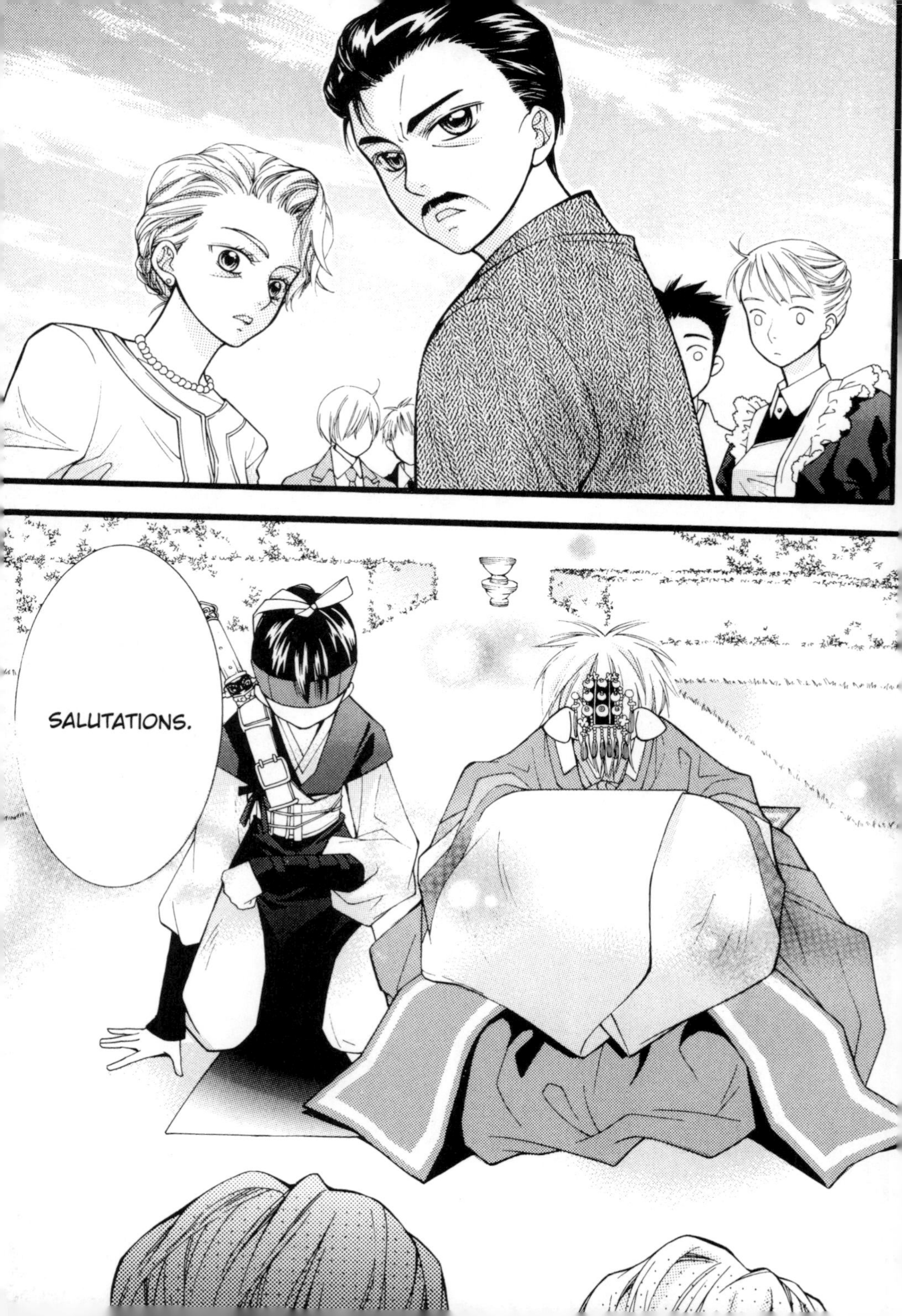
SALUTATIONS.

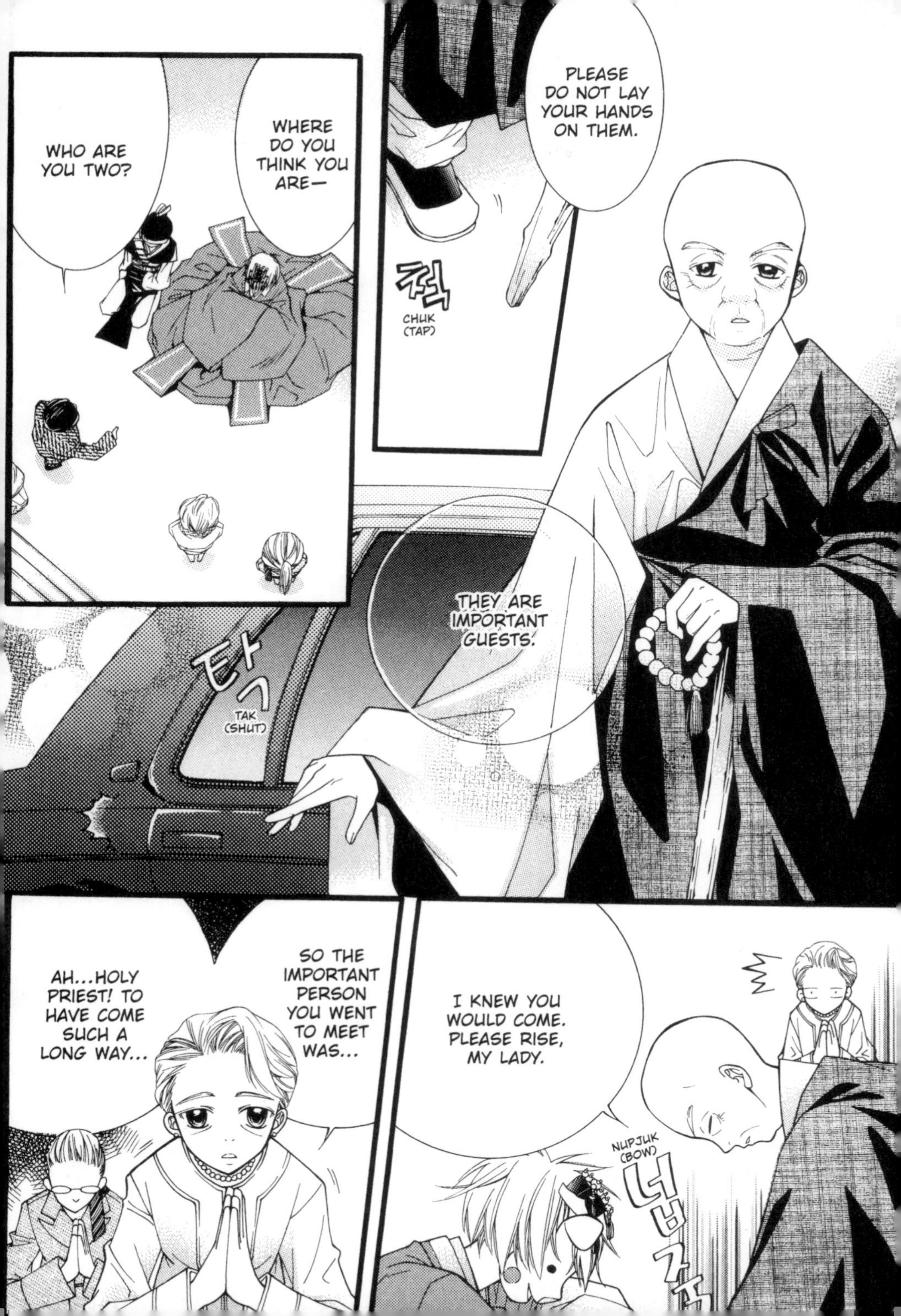
WHERE DO YOU THINK YOU ARE—
WHO ARE YOU TWO?
PLEASE DO NOT LAY YOUR HANDS ON THEM.
척
CHUK (TAP)
THEY ARE IMPORTANT GUESTS.
탁
TAK (SHUT)
SO THE IMPORTANT PERSON YOU WENT TO MEET WAS...
AH...HOLY PRIEST! TO HAVE COME SUCH A LONG WAY...
I KNEW YOU WOULD COME. PLEASE RISE, MY LADY.
NUPJUK (BOW)
넙죽

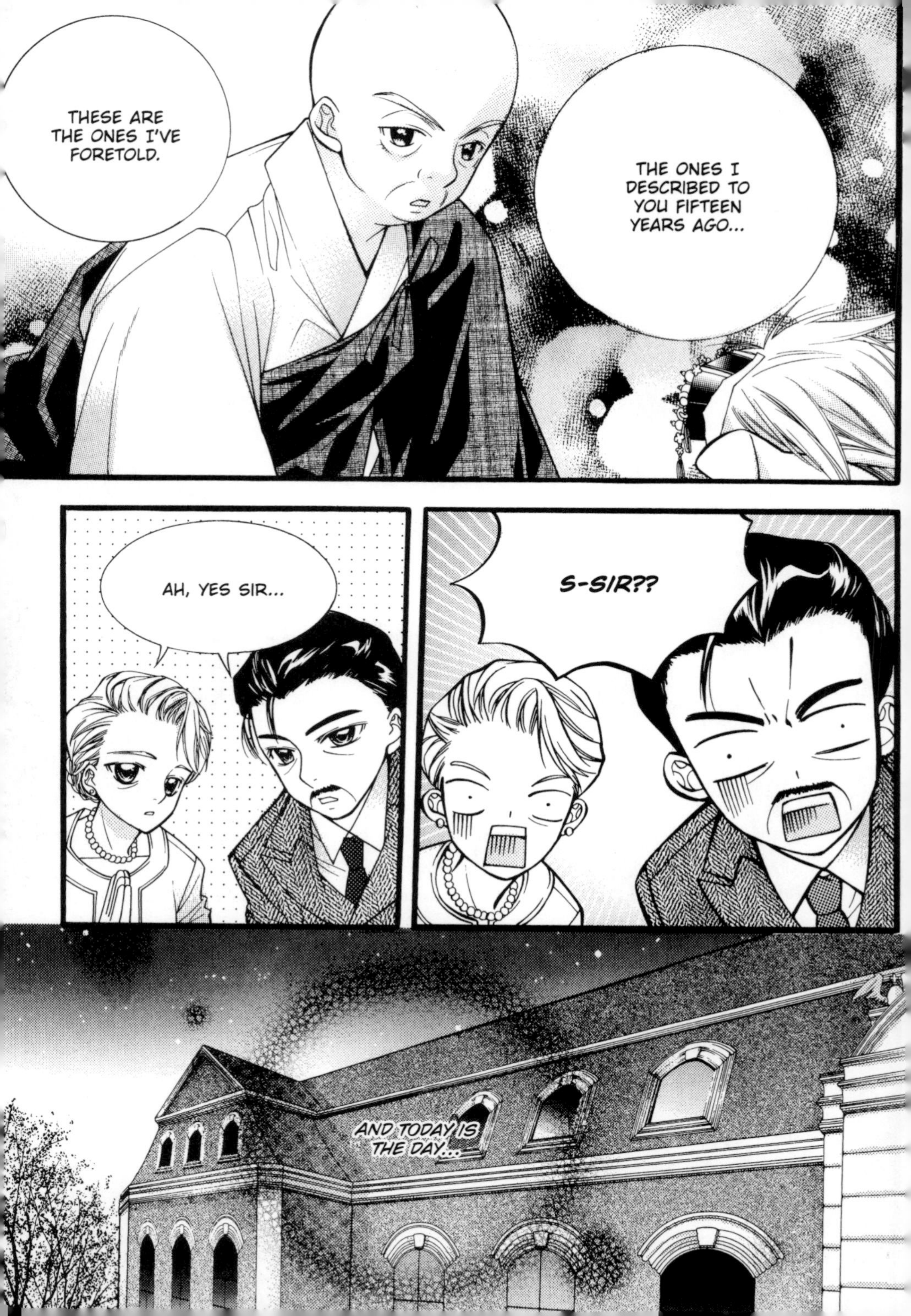
THESE ARE THE ONES I'VE FORETOLD.
THE ONES I DESCRIBED TO YOU FIFTEEN YEARS AGO...
AH, YES SIR...
S-SIR??
AND TODAY IS THE DAY...

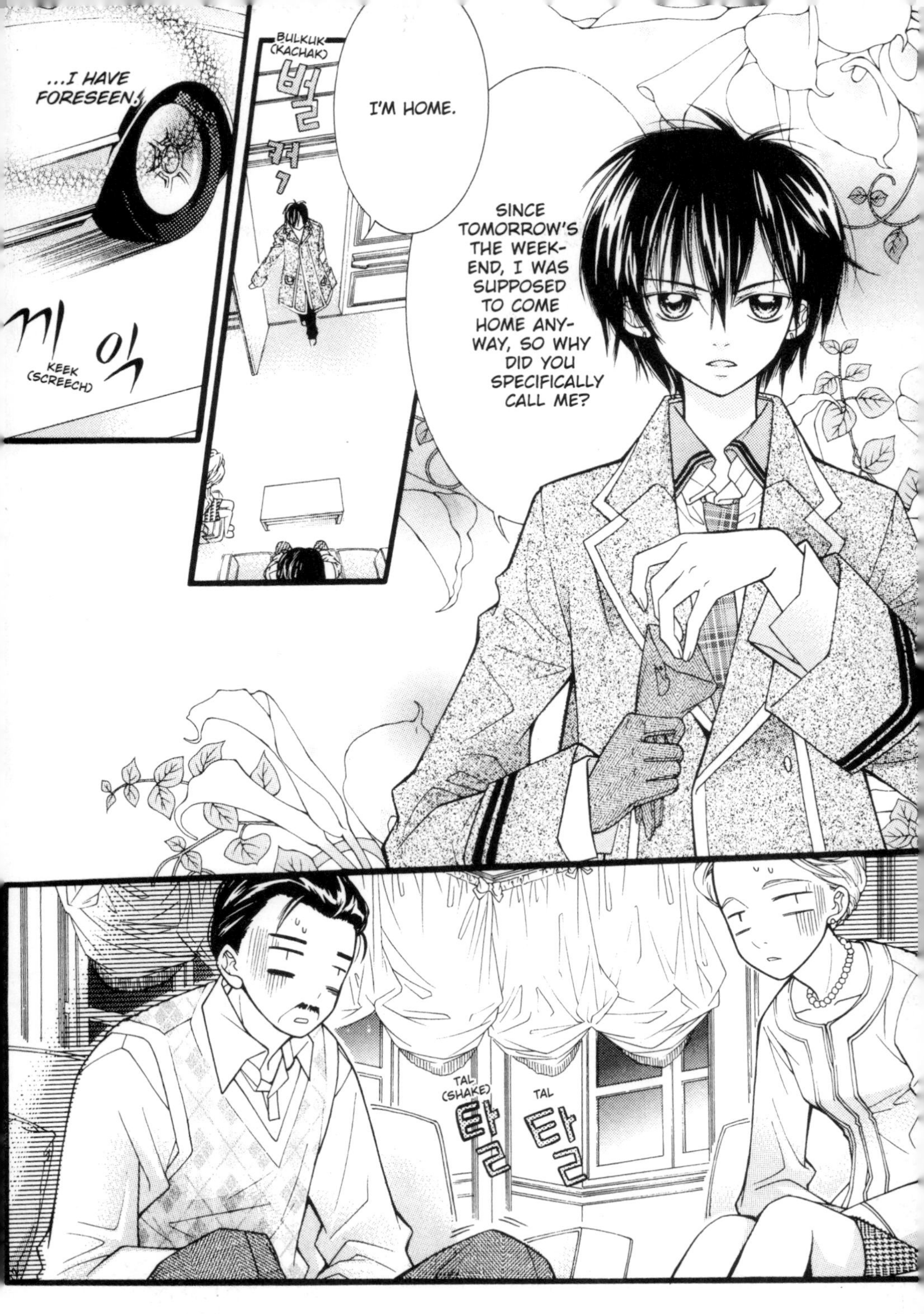

I'M HOME.
BULKUK (KACHAK)
벌컥
...I HAVE FORESEEN.
끼익
KEEK (SCREECH)
SINCE TOMORROW'S THE WEEK-END, I WAS SUPPOSED TO COME HOME ANY-WAY, SO WHY DID YOU SPECIFICALLY CALL ME?
TAL (SHAKE) TAL
탈 탈

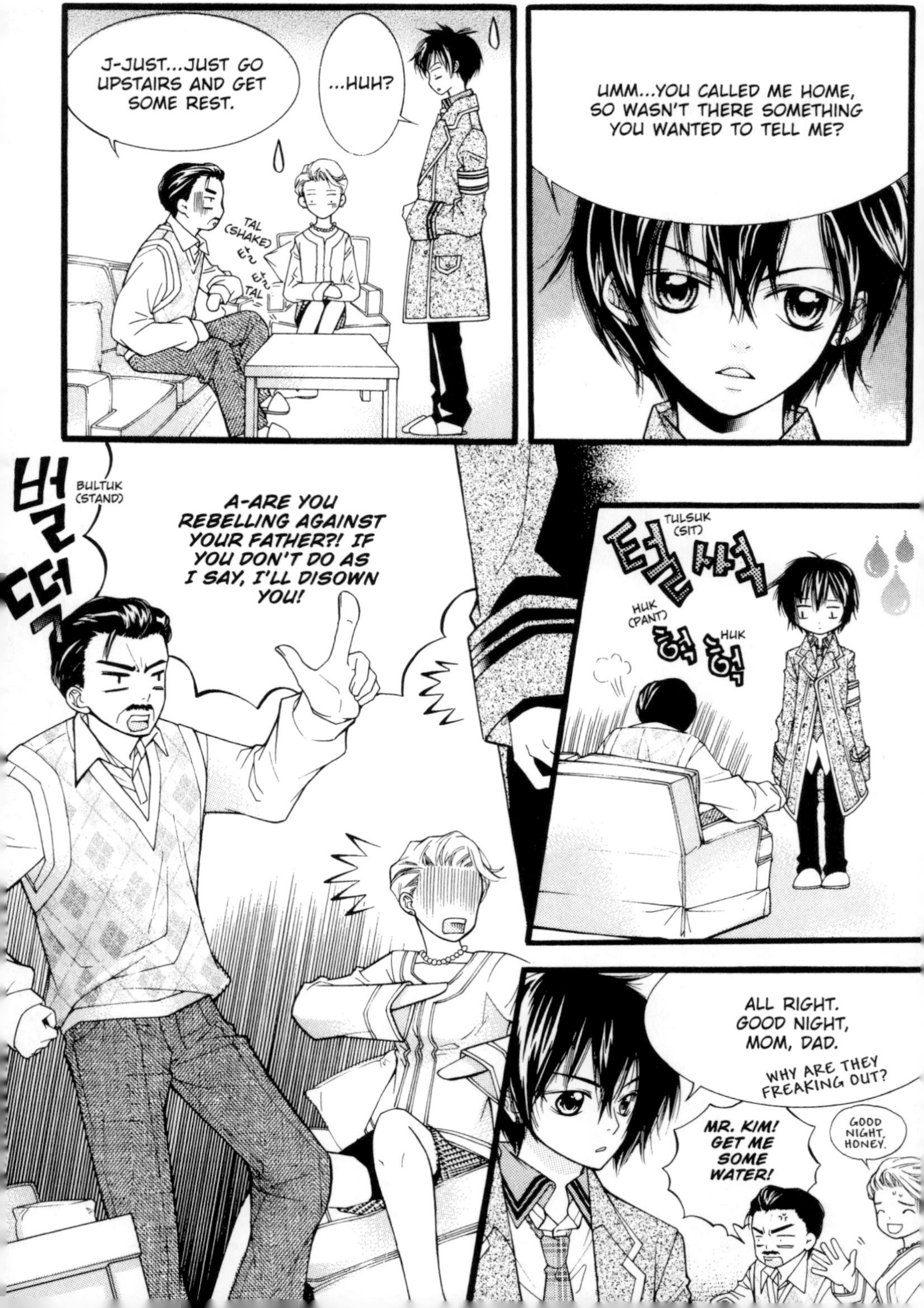
J-JUST...JUST GO UPSTAIRS AND GET SOME REST.
...HUH?
TAL (SHAKE)
탈
탈
TAL
UMM...YOU CALLED ME HOME, SO WASN'T THERE SOMETHING YOU WANTED TO TELL ME?
벌떡
BULTUK (STAND)
A-ARE YOU REBELLING AGAINST YOUR FATHER?! IF YOU DON'T DO AS I SAY, I'LL DISOWN YOU!
털썩
TULSUK (SIT)
HUK (PANT)
헉
헉
HUK
ALL RIGHT. GOOD NIGHT, MOM, DAD.
WHY ARE THEY FREAKING OUT?
MR. KIM! GET ME SOME WATER!
GOOD NIGHT, HONEY.

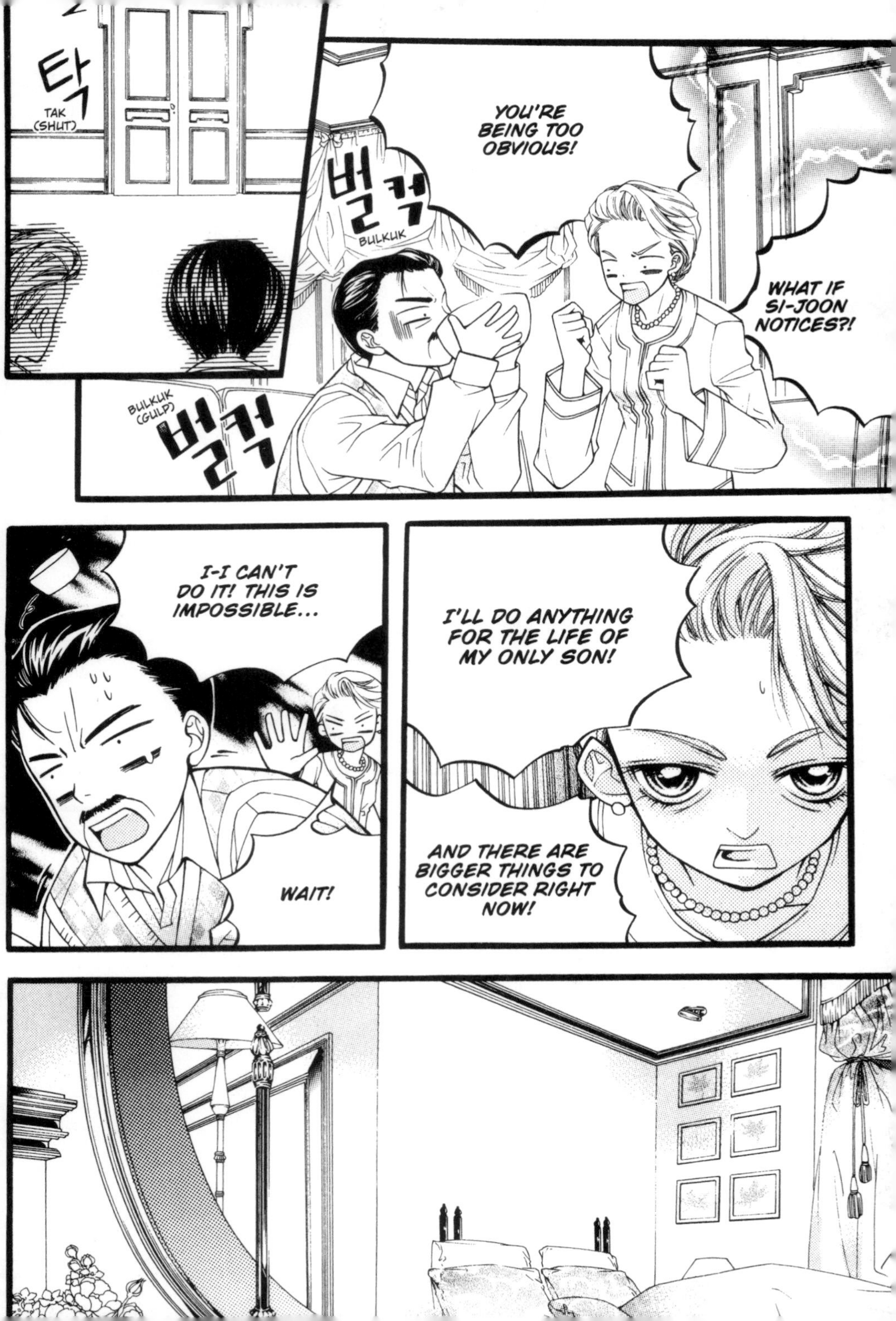
탁
TAK (SHUT)
벌컥
BULKUK
YOU'RE BEING TOO OBVIOUS!
WHAT IF SI-JOON NOTICES?!
BULKUK (GULP)
벌컥
I-I CAN'T DO IT! THIS IS IMPOSSIBLE...
WAIT!
I'LL DO ANYTHING FOR THE LIFE OF MY ONLY SON!
AND THERE ARE BIGGER THINGS TO CONSIDER RIGHT NOW!

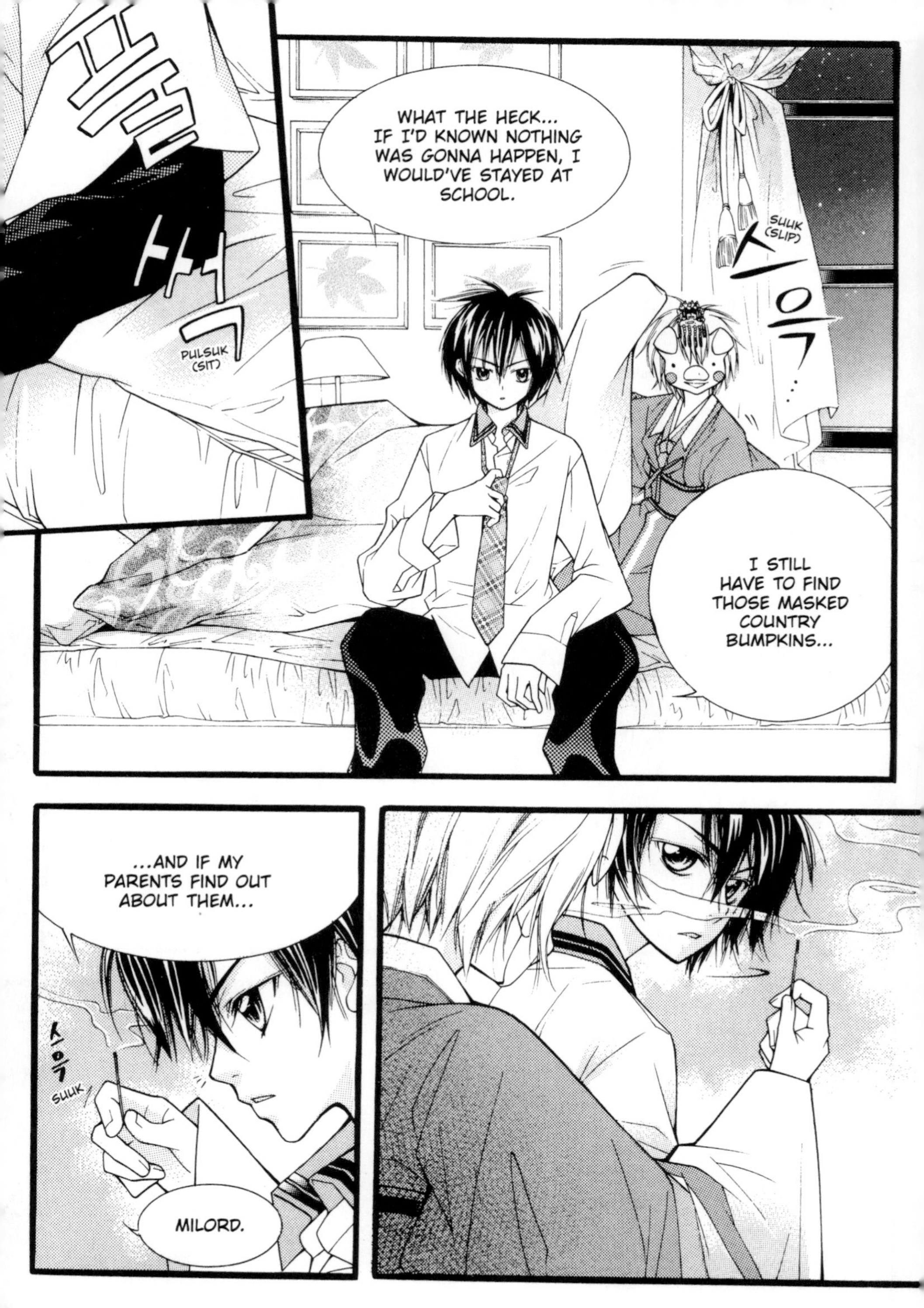
PULSUK (SIT)
WHAT THE HECK... IF I'D KNOWN NOTHING WAS GONNA HAPPEN, I WOULD'VE STAYED AT SCHOOL.
SUUK (SLIP)
I STILL HAVE TO FIND THOSE MASKED COUNTRY BUMPKINS...
...AND IF MY PARENTS FIND OUT ABOUT THEM...
SUUK
MILORD.

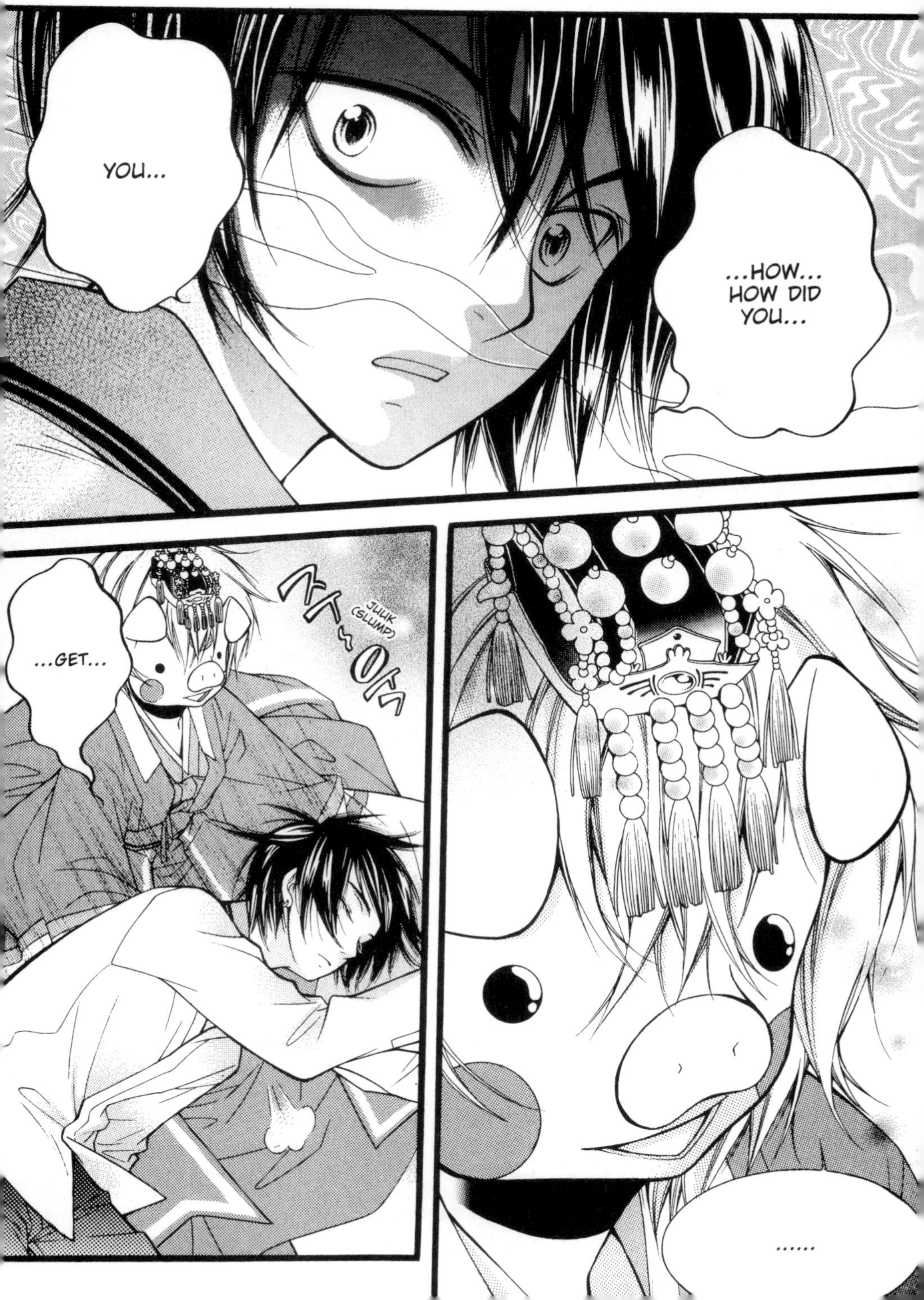
...HOW... HOW DID YOU...
YOU...
JUUK (SLUMP)
...GET...
......

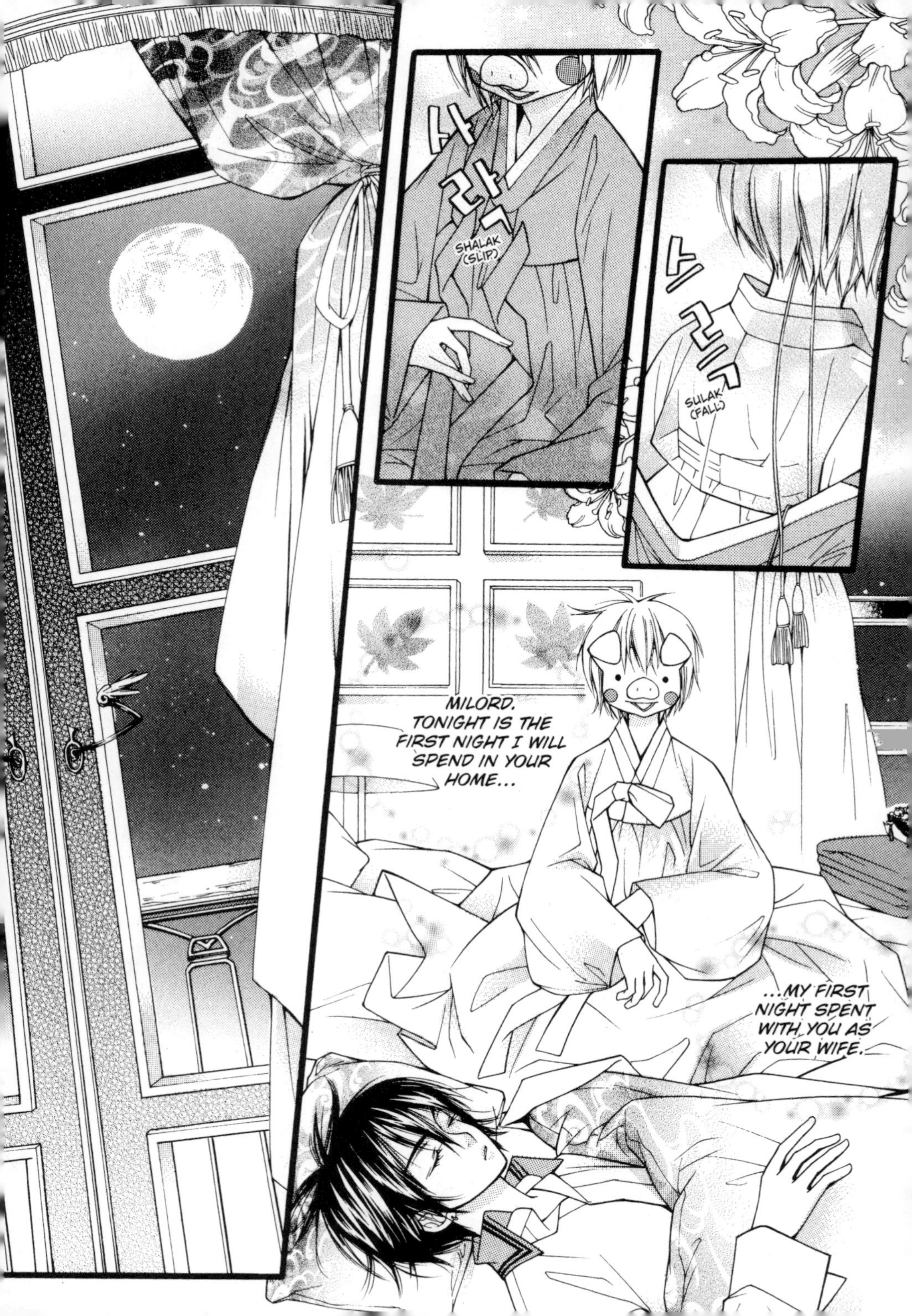
사락
SHALAK (SLIP)
스르륵
SULAK (FALL)
MILORD. TONIGHT IS THE FIRST NIGHT I WILL SPEND IN YOUR HOME...
...MY FIRST NIGHT SPENT WITH YOU AS YOUR WIFE.

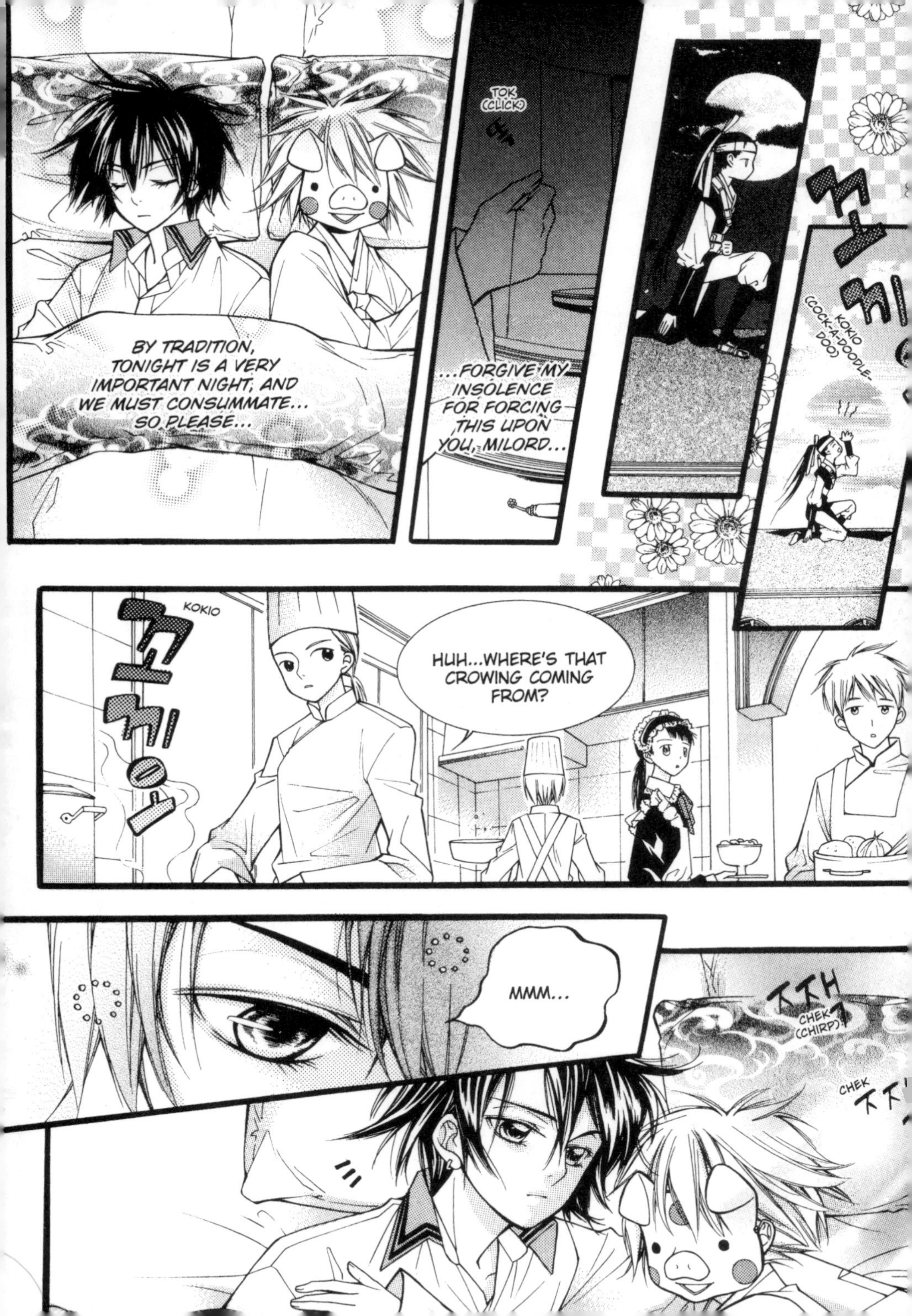
BY TRADITION, TONIGHT IS A VERY IMPORTANT NIGHT, AND WE MUST CONSUMMATE... SO PLEASE...
TOK (CLICK)
...FORGIVE MY INSOLENCE FOR FORCING THIS UPON YOU, MILORD...
KOKIO (COCK-A-DOODLE-DOO)
KOKIO
HUH...WHERE'S THAT CROWING COMING FROM?
MMM...
CHEK (CHIRP)
CHEK

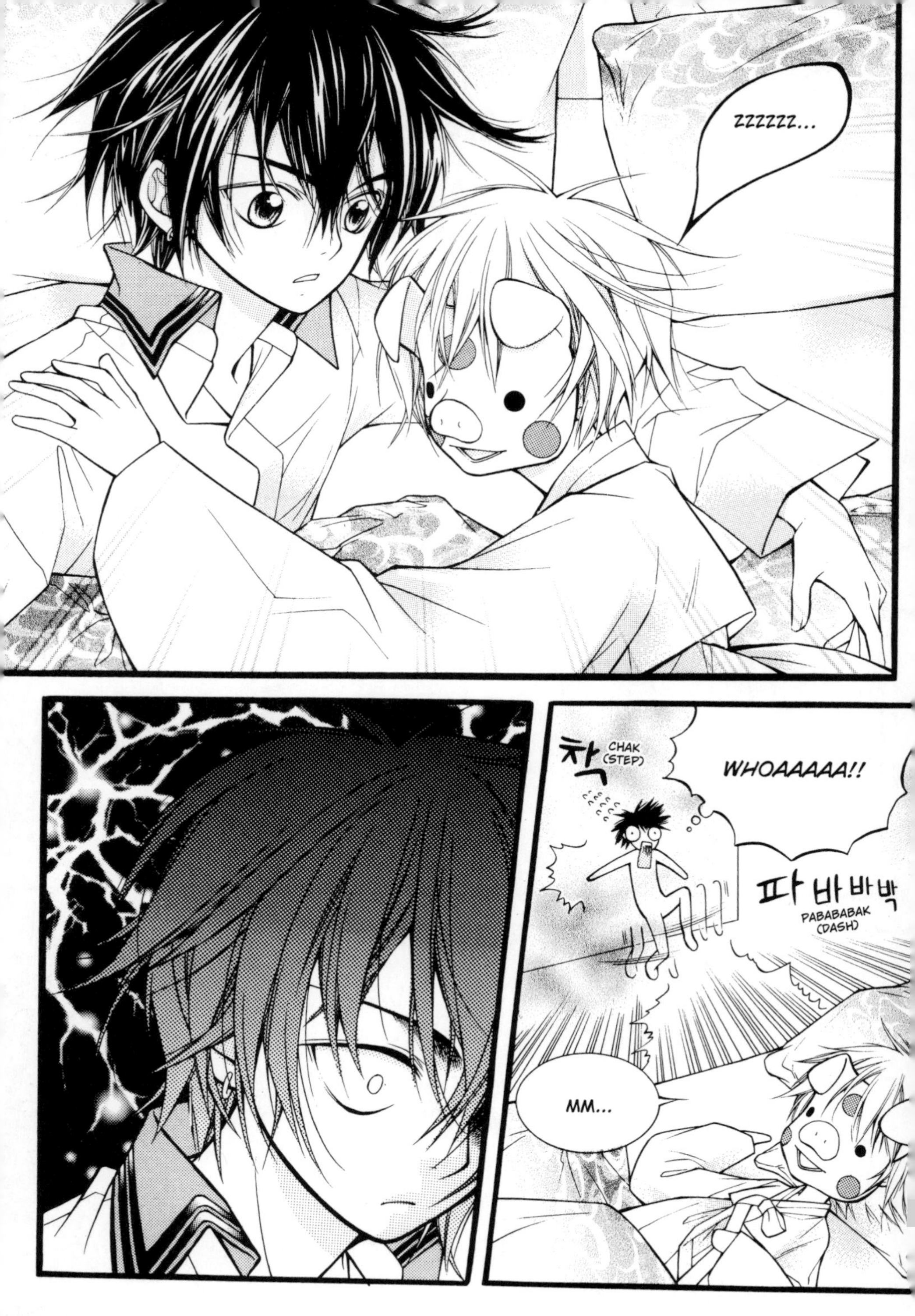
ZZZZZZ...
착
CHAK (STEP)
WHOAAAAA!!
파바바박
PABABABAK (DASH)
MM...

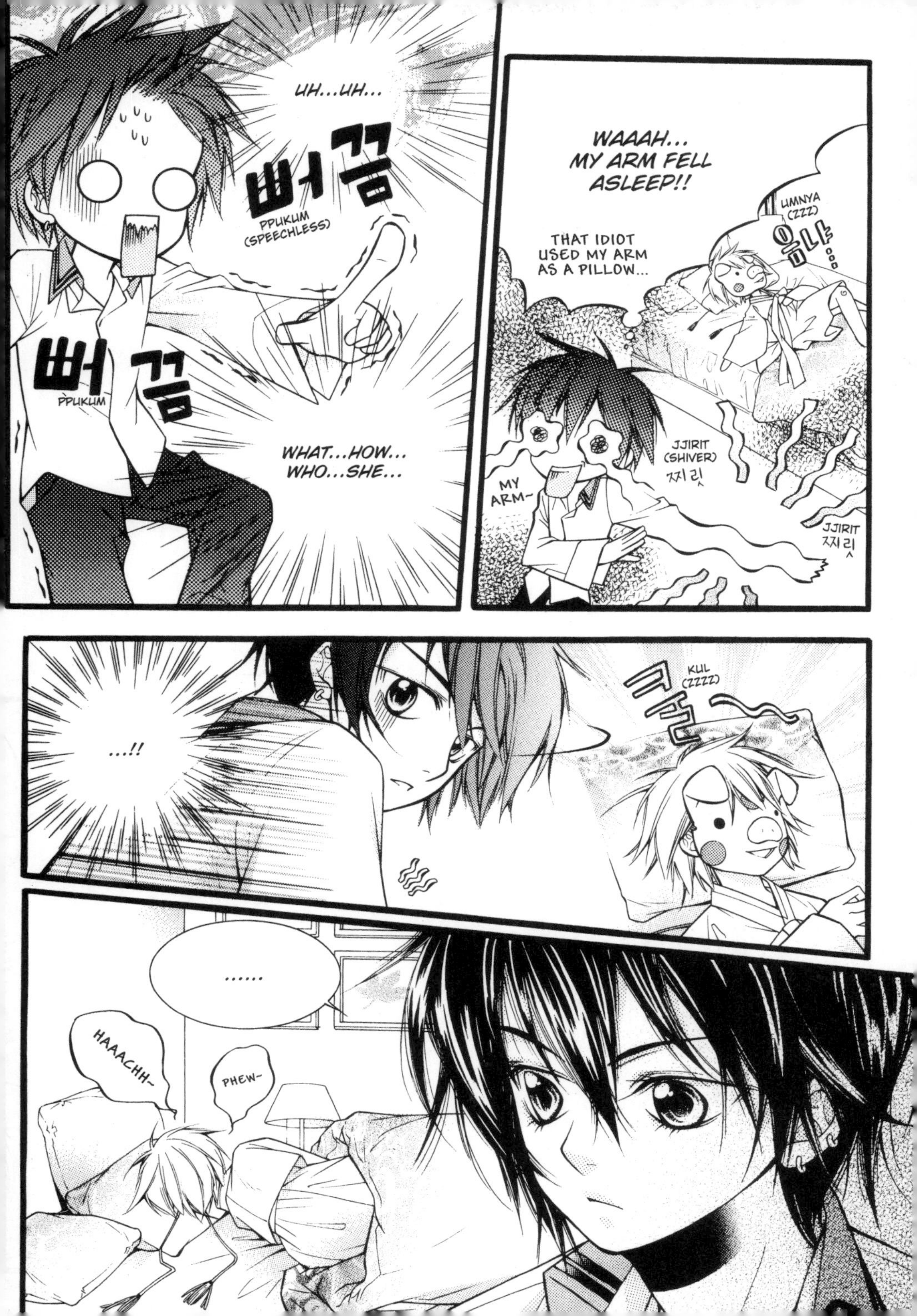

UH...UH...
뻐끔
PPUKUM (SPEECHLESS)
뻐끔
PPUKUM
WHAT...HOW... WHO...SHE...
WAAAH... MY ARM FELL ASLEEP!!
THAT IDIOT USED MY ARM AS A PILLOW...
UMNYA (ZZZ)
음냐...
MY ARM~
JJIRIT (SHIVER)
찌릿
JJIRIT
찌릿
...!!
KUL (ZZZZ)
......
HAAACHH~
PHEW~

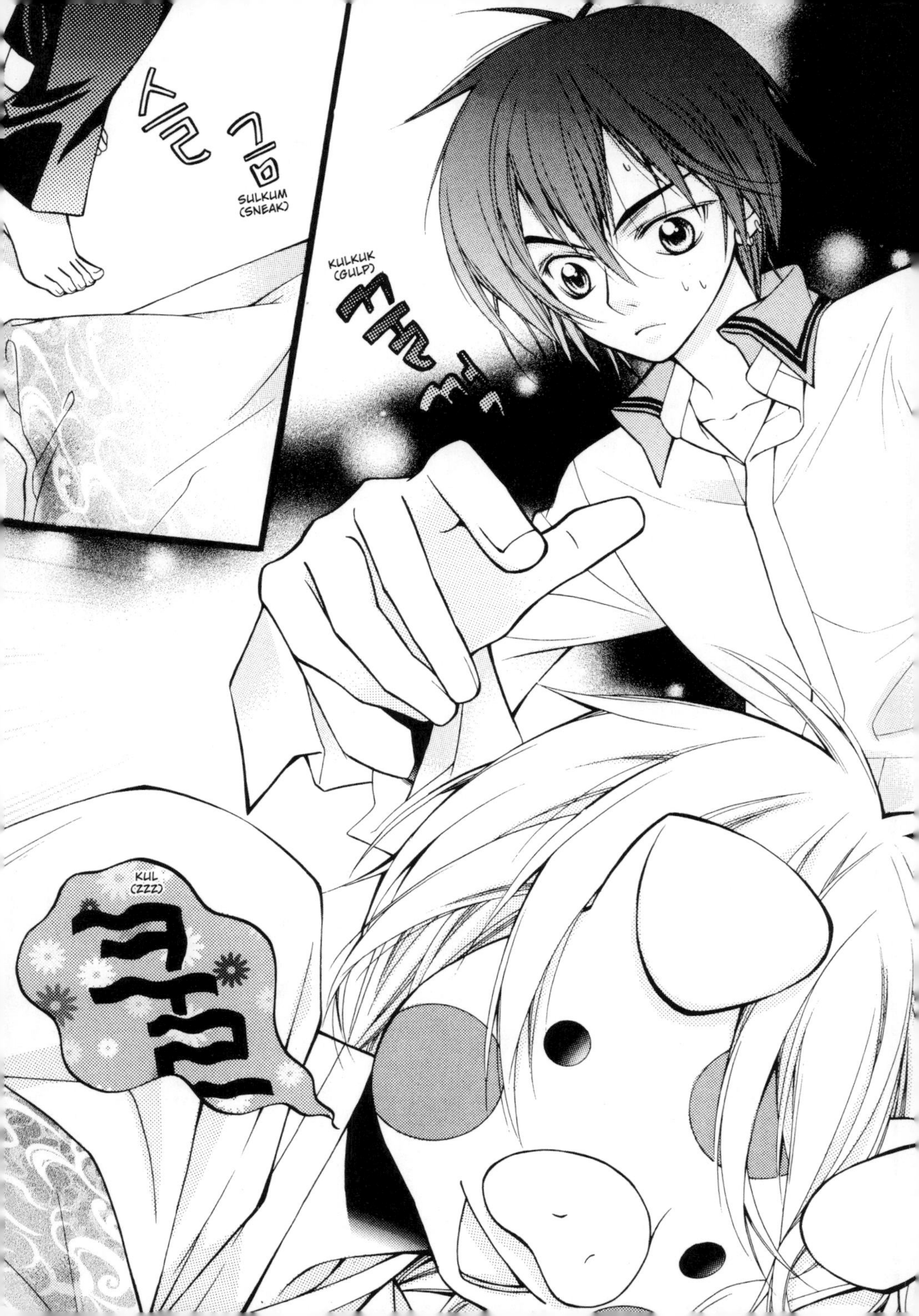
SULKUM
(SNEAK)
KULKUK
(GULP)
KUL
(ZZZ)

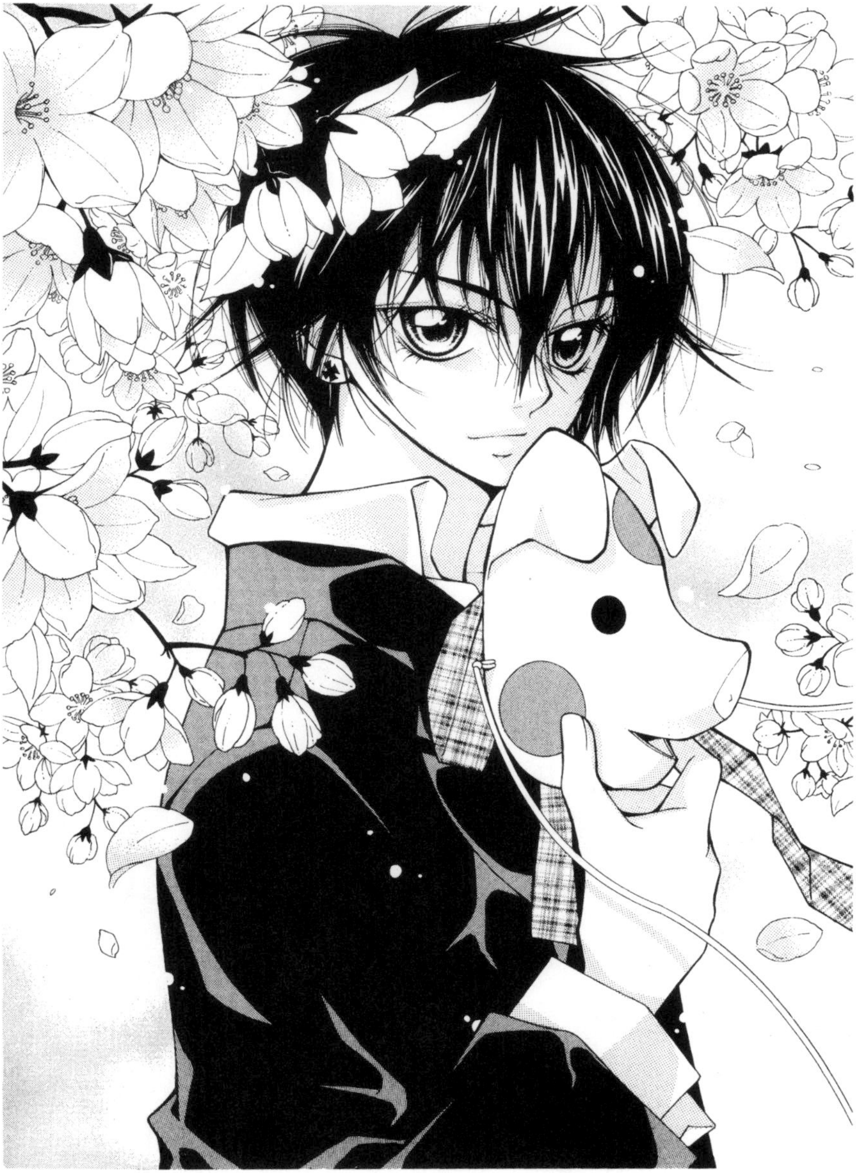

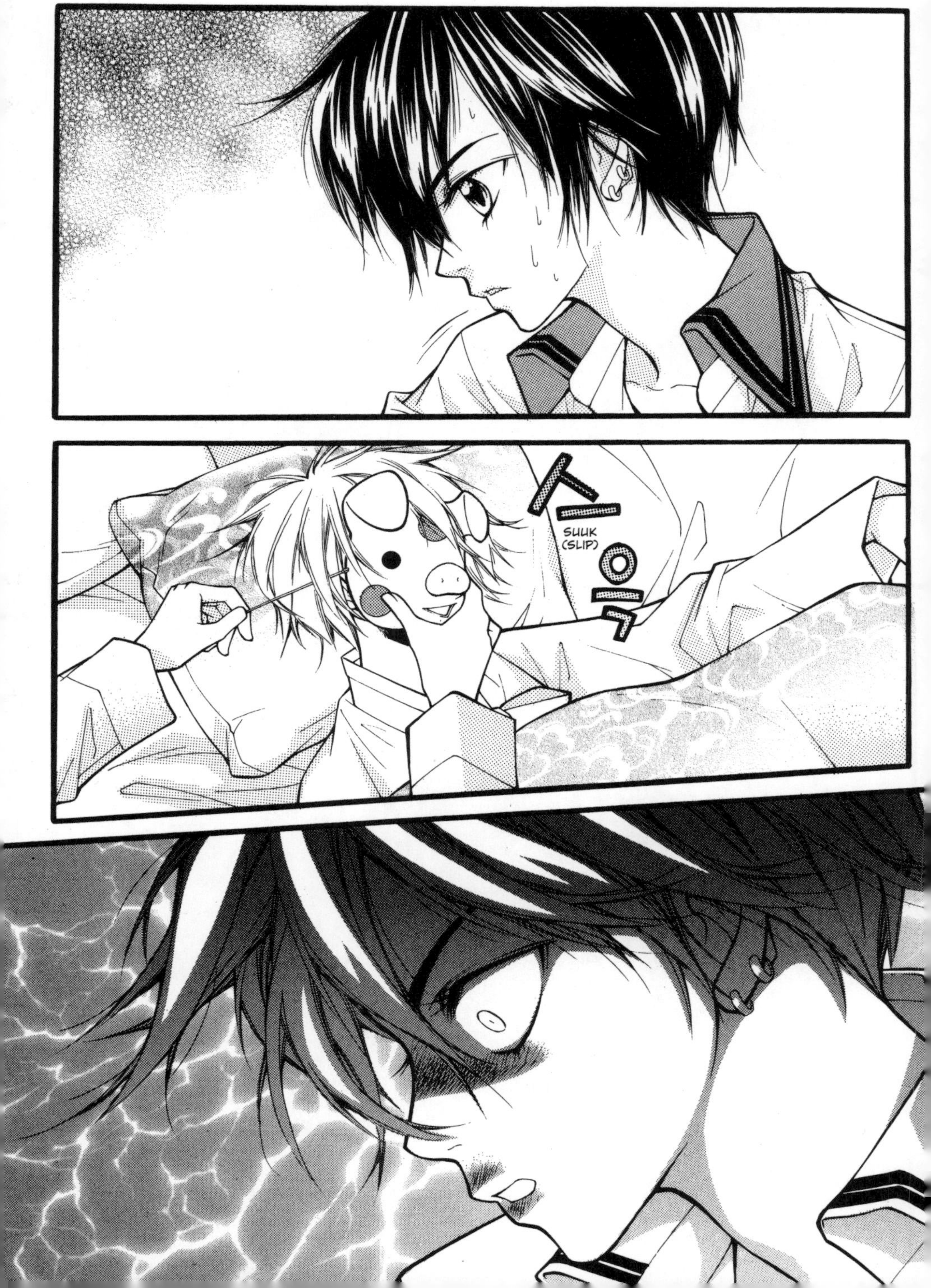
SUUK
(SLIP)

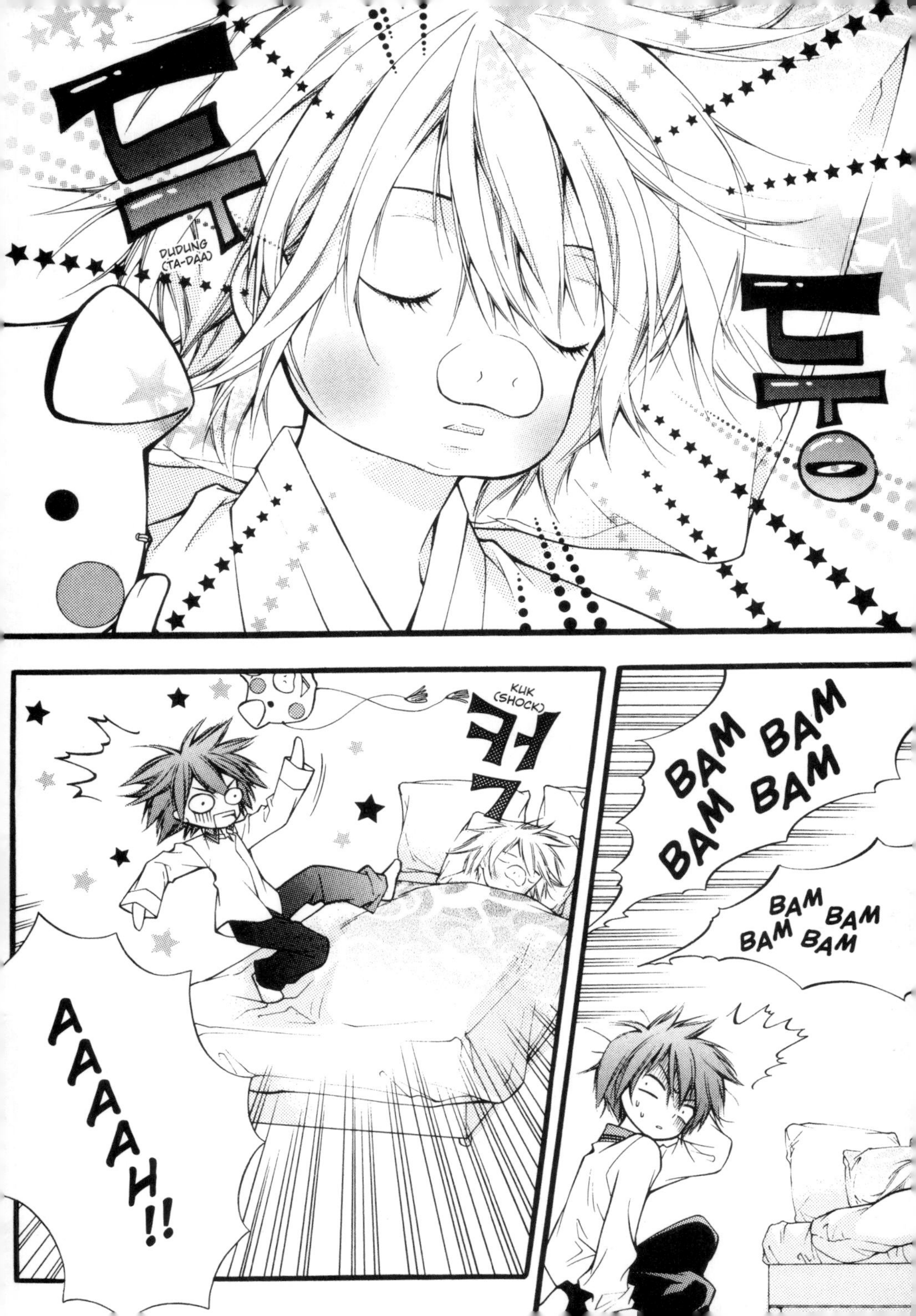
DUDUNG (TA-DAA)
BAM BAM BAM BAM
BAM BAM BAM BAM
KUK (SHOCK)
AAAAH!!

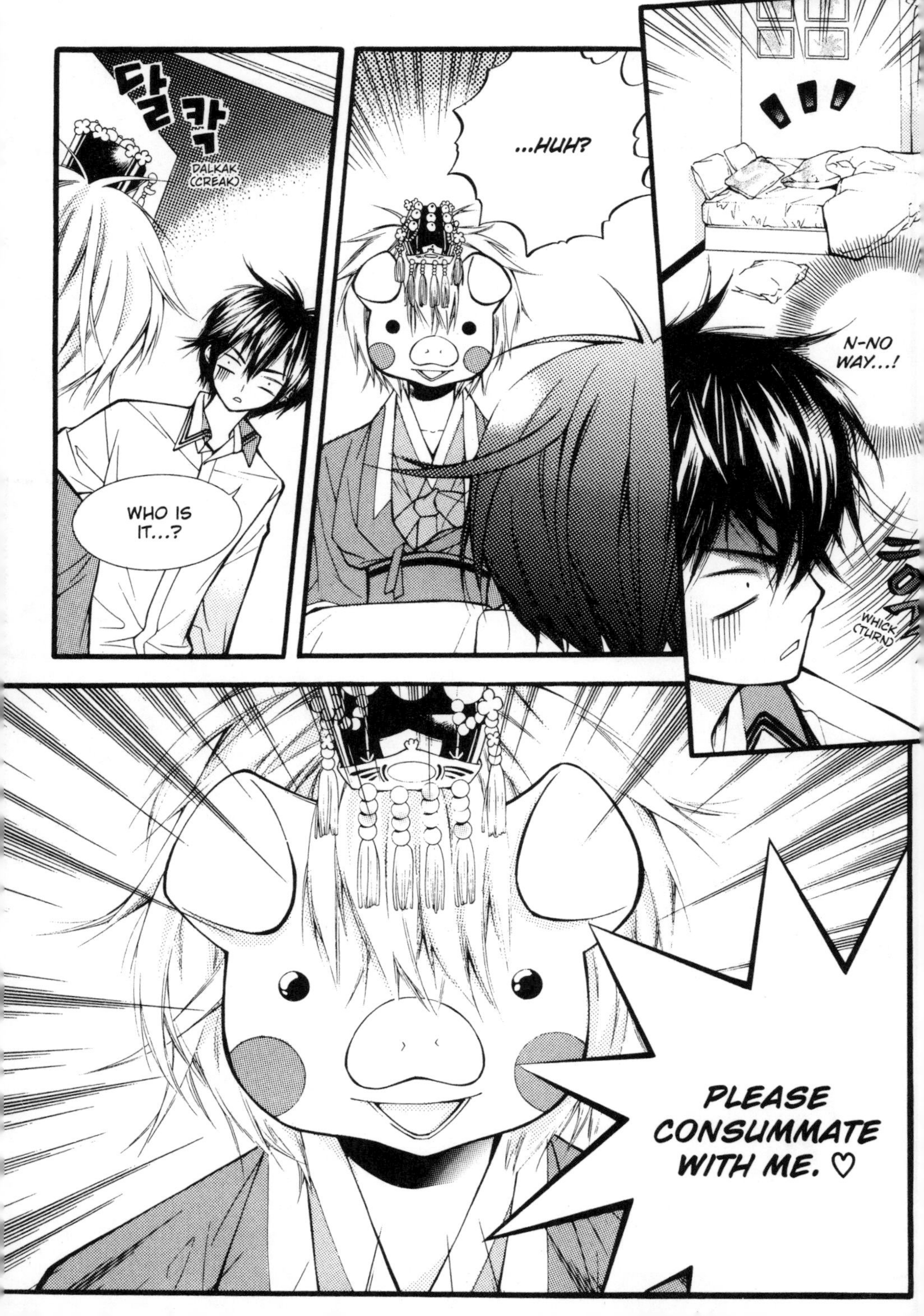
달칵
DALKAK (CREAK)
WHO IS IT...?
...HUH?
N-NO WAY...!
WHICK (TURN)
PLEASE CONSUMMATE WITH ME. ♡

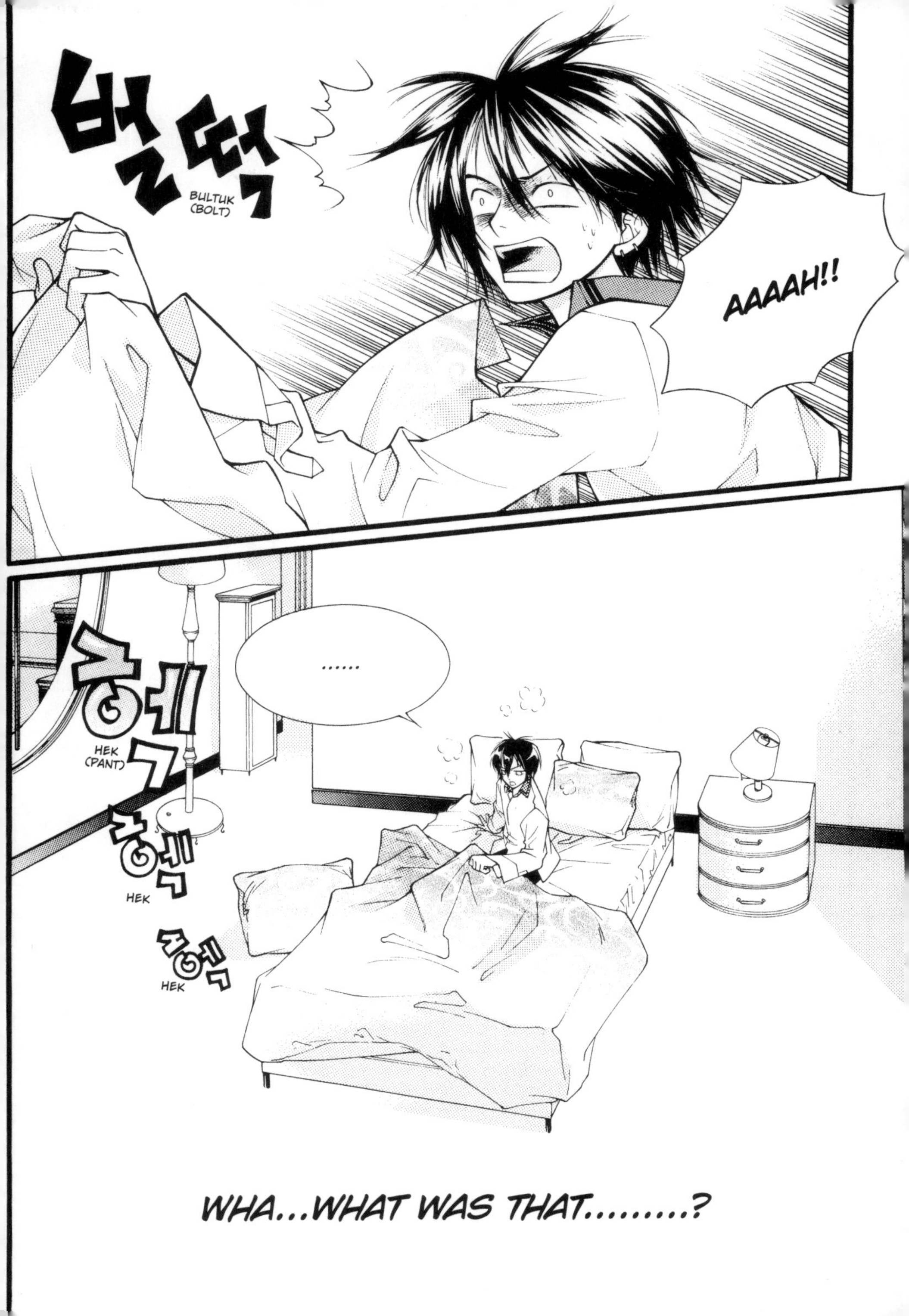
벌떡
BULTUK (BOLT)
AAAAH!!
헤
HEK (PANT)
헥
HEK
헥
HEK
......
WHA...WHAT WAS THAT........?

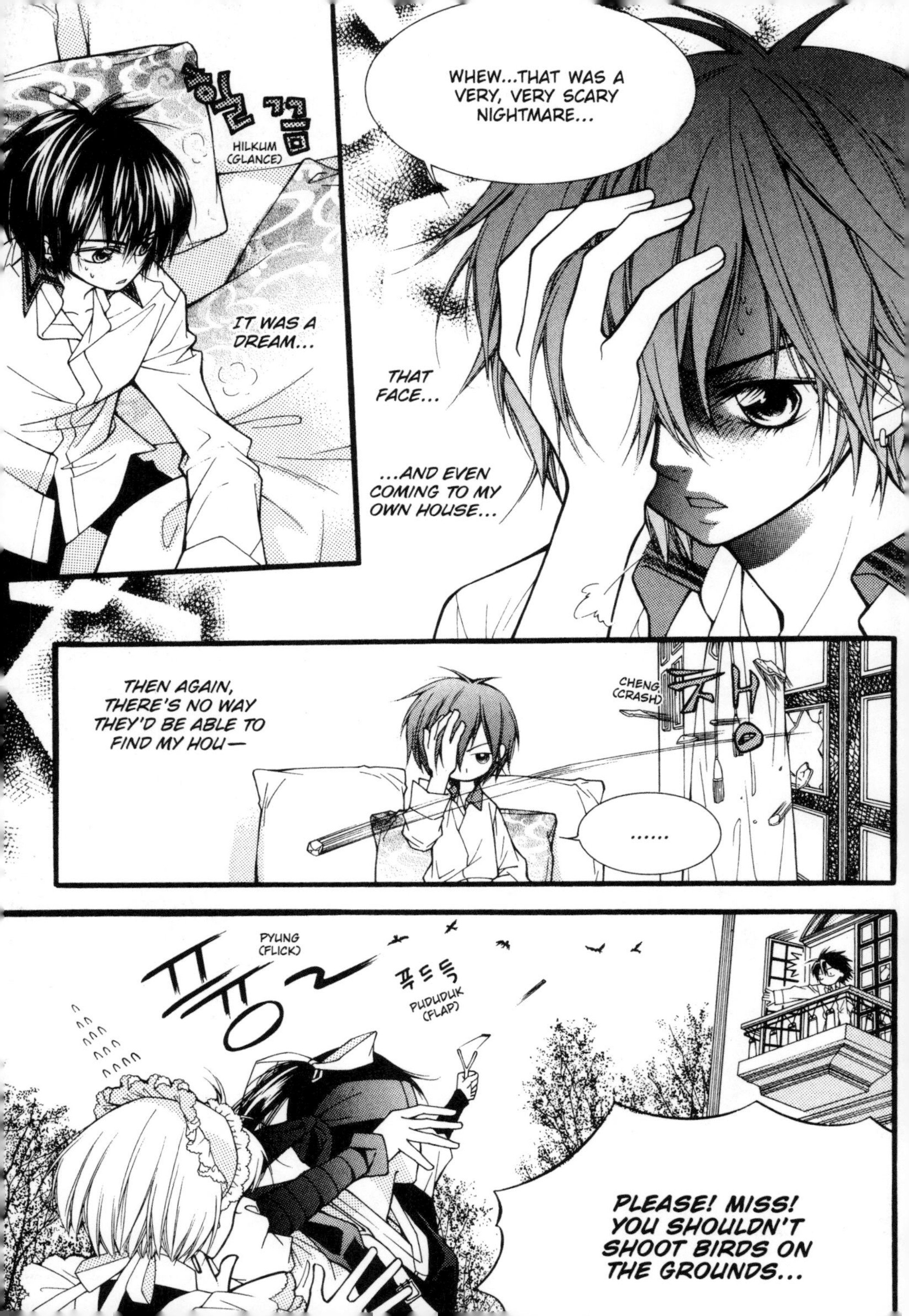

HILKUM (GLANCE)
IT WAS A DREAM...
WHEW...THAT WAS A VERY, VERY SCARY NIGHTMARE...
THAT FACE...
...AND EVEN COMING TO MY OWN HOUSE...
THEN AGAIN, THERE'S NO WAY THEY'D BE ABLE TO FIND MY HOU—
CHENG (CRASH)
......
PYUNG (FLICK)
푸드득
PUDUDUK (FLAP)
PLEASE! MISS! YOU SHOULDN'T SHOOT BIRDS ON THE GROUNDS...

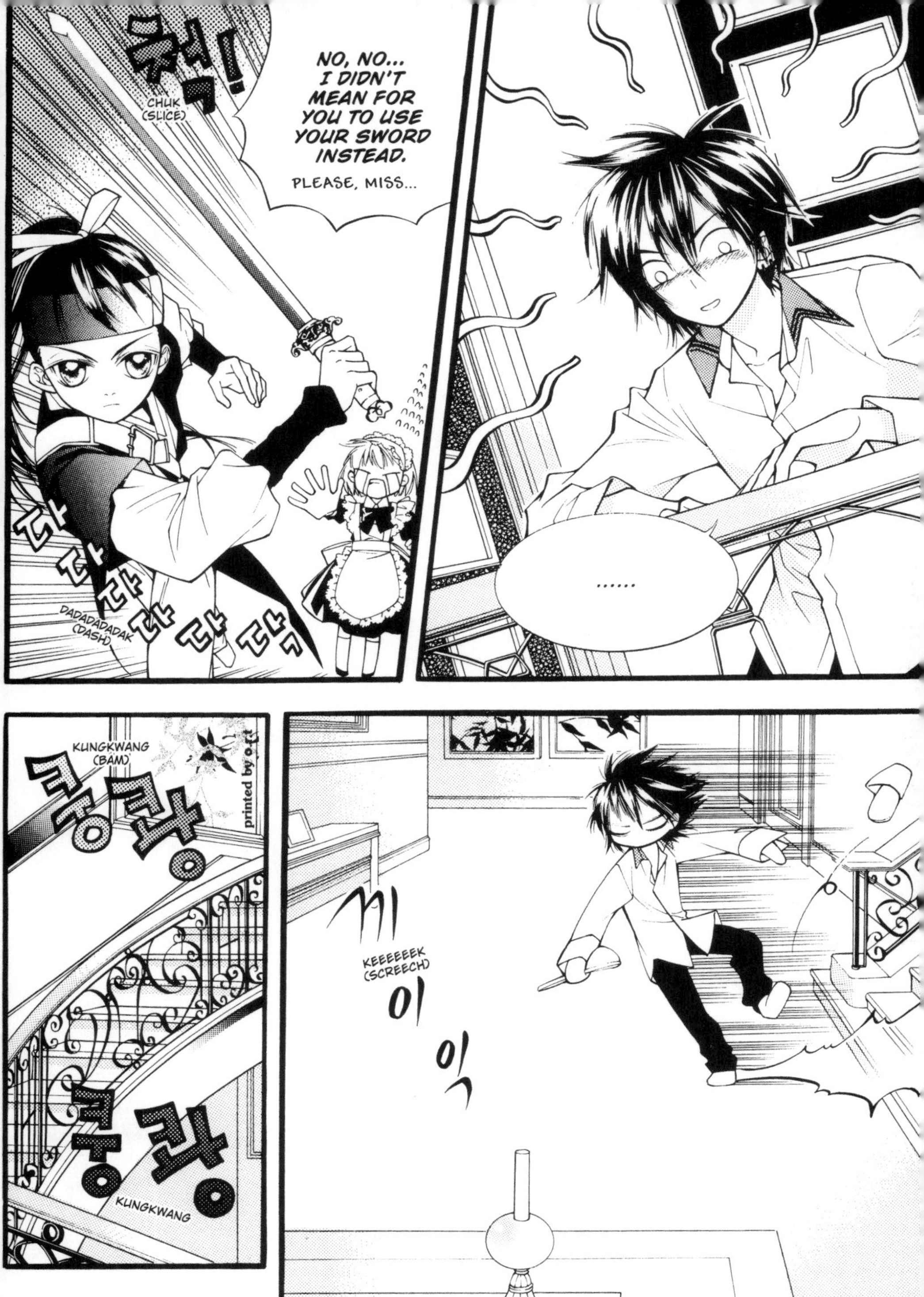
척!
CHUK (SLICE)
NO, NO... I DIDN'T MEAN FOR YOU TO USE YOUR SWORD INSTEAD.
PLEASE, MISS...
DADADADADAK (DASH)
......
KUNGKWANG (BAM)
KUNGKWANG
KEEEEEEK (SCREECH)

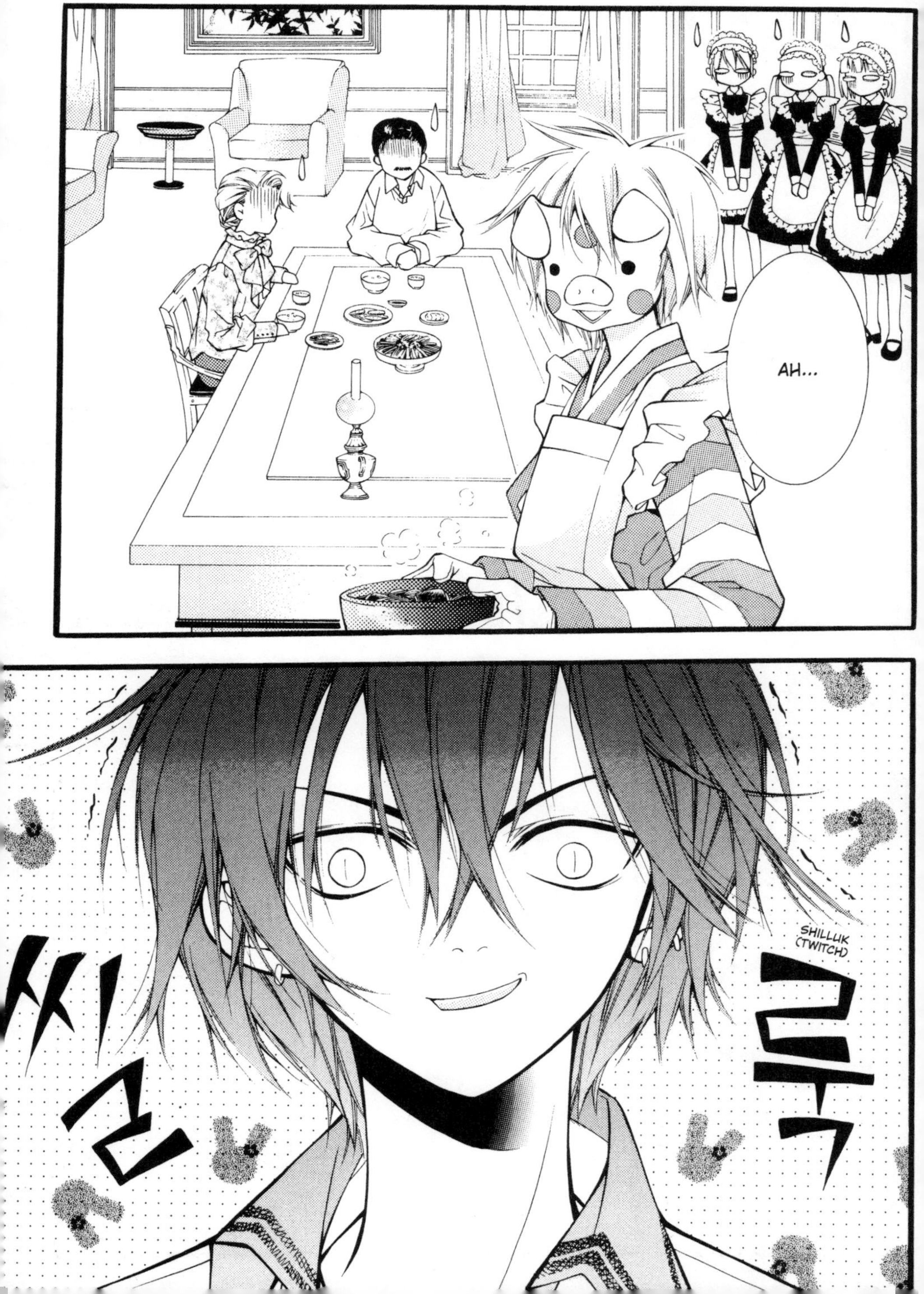
AH...
SHILLUK
(TWITCH)

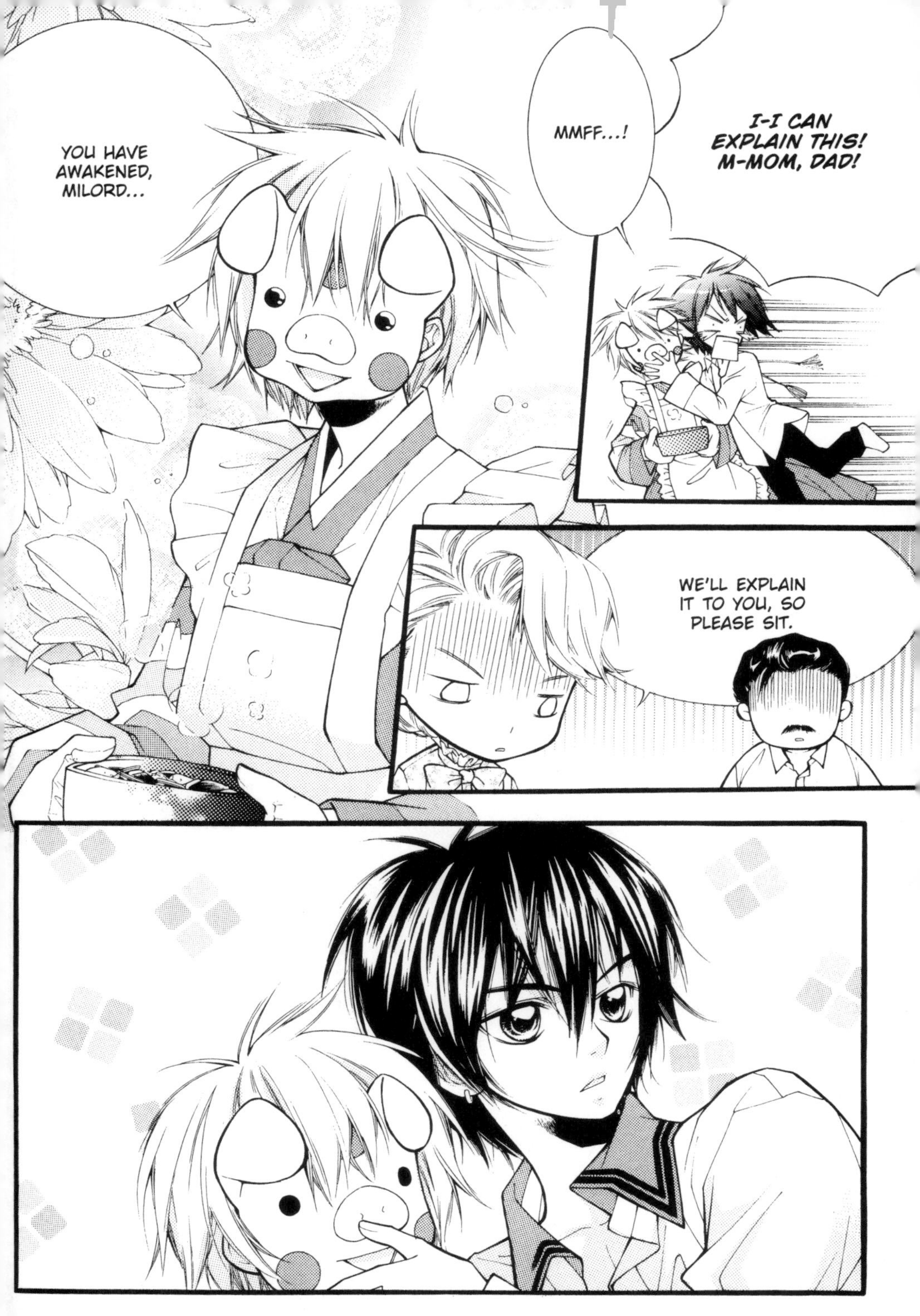

YOU HAVE AWAKENED, MILORD...
I-I CAN EXPLAIN THIS! M-MOM, DAD!
MMFF...!
WE'LL EXPLAIN IT TO YOU, SO PLEASE SIT.

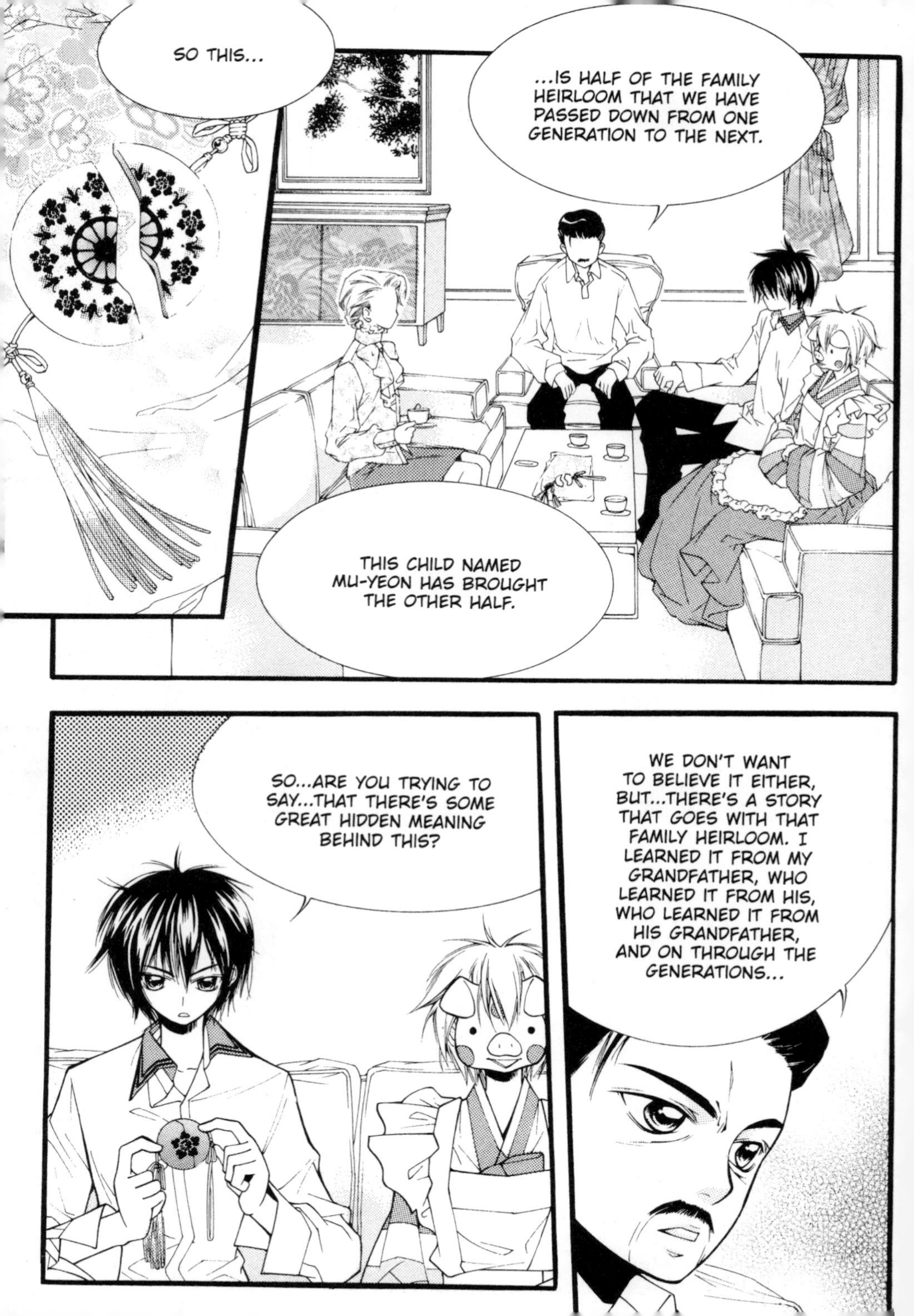
SO THIS...
...IS HALF OF THE FAMILY HEIRLOOM THAT WE HAVE PASSED DOWN FROM ONE GENERATION TO THE NEXT.
THIS CHILD NAMED MU-YEON HAS BROUGHT THE OTHER HALF.
SO...ARE YOU TRYING TO SAY...THAT THERE'S SOME GREAT HIDDEN MEANING BEHIND THIS?
WE DON'T WANT TO BELIEVE IT EITHER, BUT...THERE'S A STORY THAT GOES WITH THAT FAMILY HEIRLOOM. I LEARNED IT FROM MY GRANDFATHER, WHO LEARNED IT FROM HIS, WHO LEARNED IT FROM HIS GRANDFATHER, AND ON THROUGH THE GENERATIONS...

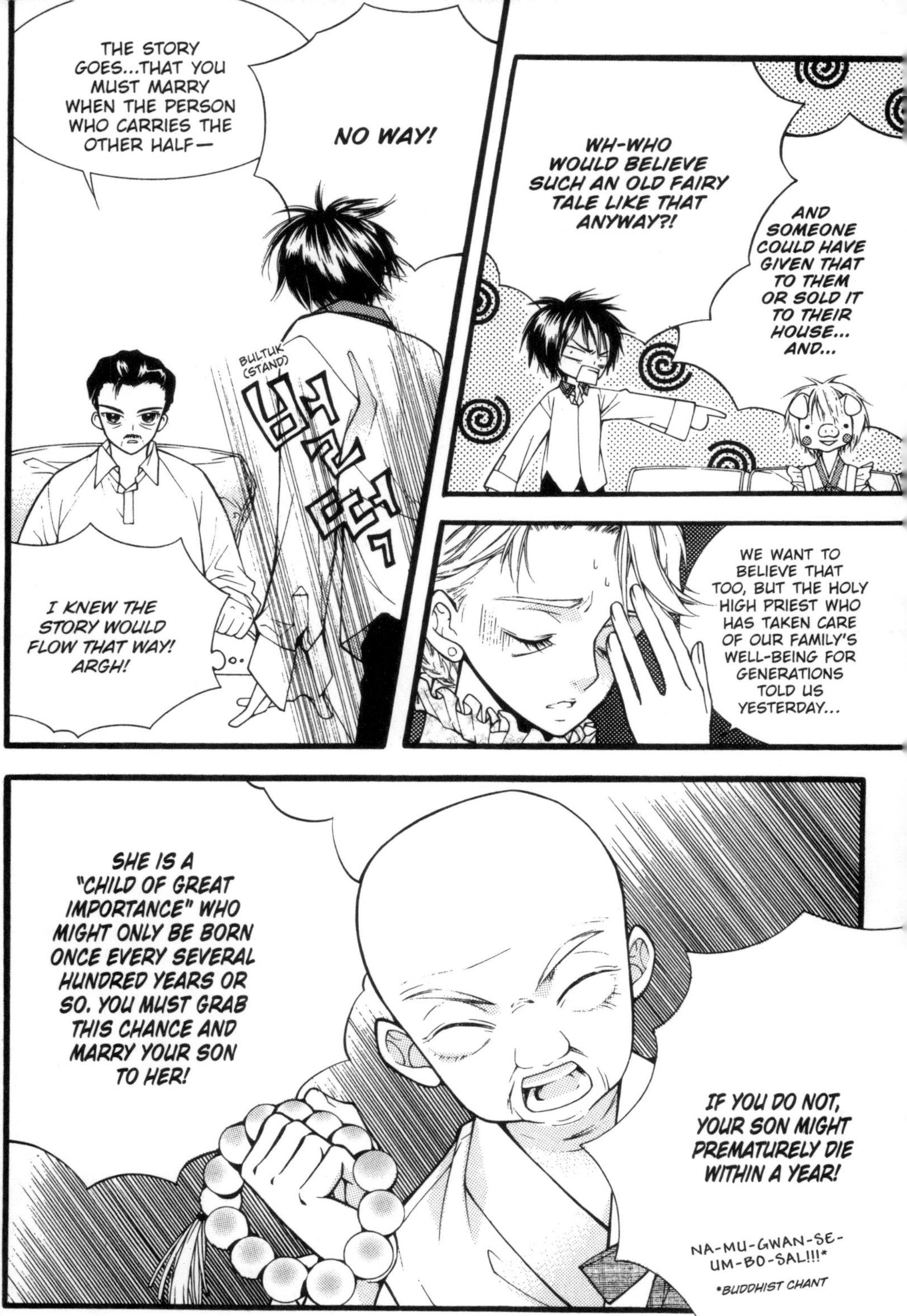
THE STORY GOES...THAT YOU MUST MARRY WHEN THE PERSON WHO CARRIES THE OTHER HALF—
NO WAY!
BULTUK (STAND)
I KNEW THE STORY WOULD FLOW THAT WAY! ARGH!
WH-WHO WOULD BELIEVE SUCH AN OLD FAIRY TALE LIKE THAT ANYWAY?!
AND SOMEONE COULD HAVE GIVEN THAT TO THEM OR SOLD IT TO THEIR HOUSE... AND...
WE WANT TO BELIEVE THAT TOO, BUT THE HOLY HIGH PRIEST WHO HAS TAKEN CARE OF OUR FAMILY'S WELL-BEING FOR GENERATIONS TOLD US YESTERDAY...
SHE IS A "CHILD OF GREAT IMPORTANCE" WHO MIGHT ONLY BE BORN ONCE EVERY SEVERAL HUNDRED YEARS OR SO. YOU MUST GRAB THIS CHANCE AND MARRY YOUR SON TO HER!
IF YOU DO NOT, YOUR SON MIGHT PREMATURELY DIE WITHIN A YEAR!
NA-MU-GWAN-SE-UM-BO-SAL!!!*
*BUDDHIST CHANT

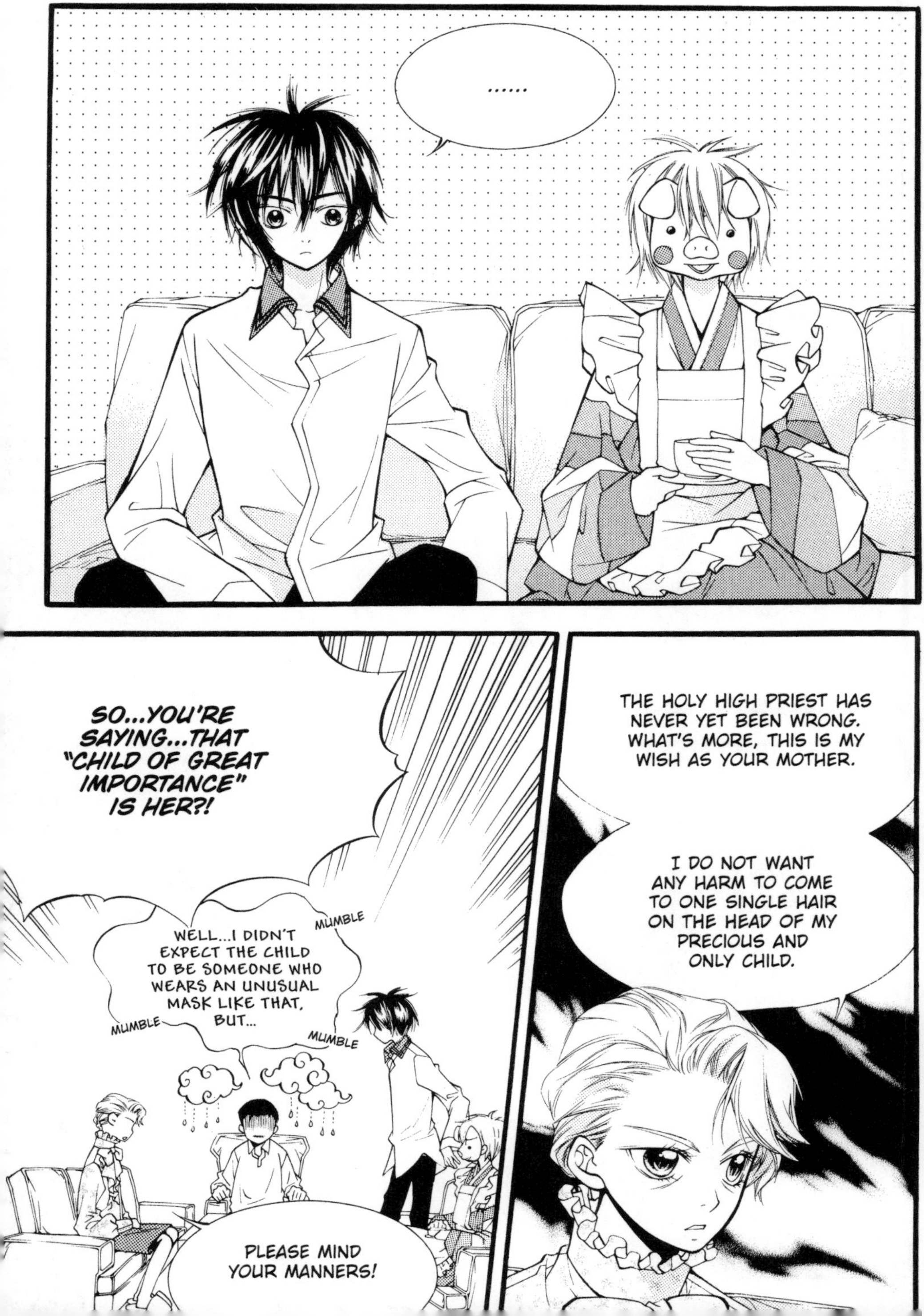
......
THE HOLY HIGH PRIEST HAS NEVER YET BEEN WRONG. WHAT'S MORE, THIS IS MY WISH AS YOUR MOTHER.
I DO NOT WANT ANY HARM TO COME TO ONE SINGLE HAIR ON THE HEAD OF MY PRECIOUS AND ONLY CHILD.
SO...YOU'RE SAYING...THAT "CHILD OF GREAT IMPORTANCE" IS HER?!
WELL...I DIDN'T EXPECT THE CHILD TO BE SOMEONE WHO WEARS AN UNUSUAL MASK LIKE THAT, BUT...
MUMBLE
MUMBLE
MUMBLE
PLEASE MIND YOUR MANNERS!

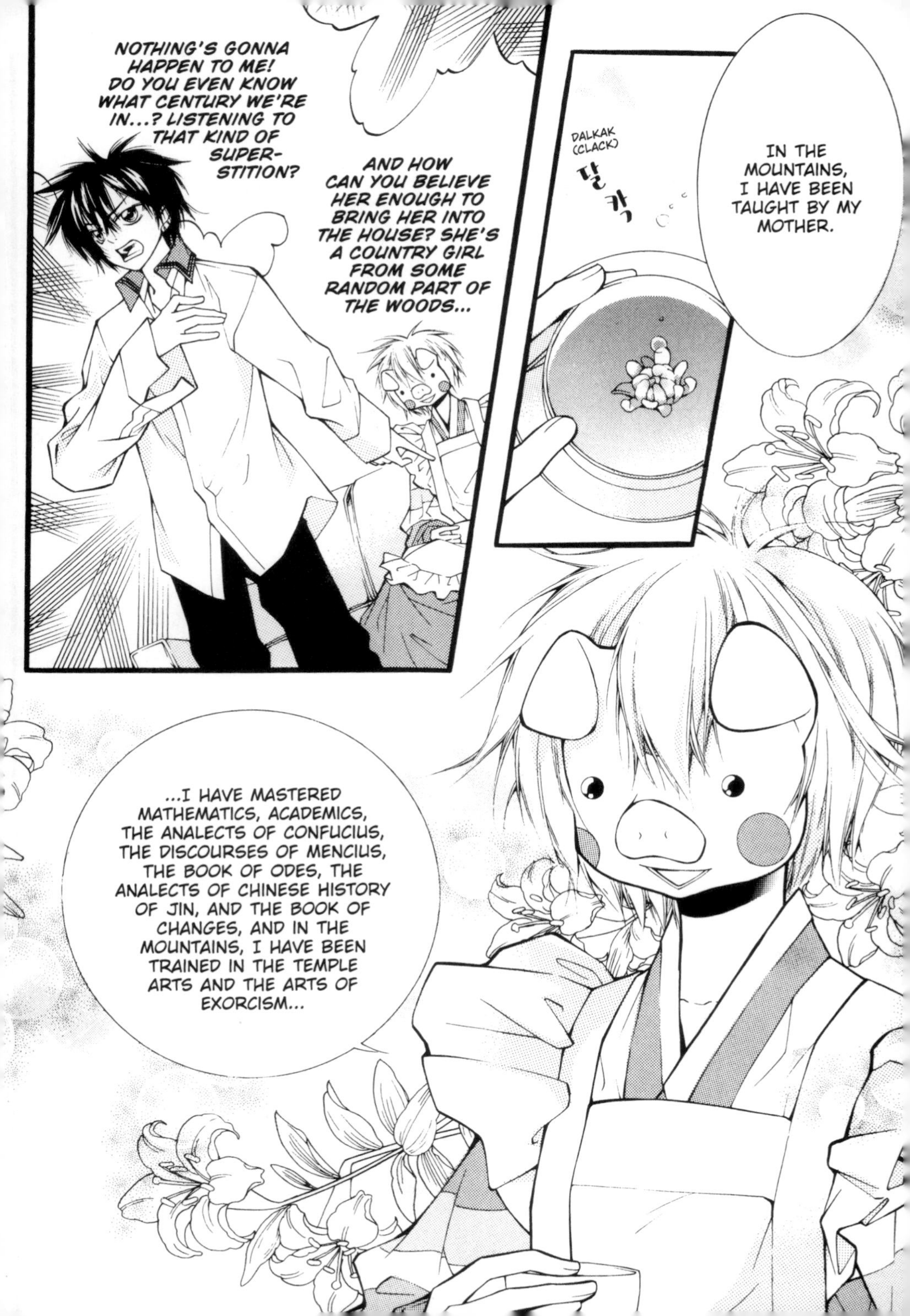
NOTHING'S GONNA HAPPEN TO ME! DO YOU EVEN KNOW WHAT CENTURY WE'RE IN...? LISTENING TO THAT KIND OF SUPER-STITION?
AND HOW CAN YOU BELIEVE HER ENOUGH TO BRING HER INTO THE HOUSE? SHE'S A COUNTRY GIRL FROM SOME RANDOM PART OF THE WOODS...
DALKAK (CLACK)
달칵
IN THE MOUNTAINS, I HAVE BEEN TAUGHT BY MY MOTHER.
...I HAVE MASTERED MATHEMATICS, ACADEMICS, THE ANALECTS OF CONFUCIUS, THE DISCOURSES OF MENCIUS, THE BOOK OF ODES, THE ANALECTS OF CHINESE HISTORY OF JIN, AND THE BOOK OF CHANGES, AND IN THE MOUNTAINS, I HAVE BEEN TRAINED IN THE TEMPLE ARTS AND THE ARTS OF EXORCISM...

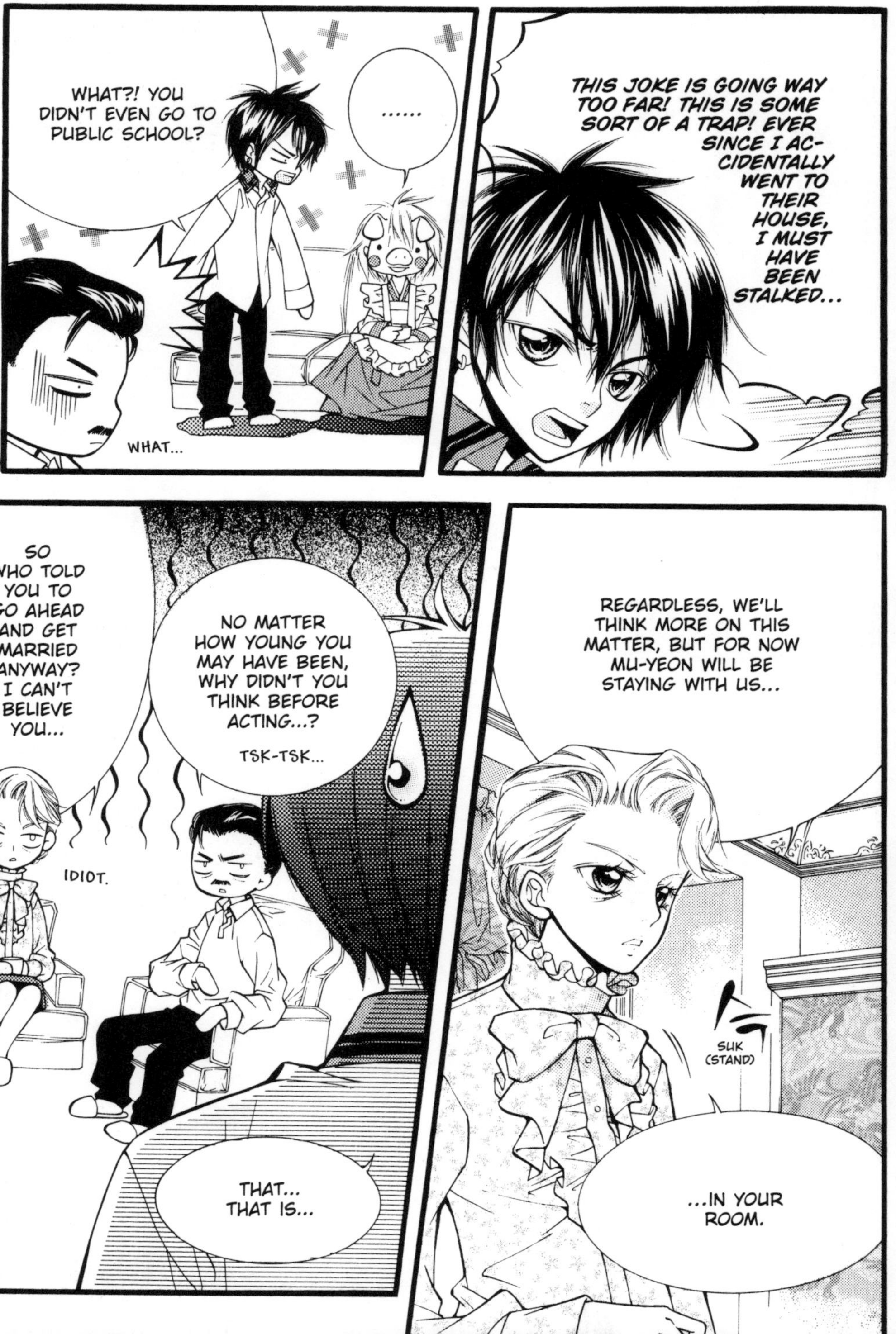
WHAT?! YOU DIDN'T EVEN GO TO PUBLIC SCHOOL?
......
WHAT...
THIS JOKE IS GOING WAY TOO FAR! THIS IS SOME SORT OF A TRAP! EVER SINCE I AC-CIDENTALLY WENT TO THEIR HOUSE, I MUST HAVE BEEN STALKED...
SO WHO TOLD YOU TO GO AHEAD AND GET MARRIED ANYWAY? I CAN'T BELIEVE YOU...
NO MATTER HOW YOUNG YOU MAY HAVE BEEN, WHY DIDN'T YOU THINK BEFORE ACTING...?
TSK-TSK...
IDIOT.
THAT... THAT IS...
REGARDLESS, WE'LL THINK MORE ON THIS MATTER, BUT FOR NOW MU-YEON WILL BE STAYING WITH US...
SUK (STAND)
...IN YOUR ROOM.

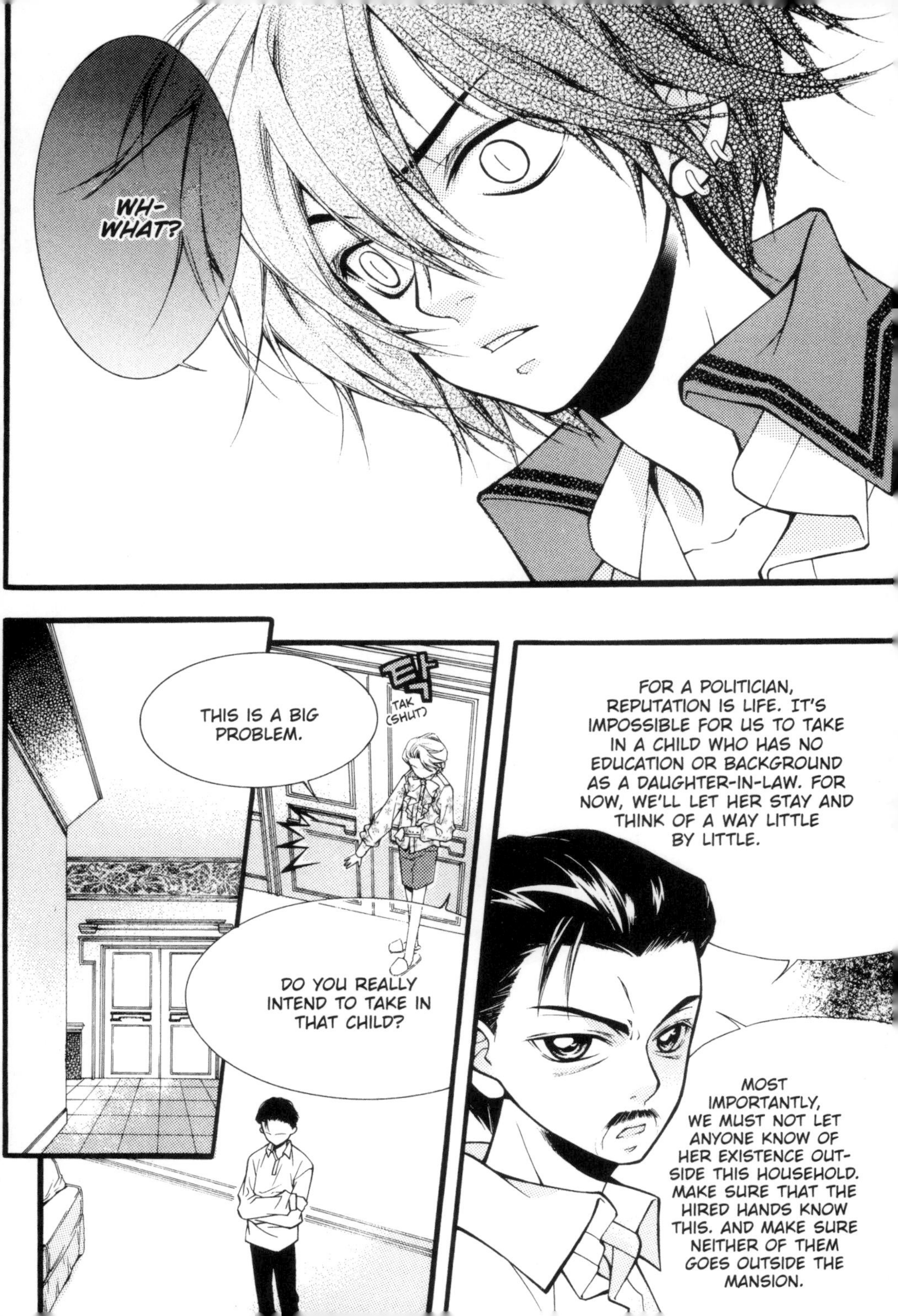
WH- WHAT?
THIS IS A BIG PROBLEM.
탁
TAK (SHUT)
DO YOU REALLY INTEND TO TAKE IN THAT CHILD?
FOR A POLITICIAN, REPUTATION IS LIFE. IT'S IMPOSSIBLE FOR US TO TAKE IN A CHILD WHO HAS NO EDUCATION OR BACKGROUND AS A DAUGHTER-IN-LAW. FOR NOW, WE'LL LET HER STAY AND THINK OF A WAY LITTLE BY LITTLE.
MOST IMPORTANTLY, WE MUST NOT LET ANYONE KNOW OF HER EXISTENCE OUTSIDE THIS HOUSEHOLD. MAKE SURE THAT THE HIRED HANDS KNOW THIS. AND MAKE SURE NEITHER OF THEM GOES OUTSIDE THE MANSION.

I UNDERSTAND.

I'LL KEEP A CLOSE WATCH ON THEM.

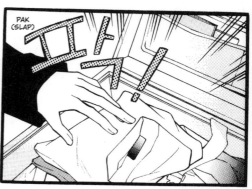

PAK (SLAP)

MILORD...WHAT ARE YOU—

DON'T CALL ME "MILORD"!

TAK (SNAP)

CHUK GTURND

I'M OUTTA HERE!

YOU MUSTN'T!

WARAK (GRAB)

WHA—!!

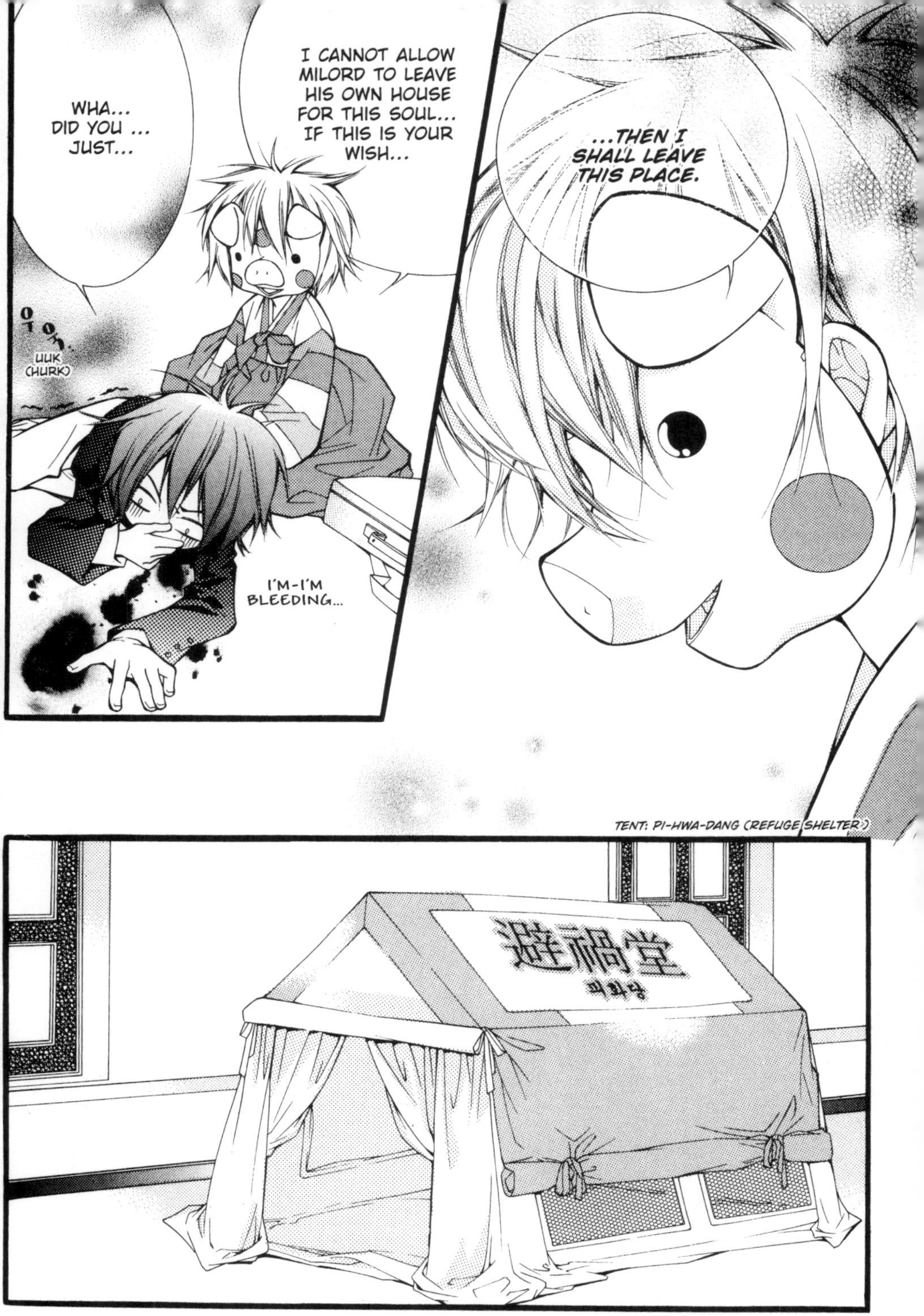
WHA... DID YOU ... JUST...
I CANNOT ALLOW MILORD TO LEAVE HIS OWN HOUSE FOR THIS SOUL... IF THIS IS YOUR WISH...
UUK (HURK)
I'M-I'M BLEEDING...
...THEN I SHALL LEAVE THIS PLACE.
TENT: PI-HWA-DANG (REFUGE SHELTER)
避禍堂
피화당

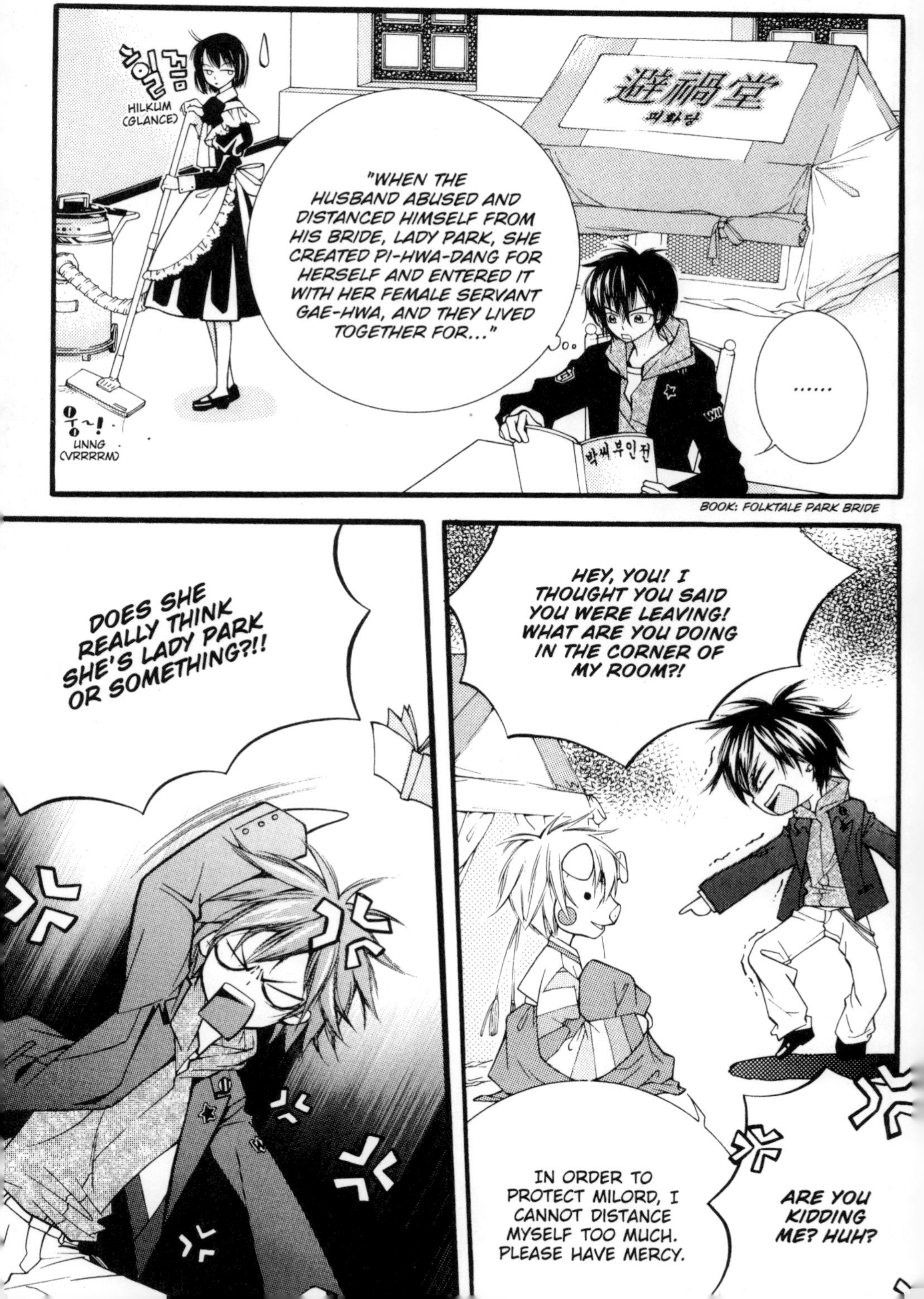
힐끔
HILKUM (GLANCE)
避禍堂
피화당
"WHEN THE HUSBAND ABUSED AND DISTANCED HIMSELF FROM HIS BRIDE, LADY PARK, SHE CREATED PI-HWA-DANG FOR HERSELF AND ENTERED IT WITH HER FEMALE SERVANT GAE-HWA, AND THEY LIVED TOGETHER FOR..."
......
웅~!
UNNG (VRRRRM)
박씨부인전
BOOK: FOLKTALE PARK BRIDE
DOES SHE REALLY THINK SHE'S LADY PARK OR SOMETHING?!!
HEY, YOU! I THOUGHT YOU SAID YOU WERE LEAVING! WHAT ARE YOU DOING IN THE CORNER OF MY ROOM?!
IN ORDER TO PROTECT MILORD, I CANNOT DISTANCE MYSELF TOO MUCH. PLEASE HAVE MERCY.
ARE YOU KIDDING ME? HUH?

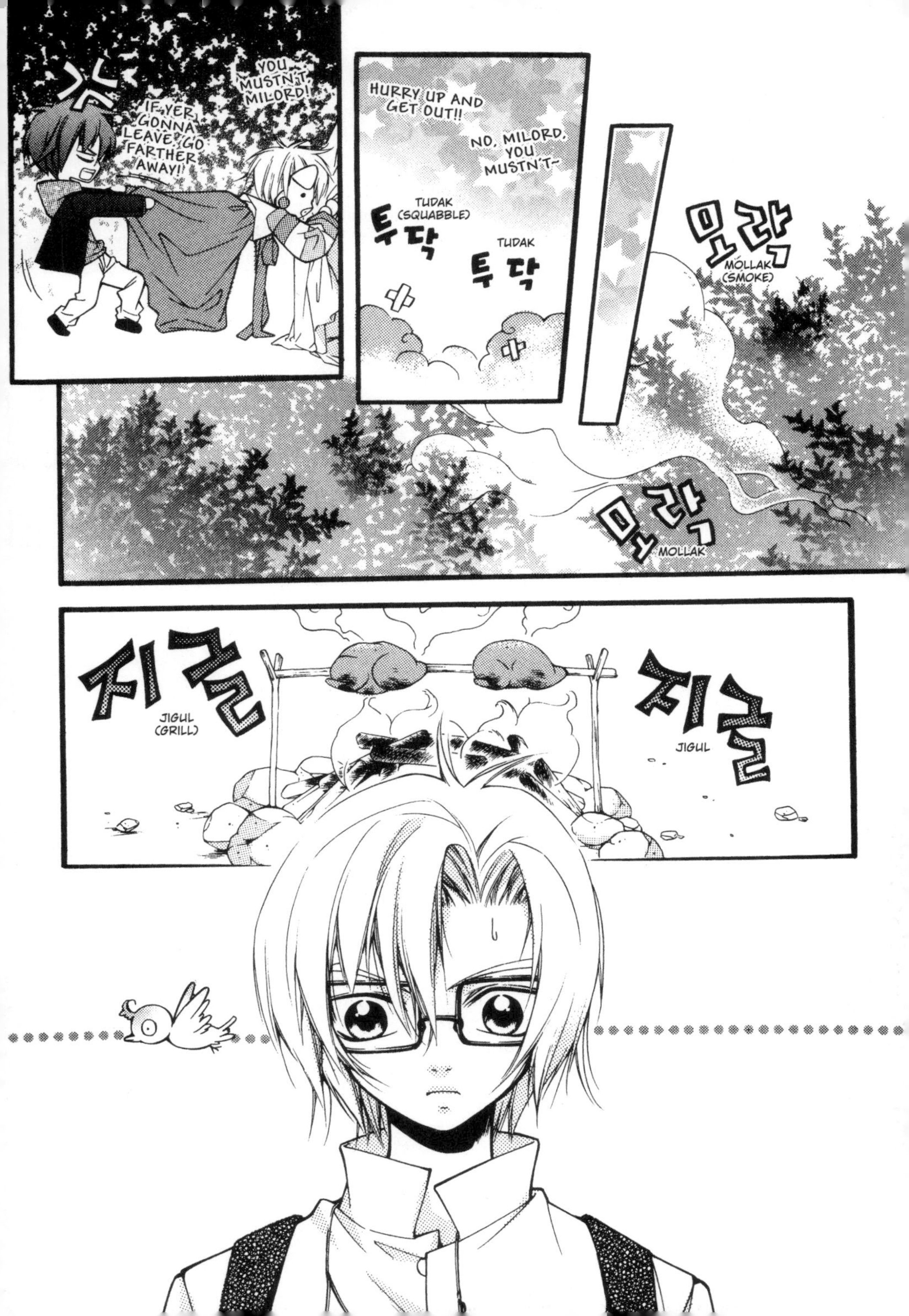

HURRY UP AND GET OUT!!
NO, MILORD, YOU MUSTN'T~
투닥
TUDAK (SQUABBLE)
투닥
TUDAK
IF YER GONNA LEAVE, GO FARTHER AWAY!!
YOU MUSTN'T, MILORD!!
모락
MOLLAK (SMOKE)
모락
MOLLAK
지글
JIGUL (GRILL)
지글
JIGUL

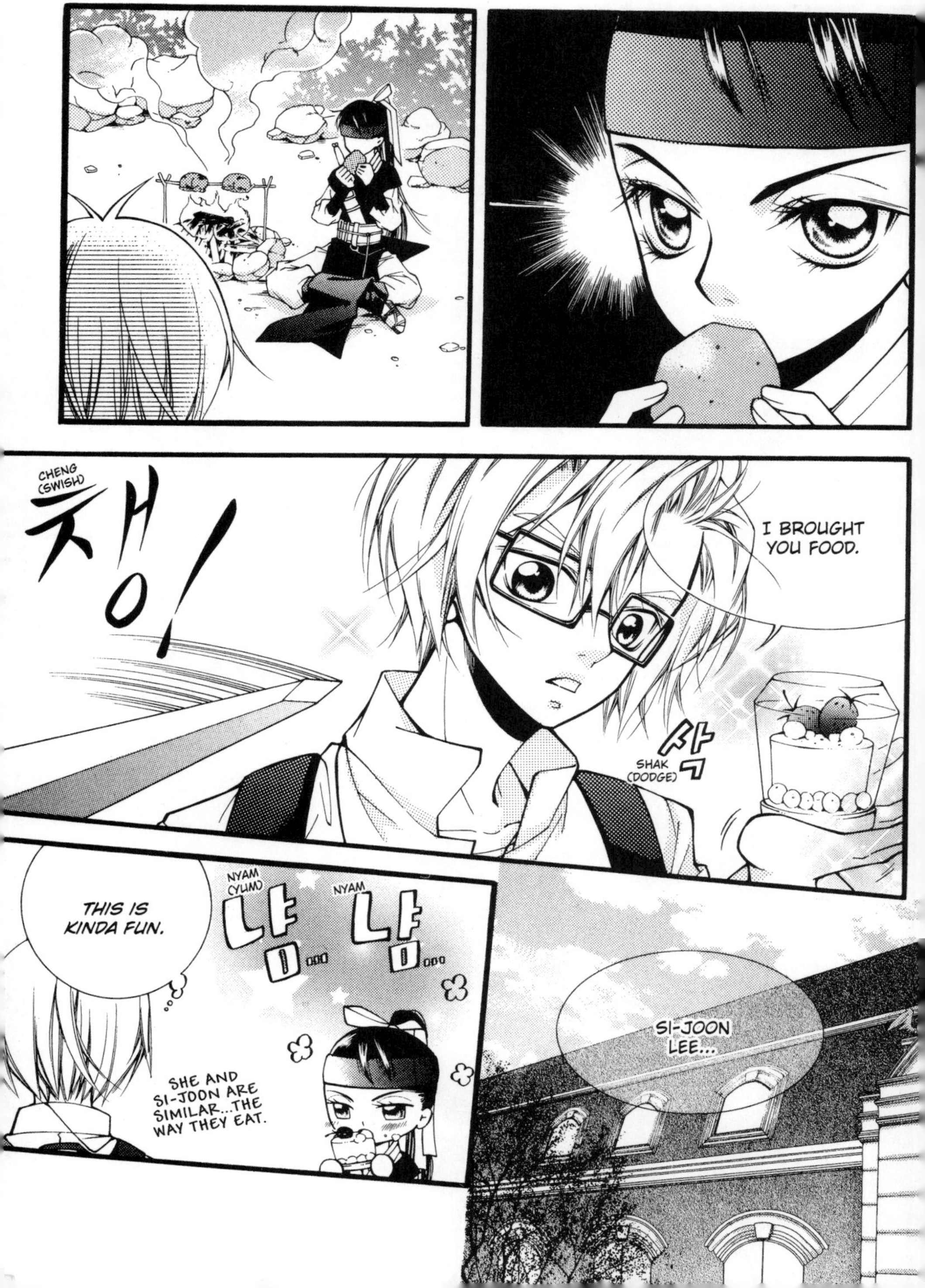

CHENG (SWISH)
쟁!
I BROUGHT YOU FOOD.
샥
SHAK (DODGE)
NYAM (YUM)
냠...
NYAM
냠...
THIS IS KINDA FUN.
SHE AND SI-JOON ARE SIMILAR...THE WAY THEY EAT.
SI-JOON LEE...

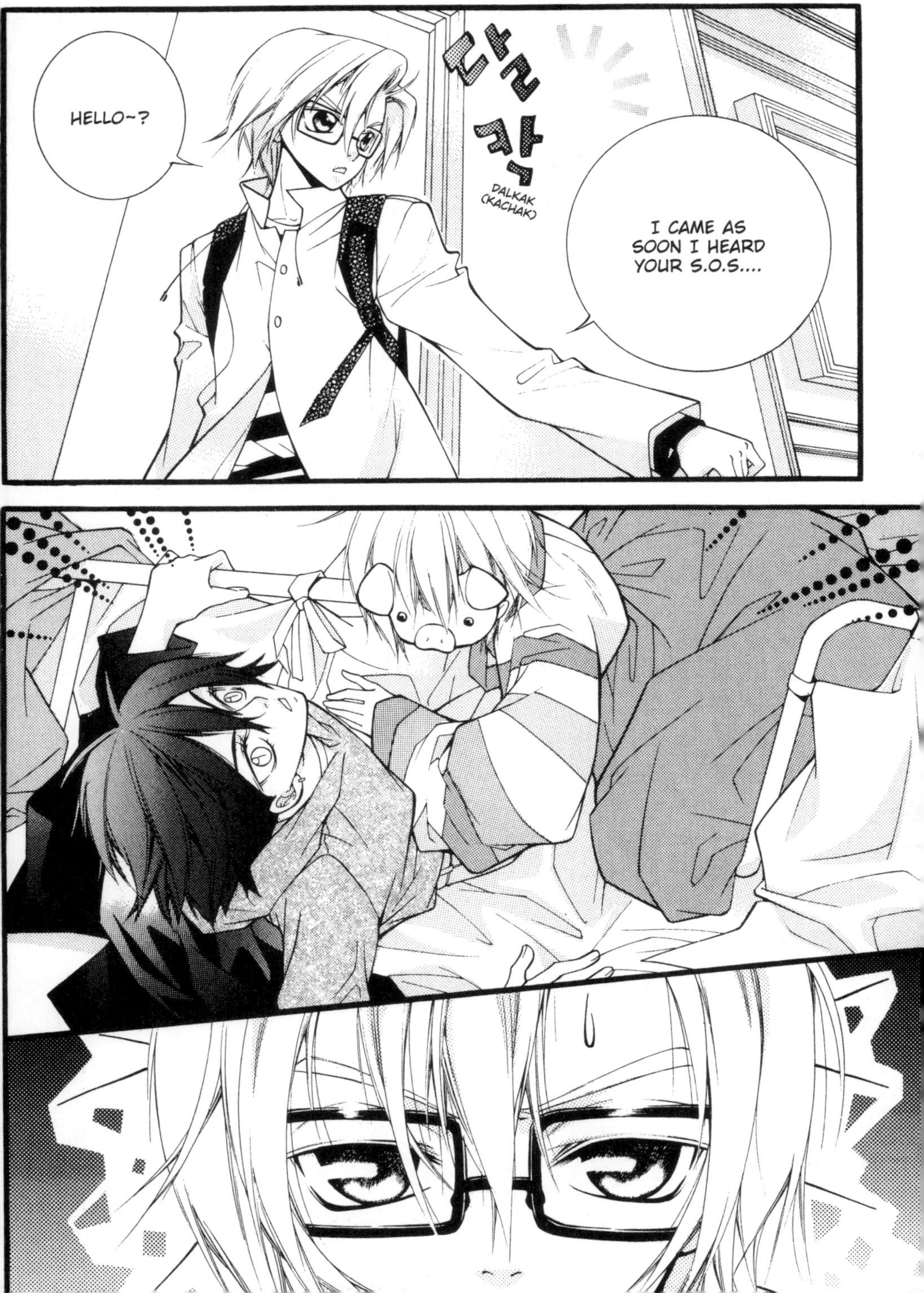
HELLO~?
달칵
DALKAK (KACHAK)
I CAME AS SOON I HEARD YOUR S.O.S....

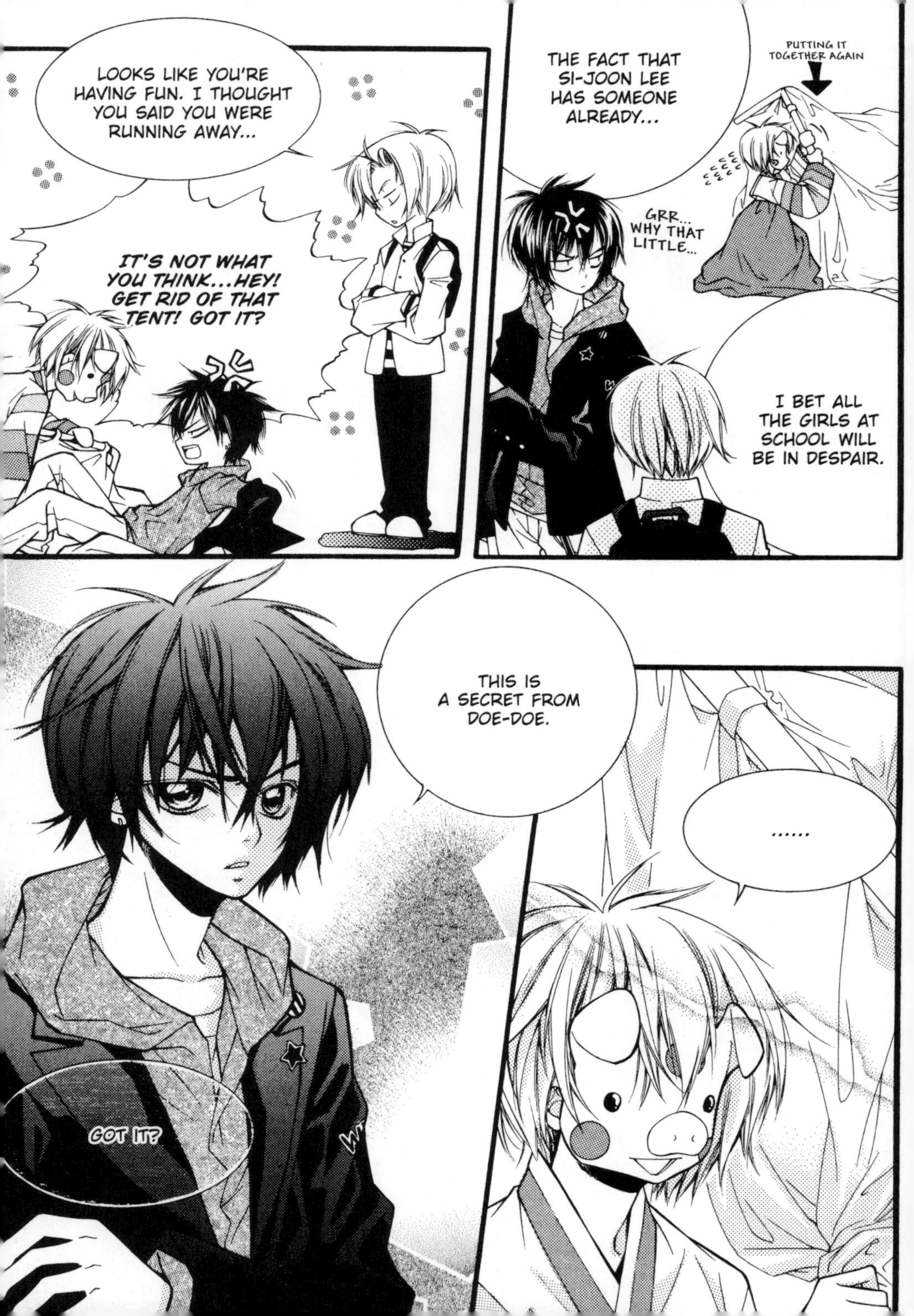
LOOKS LIKE YOU'RE HAVING FUN. I THOUGHT YOU SAID YOU WERE RUNNING AWAY...
IT'S NOT WHAT YOU THINK...HEY! GET RID OF THAT TENT! GOT IT?
THE FACT THAT SI-JOON LEE HAS SOMEONE ALREADY...
PUTTING IT TOGETHER AGAIN
GRR... WHY THAT LITTLE...
I BET ALL THE GIRLS AT SCHOOL WILL BE IN DESPAIR.
THIS IS A SECRET FROM DOE-DOE.
GOT IT?
......

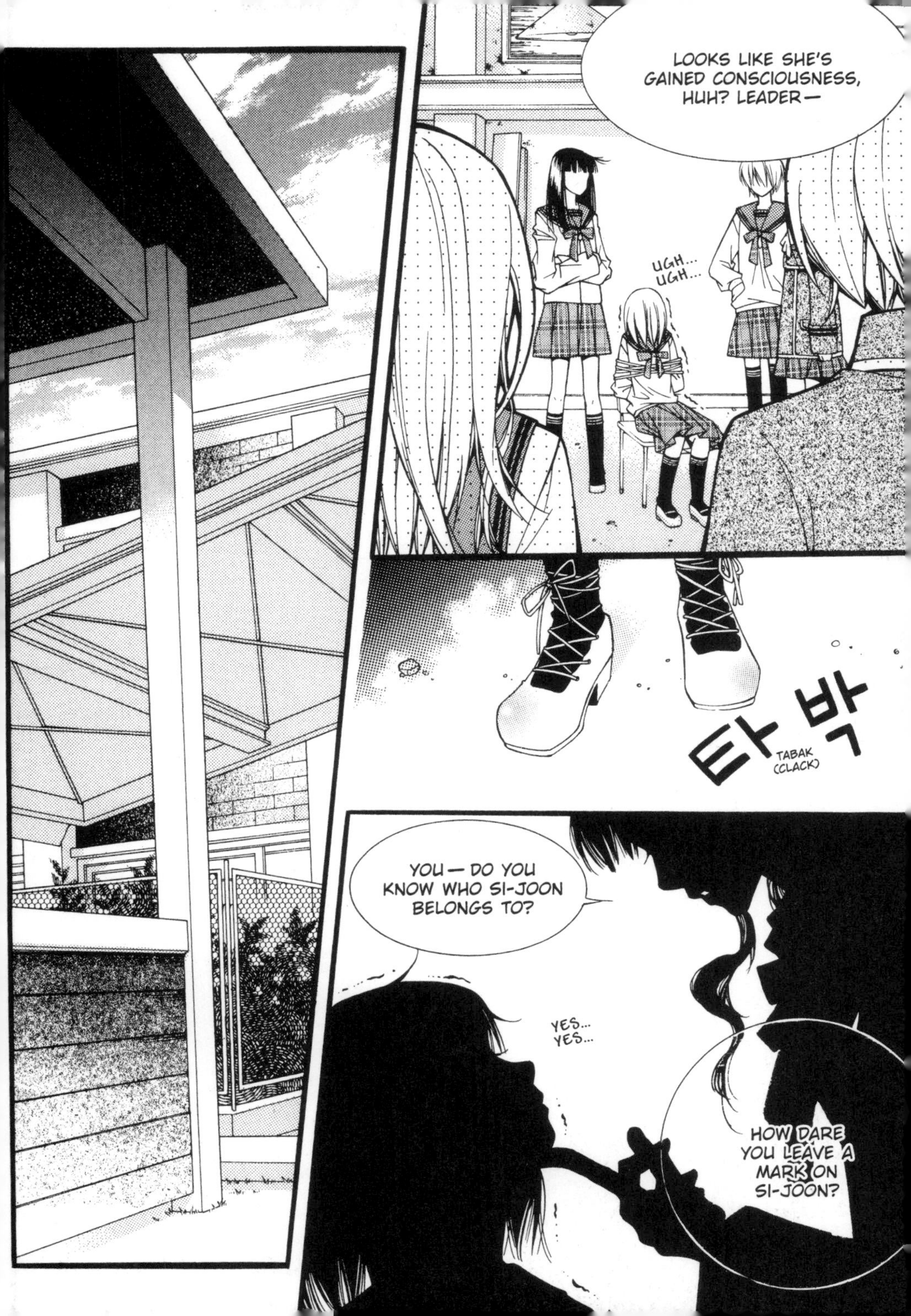
LOOKS LIKE SHE'S GAINED CONSCIOUSNESS, HUH? LEADER—
UGH... UGH...
타박
TABAK (CLACK)
YOU— DO YOU KNOW WHO SI-JOON BELONGS TO?
YES... YES...
HOW DARE YOU LEAVE A MARK ON SI-JOON?

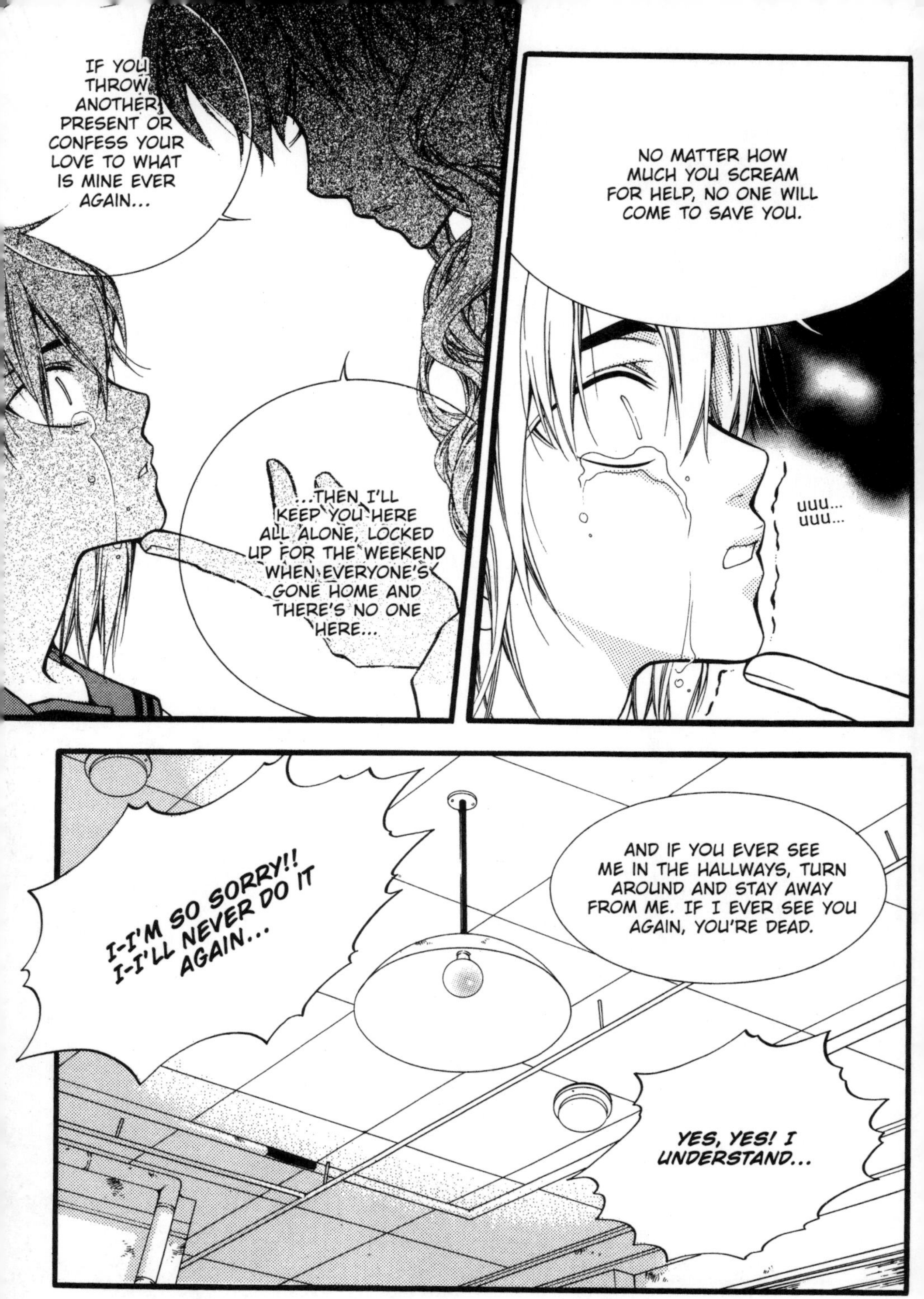
IF YOU THROW ANOTHER PRESENT OR CONFESS YOUR LOVE TO WHAT IS MINE EVER AGAIN...
...THEN I'LL KEEP YOU HERE ALL ALONE, LOCKED UP FOR THE WEEKEND WHEN EVERYONE'S GONE HOME AND THERE'S NO ONE HERE...
NO MATTER HOW MUCH YOU SCREAM FOR HELP, NO ONE WILL COME TO SAVE YOU.
UUU... UUU...
AND IF YOU EVER SEE ME IN THE HALLWAYS, TURN AROUND AND STAY AWAY FROM ME. IF I EVER SEE YOU AGAIN, YOU'RE DEAD.
I-I'M SO SORRY!! I-I'LL NEVER DO IT AGAIN...
YES, YES! I UNDERSTAND...

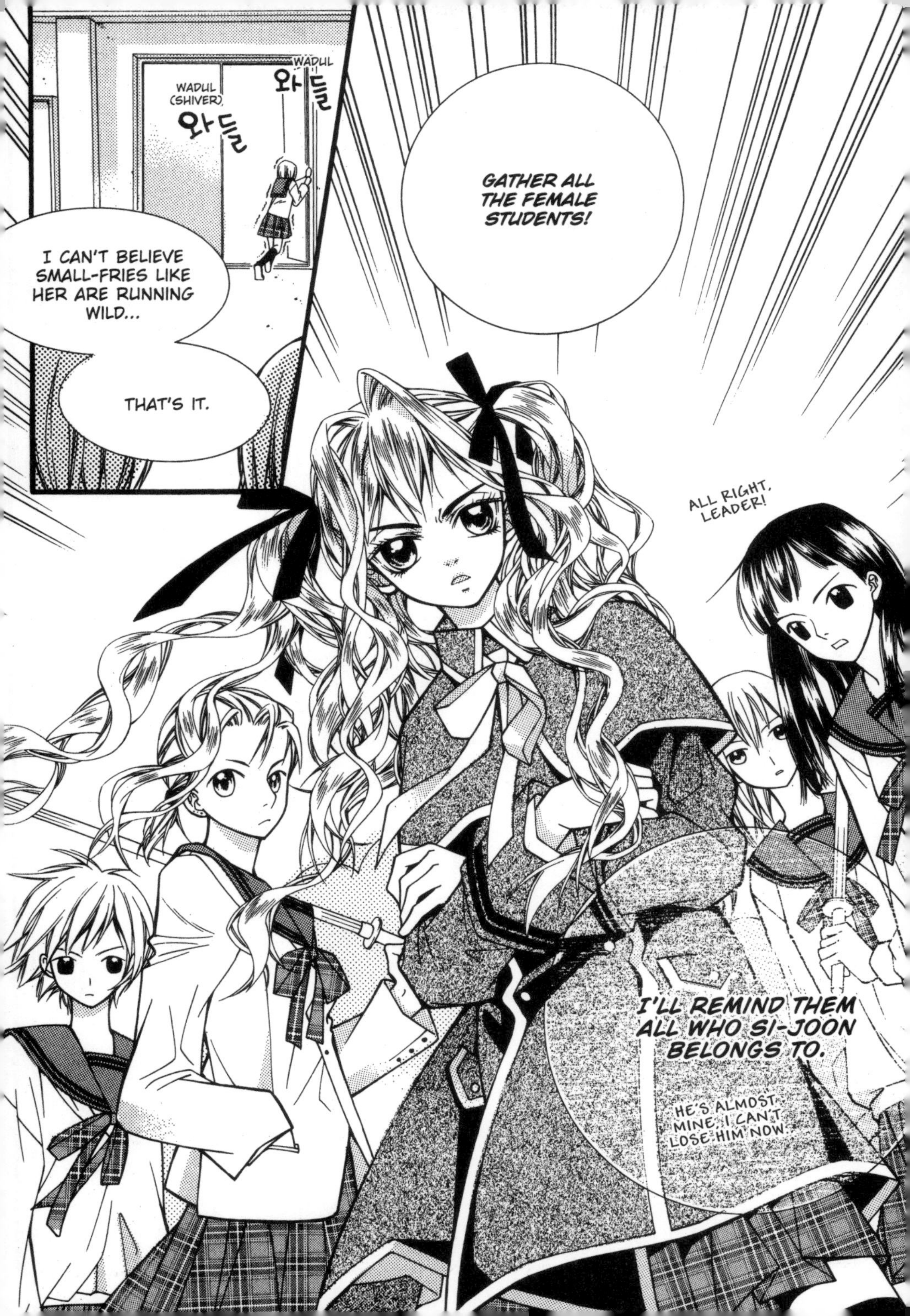
WADUL
와들
WADUL (SHIVER)
와들
I CAN'T BELIEVE SMALL-FRIES LIKE HER ARE RUNNING WILD...
THAT'S IT.
GATHER ALL THE FEMALE STUDENTS!
ALL RIGHT, LEADER!
I'LL REMIND THEM ALL WHO SI-JOON BELONGS TO.
HE'S ALMOST MINE. I CAN'T LOSE HIM NOW.

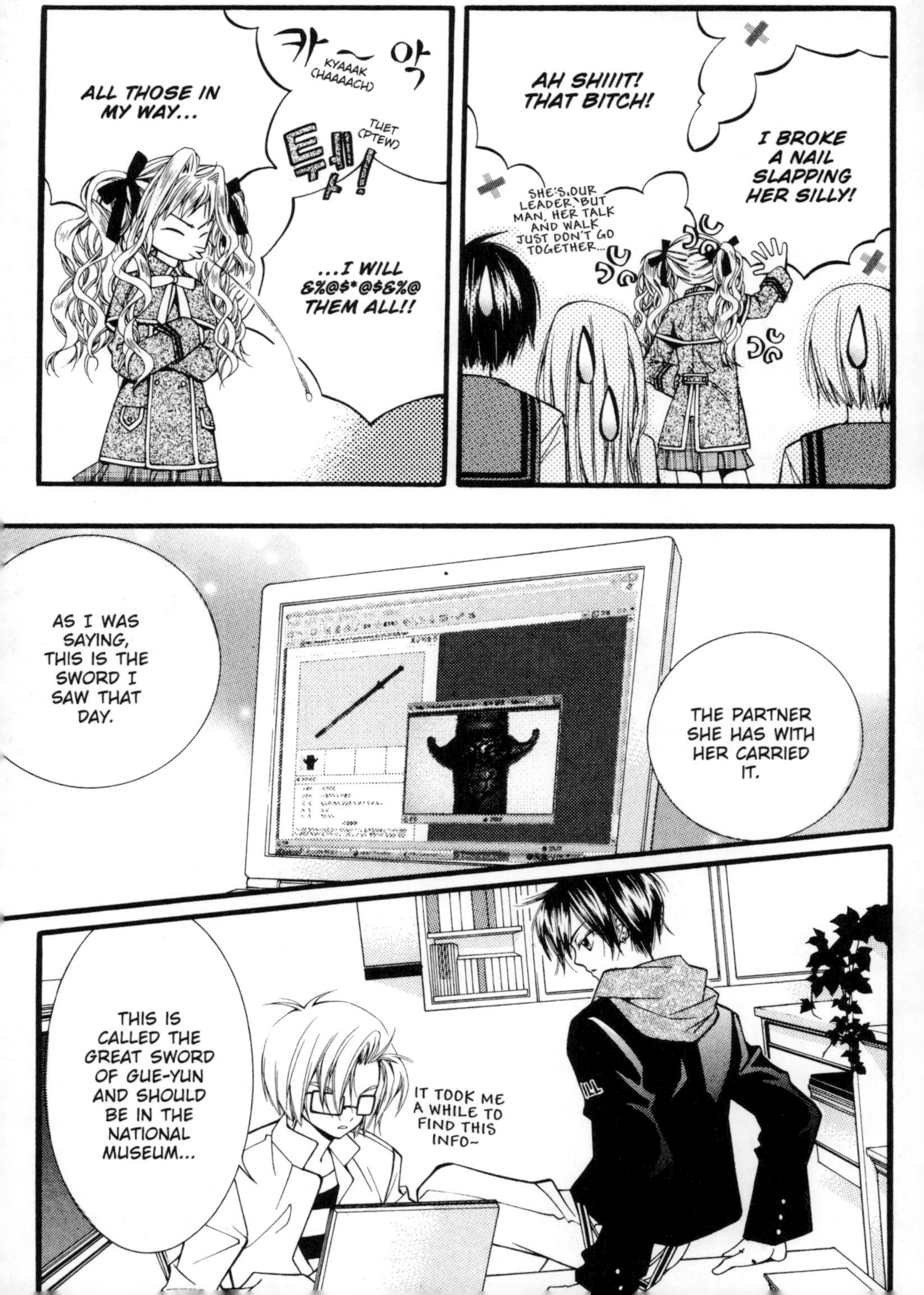

ALL THOSE IN MY WAY...
카~악
KYAAAK (HAAAACH)
퉤!
TUET (PTEW)
...I WILL &%@$*@$&%@ THEM ALL!!
AH SHIIIT! THAT BITCH!
I BROKE A NAIL SLAPPING HER SILLY!
SHE'S OUR LEADER, BUT MAN, HER TALK AND WALK JUST DON'T GO TOGETHER...
AS I WAS SAYING, THIS IS THE SWORD I SAW THAT DAY.
THE PARTNER SHE HAS WITH HER CARRIED IT.
THIS IS CALLED THE GREAT SWORD OF GUE-YUN AND SHOULD BE IN THE NATIONAL MUSEUM...
IT TOOK ME A WHILE TO FIND THIS INFO~

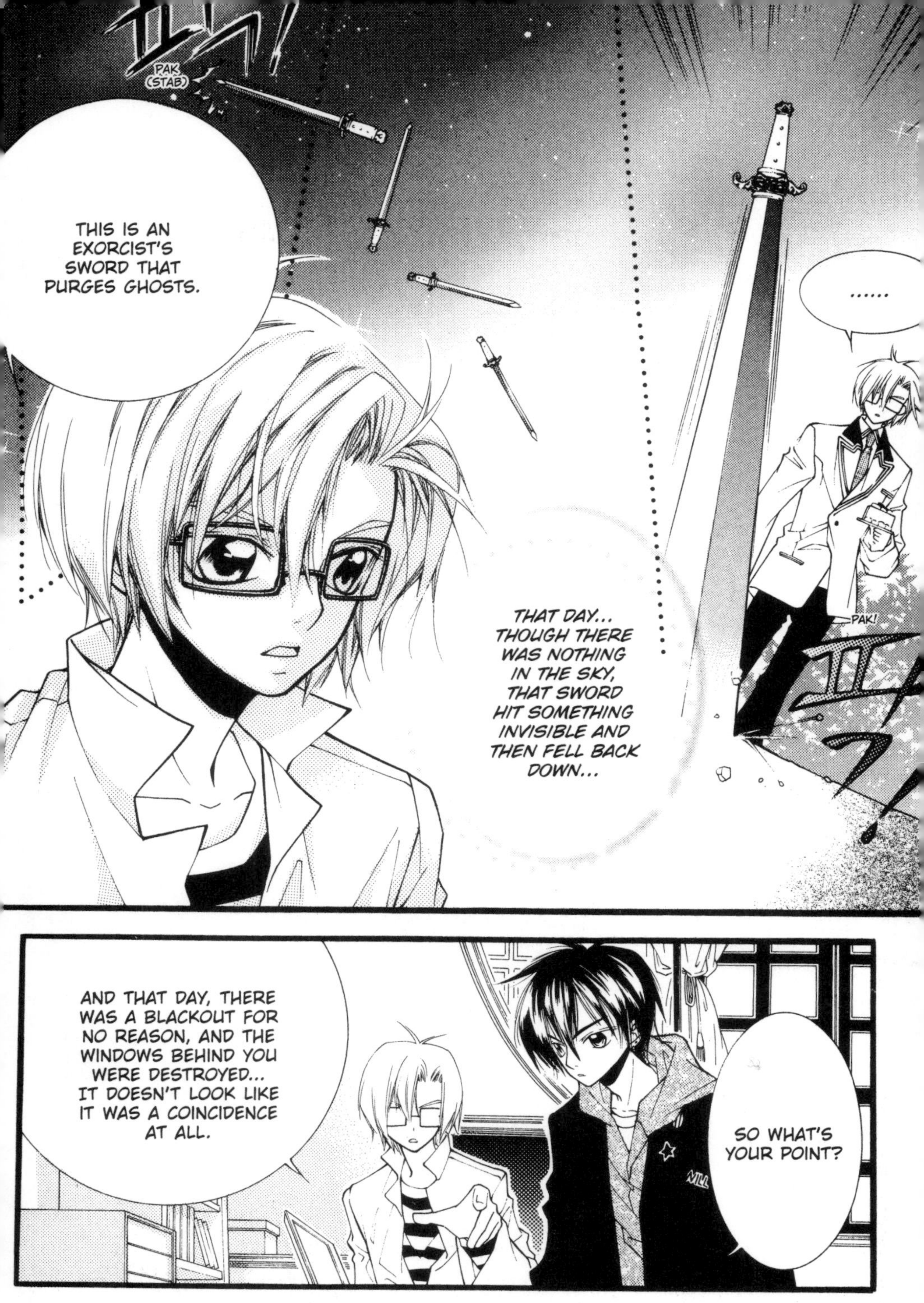
PAK (STAB)
THIS IS AN EXORCIST'S SWORD THAT PURGES GHOSTS.
THAT DAY... THOUGH THERE WAS NOTHING IN THE SKY, THAT SWORD HIT SOMETHING INVISIBLE AND THEN FELL BACK DOWN...
......
PAK!
AND THAT DAY, THERE WAS A BLACKOUT FOR NO REASON, AND THE WINDOWS BEHIND YOU WERE DESTROYED... IT DOESN'T LOOK LIKE IT WAS A COINCIDENCE AT ALL.
SO WHAT'S YOUR POINT?

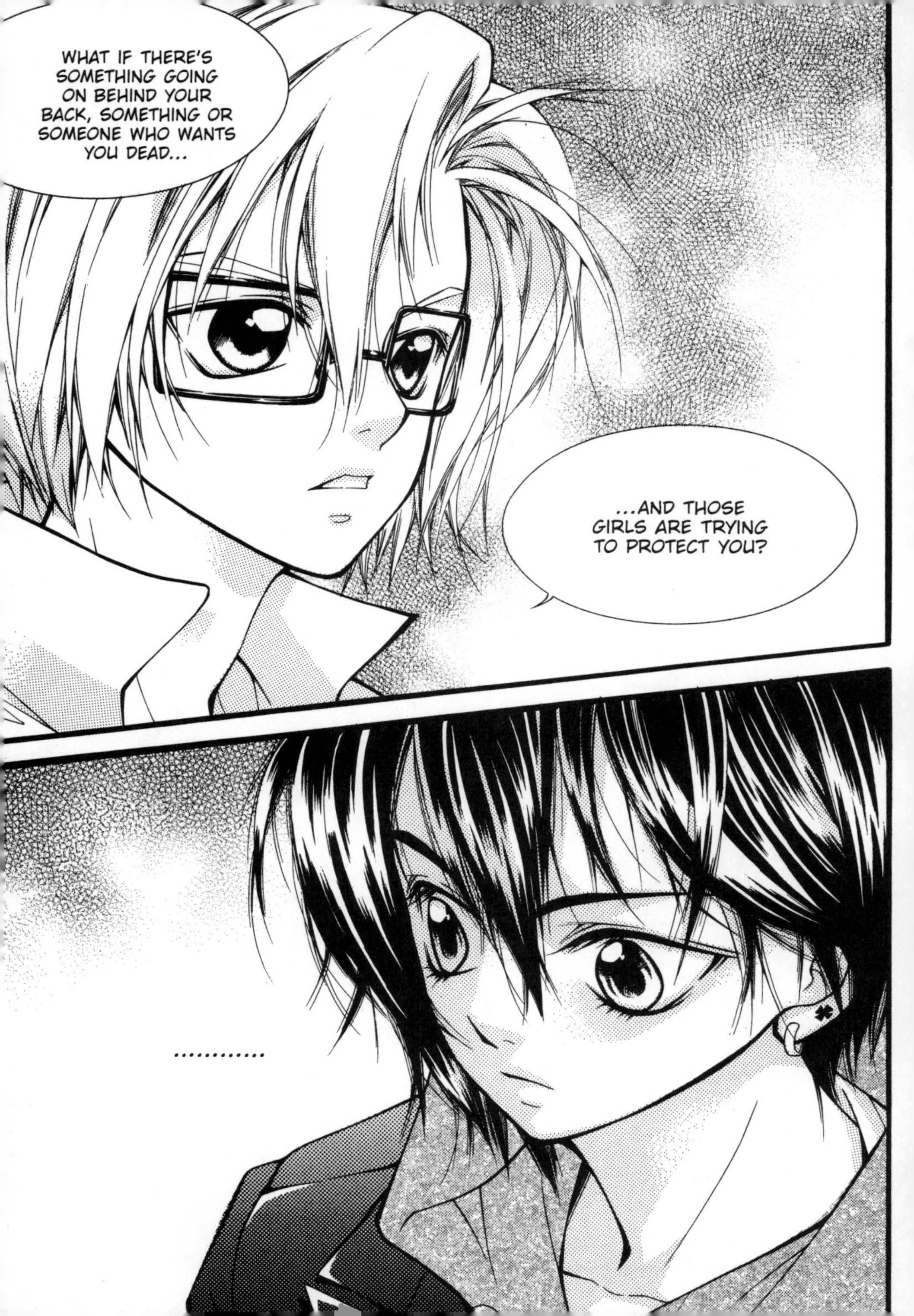
WHAT IF THERE'S SOMETHING GOING ON BEHIND YOUR BACK, SOMETHING OR SOMEONE WHO WANTS YOU DEAD...
...AND THOSE GIRLS ARE TRYING TO PROTECT YOU?
....

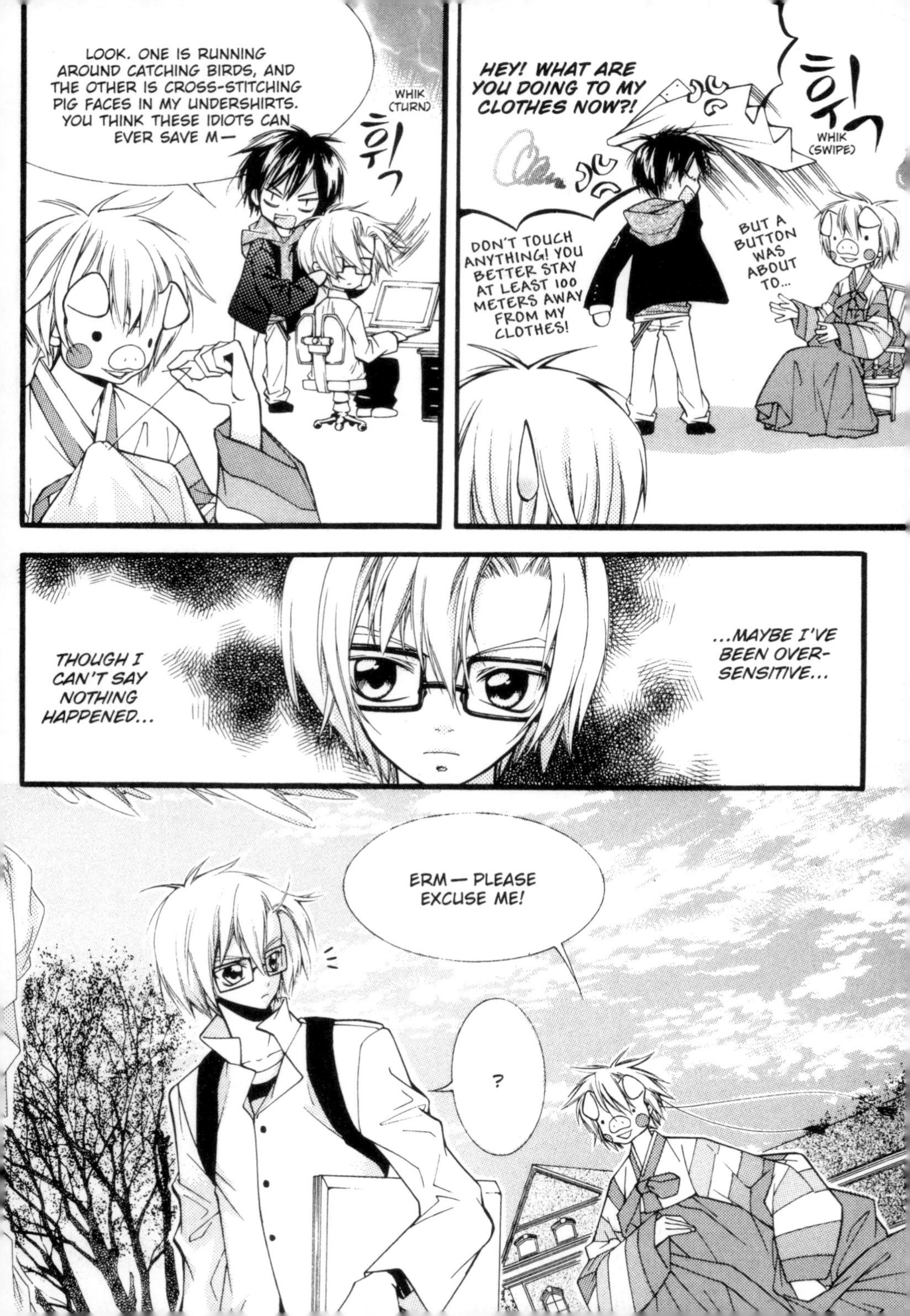

LOOK. ONE IS RUNNING AROUND CATCHING BIRDS, AND THE OTHER IS CROSS-STITCHING PIG FACES IN MY UNDERSHIRTS. YOU THINK THESE IDIOTS CAN EVER SAVE M—
휘익
WHIK (TURN)
휘익
WHIK (SWIPE)
HEY! WHAT ARE YOU DOING TO MY CLOTHES NOW?!
BUT A BUTTON WAS ABOUT TO...
DON'T TOUCH ANYTHING! YOU BETTER STAY AT LEAST 100 METERS AWAY FROM MY CLOTHES!
...MAYBE I'VE BEEN OVER-SENSITIVE...
THOUGH I CAN'T SAY NOTHING HAPPENED...
ERM— PLEASE EXCUSE ME!
?

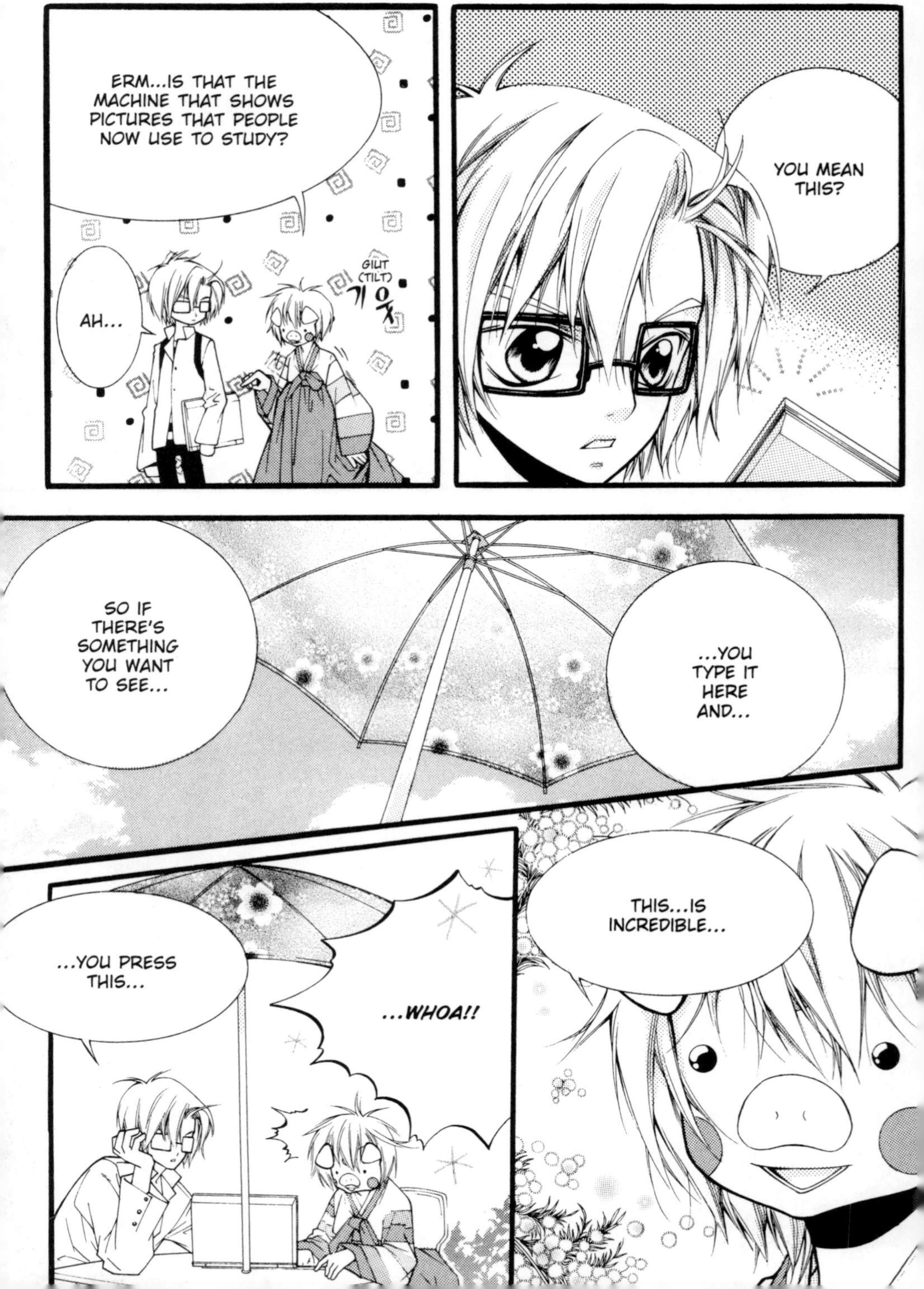

ERM...IS THAT THE MACHINE THAT SHOWS PICTURES THAT PEOPLE NOW USE TO STUDY?
AH...
GIUT (TILT)
기웃
YOU MEAN THIS?
SO IF THERE'S SOMETHING YOU WANT TO SEE...
...YOU TYPE IT HERE AND...
...YOU PRESS THIS...
...WHOA!!
THIS...IS INCREDIBLE...

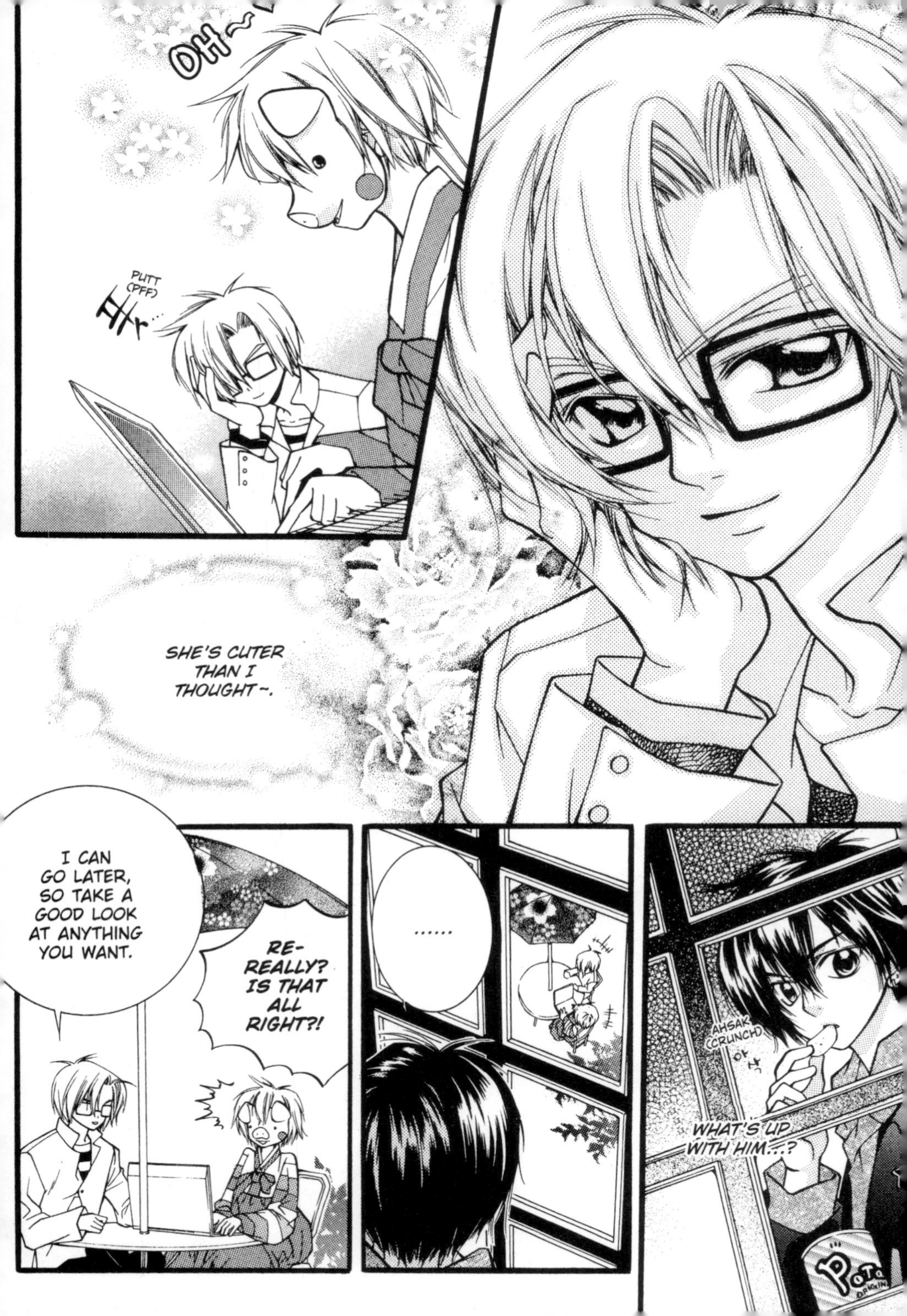

OH~
PUTT (PFF)
SHE'S CUTER THAN I THOUGHT~.
I CAN GO LATER, SO TAKE A GOOD LOOK AT ANYTHING YOU WANT.
RE-REALLY? IS THAT ALL RIGHT?!
......
AHSAK (CRUNCH)
WHAT'S UP WITH HIM...?

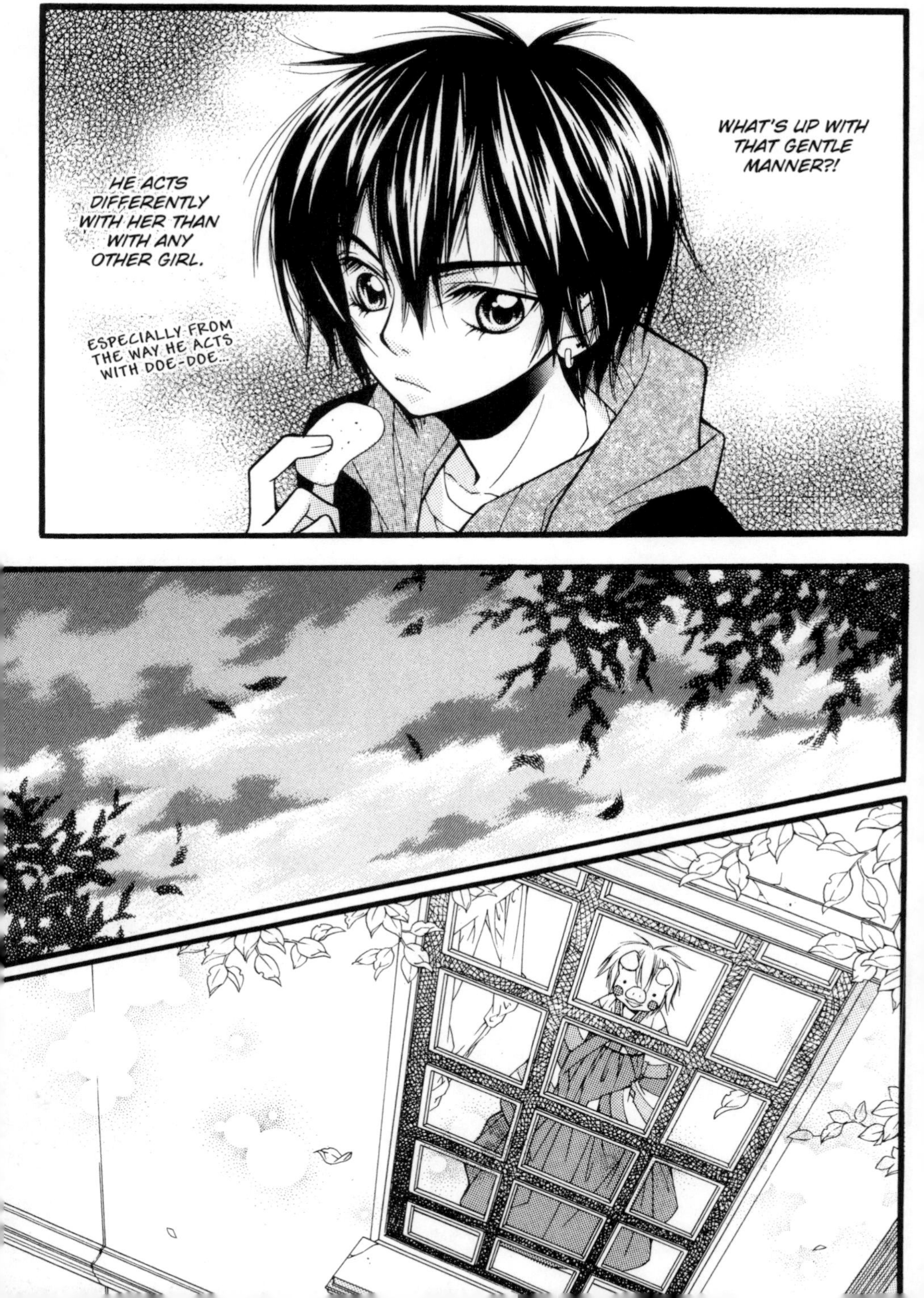
WHAT'S UP WITH THAT GENTLE MANNER?!
HE ACTS DIFFERENTLY WITH HER THAN WITH ANY OTHER GIRL.
ESPECIALLY FROM THE WAY HE ACTS WITH DOE-DOE...

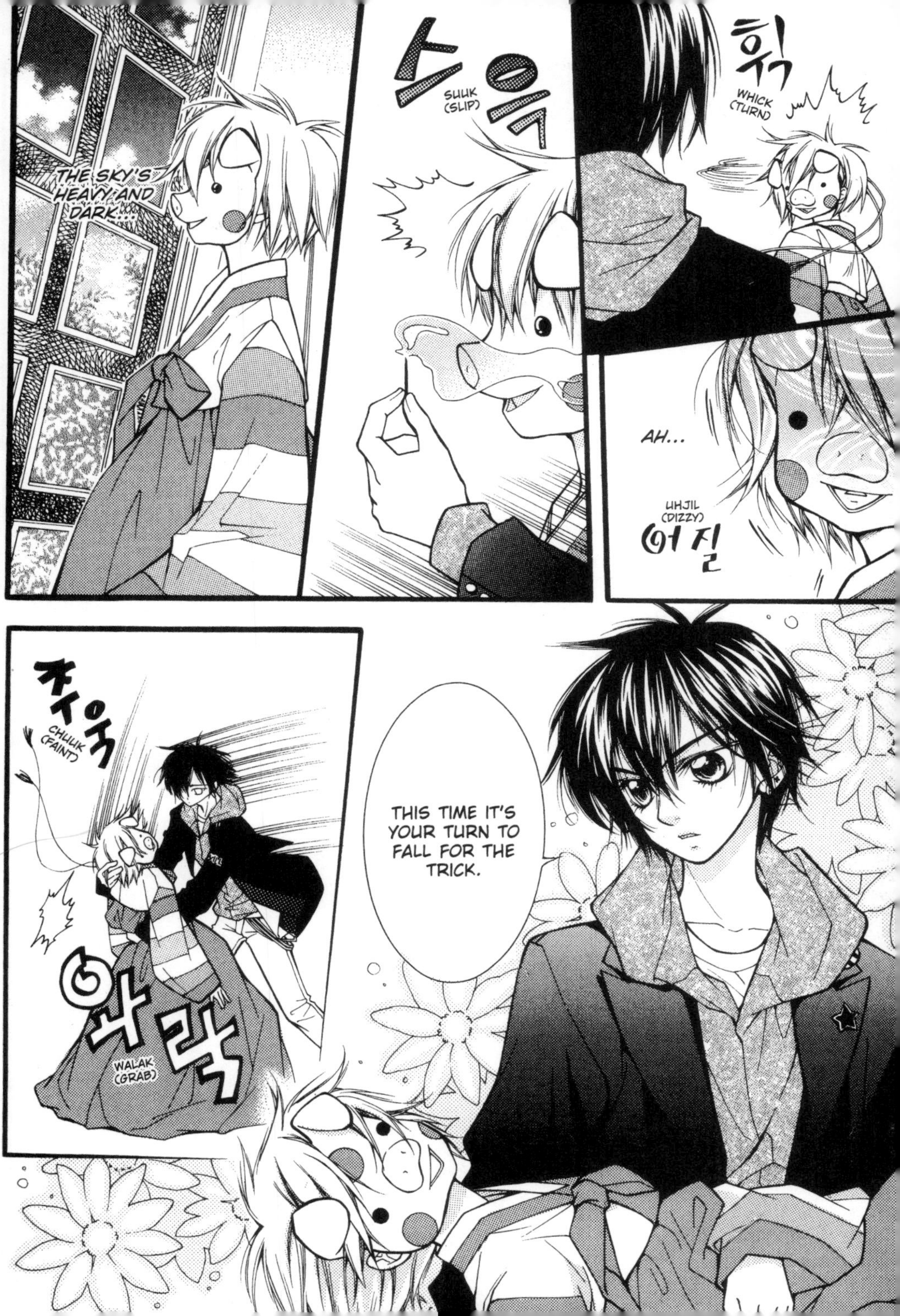
THE SKY'S HEAVY AND DARK...
스윽
SUUK (SLIP)
휙
WHICK (TURN)
AH...
UHJIL (DIZZY)
어질
추욱
CHUUK (FAINT)
와락
WALAK (GRAB)
THIS TIME IT'S YOUR TURN TO FALL FOR THE TRICK.

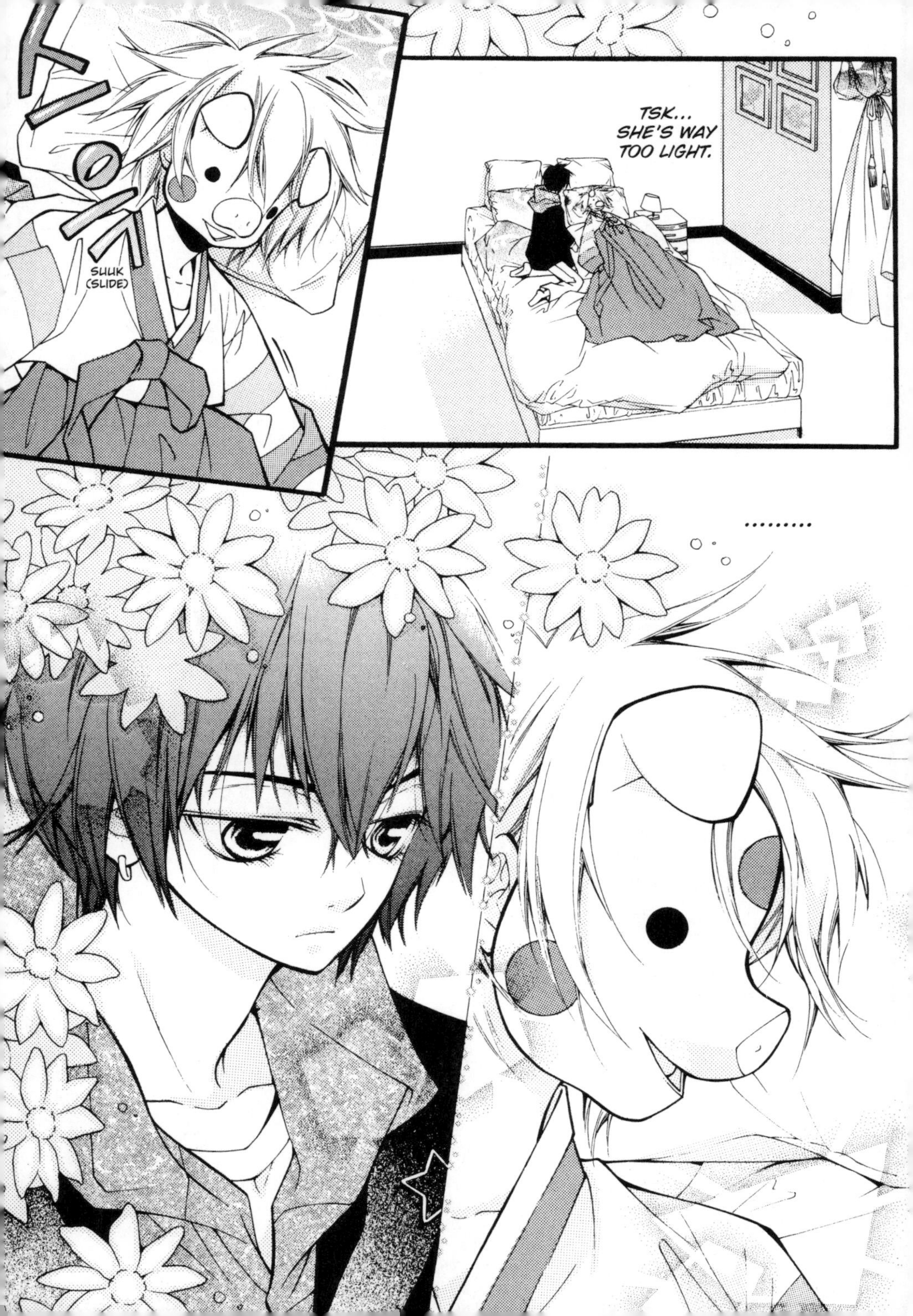
TSK... SHE'S WAY TOO LIGHT.
SUUK (SLIDE)
....

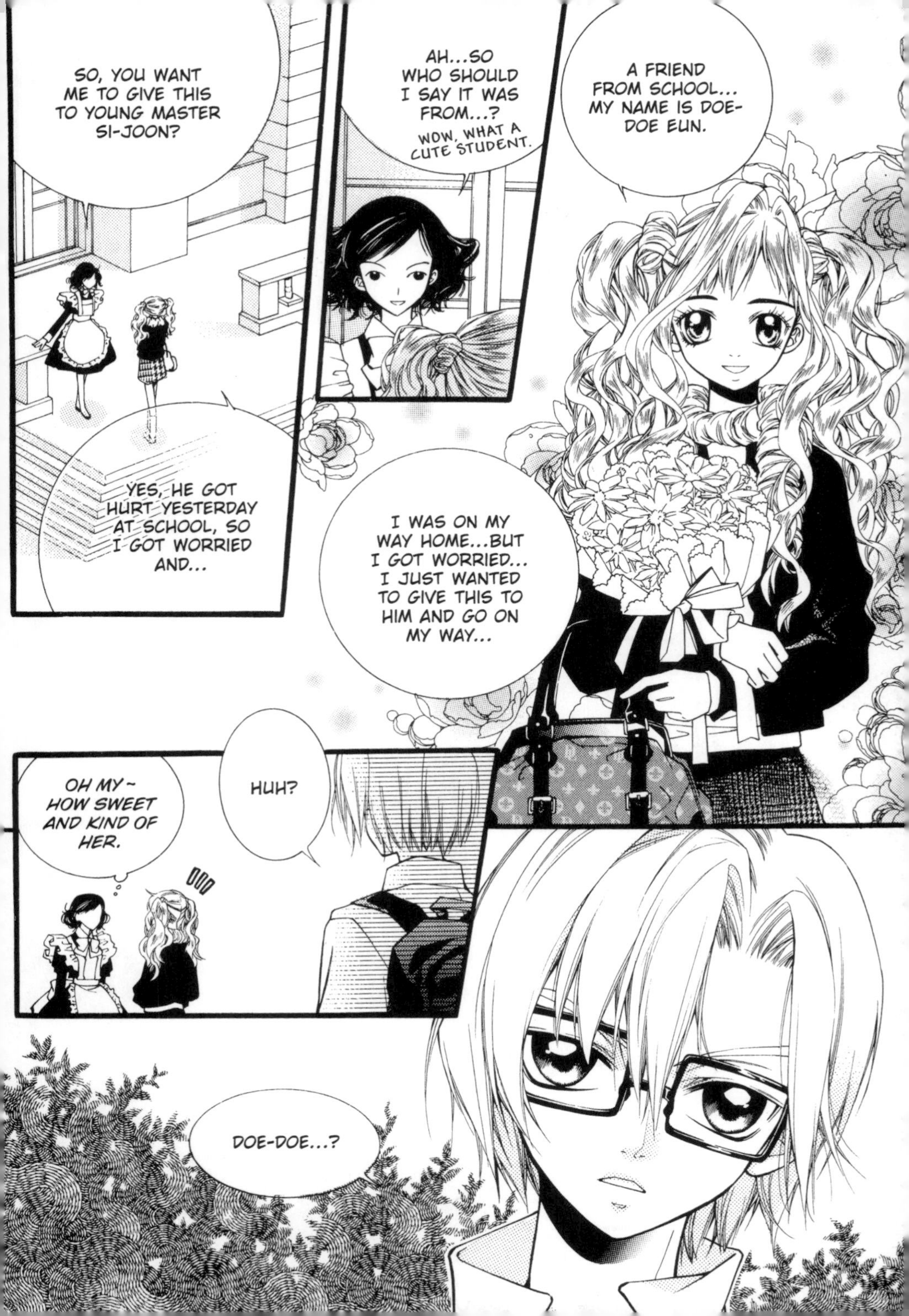
SO, YOU WANT ME TO GIVE THIS TO YOUNG MASTER SI-JOON?
YES, HE GOT HURT YESTERDAY AT SCHOOL, SO I GOT WORRIED AND...
AH...SO WHO SHOULD I SAY IT WAS FROM...?
WOW, WHAT A CUTE STUDENT.
A FRIEND FROM SCHOOL... MY NAME IS DOE-DOE EUN.
I WAS ON MY WAY HOME...BUT I GOT WORRIED... I JUST WANTED TO GIVE THIS TO HIM AND GO ON MY WAY...
OH MY~ HOW SWEET AND KIND OF HER.
HUH?
DOE-DOE...?

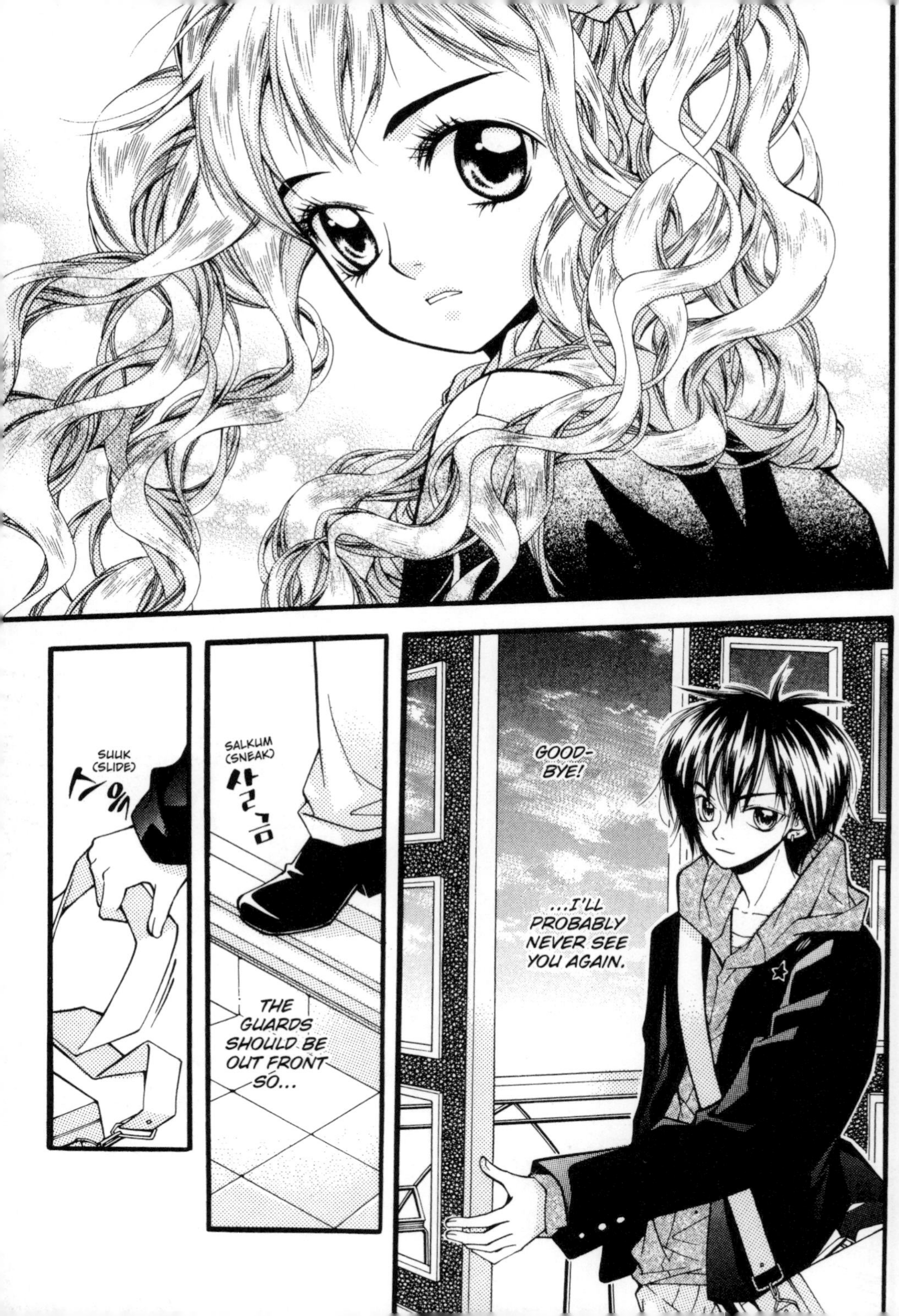
SUUK (SLIDE)
SALKUM (SNEAK)
THE GUARDS SHOULD BE OUT FRONT SO...
GOOD-BYE!
...I'LL PROBABLY NEVER SEE YOU AGAIN.

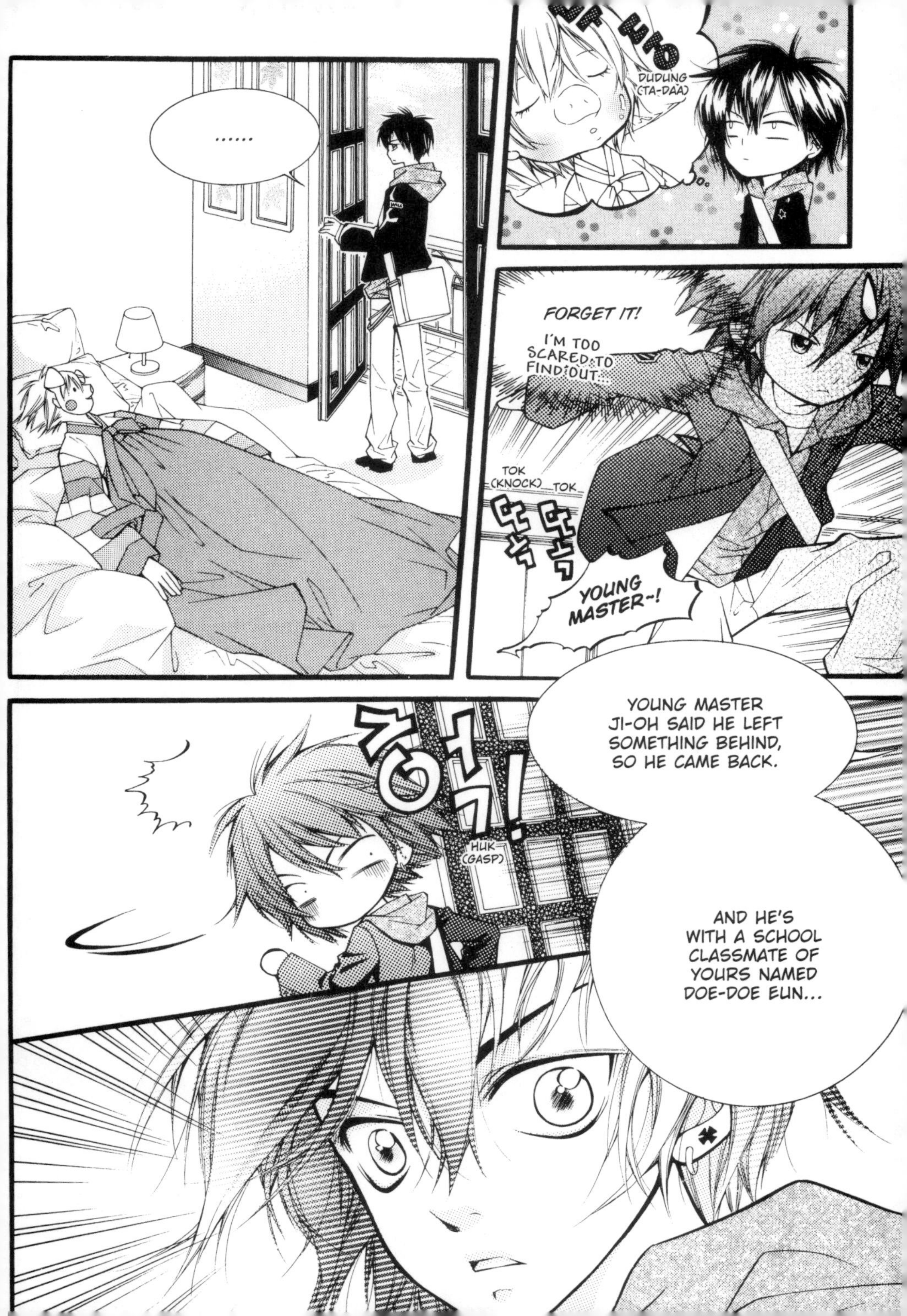
......
DUDUNG (TA-DAA)
FORGET IT!
I'M TOO SCARED TO FIND OUT...
TOK (KNOCK) TOK
YOUNG MASTER~!
HUK (GASP)
YOUNG MASTER JI-OH SAID HE LEFT SOMETHING BEHIND, SO HE CAME BACK.
AND HE'S WITH A SCHOOL CLASSMATE OF YOURS NAMED DOE-DOE EUN...

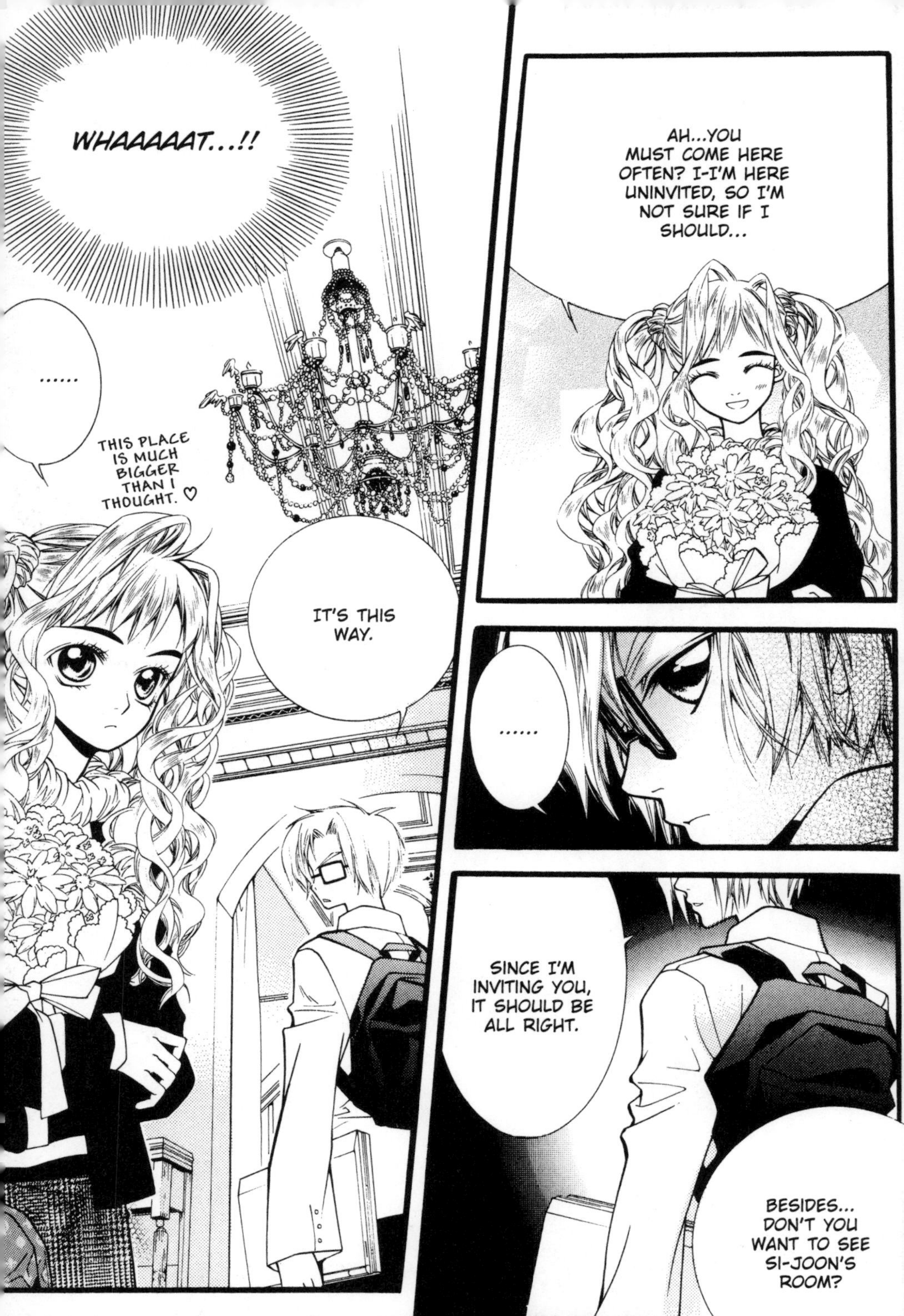
WHAAAAAT...!!
......
THIS PLACE IS MUCH BIGGER THAN I THOUGHT. ♡
IT'S THIS WAY.
AH...YOU MUST COME HERE OFTEN? I-I'M HERE UNINVITED, SO I'M NOT SURE IF I SHOULD...
......
SINCE I'M INVITING YOU, IT SHOULD BE ALL RIGHT.
BESIDES... DON'T YOU WANT TO SEE SI-JOON'S ROOM?

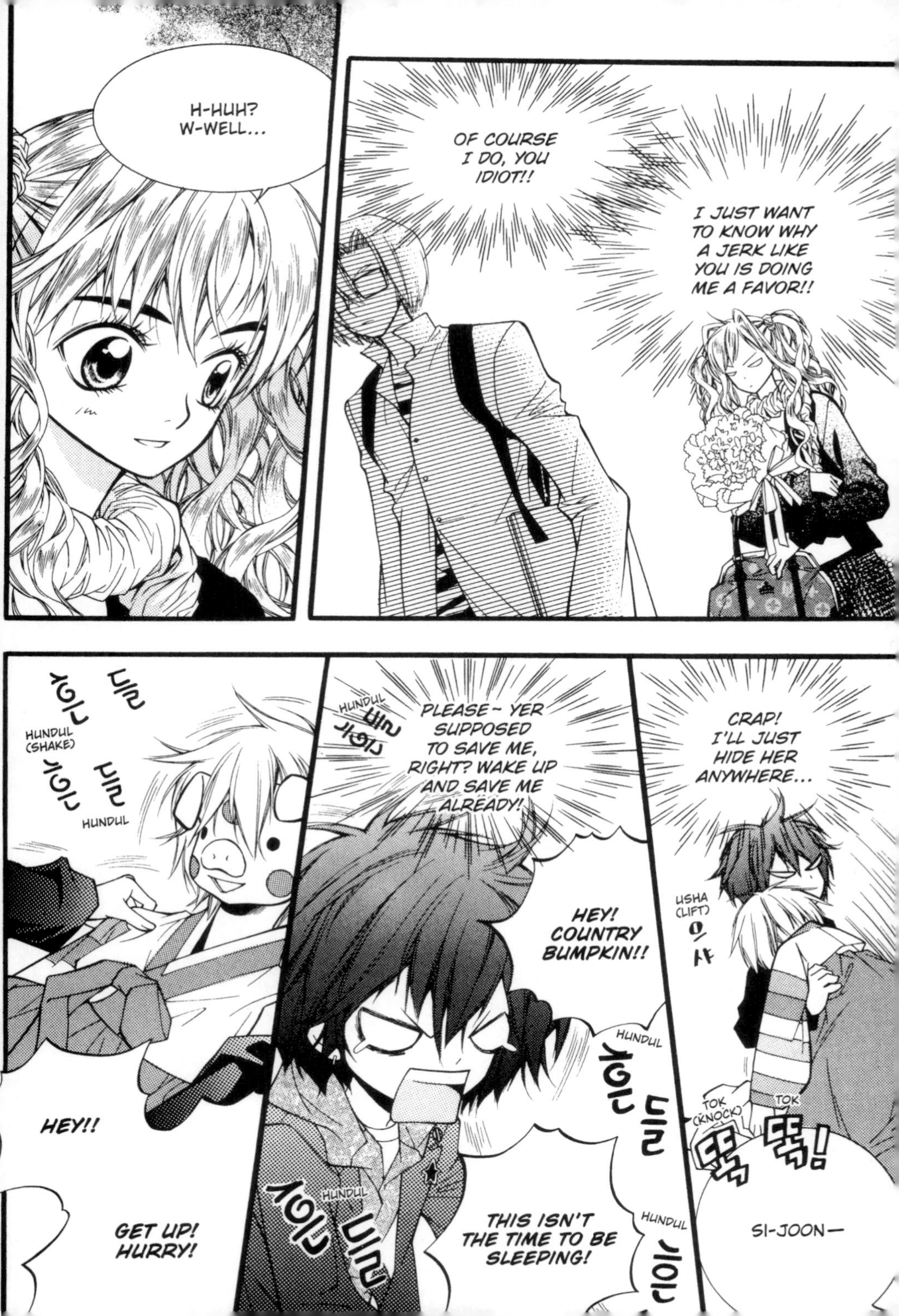
H-HUH? W-WELL...
OF COURSE I DO, YOU IDIOT!!
I JUST WANT TO KNOW WHY A JERK LIKE YOU IS DOING ME A FAVOR!!
HUNDUL (SHAKE)
HUNDUL
HEY!!
GET UP! HURRY!
HUNDUL
PLEASE~ YER SUPPOSED TO SAVE ME, RIGHT? WAKE UP AND SAVE ME ALREADY!
HEY! COUNTRY BUMPKIN!!
HUNDUL
HUNDUL
THIS ISN'T THE TIME TO BE SLEEPING!
HUNDUL
CRAP! I'LL JUST HIDE HER ANYWHERE...
USHA (LIFT)
TOK (KNOCK)
TOK
SI-JOON—

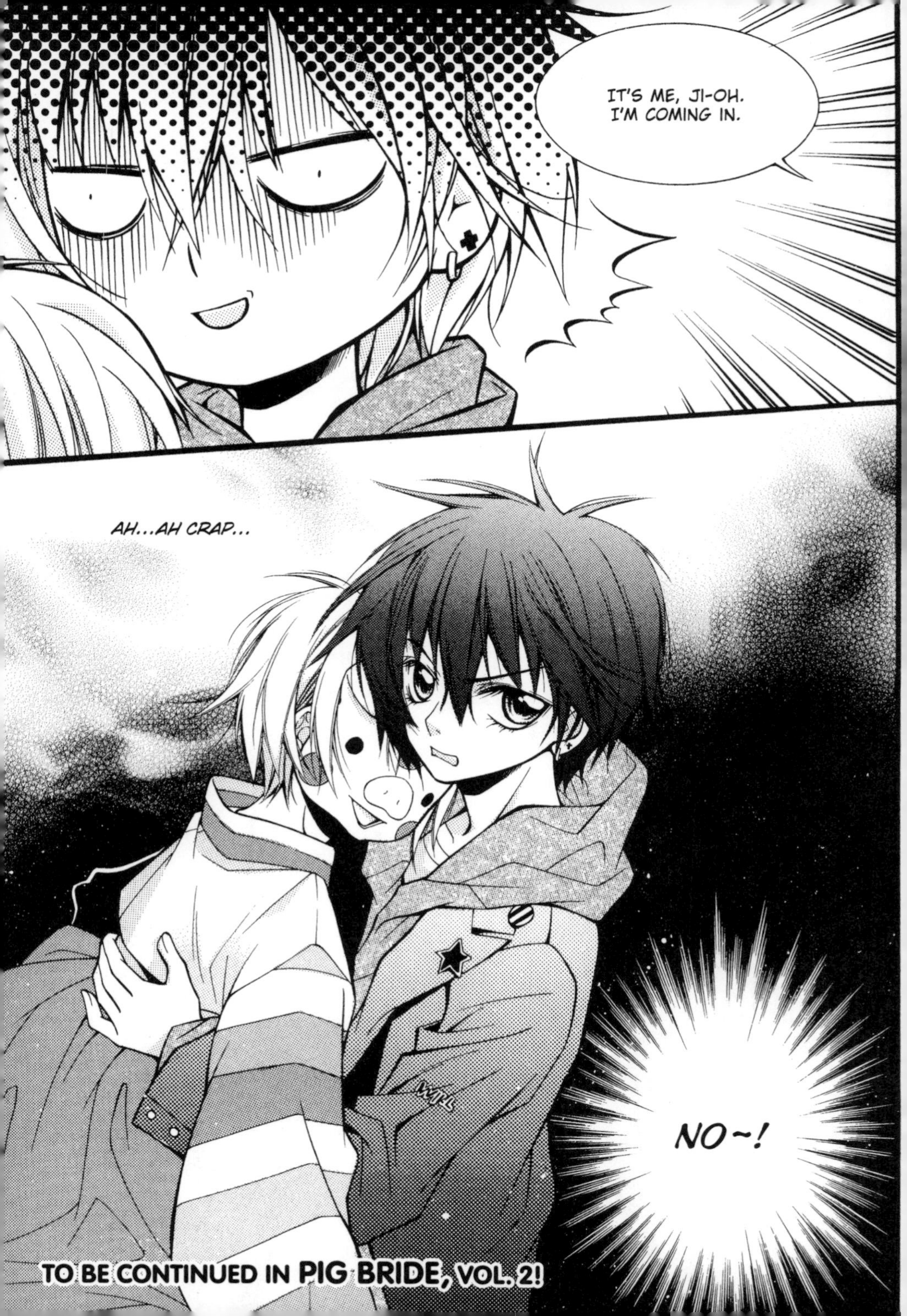
IT'S ME, JI-OH. I'M COMING IN.
AH...AH CRAP...
NO~!
TO BE CONTINUED IN PIG BRIDE, VOL. 2!

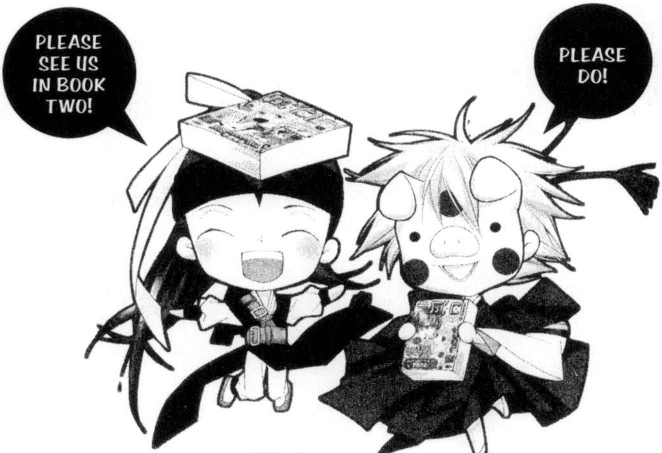
PLEASE DO!
PLEASE SEE US IN BOOK TWO!

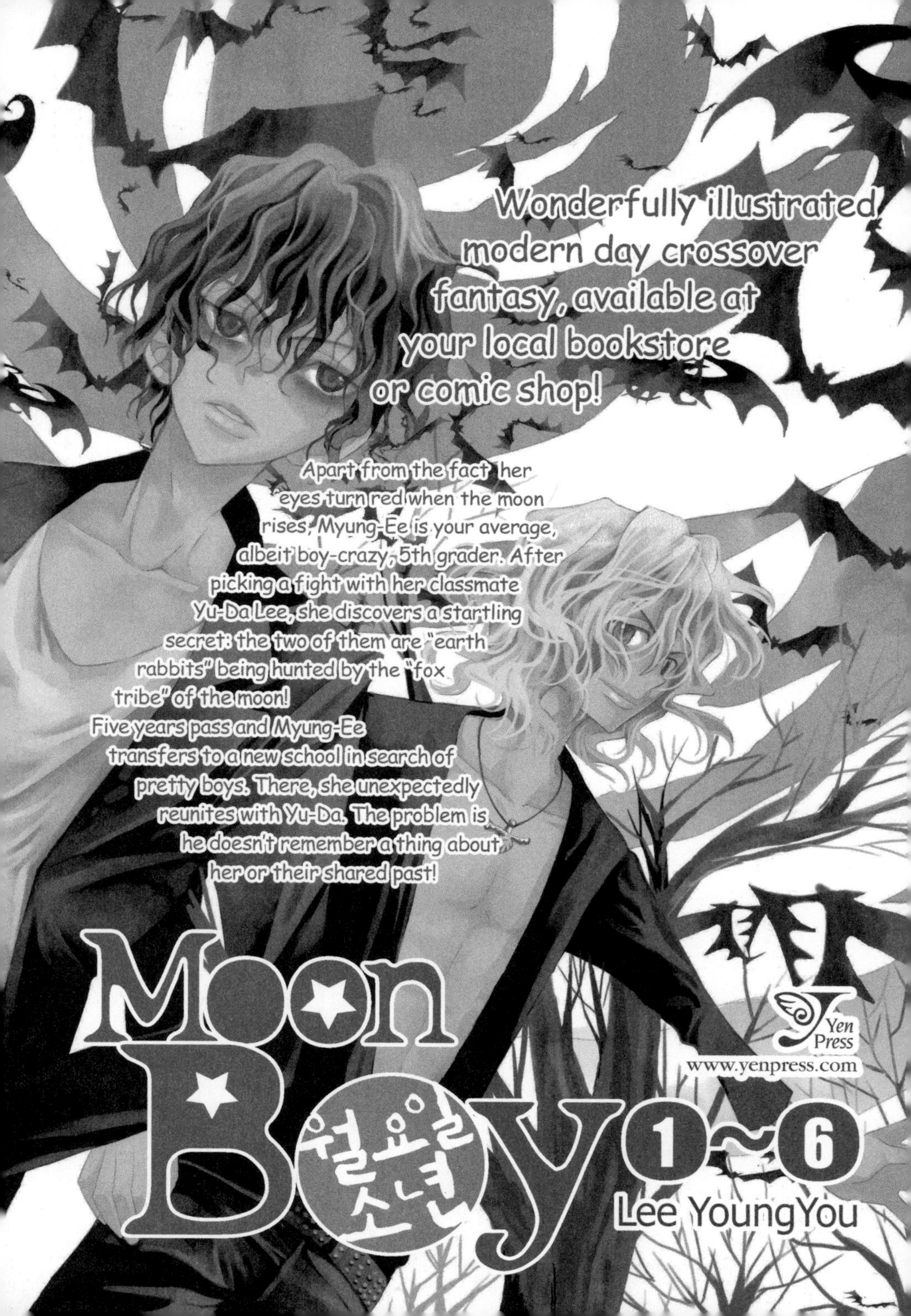
Wonderfully illustrated modern day crossover fantasy, available at your local bookstore or comic shop!
Apart from the fact her eyes turn red when the moon rises, Myung-Ee is your average, albeit boy-crazy, 5th grader. After picking a fight with her classmate Yu-Da Lee, she discovers a startling secret: the two of them are "earth rabbits" being hunted by the "fox tribe" of the moon!
Five years pass and Myung-Ee transfers to a new school in search of pretty boys. There, she unexpectedly reunites with Yu-Da. The problem is he doesn't remember a thing about her or their shared past!
Moon Boy
월요일 소년
1~6
Lee YoungYou
Yen Press
www.yenpress.com

Yen
Press
www.yenpress.com

Becoming the princess... Isn't that every girl's dream?!

Monarchy rule ended long ago in Korea, but there are still other countries with kings, queens, princes and princesses. What if Korea had continued monarchism? What if all the beautiful palaces, which are now only historical relics, were actually filled with people? What if the glamorous royal family still maintained the palace customs? Welcome to a world where Korea still has the royal family living in their everyday lives! Only for this one high school girl, Chae-Kyung, is this a tragedy, since she has to marry the prince — who apparently is a total bastard!

THE ROYAL PALACE

Goong
vol.1 ~ 4

Park SoHee

Available at bookstores near you!

CHOCOLAT
1~7

Shin JiSang · Geo

Kum-ji was a little late getting under the spell of the chart-topping band, DDL. Unable to join the DDL fan club, she almost gives up on meeting her idols, until she develops a cunning plan–to become a member of a rival fan club for the brand-new boy band Yo-I. This way she can act as Yo-I's fan club member and also be near Yo-I,

How far would you go to meet your favorite boy band?

who always seem to be in the same shows as DDL. Perfect plan...except being a fanatic is a lot more complicated than she expects. Especially when you're actually a fan of someone else. This full-blown love comedy about a fan club will make you laugh, cry, and laugh some more.

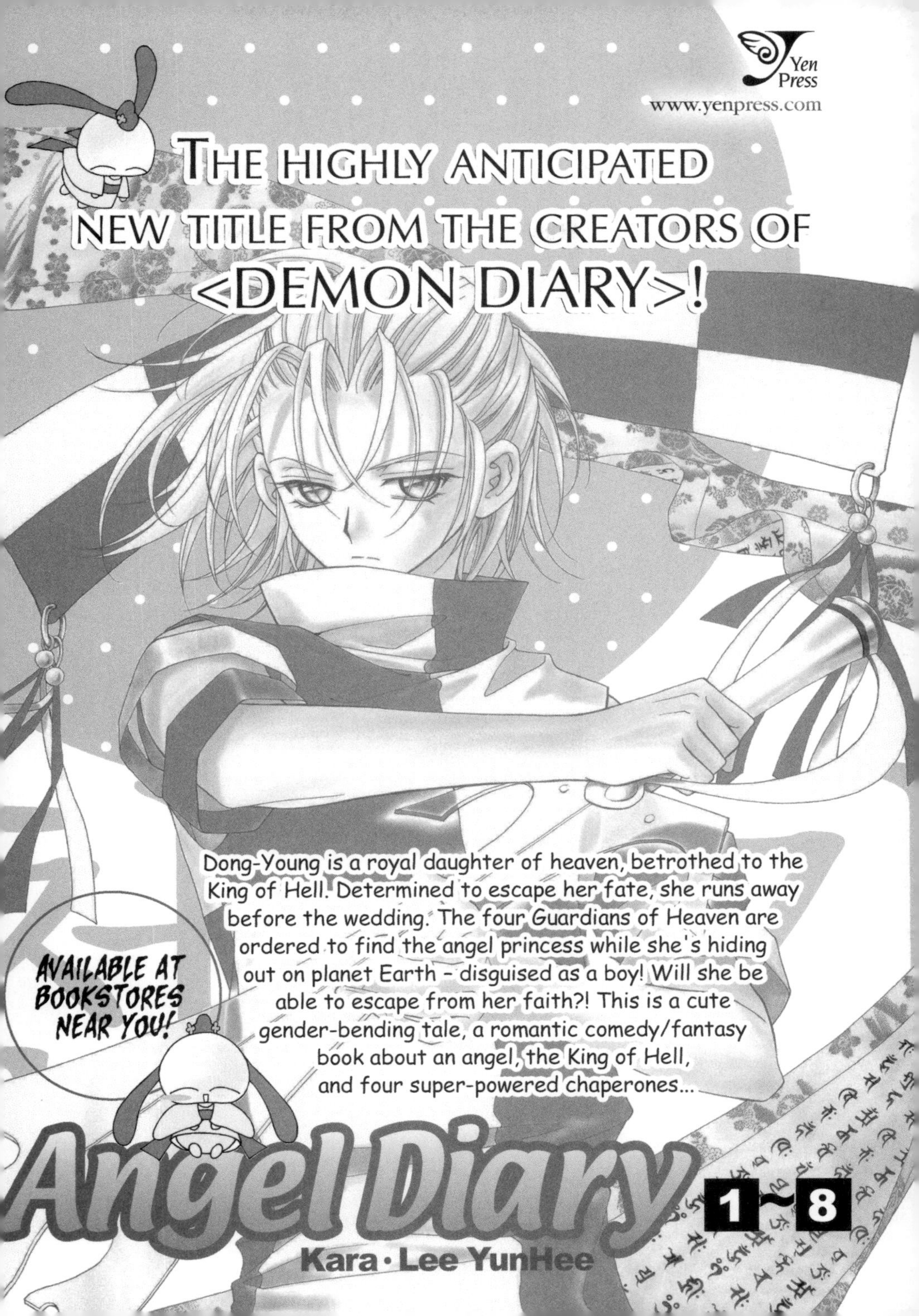
Yen Press
www.yenpress.com
THE HIGHLY ANTICIPATED NEW TITLE FROM THE CREATORS OF <DEMON DIARY>!
Dong-Young is a royal daughter of heaven, betrothed to the King of Hell. Determined to escape her fate, she runs away before the wedding. The four Guardians of Heaven are ordered to find the angel princess while she's hiding out on planet Earth – disguised as a boy! Will she be able to escape from her faith?! This is a cute gender-bending tale, a romantic comedy/fantasy book about an angel, the King of Hell, and four super-powered chaperones...
AVAILABLE AT BOOKSTORES NEAR YOU!
Angel Diary
1~8
Kara · Lee YunHee

Totally new Arabian nights, where Shahrazad is a guy!

Everyone knows the story of Shahrazad and her wonderful tales from the Arabian Nights. For one thousand and one nights, the stories that she created entertained the mad Sultan and eventually saved her life. In this version, Shahrazad is a guy who wanted to save his sister from the mad Sultan by disguising himself as a woman. When he puts his life on the line, what kind of strange and unique stories would he tell? This new twist on one of the greatest classical tales might just keep you awake for another ONE THOUSAND AND ONE NIGHTS.

Yen Press

www.yenpress.com

Available at bookstores near you!

One thousand and one nights 1~7

Han SeungHee · Jeon JinSeok

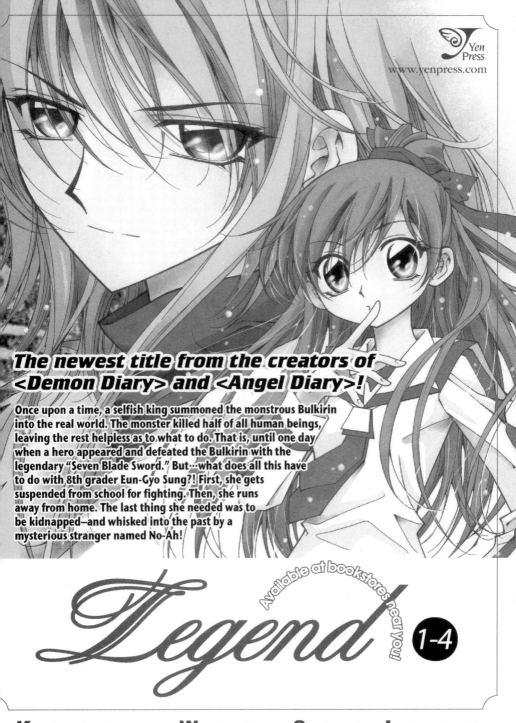

Yen Press
www.yenpress.com

The newest title from the creators of <Demon Diary> and <Angel Diary>!

Once upon a time, a selfish king summoned the monstrous Bulkirin into the real world. The monster killed half of all human beings, leaving the rest helpless as to what to do. That is, until one day when a hero appeared and defeated the Bulkirin with the legendary "Seven Blade Sword." But...what does all this have to do with 8th grader Eun-Gyo Sung?! First, she gets suspended from school for fighting. Then, she runs away from home. The last thing she needed was to be kidnapped—and whisked into the past by a mysterious stranger named No-Ah!

Available at bookstores near you!

Legend 1-4

K a r a · W o o S o o J u n g

Yen Press
www.yenpress.com

THE MOST BEAUTIFUL FACE, THE PERFECT BODY,
AND A SINCERE PERSONALITY...THAT'S WHAT HYE-MIN HWANG HAS.
NATURALLY, SHE'S THE CENTER OF EVERYONE'S ATTENTION.
EVERY BOY IN SCHOOL LOVES HER, WHILE EVERY GIRL HATES HER OUT OF JEALOUSY.
EVERY SINGLE DAY, SHE HAS TO ENDURE TORTURES AND HARDSHIPS FROM THE GIRLS.

A PRETTY FACE COMES WITH A PRICE.

THERE IS NOTHING MORE SATISFYING THAN GETTING THEM BACK.
WELL, EXCEPT FOR ONE PROBLEM...HER SECRET CRUSH, JUNG-YUN.
BECAUSE OF HIM, SHE HAS TO HIDE HER CYNICAL AND DARK SIDE
AND DAILY PUT ON AN INNOCENT FACE. THEN ONE DAY, SHE FINDS OUT
THAT HE DISLIKES HER ANYWAY!! WHAT?! THAT'S IT! NO MORE NICE GIRL!
AND THE FIRST VICTIM OF HER RAGE IS A PLAYBOY SHE JUST MET, MA-HA.

vol.1~6

Cynical Orange

Yun JiUn

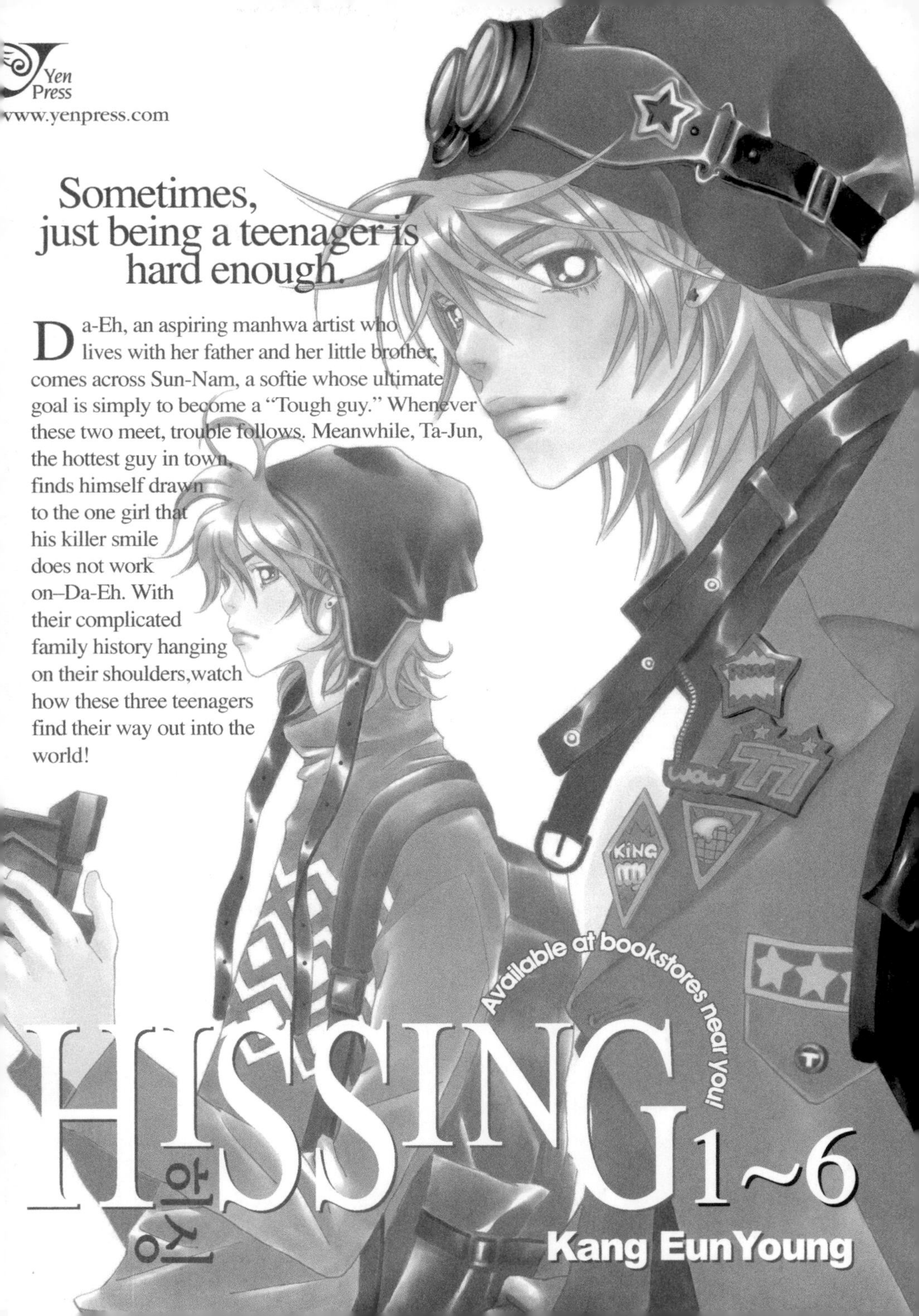
Yen Press
www.yenpress.com
Sometimes, just being a teenager is hard enough.
Da-Eh, an aspiring manhwa artist who lives with her father and her little brother, comes across Sun-Nam, a softie whose ultimate goal is simply to become a "Tough guy." Whenever these two meet, trouble follows. Meanwhile, Ta-Jun, the hottest guy in town, finds himself drawn to the one girl that his killer smile does not work on–Da-Eh. With their complicated family history hanging on their shoulders,watch how these three teenagers find their way out into the world!
Available at bookstores near you!
HISSING 1~6
히싱
Kang EunYoung

PIG BRIDE ①

KOOKHWA HUH
SUJIN KIM

Translation: Jackie Oh

Lettering: Erika T.

PIG BRIDE, Vol. 1 © 2007 KookHwa Huh & SuJin Kim. All rights reserved. First published in Korea in 2007 by Haksan Publishing Co., Ltd. English translation rights in U.S.A., Canada, UK, and Republic of Ireland arranged with Haksan Publishing Co., Ltd.

English translation © 2009 Hachette Book Group, Inc.

Yen Press
Hachette Book Group
237 Park Avenue, New York, NY 10017

Visit our Web sites at www.HachetteBookGroup.com and www.YenPress.com.

Yen Press is an imprint of Hachette Book Group, Inc. The Yen Press name and logo are trademarks of Hachette Book Group, Inc.

First Yen Press Edition: April 2009

ISBN: 978-0-7595-2956-4

10 9 8 7 6 5 4 3 2 1

BVG

Printed in the United States of America